NATURE, GOD AND HUMANITY

Nature, God and Humanity weaves together philosophical, scientific, religious, and cultural considerations to show why non-human animals and nature in general are proper objects of moral concern, and how our well-being depends on harmony with nature-as-created. The book clarifies the task of forming an ethics of nature, thereby empowering readers to develop their own critical, faith-based ethics.

Calling on original, thought-provoking analyses and arguments, Richard L. Fern frames a philosophical ethics of nature, assesses it scientifically, finds support for it in traditional biblical theism, and situates it culturally. Though defending the moral value of beliefs affirming the radical Otherness of God and human uniqueness, his book aims not to compel the adoption of any particular ethic but rather to illumine the contribution diverse forms of inquiry make to an ethics of nature. How does philosophy clarify moral conviction? What does science tell us about nature? Why does religious faith matter? Rejecting the illusion of a single, rationally compelling ethics, Fern answers these questions in a way that fosters both agreement and disagreement, allowing those holding conflicting ethics of nature to work together to end our current, foolish abuse of wild nature.

RICHARD L. FERN taught ethics for many years at the University of Illinois and Yale Divinity School. He is currently taking advantage of an early retirement to write on topics of interest.

NATURE, GOD AND HUMANITY

Envisioning an Ethics of Nature

RICHARD L. FERN

CAMBRIDGE
UNIVERSITY PRESS

PUBLISHED BY THE PRESS SYNDICATE OF THE UNIVERSITY OF CAMBRIDGE
The Pitt Building, Trumpington Street, Cambridge, United Kingdom

CAMBRIDGE UNIVERSITY PRESS
The Edinburgh Building, Cambridge CB2 2RU, UK
40 West 20th Street, New York, NY 10011-4211, USA
477 Williamstown Road, Port Melbourne, VIC 3207, Australia
Ruiz de Alarcón 13, 28014 Madrid, Spain
Dock House, The Waterfront, Cape Town 8001, South Africa

http://www.cambridge.org

First published 2002

Printed in the United Kingdom at the University Press, Cambridge

Typeface Baskerville Monotype 11 / 12.5 pt.   *System* LaTeX 2$_\varepsilon$ [TB]

A catalogue record for this book is available from the British Library

Library of Congress Cataloguing in Publication data
Fren, Richard L.
Nature, God and humanity : envisioning an ethics of nature / by Richard L. Fern.
p.   cm.
Includes bibliographical references and index.
ISBN 0 521 81122 8 – ISBN 0 521 00970 7 (pbk.)
1. Philosophy of nature.   2. Ethics.   I. Title.
BD581.F39 2002
179′.1–dc21   2001043658

ISBN 0 521 81122 8 hardback
ISBN 0 521 00970 7 paperback

To Sally
In memory of our parents
Alex and Arden Post
Thelma and Ray Fern

We should understand well that all things are the works of the Great Spirit. We should know that He is within all things: the trees, the grasses, the rivers, the mountains, and all the four-legged animals, and the winged peoples; and even more important, we should understand that He is also above all these things and peoples. When we do understand all this deeply in our hearts, then we will fear, and love, and know the Great Spirit, and then we will be and act and live as He intends.

Black Elk (Brown 1971: *xx*)

Contents

Preface

This book originated in environmental ethics courses taught at Yale University during the years 1989 to 2000. As such, it owes a large debt to the students, undergraduate and graduate, mostly divinity and forestry, who listened and engaged, agreeing here, disagreeing there, forcing me to re-think and clarify one issue after the other. I trust that what follows repays some of that debt and, especially, makes clear why I asked them to read more than the standard texts, to wade through histories of ecology, philosophical arguments about the moral standing of animals and plants, theologies of creation, socio-political assessments of the environmental movement, so forth and so on. They were a hardy lot and I owe them much.

One thing I learned from them is that deep tensions exist in the way people think about nature. One tension appears in relation to modern science: a respect for and virtually automatic deference to what science tells us about nature is often combined with a no less genuine conviction that there is more to nature than a merely quantitative science can tell us. As to what this "more" might involve, lively affirmations of ecological spirituality appear arm-in-arm with a zealous distrust of religion. In both cases, science and religion, established ways of thinking, are affirmed with reservations, reservations tied to ethical concerns. In the first case, these concerns lead people to look for more in a recognized authority than is there; in the second, to a longing for the icing of faith apart from the hard cake of church and theology.

A third tension appeared as regards ethical concern itself. Many students whose ethical seriousness was evident saw virtually no value in the painstaking analyses and arguments of professional ethicists. At first, being an ethicist, I attributed this opinion to an intellectual vice, a lack of rigor, a prejudice. Attempting to do ethics without engaging moral philosophy makes no more sense than studying natural history while ignoring evolutionary biology. You may learn some interesting things from medieval bestiaries but you can certainly never expect to understand, yet alone master the subject. Why, then, I asked myself, do so many, not only students but otherwise learned books, assume it is possible to resolve moral questions about nature without engaging the studied delibera- tions of ethicists regarding such things as the moral status of animals, species, or nature-as-a-whole?

With time I realized ethical earnestness itself, oddly enough, prevents people from appreciating the seemingly endless analyses and arguments of ethicists, just as a desire to know and experience the deep, spiri- tual truth about nature can make people dissatisfied with the number- crunching of scientists and metaphysical musings of theologians. This, in turn, keyed my awareness of a fourth and comprehending tension. Whether my students envisioned the future in terms of a left-leaning ecological democracy, a right-leaning enlightened market, a return to the ways of native peoples, or, my own preference, the second coming of bioregional federalism, almost all agreed on the need for strong, morally limed communities – yet, at the same time, had a hard time imagining a life more constrained by oughts or others than the one they were cur- rently living. Once again, they wanted a benefit without the institutional consequences or limitations. Science without numbers, God without sa- cred texts, ethics without argument, community without constraint.

In part, of course, this is a point about self-indulgence and it may seem I am about to launch into still another critique of modernity. That is not my intent. While there is clearly much to criticize, there is also something right, even profound, about the contradictory impulses of modernity. The tensions which appear are both moral and conceptual and, as such, reveal complex truths about human nature and good, truths that point toward a more wise and rewarding engagement with nature and, no less, ourselves. What I hope to show is not a way to escape these tensions by means of a heightened morality, a re-formulated science, or, even, a new conception of God, but, more modestly, a way to live with them, learn from them, keep them and us in balance.

My students, like all of us, were caught up in a cultural process char- acteristic of modernity, blinding them to the relevance of one specialized endeavor to another and, more tellingly, the relevance of specialized endeavors – science, theology, even ethics – to the fundamental, ethi- cal task of living, here-and-now, day-by-day, with those we love, a truly good, fully human life, a life of which we can be justifiably proud. That is why they so often failed to see that smashing the world to bits and re-shaping it nearer to the heart's desire, life without limits, is not a live option – not only because the enemy is us but, more profoundly, because our critical awareness is rooted in and sustained by the institutions, the patterns of thought and behavior, the nature, our nature, we seek, rightly, to transcend.

That, in a nutshell, is the lesson on which I will expand in what follows. As regards the way in which I do, I need to say three things. First, with regard to the large number of references and footnotes: these situate points made, positions taken, in relation to the larger, often but not always academic literature; if you want to find valuable reflection, supporting or questioning what I claim, this is a good place to look. They do not "prove" the truth of my claims (by appeal to the authority of others) nor, counterwise, "disprove" the claims of those with whom I disagree. The value of this book lies in its overarching, synthetic vision, not a polemical engagement with other positions. While I do not hesitate to draw contrasts or make critical comments by way of developing my own contentious position, I realize that in virtually every case more has been and needs to be said – which leads me to my second and third points.

While I make and depend throughout on substantive, contentious claims about nature, God, and humanity, my primary goal is not to develop or defend any particular view but, rather, illuminate ways of thinking and arguing about such matters. How are we to bring philosophical ethics to bear on our ethical concerns about nature? What can and cannot modern science tell us about nature? What if any relevance does religious faith have to these concerns? How are we to put all this together and go about making the world a better place? My aim as regards each of these methodological concerns is to facilitate disagreement as much as agreement. Where substantive claims enter the picture is predominately by way of opening up this dialogue to those who have for various reasons been excluded in the recent past. Here we encounter a third, broader point and with it, a set of convictions regarding human life and society.

I write under the presumption that traditional biblical theism and, with it, the historic religions – Judaism, Christianity, and Islam – by which Western society has been shaped for better and for worse are an invaluable resource in coming to terms with the social and ecological crises of our time. In part, they are required to break the hold of falsely reductionist, sub-human ways of thinking about nature, God, and humanity. More important, they are needed to formulate positive visions of the future, visions of a just and good world erected on the inevitable ruins of yesterday's society, our society, the shifting sands of history. We need in this regard to get people of faith involved, intellectually and socially. This is not an easy matter and here I seek to do only two things: one, reveal a little of what traditional theists can contribute to that endeavor and, two, show to all, especially traditional theists, the value of dialogue among Jews, Christians, and Muslims. It is only by coming together, honoring our agreements and disagreements, that we can advance, together and apart, our common interest in the good of creation.

That, then, is the project undertaken. In reaching the point where it now stands, I am indebted to many persons, ranging from Brother Brown, who shared with a small boy the mysteries of the Great Pyramid (and gave him his first book of theology), to Kevin Taylor, my editor at Cambridge, who saw value in the project and believed it possible to reduce a typescript three times longer to its current size and cohesion – a task much facilitated by Audrey Cotterell, my incisive copy-editor. The time does not exist (Kevin insists) to mention by name all those who enlightened the way in between, though note must be taken of my inspired teachers at North Hollywood High School, Oral Roberts University, and Perkins School of Theology (SMU), especially Joe Jones, who introduced me to the wit and wisdom of Wittgenstein, that indispensable modern; William Babcock, who put me in touch with the Irish saints, among whose spiritual descendants I was fortunate to be raised; Albert Outler, who uncovered the charismatic roots of apophatic theology; and Herndon Wagers, who insisted I take a closer look at Tillich's doctrine of the Trinity.

My greatest debt, academically, is to the philosophers and theologians with whom I studied at Yale during the 1970s and later taught during the 1980s and 1990s. It was a truly wonderful place to be, full of knowledge and, invariably, fruitful tension. Those familiar with their work will recognize the pleasure of being able to study with such strong and different individuals as Paul Holmer and William Christian, Michael Williams and Karsten Harries, John Smith and Ruth Barcan Marcus. I am sure I would have been unable to digest it were it not for the synthesizing conversations with my fellow graduate students, especially Phil Glotzbach. During those years I absorbed and, hopefully, develop herein something of "the Yale School." In that regard, I owe a special debt to two individuals, Hans Frei and Gene Outka. The position of theistic naturalism is at core an exercise in "figural interpretation," something I would never have imagined myself doing at the time I studied hermeneutics with Frei. In coming to appreciate the "generous orthodoxy" of Frei I have benefited immensely from studying and teaching with Outka. While no one in my experience values analytic distinctions more than he, all who know him will agree that in the end he, like his mentor Augustine, gives priority to a "both-and," insisting, along with Frei and Barth, that God's "yes" runs deeper than the "no" of human sin.

There are others still. James Wallace, a colleague at the University of Illinois, who taught me there had to be more to moral realism than compelling intuitions. In this regard, I was also fortunate, while a student at the Yale Law School, to study with a number of "Niebuhrian realists," most especially, Steve Wizner and the late Robert Cover, both of whom, moved by their heritage and faith, gave priority to "people" over "theory," allowing me to see that the fundamental harmony of faith and reason is not theoretical but practical and, therewith, moral. In putting the material together on which this book is based, I was advantaged greatly by the opportunity to teach with Steve Kellert, whose work on biophilia led me to look deeper into my own, Christian heritage and, in so doing, beyond standard appeals to stewardship. I was also fortunate during this time to meet and converse with Holmes Rolston, who encouraged me and on whose intellectual shoulders I have attempted to climb in my account of sentiosis. I am also much indebted to Peter Singer and Tom Regan, whose work first got me interested in these matters and to whom all the world, wild and human, owes a great debt. They represent a wide range of scholars, many cited in what follows, by way of agreement and disagreement, who have not forgotten the things that matter. This is especially true of Peter Ochs, whose careful, critical reading of the text not only made it better but led me to see more clearly the conceptual underpinnings and motivating concerns of this project.

The reference to origins and ends brings to mind the larger context of my life and with it the personal debt I owe to family and friends, many already mentioned. The most fortunate aspect of my life has been the number of good friends with whom I have been blessed from childhood. The saddest part has been the recurrent movement, the leaving behind of place after place, friend after friend. I cannot mention all, so let me simply say, to one and all, my deepest thanks. In each of you, I experienced a love and forbearance greater than I deserved, a grace greater than I gave in return. The same has proved true with regard to my family. My twin sister Annette and brother Bill, my stepson Clint, have given me much. Above all, without the encouragement and faith of my mother, Thelma Beesley Fern, I would never have dared pursue the education she was denied by the hard necessities of life. Caring for my father, Raymond William Fern, during the final four years of his life, while he struggled with cancer and

Alzheimer's disease, delayed but greatly strengthened this project, teaching me that God is present in times of sorrow no less than joy – thanks in large measure to the wise counsel and helping hand of our good friend, Gregor Barnum. My wife Sally has been there in good times and bad, making all this possible and, in the process, enriching my life immeasurably. It is to her and, with her, all those, human and non-human, who have opened for me the rich wonder of God's strange creation that I dedicate this book.

Introduction

This book has two goals. The first and primary is to develop a framework for reflection. How are we, as a society, to come to terms with nature, wild and human? This "coming to terms" is not simply a matter of addressing the current ecological crisis. More fundamentally, it is a matter of determining our place in the world of nature and, therewith, our relation to the wild creatures with whom we share the planet and its formative, natural processes. Who are we? Who are they? What makes us different? What do we have in common? Addressing these and related questions requires us to take into account not only "the facts" but, no less, "our values." What do we care about? Is there any reason we ought to care about the well-being of other creatures? Of nature-as-a-whole? What follows attempts to remove some of the confusion and disagreement surrounding these matters and, therewith, our normatively laden relation to nature not by providing a short-cut to the truth but, rather, helping those who care enough to think hard make their way through the labyrinth of complexities involved.

A second, related goal is to develop and defend claims about our relation to nature. Some of these, such as those affirming animal awareness, the inherent purposefulness of natural processes, religious naturalism, and our own, irreducibly communal identity, are integral to the proposed framework for reflection. It makes little sense apart from them. Other claims, such as those about predation and modern agribusiness, are illustrative; their truth, relative to the framework, is wide-open. Still other claims lie somewhere in between. This holds true for both the account given of modern science and, more fundamentally, theistic naturalism. While I believe these valid, especially the latter, it is possible to be a religious believer and, even, believe in divine creation while disagreeing with them, in whole or in part. There is room for variation. This does not mean these claims are unimportant. To the contrary, simply repudiating them, would leave the abstract framework less plausible, unsupported, and undeveloped. Thus, those who reject them while retaining the ethical stance of humane holism will need to find analogous support and elucidation elsewhere. That this possibility exists is a good thing, allowing for affirmation of the proposed framework by not only traditional theists but other religious believers and, even, in many respects, those who hold no religious beliefs whatsoever.

The text itself is divided into three Parts. Part I outlines our ethics of nature, establishing the moral standing of wild nature from the standpoint of philosophical ethics; it does this in three steps, engaging, first, questions regarding the moral status of non-human animals, second, the same questions regarding nature-as-a-whole, and, third, methodological concerns regarding plausibility and determinacy – thereby setting the stage for Parts II and III. Part II inquires as to the relevance of religious faith for an ethics of nature and offers in this regard a faith-based stance, theistic naturalism, supporting the conclusions drawn in Part I. Part III considers the relevance of cultural traditions for moral reflection, showing how the ethics and politics of nature come to fruition in contentious, more-or-less plausible ways of life. Since the path forward is long and intricate, let me briefly summarize the argument of and conclusions drawn in each chapter.

Chapter one sets forth two basic principles, one of decency, the other necessity. As regards the first, I argue, following a well-trod path, that some non-human animals, those living a life which goes for them better-or-worse and, thereby, having a well-being of their own, count morally. This "ethics of well-being" does not, however, so I argue, extend the same protection to all selves and sentients. The second principle, that of necessity, justifies us in giving preferential consideration to the life and interests of humans. This rejection of "biotic egalitarianism" is grounded not in claims about moral worth but, rather, the unique, constitutive relation existing, so I argue (in Parts II and III), between all and only human beings. I conclude that we ought, as common sense dictates, to take the interests of non-human selves and sentients into account while granting priority to our own life and interests. What remains unsettled, a matter of great import, is the extent of preference justified and, correspondingly, what decency and necessity require in situations of conflict. While the argument for attributing moral standing to all selves and sentients is as close to rationally compelling as an ethical argument gets, there is no rationally compelling account of how much non-humans count morally compared to humans.

Chapter two considers the moral standing of nature-as-a-whole and, therewith, all living creatures. After showing that appeals to natural beauty, even if successful, provide at most *de minimis* protection, I argue the same holds for appeals to the objectively determined good of living creatures and natural processes. Efforts to ground an ethics of nature in this manner fail not because there is no such good but due to morally significant disanalogies between these goods and the well-being of selves and sentients. If we are to move beyond an ethics of well-being, we will require an account of moral standing that does not depend, by way of intentionality or sentience, on the living of a life that goes better-or-worse. Here, presuming a truly holistic ethics of nature will ground the moral worth of protected "wholes" in their relation to encompassed, individual selves and sentients, I argue that nature-as-a-whole is entitled to moral respect because it is "sentiotic," a creative, life-sustaining process, the well-functioning of which is not only vital to but constitutive of human and non-human well-being. This "ethics of preservation" rests on paradigmatically moral concerns about well-being indirectly – by virtue of an inherent orientation toward the good of well-being. I conclude that we have a duty to preserve and protect natural processes. Adding this principle of deference to those of decency and necessity generates the ethic of humane holism. This addresses the problem of indeterminacy at one level, by providing an encompassing framework in which to view conflicting interests. At the same time, it introduces additional indeterminacy regarding the object of deference: since this cannot be identified with the beauty or relentless regularity of nature, how are we to ascertain what morality requires of us?

This question is addressed in Parts II and III. Before going there, however, we need to consider the relevance of modern science for our presumptions in Part I regarding animal awareness and, more contentiously, the inherent orientation of natural processes toward well-being. Here, I argue, in chapter three, that scientific theories, while describing the world as it really is, do so in a necessarily abstract manner. Modern science succeeds so well at what it does by systematically ignoring whatever cannot be made an object of scientific study. One consequence is that it cannot confirm or disconfirm either the existence of consciousness, human or non-human, or the inherent purposefulness of nature. It follows that not only grand schemes to scientize ethics but more low-flying efforts to ground an ethics of nature in what ecological and evolutionary theories tell us about the workings of nature are methodologically flawed.

The ethics of nature cannot avoid, by way of philosophy or science, a reliance on faith-based convictions. This, far from disabling moral reason, enables it and, therewith, as I show in Parts II and III, the effort to live, as morality directs, a truly good, fully human life. I conclude chapter three by explaining why and how the three parts of the text are correlated with three forms of moral reflection: philosophical, religious, and commonsensical, or, cultural.

Part II explores the contribution of religious faith to an ethics of nature. In so doing it provides faith-based reasons for adopting the ethic developed in Part I, humane holism. Chapter four begins this endeavor by clarifying the notion of "religious naturalism," arguing that religious faith assumes this shape when nature, in whole or in part, is taken to provide an indispensable medium of engagement with a fundamental, sacred reality. Examples abound in so-called "primitive religions." Religious naturalism assumes a theistic form when the Sacred is understood theistically, as a Supreme Person. Theism is distinguished from other religious perspectives by its belief that the Sacred is like us personal, yet radically Other. A more precise characterization is achieved by contrasting historic theism with four quasi-theisms: polytheism, pantheism, deism, and emanationism. Having clarified what it means to be a theist, we engage the issue of plausibility: what if any reasons are there for believing that God exists?

Addressing this question is of interest not because it removes the need for faith but, rather, because it calls to mind aspects of and places in nature where theists encounter the living reality of God. Ultimately the appeal of theistic naturalism, like every form of religious faith, rests on charismatically compelling, life-transforming encounters. This, in turn, brings us into the domain of theology: dogmatic, systematic, and imaginative. It is here we engage the basic reasonableness of faith, that is, the operation of critical reason in a context of faith. This dynamic appears in the modernist critique of belief in divine miracles as well as the traditionalist reply. While the resultant interplay of arguments occasionally results in changing images of God and God's creative activity in the world, it typically and quite properly results in more refined, reasonable versions of the faith by which believers are grasped at the start of their quest for understanding: reason and (charismatic) faith work arm-in-arm. This, in turn, allows us to see how belief in a radically transcendent sacred reality can incorporate and learn from an on-going experience of God in nature, be it abstract, as in modern science, or concrete, as in everyday life.

Chapter five turns to the theological task of developing a faith-based, overtly theistic perspective on nature. I do so by explicating the traditional belief in a *creatio ex nihilo*. This doctrine holds that God created the world freely, out of nothing, and, thus, might not have created it without any loss to himself. The radical freedom of this act is, I argue a mark of love, not indifference. This love, being constitutive of finite reality, is present in all times and places. I analogize it to the sustaining word of a cosmic storyteller. God speaks the world into existence. This is only possible given a self-limitation by God, one that produces a "relative nothingness" from which to create and in which to place the inherently limited, contingent reality of nature. In so doing, God brings into being, along with the world, imperfection and the possibility of natural evil. This possibility is realized with the appearance of finite selves and sentients, creatures with a genuine but limited capacity to experience the unity and good of existence.

That God creates and sustains such a world is justified by the good realized in its existence and, especially, a mutuality of love involving God and his creatures, all of whose stories are treasured by God in the infinite, unlimited fullness of his eternal Being. For this mutuality to be complete requires, in addition, a freedom of response on the part of creation. This, in turn, introduces into creation, along with agency, the possibility of moral evil, a rejection of the love manifest in creation. This possibility becomes a reality in the Fall of humanity, the freedom of nature. In response, God supplements the constitutive grace present in creation with a consequent, restorative grace, thereby allowing to continue the weaving together of our stories, our own broken creativity, with his redemptive love. The wonder of that love consists in its free, unnecessitated availability: like us, God must be able to walk away for there to be a genuine mutuality of love.

Part III asks how an ethics of nature moves from faith-based, generic ideality to a culturally specific determinacy. Here we encounter one of the many paradoxes of modernity: a heightened awareness of the role culture plays in human formation and life co-exists with a desire to escape the constraint of traditional norms and ideals. In response, I argue that our capacity for self-transcendence, through reason and faith, is not only dependent on but inherent in the authority of tradition. That we see this is not incidental to an ethics of nature; it is the methodological analogue of our own constitutive relation to wild nature. Here, there appears a parallel between a holistic ethic of nature and its upshot, ecological conservationism, and a holistic ethic of culture and its upshot, cultural conservatism.[1] Bearing this in mind, Part III situates our relation with nature culturally, revealing as it does the commonality and diversity of human nature. Culture, so viewed, becomes the sentiotic flowering of wild nature, which, in turn, becomes the extended body of humanity.

Chapter six develops, toward this end, a relational, communal view of the *imago Dei*: humans are given responsibility to speak for and mirror God in nature. Rather than deny the uniquely god-like quality of human life and freedom, as many do, we affirm this as an essential condition of the above task while denying it leaves us free to abuse the good of other creatures. Everything turns on how we understand the task to which we are called. Here, by way of developing the notion of an irreducibly communal identity, I defend the notion of corporate responsibility, linking it to the existence of communities with a shared, common good. Such thick communities play a vital role in the natural process whereby human selves are formed, that is, enculturation. This process, I argue, occurs in three stages, corresponding to three dimensions of every cultural *ethos*: ecotic, alethic, and teleotic. Unpacking these allows us to see the indispensable role cultural traditions play in human life: apart from the particularities of culture there are no particularized, actual human selves.

Given this, I argue, along lines laid down in chapter two, that cultural traditions, being sentiotic, not only deserve moral respect but, also and crucially, possess a non-derivative normative authority for their adherents. Neither reason nor experience can provide an Archimedean point on which to dry-dock and reformulate the constitutive faith by which we live. Far from precluding critical reflection, this makes it possible. Thus, the natural diversity of cultures, like that of biotic communities, is a good part of creation, essential to the unity of difference that makes for a true mutuality.

Chapter seven turns its attention to that larger unity, the all-encompassing fellowship of creation. Here I argue, contrary to those theanthropocentrists who claim creation was for the sake of humanity alone, that all of nature, in whole and in part, is known and loved by God as integral parts of a single, indivisible whole, the on-going story of creation. This "big hug" theory of creation grounds human dominion in the unique role of humans in that story, not in any greater love for humans on the part of God: human uniqueness and dominion, the *imago Dei*, are part and parcel of God's structuring of nature for the good of

---

[1] It is important to distinguish cultural conservatism, as developed herein, from both economic and *status quo* conservatism; not only do the latter two positions not follow from the first, they are arguably inconsistent with it.

all. As argued in Part I, the priority of human life and interests, morally, rests on the special relation in which all and only humans stand to one another, not on human uniqueness, dominion, or an allegedly greater love of God for humanity.

It follows, relative to the encompassing unity of creation, that in wrongfully harming wild nature we harm ourselves, whatever the extrinsic or intrinsic consequences. It also follows, if we are to ascertain what this constitutive harm involves, we will have to engage moral concerns from a culturally informed point of view. By way of illuminating what this involves, I raise questions about the morality of predation, wild and human. As regards predation in the wild, I argue this hard reality is integral to the identity of predator and prey and, therefore, like politics among humans, part of God's good creation. The case as regards human predation is more complex given the need to ascertain what makes for human well-being and, therewith, necessity. Engaging questions about nature hunting and modern agribusiness, I conclude by advocating a political pluralism that is principled and pragmatic, arguing this holds out the best hope for a life in accord with the created nature and good of humanity.

That completes the argument, leaving us with a framework for critical reflection on our constitutive relation to that nature by which we are what we are. Apprehending the shape and force of this framework is not easy. The analyses and arguments offered require an effort to follow and assess; these convolutions and difficulties cannot, however, be avoided. Equally essential, though, is the realization that these analyses and arguments – more points, as Shakespeare put it, than all the lawyers in Bohemia can learnedly handle – will not provide a single, rationally compelling answer to our concerns. There are no such answers. Accordingly, no easy task, we must learn to take analysis and argument seriously, while recognizing their ultimate inadequacy. In the end, we are cast back on charismatic insight and cultural tradition – and, thereby, a multiplicity of reasonable positions, though not an unlimited multiplicity. Ethical maturity requires us to continue our search for clarity while living with the inevitable ambiguity. Hence, the overriding importance of a good will and strong character. We live in anticipation of a future we can never grasp entire, never call our own apart from a love, a faith and hope, that calls into being a nature that is, yet-not-yet.

In a sense, this book leaves us where we began. Though the ethic it proposes, humane holism, strongly suggests the need for change in our lives, perhaps radical change, there are not only no easy answers here – of which there are none in any case – there are no concrete proposals, no worked-out agendas for the future. In that sense, the real work remains to be done, the real dialogue to begin. My hope is that what follows will help us move forward by breaking the current conceptual and political logjam. To move the former, we need to see more clearly than is now common what can and cannot be provided by the various epistemic authorities to which appeal is made, be this philosophical ethics, scientific inquiry, spirituality, theological reflection, cultural tradition, whatever. We cannot move forward until we realize, as Joseph Butler (1950: 15) put so well, that everything is what it is and not another thing. The secret of ethics, like nature, lies in the harmonizing of a great many, irreducibly diverse, yet all vital parts. Much the same holds with regard to the prospects of political and social reform. We need to not only affirm cultural diversity in the abstract but, more concretely, nourish into being a genuinely diverse coalition of concerned individuals and communities, one that encompasses deep-cutting differences of interest and conviction. The secret of cultural change, like change in wild nature, lies in a mutually rewarding, symbiotic cooperation, not competition, as good a part of creation as that is.

PART I
The ethics of nature

CHAPTER ONE

Moral concerns

POSING THE QUESTION

That we ought to care about nature is evident.[1] Wild nature has unparalleled *instrumental value* – the water we drink, the air we breathe, the silicon chips we rely on. Human life cannot be sustained, let alone achieve well-being, apart from the multifold goods of wild nature. In addition, independent of its contribution to other goods, wild nature itself has value for us – mountain lions and otters, rivers and towering mountains, the wind blowing through pine trees. Even if we left this world to live on self-sustaining star-ships, wild nature would retain this *intrinsic value* for those who knew and remembered the wonders of earth.

That wild nature has this value makes it an obvious *indirect* object of moral concern relative to the good of humans. These concerns may be large – involving the devastation of an entire continent – or small – involving a town's hesitancy to share access to its beach with land-locked others. Such issues arise because natural goods and ills, weal and woe, are unevenly distributed and, on occasion, unfairly appropriated. The colonizing power, state or business, that extracts natural resources without consent or recompense acts unjustly. Even with consent and fair recompense, parties to "the deal" may act unjustly with regard to humans

---

[1] Rosemary Ruether (1992: 5) observes: "The word *nature* is used in four distinct senses in Western culture: (1) as that which is 'essential' to a being; (2) as the sum total of physical reality, including humans; (3) as the sum total of physical reality apart from humans; and (4) the 'created' world apart from God and divine grace." Similarly, C. S. Lewis (1947: 8of.) lists as contrast terms for "nature" and its correlate "natural": "artificial," "civil," "human," "spiritual," and "supernatural." In what follows I distinguish three progressively narrower usages. In the first, broadest sense, "nature" refers to the entire universe, everything that is other than God: *nature-as-creation* encompasses all finite entities and processes. A second, narrower sense designates the organic processes and inorganic substratum found on earth, *nature-as-biosphere*; like the first, it includes the distinctively human. A third sense, *wild nature*, signifies nature-as-biosphere-apart-from-the-distinctively-human. It is important to keep these distinctions in mind (Bookchin 1991: xx): "The greatest confusion has arisen as a result of the many and often-contradictory meanings imputed to the word ['nature']."

not-yet-present at the table, the posterity to whom they leave a world depleted of value. Setting aside these vital issues, the question I want to pose here concerns the extent, if any, to which wild nature itself is a *direct* object of moral concern, a moral subject in its own right.

Consider moral constraints on our treatment of one another. As every sports-fan and employer is aware, some humans have more instrumental value than others. The survival and well-being of businesses and athletic teams depends on tapping this talent. In addition, many humans have value for others in their own right, intrinsic value. The value of children for their parents is non-derivative. Virtually everyone has instrumental and intrinsic value for someone. Even, however, were there a human so sad as to lack both, that individual would still have moral worth. This *inherent value* grounds the claim all humans, however talented, however lovable, ought to be treated with moral respect.

The question I want to pose is whether wild nature, whatever its instrumental or intrinsic value for us, has inherent value in this sense. If it does and, thus, turns out to be a direct object of moral concern, it will have a claim to be treated with moral respect. This, in turn, will mean that we may act immorally with regard to wild nature even where we treat other humans without fault, as thieves who fairly divide ill-gotten gain. If nature has moral worth, then, as Holmes Rolston affirms (1988: 226), "humans are not free to make whatever uses of nature suit their fancy, amusement, need, or profit."

Does wild nature have value independent of its value for us? One reason for thinking it does lies in its awe-inspiring beauty. In *Desert Solitaire* (1971: 40ff.), Edward Abbey asserts that natural objects such as Delicate Arch, "a fragile ring of stone on the far side of a natural amphitheater, set on its edge at the brink of a five hundred foot drop-off," enable us "to see, as the child sees, a world of marvels," and, thereby, quicken our awareness that "*out there* is a different world, older and greater and deeper by far than ours, a world which surrounds and sustains the little world of men as sea and sky surround and sustain a ship." A similar fascination with the aesthetic value of wilderness drives the land ethic of Aldo Leopold, leading him to claim (1970: 262) in his now-famous "key log," that "a thing is right when it tends to preserve the integrity, stability, and beauty of the biotic community." Intuitions and experiences of this sort are common among nature writers, from Muir to Nabham. Together they affirm what John E. Smith puts in more general terms (1978: 57): "Nature is disclosed in its aesthetic capacity as a reality surpassing the status of object and even of environment; as such it has a claim on man as a responsible being." The beauty of nature compels respect.[2]

To some this claim will appear, upon explication, to involve no more than an appeal to intrinsic value, a value that nature has for individual nature-lovers such as Abbey and Leopold. Others see here a basis for inherent value and moral standing. The English philosopher G. E. Moore poses in this regard a hypothetical choice between the creation of two worlds, neither inhabited by sentient creatures. Moore describes these worlds this way (1968: 83f.):

Let us imagine one world exceedingly beautiful. Imagine it as beautiful as you can; put into it whatever on this earth you most admire – mountains, rivers, the sea; trees and sunsets, stars and moon. Imagine these all combined in the most exquisite proportions, so that no one thing jars against another, but each contributes to increase the beauty of the whole. And then imagine the ugliest world you can possibly conceive. Imagine it simply one heap of filth, containing everything that is most disgusting to us, for whatever reason, and the whole, as far as may be, without one redeeming feature.

Assuming, correctly I think, that no one in his right mind would choose the second world, Moore takes this as support for the claim beauty has inherent value and, accordingly, that a moral obligation exists to preserve natural beauty.

Other ethicists have strongly disagreed. According to Robin Attfield (1994: 186f.), once we rule out the possibility some creature will benefit from our creating a beautiful as opposed to an ugly world, Moore's intuition fades and, along with it, "the assumption that the mere existence of beauty is of [inherent] value."[3] Similarly, Peter Singer asks, rhetorically (1979: 204): "If . . . I were the last sentient being on earth, would it matter if, in a moment of boredom, I entertained myself by making a bonfire of all the paintings in the Louvre?" Like Attfield, Singer believes there is no ethical issue apart from an impact on individual well-being. If there is no one around who cares, no one who will suffer as a result of my behavior, then, if I get pleasure out of destroying beautiful objects, there is no *moral* wrong in it (even if we allow, as I suspect Attfield and Singer would, that acting this way betrays a flawed character). The disagreement between

---

[2] Eugene Hargrove (1989: 165ff.) develops along similar lines an "ontological argument" concluding we have a moral duty to protect and preserve natural beauty "simply because it is good." Hargrove also argues (77–104) the environmental movement arose as a result of developing aesthetic sensitivities; see Thomas (1983: 192ff.) and Worster (1993: 199f.).

[3] Attfield uses the term "intrinsic" to designate what I label "inherent" and vice versa. To avoid confusion I have substituted the term "inherent" in square brackets. This practice is adopted throughout the text wherever a similar shift in usage occurs.

Moore and his critics comes down to a disagreement about what is and is not a *moral* value.

Is there any way to get hold of this disagreement and move the discussion forward? To begin, it is worth noting the oddity of appeals to beauty in a moral context. The point is not simply that common usage distinguishes these two kinds of considerations, as in Kierkegaard's contrast between the aesthetic meanderings of "a seducer" (1959; vol. I) and the ethical seriousness of Judge William (1959; vol. II). No one ever accused Moore of lacking ethical seriousness. The point is that in some, paradigmatic moral situations taking beauty into account is not only out of place but confused. We can understand a choice to save a beautiful person rather than an ugly one on the grounds of personal preference or, even, love. Attempts to justify that choice on moral grounds, however, as one might, for instance, justify the decision to save a mother of six rather than an elderly widow, are misguided, if not absurd, as if movie stars had a greater right to life than other, more ordinary people.

It does not follow that beauty has no moral significance, only that it is not a paradigmatic moral value and, accordingly, that even supposing appeals to natural beauty survive close analysis, their force will be weak in comparison to those based on human life and well-being. Thus, Elliot Sober, while agreeing with Moore that beauty has inherent value, argues (1986: 191): "It would be the height of condescension to expect a nation experiencing hunger and chronic disease to be inordinately concerned with the autonomous value of ecosystems or with creating and preserving works of art. Such values are not frivolous, but they can become important to us only after certain fundamental human needs are satisfied." Similarly, Lawrence Johnson, while arguing that we ought to value striking instances of natural beauty like Ayer's Rock, concludes (1991: 273), "valuing nature for its beauty, like valuing a woman for her beauty, tends to trivialize the object, valuing it not for what it is in itself but for how it pleases us." The crucial point is that arguments for the moral worth of wild nature need to do more than propose or even establish a moral obligation to preserve natural beauty.

WHY PEOPLE MATTER

What it is about human beings that makes us such perspicuous objects of moral concern? If anything possesses moral worth, we do. The claim that this worth or, derivatively, its perspicuity is merely a result of human bias falters before the diversity and frequent conflict of human interests.

Regarding human beings as moral subjects places moral constraints on the way we treat them, which explains why, historically, some humans have discounted or denied altogether the moral worth of others. We need, then, by way of coming to terms with the general notion of moral concern, to ask why humans are so strongly inclined to view their fellow humans as direct objects of moral concern, moral subjects, even when doing so conflicts with their own perceived interests.[4]

One obvious answer is that what we do to our fellow humans matters to them and, thereby, us. If we harm them, they are not only damaged, like the Mona Lisa, they typically experience a loss, suffer pain, find themselves hurt. Further, unlike the Mona Lisa, which keeps smiling whatever we do, they are likely to respond, to let us know we are not only hurting them but doing something wrong, something immoral. The touch, the look, the word, all create a morally laden community of encounter. This, in turn, matters to us for a variety of reasons. For one, accusations of immorality threaten our sense of personal excellence and, thereby, well-being. Typically we feel good about ourselves and our endeavors only when success comes without a loss of moral propriety. Of course, if we do not care about moral propriety, moral encounter will not have for us the significance it has for those who adopt a moral point of view. At the same time, this removes not only a burden but a good: our concerns so limited, we lose the capacity to feel good about ourselves because we have done the right thing. This flags a second reason why moral engagement matters: not caring about what matters to others, diminishes the scope and depth of our own good, our own humanity. In addition, a third reason, by opting out of moral community we preempt our own morally laden judgment: we no longer have a principled basis from which to object when others treat us wrongly.

Whatever the force of these reasons, situating moral concern in the context of moral community is important because it allows us to see that the compellingness of such concern is rooted not in isolated convictions but, rather, the entirety of our life as human beings (Wallace 1978: esp. 15–38). Caring, morally, about what matters to our fellow human beings is vital to the normative fabric of human life, an essential part of our humanity. That we care in this way makes possible the particular communities in which we live and, thereby, the lives we live as individuals-in-community. This, I suggest, is what makes us such perspicuous objects of moral concern. We cannot avoid such concern so long as we intend to

---

4 Here I agree with Attfield (1983: *x*) that "environmental ethics can only proceed by reasoning outwards from received moral judgments about familiar cases."

live a proto-typically human life. People matter the way they do because mattering to one another, moral community, is an integral part of human nature and good. It is hardly surprising, then, that the paradigmatic form taken by moral concern is a reciprocating community of adult human beings, or, put abstractly, moral agents.

Some ethicists have taken the significance of moral community to imply that only fully reciprocating members of moral community, moral agents, are moral subjects.[5] This follows, however, only if what makes for moral perspicuity is a necessary condition of moral concern. There are strong reasons, though, to believe this false. One reason, much commented on, is that some humans are not moral agents and, thus, unable to participate fully in the give-and-take of moral community; consigning these so-called "marginal humans" to a derivative moral status runs contrary to our basic commitment to human equality and rights. A more positive reason derives from the very nature of moral community. Reciprocity of concern makes no sense apart from the underlying fact that what happens to human beings matters to them, makes a difference in the quality of their lives. The roots of moral concern lie not in moral community, *per absurdum*, but, rather, human needs and interests. Apart from these, reciprocity – relative to our interests – has no point. It is our affectivity, our vulnerability to the action of others, that gives rise to morally laden looks and words. Accordingly, it makes good sense to believe, as many have argued, that the scope of moral concern extends beyond a full reciprocity to encompass all human beings whose existence, like that of ordinary persons, goes, for them, better-or-worse from the inside-out. We need, then, by way of identifying direct objects of moral concern to note the ways our life can go better-or-worse. Here, two encompassing categories come into play, experience and agency. Let me comment briefly on each, beginning with the second.

One general way in which a human life may go better-or-worse concerns its agency, or, broadly put, intentionality. How well a typical human life goes depends on the shape of its intentions and, more particularly, its success in realizing those intentions, which is to say, achieving the ends for which we act. It is a bad thing when our actions, our goals, are frustrated, a good thing when they are realized. Of course, there may be larger considerations which make us in retrospect glad for failure, as in the case of a would-be murderer foiled by a flat tire, an investor frustrated in his

5 For recent arguments to this end, see Frey 1980, Leahy 1994, and Carruthers 1992. For critical discussions see Attfield 1983, Clark 1984, DeGrazia 1996, Johnson 1991, Pluhar 1995, Regan 1983, Rollin 1992, Sapontzis 1987, Singer 1975, and Wenz 1988.

effort to buy stock in a company whose value subsequently plummets, so forth and so on. The point remains that all else being equal success in the realization of worthy ends is a vital part of human well-being and, accordingly, one of the reasons why we value moral community. The likelihood of achieving worthy ends is increased when others respect us and our endeavors. What triggers a concern with justice, however, is not reciprocity alone but the difference reciprocity and, therewith, agency make to well-being, the way our life goes.

Intentionality, purposefulness, gives a life depth, means that it is not exhausted by the things done to it. Its good encompasses that of agency, the pursuit of one's own ends, the living of life as one chooses. As a result, agents care about their life, judge it to be going better-or-worse and, in accord with their capacity, adjust their plans and actions accordingly. Here, it must be borne in mind that agency is not an all-or-nothing proposition. Human socio-paths, even where highly intelligent and capable of otherwise fully intentional behavior, lack moral agency. Nevertheless, they are objects of moral concern and, correspondingly, have a moral and legal right to be treated justly. A socio-path who works in return for the promise of payment has a just claim to the sum agreed upon. Though unable to grasp the moral force of that promise, it matters to him, to his agency, that his intentions and actions be honored. Similarly, individuals incapable of a full, reflective agency are, nevertheless, entitled to the fruits of their endeavors, as can be readily seen in the Special Olympics.[6]

Intentionality is a morally constitutive property. Given the importance of agency for human well-being, its presence in humans triggers moral concern. We care about our intentions and the way these play out in the world. In addition, of course, we care about the quality of our experience. Sentience, like intentionality, is a morally constitutive property, one whose presence always triggers moral concern. Typically, concerns of this sort are quickened by attention-consuming, physically embodied sensations, intense, raw feelings and graphically present emotions, the pains we are eager to avoid, the pleasures we long to embrace. This allows us to see even more vividly than in the case of intentionality why "how

---

[6] Though possessing diminished responsibility, such individuals are at the least (what I will call) "mere selves" or, following Tom Regan, "subjects of a life." According to Regan (1983: 243):

individuals are subjects-of-a-life if they have beliefs and desires; perception, memory, and a sense of the future, including their own future; an emotional life together with feelings of pleasure and pain; preference- and welfare-interests; the ability to initiate action in pursuit of their desires and goals; a psychophysical identity over time; and an individual welfare in the sense that their experiential life fares well or ill for them, logically independently of their utility for others and logically independently of their being the object of anyone else's interests.

their life is going" matters to sentient beings. It also allows us to envision the existence of humans who lack agency in any meaningful sense yet experience life as better-or-worse, who have an inside-out without reflective thought or intentional action – third-term fetuses, anencephalic children, severely brain-damaged adults, so forth and so on. What makes such mere sentience a compelling source of moral concern is the evident manner and extent to which the felt quality of its life matters to any individual who experiences life as better-or-worse. As Mary Midgley puts it (1984: 91): "The special importance of sentience or consciousness in a being outside ourselves is that it can give that being experiences sufficiently like our own to bring into play the Golden Rule – 'treat others as you would wish them to treat you'."[7] Here, as in the more abstract case of intentionality, moral concern has its origin in the awareness that what we do makes a difference to others, causes their lives to go better-or-worse. While this does not tell us by itself what we ought to do, it generates and sustains an ethics of well-being encompassing all human selves and sentients. To deny that is not morally plausible.

SELVES AND SENTIENTS

This ethics of well-being embraces all humans for whom life goes better-or-worse. I want now to argue, following a well-trod path, that it also embraces numerous non-human animals. To begin, it must be allowed that, so far as we know, no wild creatures are moral agents nor, thereby, capable of a full-fledged participation in moral community. Accordingly, we do not hold non-human animals, yet alone plants, morally responsible. If great apes and possibly other non-humans are capable of learning and speaking a human language, this may change, though, even then, it is likely these animals will turn out to lack the mental capacity essential for a full agency. Supposing no non-humans possess even this limited capacity, however, it is nevertheless evident, as the eighteenth-century French philosopher Jean Jacques Rousseau argues (1950: 194) that many non-human animals, though "destitute of intelligence and liberty," possess a "sensibility" similar to our own and, accordingly, "partake of natural

---

[7] Midgley adds (1984: 91), apropos our argument in the next section:

> Nearly all of us would, I think, put that point to our small children if we found them tormenting animals, even animals with very limited nervous systems . . . The Golden Rule does not, however, seem to apply to forests. If we have duties to forests, they are not of that kind. But there are in any case other sorts of duties, so this need not surprise us.

We return to this important point in chapter two.

right" as a result of which humans are "subjected to a kind of obligation even toward the brutes."[8] Rousseau is not alone in drawing this conclusion (see Glacken 1967, Brumbaugh 1978, and Thomas 1983).

Recalling our earlier discussion of natural beauty, we can ask by contrast who could be so callous as not to think that it matters morally should the last person, driven by boredom, inflict pain on the lowliest of creatures. Thus, the American philosopher William James claimed, with typical flourish, that the world is not as good a place as it might be so long as "a single cockroach suffers the pain of unrequited love."[9] Similarly, Singer argues (1975: 8), "if a being suffers there is no moral justification for refusing to take that suffering into consideration." This reflects the defining importance of well-being for morality. The first and most indisputable principle for any ethics of nature is simply this: the well-being of every creature with a well-being matters morally. Well-being has moral value in and of itself and must, therefore, be taken into account wherever, for whatever, it is at issue. This extends moral concern beyond humanity, encompassing not only our fellow mammals but vast numbers of less advanced creatures, fish, reptiles, possibly, even, earthworms and cockroaches. Before inquiring as to the significance of this conclusion, however, we need to ask what, if any, role non-human animals play in our own, distinctively human moral communities. Can they be not only harmed but treated unjustly?[10] While the capacity to suffer establishes moral standing for non-human animals, too close an attention to sentience alone can distort the shape and range of our relations and obligations.

The naturalist John Muir tells of reading, as a child in Scotland, the story of a dog, Gelert, "slain by his own master, who imagined the dog . . . had devoured his son because he came to him all bloody when the boy was lost"; the truth, however, was that Gelert had been bloodied by a large wolf while saving the boy's life. Muir remarks (1954: 5):

---

[8] Anticipating Bentham's oft-cited observation, Rousseau remarks (1950: 194): "It appears, in fact, that if I am bound to do no injury to my fellow-creatures, this is less because they are rational than because they are sentient beings; and this quality, being common to men and beasts, ought to entitle the latter at least to the privilege of not being wantonly ill-treated by the former."

[9] Cited in Feinberg 1978: 65. Rosemary Rodd observes (1990: 176f.), "it is unlikely that anyone would seriously dispute the suggestion that a world in which animal suffering was reduced would be preferable to present conditions if this could be achieved without even the slightest inconvenience to humans."

[10] William Galston observes (1980: 124): "The contention that we are not free to treat animals in any way we choose has great intuitive force. But we must inquire into the principles of right conduct toward animals to determine whether animals stand within the sphere of justice, for not all moral restraints are founded on justice." Galston concludes some non-human animals are subjects of justice, though not in the same way or to the same extent as human beings.

This auld-lang-syne story stands out in the throng of old school day memories as clearly as if I had myself been one of that Welsh hunting-party – heard the bugles blowing, seen Gelert slain, joined in the search for the lost child, discovered it at last happy and smiling among the grass and bushes beside the dead, mangled wolf, and wept with Llewellyn over the sad fate of his noble, faithful dog friend.

Muir's response is not atypical. Most would agree that the heroic Gelert was not only harmed but treated unjustly.[11]

Speaking of Washoe, a chimpanzee taught to use Ameslan to communicate with her trainers, Johnson remarks (1991: 30): "The mere fact that she does communicate with humans and has entered into personal relationships of trust and affection with humans does seem to me to carry some moral weight. For those who have dealings with Washoe, failing to act toward her with goodwill would, I believe, amount to betrayal of trust, a double-cross." Johnson's intuitions are widely shared. Many hunter-gatherer societies have believed there exist "implicit agreements between humans and animals"; in addition, societies dependent on work animals commonly see them "as group members to the extent of refusing to eat them even when killed or disabled by accident, disease, or age" (Rodd 1990: 242f., 233; see 223–255 for examples, including the outcry in Britain over the sale of ex-cavalry horses for pet food). In such cases we find reasoning of the following sort, offered by a devout Hindu in explanation of his people's respect for cows (Rodd 1990: 235, citing Lodrick 1981: 14f.):

One does not ... kill one's mother once her useful life is over and she can no longer contribute anything to the household. Even so with Mother Cow – she gives us life through her milk and is a tender and faithful companion. She deserves better than death once her useful economic life is over, and so she should be cared for and fed in her old age.

Non-human animals are not only vulnerable and, thereby, worthy of moral respect, they enter into reciprocating relationship with us, becoming, thereby, associate members of our own, moral communities.

In recognizing this we need not deny the importance of moral agency for moral community nor, therewith, its distinctively human character. Too often ethicists, eager to save by praising a wild nature in danger of destruction, downplay the uniquely wonderful nature of human life

---

[11] VanDeVeer asks (1986: 65): "Who would not feel some sense of betrayal when an aged dog eagerly gets in the car for a ride but does not know that it is being taken to be put to death (commonly: 'to sleep')?" See Johnson on "Disposapup Ltd" (1991: 121f.).

and society. One consequence is they fail to appreciate fully the true wonder of nature: humans are no less a product of nature than wolves and dolphins.

Only human societies possess the level of reflectivity needed for the existence of moral community. In this respect humanity is uniquely, remarkably wonderful. In us it becomes possible for the first time to realize self-reflective, morally limed goods such as family, friendship, and political association, goods found nowhere else in the universe – so far as we know. The complex forms of relationship found among social animals such as elephants, wolves, chimpanzees, and bees provide mere analogues of these irreducibly communal goods. Hence, the total absence in animal societies of those legal and moral institutions which give human society its distinctive form and flavor. Accordingly, ethicists like Thomas Aquinas and Immanuel Kant are correct to stress human uniqueness.[12] It cannot be denied. There is nothing in our uniqueness, however, contrary to Aquinas and Kant, which precludes those who lack a full agency, mere selves, from being caught up, as direct objects of moral concern in the normative web of human life. It happens all the time.[13]

To grasp fully the place of mere selves in moral community, we need to pay closer attention to the role feelings and emotions play in the moral life.[14] A society of individuals who invariably did the right thing but failed to care, emotionally, about each other, would not add up to a truly moral community. While it is a mistake to overlook the role moral principles play in morality, it is no less a mistake to overlook the extent

---

[12] See Thomas Aquinas (1975: 115–19 [3rd Bk., Pt. II, c. 112]), (1964, vol. XIII: 122–35 [I, Q.96]) and (1964, vol. XXXVIII: 19–21 [II–II, Q.64, a.1]); also Immanuel Kant (1997: 147, 212–213, 218, 404; 434–5). Selections can be found in Regan and Singer (eds.) 1976 and Linzey and Regan (eds.) 1988.

[13] See the exquisite account of such relationships in Weston 1994: 15–58. Also the sensitive, informed discussion of zoos in Bostock 1993. Both books contain a wealth of information on "mixed communities."

[14] The fundamental error of Kantian moral theory lies not in what Schopenhauer rightly called the "revolting and abominable" view "that beings devoid of reason (hence animals) are *things* and therefore should be treated merely as *means* that are not at the same time an *end*"; nor even the correlative notion that "only for practice are we to have sympathy for animals" (see Regan and Singer [eds.] 1976: 125). The acceptance of these gross errors by otherwise morally sensitive individuals reflects a more basic, epistemic error, namely, the belief that human life and morality consists at core in a community of "pure reason." While brilliantly perceiving the importance of critical reason for human life, Kant distorts thereby the inherently limited role played in human life by critical reason, treating the academy (*qua* Enlightenment) as though it were the very fulfillment of human life, rather than a more-or-less interesting, more-or-less valuable addition. In this respect, Kant, far from breaking with medieval scholasticism, resurrects its overly rationalistic view of nature, God, and humanity. The moral error of Aquinas and Kant stems from a common, epistemic confusion. On the vital role feelings and emotions play in morality, see Blum 1980 and 1994, Noddings 1984, Kupperman 1991, and Nussbaum 1994.

to which being moral is a matter of having one's character, one's entire self shaped in an appropriate manner. That is why it is possible to recognize a genuine moral sensitivity in creatures who lack the conceptual sophistication to apprehend and act on moral principle. Though lacking the reflectivity characteristic of a full agency, mere selves may be and frequently are moved by concerns about the well-being of others. This allows for their partial incorporation into distinctively human moral communities. Failure to acknowledge this moral sensitivity distorts our own nature, making it appear as if moral concerns spring directly from the head of Zeus – rather than coming to be through a complex, biologically rooted, emotionally laden process of moral development. We cannot understand the moral community of moral agents until we see that it encompasses not only moral agents but those creatures who display in raw form the roots of our own humanity (Midgley 1986: 60f.).

Mere selves are entitled not only to moral respect but, therewith, *moral engagement*. The basic moral fact about such beings, human and non-human, is not their capacity to suffer but, rather, to *relate*, look us in the eye, express an opinion about us, the kind of people we are. Treating such beings as mere things shuts us off from a valuable source of moral insight regarding not only them but ourselves. We ought, rather, to engage them, watch them, listen to them, try to understand how the world and we appear to them.[15] As to what this engagement might look like, it is worth noting the role moral engagement plays in the "breaking" of wild horses. Getting a wild horse to submit involves, negatively, overcoming the horse's will to resist. More positively, it involves bringing the horse to recognize and accept a role and, therewith, responsibility in human society, one that requires it to trust and accept human direction. For this to occur the horse must understand verbal commands and, more fundamentally, react appropriately to human emotions, emotions integral to the moral life. One result is that in the process of domestication horses come to exhibit in relation to human beings a proto-morality similar to but more expansive than that which they exhibit in their relation to other horses. A horse that has been well trained knows its master and responds accordingly when it has not been treated right.[16]

---

[15] It is not necessary in doing this that we anthropomorphize non-human animals – anymore than it is that we bestialize human mere selves. See Midgley (1978: 344ff., and 1984, 125ff.); also Rodd (1990: 173f.).

[16] A similarly instructive process occurs in the domestication of wild elephants. As Midgley points out (1984: 115):

working elephants can still only be successfully handled by mahouts who live in close and life-long one-to-one relations with them. Each mahout treats his elephant, not like a tractor, but like

Keeping the process of domestication in mind reminds us that engaging animals morally is not a new or strange idea. To the contrary, it is a vital element in all traditional societies, familiar to anyone who has ever had to rely on the good will and cooperation of non-human animals. Just as there is good reason to believe a great many non-human animals are direct objects of moral concern, so there is good reason to believe human moral community encompasses, as associate members, many of those same animals. These wild creatures live lives of their own, formed by social and moral sensitivities; as such, they are capable of a limited reciprocity and, thus, rendered vulnerable to not only harm but injustice. Correspondingly, just as we are diminished by callously ignoring the plaintive cry of a suffering beast, so we become less than we might otherwise be when we think ourselves too learned to spend time communicating with our fellow animals. That they are unable to talk, literally, does not mean they have nothing to say about us and what we are doing to a world that is no less theirs than ours.

BIOTIC EGALITARIANISM

"Radical speciesism," as defined by Donald VanDeVeer (1986: 53), holds that no non-human animals are direct objects of moral concern; thus, "it is morally permissible, *ceteris paribus*, to treat animals in any fashion one chooses."[17] Showing this false is a matter of no small import. As Johnson observes (1991: 9): "once we recognize that there are interests in the nonhuman world, and that they are morally significant, we will have come a long way." The question remains, however, as to how significant

a basically benevolent if often tiresome uncle, whose moods must be understood and handled very much like those of a human colleague. If there were any less expensive and time-consuming way of getting work out of elephants, the Sri Lankan timber trade would by now certainly have discovered it.

Midgley (112f.) argues domestication in general depends on treating animals as individuals rather like us and observes, "all creatures which have been successfully domesticated are ones which were originally social," the one apparent counter-example, domestic cats, being descended from Egyptian cats, "unique among the small-cat group in their sociability."

[17] VanDeVeer (1986: 53ff.) distinguishes this position from two other varieties of speciesism, extreme and interest-specific; he contrasts these three positions with two non-speciesistic views, species egalitarianism and two-factor egalitarianism. I discuss these in the text to follow. The term "speciesism" is introduced by Singer (1975: 7) who, drawing on an analogy with racism and sexism, defines it as "a prejudice or attitude of bias toward the interests of members of one's own species and against those of other species." Similarly, Evelyn Pluhar (1995: 139; 165) characterizes speciesism as a form of exploitation while DeGrazia (1996: 28) labels it "unjustified discrimination against animals." Such definitions are unfortunate insofar as they tar by association those who affirm the moral priority of human life and interests, yet oppose exploitation and unjustified discrimination in any form.

non-human interests are compared to those of humans. Resolving the issue of *moral standing* does not, by itself, resolve that of *moral significance*.[18] The repudiation of radical speciesism is consistent with both "extreme speciesism," the view that non-human interests, while counting morally, count for nothing by comparison with human interests, and "species egalitarianism," the contrary view that non-human interests count the same, morally, as comparable human interests. How are we to resolve this problem of comparative moral force?

To begin, it is clear, given the role non-human animals play in human society and, thereby, moral community, that we must reject not only radical but extreme speciesism. If, as argued above, non-human selves possess claims of justice, their interests cannot be dismissed as trivial. Indeed, common-sense moralities, supported by traditional religious faiths, typically hold that while human interests count for more, we ought not to harm other animals for trivial reasons.[19] Depending on how we understand the good of humanity and, therewith, triviality, this establishes a potentially high standard of treatment. The reality, of course, has been and continues to be that many humans, ignoring morality altogether or taking a very lax view of their "necessities," act like extreme speciesists. This, in turn, has led others, moved by the plight of non-humans, to advocate species egalitarianism. Thus, that great nineteenth-century crusader for human and animal welfare, Henry Salt argued (1980: 10), "if we are ever to do justice to the lower races, we must get rid of the antiquated notion of a 'great gulf' fixed between them and mankind, and must recognize the common bond of humanity

---

[18] Kenneth Goodpaster observes (1978: 311):

Whether a tree, say, deserves any moral consideration is a question that must be kept separate from the question of whether trees deserve more or less consideration than dogs, or dogs than human persons. We should not expect the criterion for having "moral standing" at all will be the same as the criterion for adjudicating competing claims to priority among beings that merit moral standing.

See also Rolston 1988: 100.

[19] VanDeVeer labels this view "interest sensitive speciesism" and characterizes it (1986: 55):

when there is a conflict of interests between an animal and a human being, it is morally permissible, *ceteris paribus*, so to act that an interest of the animal is subordinated for the sake of promoting a *like* interest of a human being (or a more basic one) but one may not subordinate a *basic* interest of an animal for the sake of promoting a *peripheral* human interest.

While applauding interest-sensitive speciesism for its sensitivity to degrees of interest, VanDeVeer rejects it on the grounds that it says nothing about the weighing of interests between non-human animals and, fundamentally, "omits consideration of another factor which is morally relevant in adjudicating conflicts of interest," the extent of a creature's "psychological capacities." I address these concerns below.

that unites all living beings in one universal brotherhood." Here Salt rejects not only radical and extreme speciesism but the common presumption that human life and interests count for more than those of non-humans.[20]

The biotic egalitarianism espoused by Salt and numerous others encompasses a wide range of opinions regarding which non-humans are moral subjects. For some the equality affirmed embraces all living creatures, for others, sentient creatures alone, for still others, only selves. All biotic egalitarians agree, however, one, that at least some non-human animals are moral subjects and, two, that all moral subjects (and/or their interests) count the same, morally speaking.[21] I want now to inquire whether biotic egalitarianism is defensible.

The initial problem with biotic egalitarianism is one of moral absurdity. Speaking of species egalitarianism, VanDeVeer argues (1986: 57): "This view is unacceptable. That we should, for example, equally weigh the interest in not being killed of an oyster, earthworm, or fruitfly with that of a human being is an implication in virtue of which we can summarily judge, I submit, that [it] indeed reduces to an absurdity." However much we care about grizzly bears or jellyfish, it is hard to see how we can seriously regard, let alone treat them as the moral equals of human beings.[22] Consider the following real-life examples. In the first, four men are adrift in a lifeboat without food or water. Early on they capture, kill, and eat a sea turtle; later, tormented by hunger and near death, two of the men kill and eat a seriously ill third. Rescued and placed on trial, the two men plead necessity; they are convicted of manslaughter and given a lenient prison term.[23] Nowhere in the debate surrounding

[20] Similarly, Dave Foreman, of Earth First! fame (in Chase 1991: 116): "a grizzly bear snuffling along Pelican Creek in Yellowstone National Park with her two cubs has just as much natural right to her life as any human has to his or hers." Elizabeth Gray (1981: 9) goes further down the evolutionary scale in approving her young daughter's conclusion that jellyfish "are just as important and enjoy this beautiful day just as much as I do." Such intuitions are put in more formal terms by James Rachels (1987: 99), who argues that Darwin's theory of evolution undermines the belief "there is something morally special about being human." See, also, Rachels 1990.

[21] There is a theoretically interesting difference packed into the parenthetical. Utilitarians, such as Singer, claim moral worth and equality for *interests* while neo-Kantians, such as Tom Regan, claim moral worth and equality for *individuals*. This difference surfaces below in the nuancing of biotic egalitarianism.

[22] Murray Bookchin worries (in Chase 1991: 125) about the extent "biocentrism" stems from misanthropy, arguing that once one allows "human beings are no different from lemmings in terms of their 'intrinsic worth' and the moral consideration we owe them . . . one can easily come to believe that Ethiopian children should be left to starve just as any animal species that uses up its food supply will starve."

[23] For more on this oft-cited English case, *Regina vs. Dudley and Stephens* (1884), see Francione 1994: 728ff.

this case is a question raised regarding the moral or legal propriety of the men killing and eating a sea turtle. The obvious reason, identified by Gary Francione (1994: 730), is that "when it comes to animals, the level of human need that results in the 'necessity' for animal suffering or death is different from the amount needed when humans have needs but can only satisfy them at the expense of other humans." The same presumption appears in a more recent, American case involving a ship captain indicted for manslaughter on the ground he refused to throw an eighty-pound Labrador retriever overboard to make room for drowning humans. The captain, though claiming "he could not bear to do it," was clearly in the wrong, morally and legally (Johnson 1984: 337; 359). He ought to have sacrificed his pet dog. The deep affection for his dog provided no excuse for his callous disregard of human life.

In response to such problems, VanDeVeer offers a nuanced egalitarianism; this position, "two factor egalitarianism" (TFE), holds (1986: 56):

When there is an interspecies conflict of interests between two beings, A and B, it is morally permissible, *ceteris paribus*:

    1 to sacrifice the interests of A to promote a like interest of B if A lacks significant psychological capacities possessed by B,

    2 to sacrifice a basic interest of A to promote a serious interest of B if A substantially lacks significant psychological capacities possessed by B,

    3 to sacrifice the peripheral interest to promote the more basic interest if the beings are similar with respect to psychological capacity (regardless of who possesses the interests).

TFE proportions the force of morally relevant interests to both the kind of interests involved and the degree of psychological capacity possessed. All else being equal, a nod is given, as in traditional morality, to more basic interests. At the same time, while unlike the case in traditional morality no automatic preference is given to humans, the greater psychological capacity of humans gives their interests, in general, priority relative to those of non-humans, thereby bringing biotic egalitarianism into line with common moral intuitions.

What are we to say about this nuanced egalitarianism? One obvious question concerns the central distinction between basic, serious, and peripheral interests; making this clear is crucial if the introduced complexity is to guide moral reflection. I want to set questions of this sort aside for the time being, however, to concentrate on the appeal to psychological capacity. While this appeal allows us to avoid moral absurdities at one level, by giving a general priority to human interests, it still results, I want to argue, in morally questionable conclusions. By way of seeing why, it will be worth our while to consider the nuanced positions set forth by two egalitarians, Tom Regan and Peter Singer. Both deny species membership has any bearing on moral worth, yet count the interests of (typical) humans more than those of (typical) non-humans.

To begin, Regan affirms the moral standing of any being with the psychological complexity required to be "the subject of a life." Such beings, in light of this capacity, possess inherent value and, therewith, moral worth. Moreover, Regan argues (1983: 240f.): "Inherent value is . . . a *categorical* concept. One either has it, or one does not. There are no in-betweens. Moreover, all those who have it, have it equally. It does not come in degrees." It follows that the moral worth of a dog is no less or more than that of a human. At the same time, Regan distinguishes (188) the question of moral worth from that of comparative harm, arguing that the harm done in killing a human (*qua* moral agent) is greater than that done in killing a dog (*qua* moral patient).[24] Regan relies heavily on this distinction in his response to a dog-in-the-lifeboat hypothetical (285):

Imagine five survivors are on a lifeboat. Because of limits of size, the boat can only support four. All weigh approximately the same and would take up approximately the same amount of space. Four of the five are normal adult human beings. The fifth is a dog. One must be thrown overboard or else all will perish. Whom should it be?

Allowing (324) that "all on board have equal inherent value and an equal prima facie right not to be harmed," Regan notes some would take this to imply, contrary to our moral intuitions, that the dog should be treated no differently than the humans; this, he argues, is mistaken: "the harm that death is, is a function of the opportunities for satisfaction that it forecloses, and no reasonable person would deny that the death of any of the four humans would be a greater prima facie loss, and thus a greater prima facie harm, than would be true in the case of the dog."

Singer, appealing directly to differences in the kind of interests involved, draws a similar conclusion. Strongly rejecting any and all forms of speciesism, he affirms (1975: 8), "no matter what the nature of the being, the principle of equality requires that its suffering be counted equally with the like suffering – in so far as rough comparisons can be made – of any other being." This claim of equality has led some to accuse Singer of demanding that human and non-human animals be

---

[24] A "moral patient" is a subject-of-a-life, human or non-human, who is not a moral agent (see Regan 1983: 151f.). Moral patients are mere selves, in my terminology.

treated the same. Singer, however, clearly states (3), "the basic principle of equality does not require equal or identical *treatment*"; what it requires is "equal *consideration*," which, in turn, will require "different treatment and different rights" for different creatures. Given this, biotic egalitarians, though denying the relevance of species membership, may "still hold," as Singer (20), "that, for instance, it is worse to kill a normal adult human, with a capacity for self-awareness, and the ability to plan for the future and have meaningful relations with others, than it is to kill a mouse, which presumably does not share all of these characteristics." For Singer, as for Regan, marked differences in treatment are justified by an appeal to the kind and extent of interests involved.

These nuances allow Regan and Singer to side-step otherwise devastating criticisms. At the same time, one cannot help but wonder what is left of the commitment to moral equality. It is easy to imagine the dog tossed overboard viewing moral equality as small compensation for her death. This problem is especially acute for Regan, who refuses to aggregate losses and, correspondingly, must be prepared to toss an unlimited number of dogs overboard to save the life of a single, normal human being.[25] As a Utilitarian, Singer will not face this problem. He does, however, face others, among them that of deciding whether the interests of many small dogs, say, thirty Chihuahuas, require us to toss one of the humans overboard. In this case, it is easy to imagine the abandoned human casting aspersions on our commitment to moral equality. In any case, these and similar examples leave us wondering what role the notion of moral equality actually plays in the deliberations of nuanced egalitarians.

Clearly non-human animals gain something from even a nuanced egalitarianism. VanDeVeer cites the following example, relative to his own position (1986: 56f.): "Suppose, contrary to fact, that an infant with Tay-Sachs disease could be saved from imminent death by a kidney transplant from a healthy chimpanzee at the expense of the chimpanzee's life; TFE prohibits this way of adjudicating the conflict of interests." The reason it does is that the impaired child lacks significant psychological capacities possessed by the chimp. Singer (1975: 20f.), noting "a chimpanzee, dog, or pig . . . will have a higher degree of self-awareness and a greater capacity for meaningful relations with others than a severely retarded infant or someone in a state of advanced senility," argues that "we must grant these animals a right to life as good as, or better than,

[25] See Regan 1983: 324f. For a similar critique, see Wenz 1988: 147ff.

such retarded or senile humans." Forced to choose, the senile derelict goes overboard, leaving room for the healthy, life-engaging chimp.

That one is prepared to bite the bullet and toss impaired humans overboard does not make this stance any less contrary to common-sense morality. Aware that the decision to let a Tay-Sachs child die when it might be saved through the sacrifice of an animal may appear morally misguided, VanDeVeer observes (1986: 64): "The Tay-Sachs infant will die 'soon' anyway, typically by the age of five or six years and will suffer in the interim. Its interests in continuing to exist may, then, be less basic than that of the healthy chimpanzee in continuing to live." This is a relevant consideration; it softens the apparent absurdity and leads us to allow the morally right choice might be to let the child die. The same conclusion, however, might be reached by not only interest-sensitive speciesists but extreme and, even, radical speciesists, based on the child's interests alone.

The problem is not that we cannot imagine situations in which we ought not to sacrifice a non-human life for a human or, even, more extreme, sacrifice a human life for a non-human. The problem is that such choices are morally plausible only when the deck is stacked, when non-human interests actually, significantly outweigh those of the humans involved. Imagine to the contrary, a forced choice in which the interests at stake are exactly equal. In this case, biotic egalitarianism has no moral advice to give; we are free to follow personal preference or, having none, toss a coin. This, however, is intuitively wrong. We ought in such a case to come down on the side of the human. We ought, in other words, only to sacrifice human interests and life for non-humans when the latter have *more* at stake, however much more is required morally. In a moment, I will argue this is not a mere prejudice. Let me first press the case against biotic egalitarianism one step further.

In particular, I want to argue that the commitment of biotic egalitarianism to equality is less, not more than it ought to be. The problem is that in nuancing species egalitarianism, to weaken the otherwise overwhelming force of non-human interests, biotic egalitarians end up relying on considerations – relative to mental complexity – which undercut our commitment to *human* equality.

Suppose that the lifeboat contains only human beings, say, four highly intelligent, well-educated professionals – a doctor, a lawyer, an architect, and an ethicist – plus a mentally impaired adult. Does it not follow from a nuanced biotic egalitarianism that the four professionals are morally justified, all else being equal, in tossing their mentally impaired companion overboard? Not because he has less moral worth but, simply and undeniably, fewer prospects for good; he is bound to get less out of life than his four more psychologically complex counterparts, who have worlds to conquer, fortunes to make. The same will hold if one of these four can be saved from death by a death-inflicting kidney transplant on their impaired companion. The problem, as VanDeVeer notes (1986: 62) relative to his own position, TFE, is that a nuanced biotic egalitarianism "may require or allow that the interests of human beings need not be assigned equal weight where it is the case that there are significant empirical differences among humans in terms of psychological capacity." Not all animals are equal after all: some – the brighter ones – are given a preference, leaving us wondering just how "egalitarian" nuanced biotic egalitarianisms are. That all, rich and poor, are free to stay at the Ritz, does not entail the substantive equality of rich and poor.

Nuanced forms of biotic egalitarianism avoid moral absurdity in conflict situations by relying on considerations which end up undermining the basic commitment to equality. Equality of worth becomes a formality; what really matters are differences in psychological capacity. That these differences are not indexed to species does not mean, given the way reality breaks, that human beings are not privileged relative to other animals; preserving that difference is, after all, why the proposed egalitarianism has to be nuanced. More disturbing, reliance on differences in mental complexity carries over to our morally laden relationships with other humans and, in so doing, establishes an undeniable ground of preference for those humans who are intellectually gifted: their life, like that of humans in general relative to other animals, has greater value and, accordingly, their life and interests count for more, morally, than those of the simple.[26]

Advocates of biotic egalitarianism are rightly concerned with the egregious abuse of non-human animals by human beings, an abuse often justified by appeal to the moral priority of human life and interests. Their intent is to protect the weak and vulnerable, not open a door to dismissal or oppression. Nor is there any reason to believe that a lively concern for the well-being of non-humans is inconsistent with or contrary to a lively concern for the well-being of humans. At the same time, it is important to see that positions such as TFE are inconsistent with a strong, truly universal notion of human rights and, as such, threaten

---

[26] Attempts to circumvent this conclusion by introducing "rights" falter. If these belong to all moral subjects, biotic egalitarians are faced, in even stronger form, with the absurdities bringing down an unnuanced egalitarianism. Yet, given the great variation in human capacity, rights cannot be viewed as distinctively human without appealing to species membership, as I will below.

our commitment to a substantive human equality. Taking a nuanced biotic egalitarianism seriously would require us to attribute less value and give less consideration to the interests and lives of those human beings whose capacities are more constrained than those of other, more talented human beings.[27] There is simply no way to defend cross-species egalitarianism from moral absurdity without construing the equality it affirms in such a weak manner that its moral significance is eviscerated. Since the dog goes overboard in any case, it is difficult to see what we gain by denying that human interests and lives count for more morally than those of our fellow animals.

MORAL PRINCIPLES

Forced to choose between the life or comparable interest of a human and non-human animal, we ought, morally, to side with the human. However much the traditional presumption of human priority has been and continues to be abused, it is correct to at least this extent. Accordingly, I propose we set aside biotic egalitarianism and accept an overtly inegalitarian position, one that affirms the moral priority of humans, yet holds humans morally accountable for the way in which they treat non-human selves and sentients. This requires, in principle, no less consideration of non-humans than biotic egalitarianism: questions regarding the relative value of human and non-human lives and interests, questions egalitarians cannot avoid, reappear within this stance as part of our attempt to understand the moral priority of humans and, correspondingly, determine how much the lives and interests of non-humans count morally. As a result, biotic inegalitarians need ascribe no less consideration to the life and interests of non-humans than biotic egalitarians.

We are justified, as individuals and societies, in using wild nature for our own good so long as we treat it with proper respect. Few, if any, will deny this. The obvious question, of course, is what makes for proper respect. I want, by way of addressing this question, to recognize three

[27] What makes sanctioning of this "talent-based elitism" so disturbing is the extent to which modern society is built around its presupposition – as seen in the widespread refusal to recognize differences in capacity and, therewith, the hard fact that not all have the ability to succeed in worldly terms. We cannot face this since we assume falsely that "losers" are not only less gifted than "winners" but that their lives have less value. Winning has become everything – as seen in the heightened concern with providing all competitors an "equal opportunity," a good in its own right, yet a woefully inadequate base on which to build a good society. What we require is not a perfected meritocracy but a social order making more readily available to all, human and non-human, opportunities to live a good life.

principles, appealing, respectively, to necessity, decency, and deference. The principle of necessity allows that humans are justified in harming non-humans (and, more generally, wild nature) when doing so is necessary to preserve or advance a critical element of their own good. The following two principles require us, in meeting our necessities, to treat (wild) nature decently and deferentially, that is, with proper respect. I want now to say a few words about the second principle, decency, and its relation to the principle of necessity. I will engage the third principle, that of deference, in chapter two. At that point, our ethic assumes the form of a "humane holism."

The principles of decency and deference apply to nature in general, human and wild, in part and in whole. The principle of decency requires moral agents to respect the life and interests of selves and sentients. This respect falls into three categories, involving kindness, fairness, and rights. The first two have been dealt with above and can be treated briefly. The first category embraces all sentient creatures, granting them a claim to kindly treatment. It is morally wrong to disregard the interest of any moral subject in not being harmed; accordingly, respecting a being requires us not to harm it without good reason and, where reason exists, seek "the least detrimental alternative" (see Orleans, *et al.* 1998). The second category grants all selves a claim to fair treatment.[28] Treating a self with respect requires that we treat it fairly, in accord with its "just deserts," be this a matter of individual excellence or social reciprocity (Fern 1993: 24ff.). The third category, involving claims of right, needs to be discussed at greater length.

Rights are associated with particularly important interests and, as such, have "exclusionary authority," normative priority, over other considerations, including claims to kindly and fair treatment. Rights are not absolute, however, and may be overridden by other considerations, as in cases of human imprisonment. Here, considerations relative to the constitutive good of community are especially important. I want now, taking the general notion of rights as a given, to distinguish "capacity" and "status rights," locating the presumption of human priority in the latter.[29]

Many rights protect interests in the exercise of capacities vital to well-being, as, for instance, rights protecting freedom of speech and religion.

---

[28] Merely sentient beings, lacking intentionality, cannot be treated unfairly; hence, it makes no sense to grant them a claim to fair treatment.

[29] For more on rights, see Feinberg 1970, Waldron 1984, Fern 1993, and Novak 2000. More needs to be said about status rights than is possible here. This "more" would begin with and expand on the discussion of normative identity found in chapter six.

All selves for whom freedom of speech and religion are basic interests possess these rights, whether they are human or not. Should we discover that elephants, for instance, are moral agents, they would be entitled to the same basic rights as human moral agents. So far as we know, the only (finite) moral agents are human beings – though it appears, as noted above, that some non-humans are selves and, even, possess a proto-morality.[30] This makes it reasonable, in turn, to believe that some non-humans possess capacity rights analogous to those of humans. If this holds true, the priority of human interests relative to theirs is correspondingly limited. Since I intend here only to sketch the parameters of our obligations to wild nature, I will not explore this possibility further – beyond noting that the existence of non-human capacity rights (even if equivalent to those of humans) would not entail that humans do not possess other, status rights (simply by virtue of being human) nor, therewith, a real, though qualified moral priority.[31]

The priority of human life and interests stems from status rights possessed by all and only human beings. These rights require us to treat fellow humans in ways we are not required to treat our fellow animals. Thus, the killing and consumption of humans for food, cannibalism, is morally prohibited, unlike the killing and consumption of non-human animals. In the case of humans, harm requires a different trigger, one less tolerant of our necessities. This holds true whether we are dealing with humans who are super-intelligent or severely retarded – which explains why it is prima facie wrong to sacrifice an anencephalic child for a normal chimp. I say "prima facie" to allow that human priority may be overridden, as when the interests of non-humans are greater and/or the non-humans involved possess countervailing, capacity-based rights of their own. That these complexities exist does not negate the significance of *human* equality, the fact that all of us, whatever our capacities (and, therewith, capacity-based rights), possess – unlike chimps, turtles and, if there are such, extra-terrestrial moral agents – status-based rights. It simply means, like moral conflict, that morality is no more tidy than human life. Nature loves redundancy.

[30] An example is provided by those rhesus monkeys who refused to shock their fellow monkeys even though put by scientists in an experimental situation where doing so was the only way to obtain food (Pluhar 1995: 55f.; see also DeGrazia 1996: 199ff.).

[31] This would justify DeGrazia's conclusion (1996: 267) that "the presumption against killing humans, Great Apes, and dolphins is virtually absolute" and explain why the presumption against killing other animals is weaker, as DeGrazia reluctantly allows. On the question of animal rights, see Regan 1983 and *The Monist* 70 (January 1987). On the developing legal rights of non-human animals, see Francione 1995 and Wise 2000.

Why does species membership matter in this way? Here, we need to note vital differences between our appeal to species membership and those found in the various forms of speciesism identified by VanDeVeer. This will make clear that even though we ascribe moral significance to species membership, this does not entangle us in morally objectionable features of radical, extreme, or interest-sensitive speciesism.

To begin we do not claim, as radical speciesists do, that species membership makes for moral standing nor, correspondingly, that the failure to belong to a particular species precludes moral standing. The morally constitutive properties to which we appeal, sentience and intentionality, are grounded, in a way species membership is not, in paradigmatically moral concerns about well-being. Further, our position is not dismissive of non-human interests, as is true of extreme speciesism. While we have not taken (and will not take) a determinate stance regarding the comparative moral force of non-human life and interests, the programmatic, three-pronged principle of decency not only allows for but encourages concern for the well-being of all selves and sentients. Just what that involves will, of course, depend on how the ethic is filled out and developed. Finally, our appeal to species membership is not speciesistic in even the limited sense true of interest-sensitive speciesism, which holds (VanDeVeer 1986: 57) that "it is permissible to give preferential treatment to humans over animals *just because* the former are human beings." To the contrary, we ground the moral priority of humans in a general moral principle affirming the significance of status rights, in this case, status rights shared by all and only humans.

Species membership matters so far as moral significance is concerned because it constitutes, at least so far as humans are concerned, a "special relation," analogous to family membership.[32] While it would be morally anomalous to claim family membership as a morally constitutive property, being a member of some particular family makes a justifiable difference in the kind and force of one's interests for other members of that particular family.[33] For one thing, family members have special

---

[32] The two dominant schools of modern moral philosophy, the Utilitarian and Kantian, have a difficult time accounting for special relations. In both, vital nuances relative to things such as family membership are overwhelmed by general(izable) moral principles. Interestingly, that branch of modern moral philosophy which deals most adequately with special relations is ethical naturalism, whether by way of "a naturalized Aristotle" or "an empathic Hume." Midgley (1984: 98–111) argues explicitly, along lines similar to what follows, that species membership makes a morally relevant difference. See, also, the "concentric circle" theory developed in Wenz 1988. For criticisms of Midgley, see DeGrazia (1996: 61 ff.) and Pluhar (1995: 130ff.). For a criticism of Wenz, see Pluhar (1995: 167f.).

[33] Pluhar observes (1995: 166): "Kinship interpreted in terms of closeness can be used to justify the favoring of one morally considerable being over another, without violating the other's

duties of care; this not only justifies but requires parents, for instance, to pay more attention to the interests of their children, even if they are comparatively better off than other children. Of course, there is a limit to preferentiality, a point at which the interests of other children outweigh those of our own, just as there is a point at which the interests of non-humans will outweigh those of humans. Special relations provide a preference, not a blank check, relative to the interests of those who stand outside the relation (see Farley 1986; also Outka 1972 and 1992).

What makes a relation *special* in the sense with which we are concerned is not its importance. Though this is typically great, persons involved in such relations may and all too often do neglect them – as in the case of parents who spend all their time at work. Special relations, normatively speaking, are relations carrying with them duties and entitlements definitive of the relationship. These relations are distinguished from other relations by the manner in which they cohere and, so cohering, create a more-or-less discrete web of normative bonds, a fabric of justice. Such relations are formed in a variety of ways. Some arise by way of a discrete choice and commitment, as do marriage and naturalized citizenship. Others develop over time, along with an increasingly well-defined passion, as may prove the case with friendship. Still others are entered at birth, as are families and states-of-origin. In all cases, however, special relations normatively contextualize and, thereby, have significance for the personal identity of those who share in them. They are not passing affairs, overnight flings, mere business relations. While such relations may be no less normatively laden, they do not give rise to continuing, personally definitive contexts of relation. By contrast, special relations have the feel of a personalized institution, a more-or-less established form of relationship, a more-or-less permanent part of one's life. They cannot be simply walked away from; we have to get divorced, officially or not. Such relations have normative weight, demand more of us than other, more ordinary relations.[34]

Such special relations – family, friendship, citizenship, whatever – demand and justify morally laden preferences. As such they can appear and, indeed, all too often become to those who live within them occasions for exploitation and abuse. This appears in nationalistic crusades attacking innocent foreigners, patriarchal oppression aimed at the

basic rights, but it cannot be used to show that a being *is* morally considerable." Pluhar, explicating this "favoring" in terms of "acquired duties," rejects its extrapolation to species-based relationships.

[34] See Walzer (1983: 31–63) on the significance of membership for norms of distributive justice: fellow citizens have a special obligation to one another. See also, on the normative weight of special relations, Farley 1986.

weak within, and, no less, exploitation and abuse by humans in general of wild nature. That, of course, is one reason some moral reformers have dismissed the normative force of special relations, aiming thereby to ensure openness and equality. Hence the understandable appeal of biotic egalitarianism to persons concerned with the historic desecration of wild nature and, more particularly, the many gross injustices done to our fellow animals in the name of humanity. The strategy I adopt here, though no less committed to reform, assumes that we cannot and, even if we could, ought not eradicate the vital role special relations play in human life and morality. Preference and exclusion are not only morally dangerous; they are indispensable goods apart from which nothing like a truly good, fully human life could exist.

My claim, then, is that a special relation holding between all and only humans justifies the presumption in favor of human life and interests: though our humanity does not count for everything, it does count for something and justifiably so. This, of course, raises the question of justification: why believe such a relation exists? It is clear this normatively laden relation cannot rest on genetics alone (Pluhar 1995: 163ff.; also DeGrazia 1996: 61 ff.). Nor can it rest on the extent of "actual or possible interactions" with other humans – given the existence of incapacitated humans (Pluhar 1995: 61 ff.). What does it rest on? I want, for the time being, to set this question aside and put my claim hypothetically: if such a special relation exists it makes sense of human priority without dismissing as inconsequential the life and interests of non-humans. Later, in chapter six, I offer faith-based reasons, rooted in the overtly religious perspective of theistic naturalism, for believing that such a relation actually exists.[35]

There is no reason why those concerned about the abuse of non-human animals need be disturbed by this conclusion. For one thing, denying speciesism provides in itself no protection for non-humans: no ethicist has ever been more strongly opposed to speciesism than Kant. For another thing, claims of biotic equality are inevitably watered-down: Singer and Regan end up, as they ought, discounting non-human life and interests relative to those of humans. Further and most important, essentially the same results can be achieved, so far as the protection of non-human interests is concerned, by overtly inegalitarian stances; that human interests count for more does not entail that non-human interests

---

[35] I address the role faith plays in moral reflection in chapter three and following. The primary reason non-humans pose such a difficult problem for philosophical ethics is, in my opinion, that they expose the philosophically ungrounded, faith-based character of our commitment to *human* equality.

count for little. Thus, David DeGrazia, commenting on his own sweeping proposals for changes in the way non-humans are treated, notes (1996: 258, 280) that these "seem to depend only on giving animals *serious* – not necessarily *equal* – consideration." In short, while appeals to equality have rhetorical value, they turn out to make little difference once we confront real-world issues and, indeed, run contrary to the hard-won presumption of a substantive human equality.

LIVING WITH MORAL INDETERMINACY

We have reached two central conclusions. One involves moral standing: all selves and sentients, wild and human, are direct objects of moral concern. Another involves moral significance: humans count more, all else being equal, than non-humans. Readers who find these relatively non-contentious claims disappointing can rest assured contention enough will appear as we proceed. Before proceeding, however, I need to flag a crucial point relative to the problem of comparative moral force.

VanDeVeer distinguishes three varieties of inegalitarianism: radical, extreme, and interest-sensitive speciesism. The latter two grant moral standing to non-humans yet differ widely in the degree of consideration accorded, the second allowing for virtually none, the third, a great deal. Lest this appear a special problem for biotic inegalitarians, however, it is important to see the same variability appears among biotic egalitarians. There is no reason, in principle, why a biotic egalitarian could not nuance the claims of non-humans to the extent their interests count no more than they do for extreme speciesists. While denying equality leaves open a wide range of possibilities, affirming equality does not by itself narrow the range. For all the furor over biotic equality, neither its affirmation nor denial resolves the problem of comparative moral force.

It is necessary for egalitarians and inegalitarians to decide, before a determinate conclusion can be drawn, how much "interests" matter to all involved. Doing so is not the same as determining whether an interest is basic, serious, or peripheral. Under normal circumstances, staying alive is a basic interest for all living creatures. The question we confront is more difficult to answer. Put in terms of the lifeboat scenarios it goes like this: how bad is death for a (typical) dog compared to a (typical) human? What I want to call into doubt is the presumption there exists a single, rationally compelling answer to this question.

In part, this is a problem of epistemic access. What is it like to be a dog – or, as Thomas Nagel (1979: 165–180) puts it, a bat? For that matter, what is it like to be a corporate executive, an Amish farmer, a Sufi mystic, the woman next door? Assuming we can work our way around this issue, there exists a long and unsettled debate regarding the extent and manner, if any, in which death is a harm for anyone (see Nagel 1979: 1–10). The issue is not merely philosophical. Insofar as we care about the value of our own life we cannot avoid asking whether and, if so, what kind of harm death will be. To what extent ought I to orient my life around avoiding death? Is there anything for which I am willing, ought to be willing to die? These questions are vital, yet equally reasonable people (and cultures) come to different conclusions, live different kinds of lives.

   One of the virtues of the ethic we are developing, humane holism, is that it remains openly programmatic with regard to this vital issue. It does not pretend to know the value of life (or any other interest). All it claims is that the interests of all selves and sentients ought to be taken seriously and, further, that in cases of conflict we ought, all else being equal, give preference to human life and interests. Questions regarding the strength of competing interests are packed into the *ceteris paribus* clause, in the unpacking of which we encounter a perplexing indeterminacy of thought and obligation. What does morality require of us? Though I have not shown it to be the case, I want to claim that – and attempt in what follows to show how – answering this question, determining the morally reasonable thing to do, be it a risk to take or a life to sacrifice, requires not only hard thinking but a complex, multi-leveled act of faith.

CHAPTER TWO

Humane holism

ALL CREATURES GREAT AND SMALL

Given that we care, morally, about the well-being of our fellow humans, the conclusion that we ought also to care, morally, about the well-being of all selves and sentients is as close to rationally compelling as a moral stance gets. What that caring involves, what it demands of us in regard to non-humans or, for that matter, humans, is, by contrast, not liable to a single, rationally compelling solution. Reasonable, well-intentioned people disagree. Thus, though it may seem and undoubtedly is in many cases a mere bias that humans give priority to their own interests, this need not be the case. For one thing, in giving preference to another human, a person may act against her own interests, as in the case of a pet-lover who saves from a burning house the landlord she despises rather than the cat she adores. For another, such decisions may be rooted in reasons of the sort explored in chapter one.

I want for now to set these issues aside and continue our inquiry regarding the scope of moral concern. We have seen that morality requires us to take into account the interests of those wild creatures whose eyes look back at us from beyond the clearing of humanity. I want now to ask whether there is anything else out there, creatures without eyes, perhaps the forest itself, to which we owe moral respect. Addressing this question is vital if we are to develop a truly comprehensive ethics of nature. One condition for an such an ethic is that it recognize the moral standing of at least some non-humans; if not, as Tom Regan observes (1982c: 187f.), we have only a "management ethic" for the use of natural resources; satisfying this condition, however, establishes at most a "kinship ethic" relative to fellow selves and sentients. While this itself is no small accomplishment morally, we need to ask whether morality requires us to be concerned with the good of entities that are not selves or, even, sentient.

Albert Schweitzer, the great humanist, claims that it does in his proclamation of a universal reverence for all life, conscious and non-conscious (1976: 133f.): "Ethics thus consists in this, that I experience the necessity of practicing the same reverence for life toward all will-to-live, as toward my own. Therein I have already the needed fundamental principle of morality. It is *good* to maintain and cherish life; it is *evil* to destroy and to check life."[1] Schweitzer offers the following examples of what this reverence for all life involves (134):

A man is really ethical only when he obeys the constraint laid on him to help all life which he is able to succour, and when he goes out of his way to avoid injuring anything living. He does not ask how far this or that life deserves sympathy as valuable in itself, nor how far it is capable of feeling. To him life as such is sacred. He shatters no ice crystal that sparkles in the sun, tears no leaf from its tree, breaks off no flower, and is careful not to crunch any insect as he walks.

There is something intuitively appealing about this generosity of spirit and I want to consider it more closely. Ought we, as moral agents, to care about the good of each and every living creature?

Regan, while like all impressed by Schweitzer's life of service, finds this ethic puzzling and unpersuasive (1983: 242): "It is not clear why we have, or how we reasonably could be said to have, direct duties to, say, individual blades of grass, potatoes, or cancer cells. Yet all are alive, and so all should be owed direct duties if all have inherent value." Regan wants to know what it is about "being-alive" that renders an object worthy of moral respect. A similar concern is expressed by Peter Singer, who, unlike Regan, views sentience as a necessary and sufficient condition for moral standing (1975: 8):

The capacity for suffering and enjoyment is *a prerequisite for having interests at all*, a condition that must be satisfied before we can speak of interests in a meaningful way. It would be nonsense to say that it was not in the interests of a stone to be kicked along the road by a schoolboy. A stone does not have interests because it cannot suffer. Nothing that we can do to it could possibly make any difference to its welfare.

This absence of a felt significance leaves us wondering, as it does William Frankena (1979: 11): "Why, if leaves and trees have no capacity to feel pleasure or to suffer, should I tear no leaf from a tree? Why should I respect its location any more than that of a stone in my driveway if no

---

[1] Schweitzer adds (134f.): "ethics is in its most unqualified form extended responsibility with regard to everything that has life." For more on Schweitzer's ethic, see Attfield 1983: 153ff.

benefit or harm comes to any person or sentient being by my moving it?" If Schweitzer's ethic of reverence for all life is to be defended against this prima facie persuasive dismissal, we need to show that there is a morally relevant difference between pulling leaves from Schweitzer's tree and kicking Singer's stone. What might this be, given the absence of sentience?[2]

Attempts to extend moral status to non-sentient entities are faced with a dilemma: an appeal to paradigmatic moral concerns with well-being is blocked by the fact non-sentient entities do not, by definition, experience anything, good or bad; yet, appeals to other good-making qualities, such as beauty, lack moral force. If the moral standing of non-sentient entities is to be established some way has to be found to overcome or circumvent this dilemma. Can this be done? One possibility is to attack the first horn, arguing that non-sentient living creatures have a well-being of their own: it matters to the tree what we do to it, even if it does not feel better-or-worse as a result. I want, in the following section, to take a closer look at this line of argument. Though unable to bear the full weight of an environmental ethic, it offers an instructive account of nature's good. In subsequent sections I call on this account to challenge the second horn of our dilemma, arguing that wild nature-as-a-whole and, therewith, all living creatures, have moral worth.

AUTOPOIESIS

Regan suggests (1982c: 183; italics added), "the reason we cannot make sense of the idea that something might be in a *stone's* interests is *not* that it cannot suffer; it is that we cannot form an intelligible conception of what its *good* could be." If so, this opens up an interesting possibility. Might living creatures in general differ from stones in having, as Regan puts it, "a good or value that can be advanced or retarded depending on what is done to them"? Regan and various other ethicists have argued that they not only can but do. Joel Feinberg observes (1974: 52) that plants, while non-sentient, are not "mere things like rocks. They grow and develop according to the laws of their own nature." Similarly, Paul Taylor argues (1986: 122): "all organisms, whether conscious or not, are teleological centers of life in the sense that each is a unified, coherently ordered system of goal-oriented activities that has a constant tendency to protect

---

[2] If trees are sentient, they are, of course, covered by the moral extensionism of chapter one. Anyone who believes this to be the case may read this section as a hypothetical precursor to the forthcoming discussion of species and ecosystems.

and maintain the organism's existence." The behavior of living entities is goal-oriented and self-regulated; it unfolds in accord with an inner plan and, as such, has purposes and needs built into it. Lawrence Johnson puts the point well (1991: 146): "living beings have an intercoherent organic wholeness that is self-defining"; this "organic wholeness" sets the good and, thereby, interests of living creatures, sentient or not.

Simply by virtue of being alive, plants and animals possess an interwoven, objectively determined set of needs, requirements for their survival and flourishing. In this they differ from mere things, such as stones, that have no needs or interests. Matters are complicated, to be sure, by the existence of non-living things, such as cars and tractors, which have needs and interests of their own. These, no less than plants, will not function properly unless their needs are met. Still, as Johnson observes (1991: 145f.), there is a difference:

A tractor has a function, an identity as a tractor, only insomuch as someone considers it a tractor, assigning it that function. It has needs only with respect to its externally assigned identity. By itself, it is only a lump without needs. In contrast, a living being has a self-identity that, within a broad range, entails its own requirements. Whereas cancer is bad for an organism, rust on a tractor is bad only for the farmer. Were there no tractor-user, rust would only be change. Were there no other being to care about or have a use for a cancer-stricken worm, cancer would still be bad for it.[3]

It follows from this internally assigned identity that what happens to living creatures matters to them in a way it does not matter to tractors and cars. Living creatures have a built-in dynamic and, therewith, objectively determined good of their own. In response to the claim that measures of thriving and flourishing as applied to plants only flag our own interests, Robin Attfield remarks (1986: 98), "trees had needs before people existed, and cannot be supposed to have lost them."[4]

Living creatures, sentient or not, have an objectively defined end and, thereby, good of their own. Given this, it is reasonable to conclude, all things considered, the world is a better place when living creatures realize the ends proper to their own being. As Attfield observes (1986: 104):

---

[3] We must not to be misled by the possibility that worms, being sentient, may suffer. Johnson's point applies across the board, to sentient and non-sentient creatures.

[4] In developing this point, Attfield (1986: 99) calls on the notion of an "essential capacity"; an essential capacity is one "in the absence of which from most members of a species that species would not *be* the species [it is]." The *good* of a species is determined by its essential capacities: "the flourishing of an x entails the development in it of the essential capacities of x's." A classic example relative to humanity is "rationality."

"If trees have a good which is not our good, then they also *constitute* a good; if they have their own form of flourishing, they are thereby of value in themselves." That is what makes it more troubling when someone pulls leaves off trees than when they wander down a driveway kicking stones. In the first case we are interfering with nature's own ends, in the second we are not. This is an important point, crucial to what Schweitzer is getting at in his call to respect all living creatures. At the same time, its force is weakened by the existence of mere things, artifacts, which, unlike stones and tractors, have ends of their own.

Many human artifacts are feed-back mechanisms the behavior of which is internally directed. Some, like thermostats, are simple; others highly complex, like Deep Blue, the chess-playing computer. Each of these teleotic artifacts, like living creatures, has an objectively defined good it works to realize and maintain. If, however, plants have moral standing in light of their built-in purposefulness, will not the same hold for all teleotic entities? That thermostats and computers are artifacts is not (contra Taylor 1986: 123f. and Rolston 1988: 104ff.) morally relevant. The issue concerns what they are, not how they came to be that way – as it would be were we to create androids with human-like capacities and feelings. We appear, then, to confront a *reductio ad absurdum*.

One possibility, in reply, is to question the comparison, the alleged similarity. According to Johnson (1991: 146), "even the most complex computer – let alone a tractor – falls far short of having a good of its own." Similarly, Attfield argues (1994: 177) all artifacts now existing have at most "a derivative good, i.e. the performance of the function for which they were contrived." This appears true in that the complexity of even our most advanced computers is combinatorial, the placing of one thermostat, one on–off switch, on top of another. In particular, as Feinberg notes (1974: 52), no artifacts "grow and develop according to the laws of their own nature." The complexity of human artifacts is not only limited; it serves externally defined ends. By contrast, as Warwick Fox has argued (1990: 169), "the primary product of the operations of living systems is themselves, not something external to themselves"; all living creatures, Fox claims, are "characterized by the property of *autopoiesis*," the continuous striving of living systems "to produce and sustain their own organizational activity and structure."[5] Similarly Holmes Rolston argues (1988: 98) the simplest organism is "a spontaneous cybernetic

---

5 The term "autopoiesis," which Fox attributes to two Chilean biologists, Humberto Maturana and Francisco Varela, comes from the Greek *autos*, "self," and *poiein*, "to produce"; hence, the process of "self-production."

system, self-maintaining . . . sustaining and reproducing itself on the basis of information about how to make a way through the world."

What makes autopoiesis morally interesting is the way it orients living creatures toward survival and flourishing, makes them alive, and, correspondingly, vulnerable to death. Where there is no analogous process, we do not have the same reason to care whether a teleotic entity achieves the ends it seeks, whether it lives or dies.[6] Existing artifacts "are not concerned with the regeneration of their own organizational activity and structure"; hence, "they cannot be thought of as mattering to themselves" and, accordingly, Fox concludes (1990: 171), "there is no reason to extend moral consideration to [them]." The effort to escape death, characteristic of living creatures, signifies the integral unity and coherence of an existence that matters to the existent. That is why we speak of thermostats and computers as malfunctioning, not dying, save in the metaphorical sense we describe car batteries as "dead." Animals and plants, on the other hand, use energy for the purpose of living and, thereby, avoiding the alternative.

Being alive makes a difference.[7] Does this difference sustain a claim for moral standing? Some, allowing the difference, have concluded it does not. Donald Regan, echoing Frankena's question regarding the harm done in tearing leaves from trees, poses a rhetorical question of his own (1986: 197):

Consider an oak tree. If someone who says that an oak tree has a good of its own is pressed to justify that claim, he will usually respond by pointing out that an oak tree is a complicated, self-regulating, self-sustaining system. Now, if that is what it means to say that an oak tree has a good of its own, I agree that an oak tree does have a good of its own. But why does it follow that I have any moral duty regarding the oak tree?[8]

Though Regan allows that oak trees have an objectively determined good of their own, he fails to see why this good should receive moral protection. Is there anything the defender of moral worth can say in reply?

Given that we are dealing with non-sentient beings, just this, namely, that the complex patterning characteristic of autopoietic entities resem-

---

[6] Fictional portrayals of androids as moral subjects invariably portray them as concerned about their "termination," the classic example being Hal, in the movie *2001*; note, also, the gunslinger in *West World*, the replicants in *Blade Runner*, the heroic android in *Terminator II*, and Data in *Star Trek*.

[7] In *What is Life?* (1967), the physicist Erwin Schrödinger claims that life is qualitatively unique in its ability to resist entropy and, thus, counter the second law of thermo-dynamics; only life can "feed on negative entropy." Cited in Bramwell 1989: 55.

[8] Tom Regan poses a similar question (1982c: 202).

bles the intentional behavior of mere selves. This resemblance fuels Schweitzer's claim all living creatures, in their effort to survive, display a will-to-live and, accordingly, ought to be included in our golden-rule morality. Such a reply, as noted by Attfield (1994: 176), clearly addresses the above concerns. The problem it faces is that attribution of a "will" to non-selves is at best metaphorical.[9] What makes this metaphor illuminating is the fact that living creatures are autopoietic. At the same time, as John Searle observes (1994: 51 f.), those living creatures which are not selves, lack both the re-active adaptability of behavior and awareness indicative of even a limited intentionality. This weakens the perceived link between well-being and the objectively determined good of living creatures, leading some, while granting autopoiesis, to conclude that plants lack genuine interests and, therefore, a well-being of their own. The way we treat a plant, whether we tear leaves with abandon or respectfully hug and go our way, cannot matter *to it*, for there is no it, no self, there.

One mark of this is that plants, though distinct individuals no less than snowflakes, lack the individuality of even mere selves. By comparison with foxes, for instance, "it is very much more plausible," as Stephen Clark notes (1984: 170), "to doubt that there are individual grass-plants or individual bacilli in any sense not covered by saying there are bits of grass, or the like."[10] The autopoietic unity of plants does not provide for the individuality of selves or, even, the merely sentient. As a result, the good of individual plants matters in different ways than that of individual selves and sentients. Cutting a limb off a tree troubles us, if it does, for different reasons than cutting a leg off a pig. No matter how much we care or ought to care about trees, trees cannot look us in the eye, cannot engage us morally. There is nothing there, no pain or joy, no hope or disappointment, no striving with which we can empathize.[11]

One consequence is that even supposing oak trees have moral standing, it remains unclear what, if anything, we owe morally to individual oak

---

9 And not analogical, as in the case of God and persons, for which see chapter four.

10 Clark (1984: 171 f.) speculates that from points of view other than the human, "some plants may be individuals, as trees most probably are; some plants may have points of view." Going further, he concludes: "Even if a plant does not feel its own destruction, I would certainly admit that some plants are 'ethical individuals' and that their wanton destruction is murder, of a sort." While agreeing with Clark that the good of plants matters morally, I see no reason to believe plants have points of view or that the killing of a plant, however wanton, is murder, even of a sort. That killing a tree is not murder does not mean it is not wrong or even, morally speaking, worse than murder in some cases.

11 Tom Regan poses the problem well relative to his own, neo-Kantian ethic (1983: 395f.): "The central importance of *the individual*, given the rights view, poses unresolved questions about the ability of those who subscribe to it to develop an environmental ethic." Our view of ethics is broader but much the same problem remains.

trees. Thus, Attfield, while arguing (1987: 21 f.) that "moral standing . . .
belongs to whatever has a good of its own," ends up qualifying the level
of concern owed to the point it virtually disappears (86): "Though [non-
sentient animals and plants] have moral standing . . . their capacities are
so limited that the main value in their lives consists in their instrumental
value for creatures of other kinds. Yet, when other considerations are
equal, they should not be harmed or killed as if their good were a matter
of total indifference." Elsewhere, Attfield remarks (1986: 104), "the good
of trees might outweigh some of our whims but it does not outweigh our
interests except where our interests depend on it." While this does not
make trees of no ethical relevance in themselves, it leaves us wondering
whether trees belong in the same ballpark, morally, as selves and sentients.
And this, it seems to me, is precisely right – so far as individual well-being
is concerned. Appeals to autopoiesis take their place alongside appeals
to natural beauty, interesting but, morally speaking, of little significance.

The resultant constraints on whimsical destruction are worlds apart
from Schweitzer's strenuous ethic (1976: 137):

> Whenever I injure life of any kind I must be quite clear as to whether this
> is necessary or not . . . The countryman who has mowed down a thousand
> blossoms in his meadow as fodder for his cows should take care that on the way
> home he does not, in wanton pastime, switch off the head of a single flower
> growing on the edge of the road, for in so doing he injures life without being
> forced to do so by necessity.

Schweitzer's goal is not to avoid indifference but, rather, as he puts it
(137): "never to pass the limits of the unavoidable, even in apparently
insignificant cases." So far we have not come close to finding a rationale
for this ethic. Nor will we so long as the case for moral respect turns on
the claim that plants, like selves and sentients, have a well-being of their
own. The reason is that the good of plants does not matter to them.

SPECIES AND ECOSYSTEMS

It is interesting that Schweitzer speaks repeatedly not only of individual
plants and animals but *life* itself, as though it were the organic process that
matters morally. By way of exploring that possibility, it is worth noting
attempts to expand the above line of argument to encompass species and
ecosystems by arguing they, too, are autopoietic.[12] While many biologists

---

[12] Positions taken regarding this issue are complex. Some (Taylor 1986: 68ff.; Attfield 1983: 150f.,
and 1987: 19ff.), while allowing that autopoiesis grounds moral standing, argue that species and

view species and ecosystems as "artifacts of processes operating at lower levels of organization" (Sober 1986: 185f.), Johnson (1991: 154f.), drawing on taxonomic biology, characterizes species as homeostatic systems shaped by and influencing genetic selection, filling environmental niches, and restricting divergence from a defining norm by their response to selective pressures. So viewed, species are "genetic lineages" preserving a determinate identity and, thus, persisting through time. "A species," Johnson says (157), "like an individual organism, but unlike a tractor or a rock, is an ongoing coherent organic whole, a thing process, with past, present, and orientation and drive toward the future."[13] Given this, it follows that species, like living creatures, have interests of their own, over and above those of their parts.

Johnson cites as an example humanity (157): "humanity is not just a collection of persons with interests but is itself a living system." Since it "has complex properties and engages in complex activities that are not just the aggregate of those of the individual species members," humanity itself can flourish or, as the case may be, suffer (157f.). Correspondingly, Rolston argues (1988: 144) the primary harm done to species by extinction is not that particular instances of that kind cease to exist or, even, never come to be but, rather, the shutting down of a "generative process," "an incremental decay" in the overall "flow of life." What we aim to preserve is not merely a form of life but, fundamentally, a *formative* process (137).

Looking at species and, by extrapolation, ecosystems in this way, as life processes encompassing and ordering individual beings separated by time and space, encourages a dynamic, process-oriented view of nature. As to whether the irreducibly composite processes found there are sufficiently similar to autopoietic processes and, thereby, rendered worthy of moral respect remains a matter of much controversy. One problem, even more evident here than in the case of plants, is that "a species has no self" (Rolston 1988: 150). Rolston's reply, that a species is, nevertheless, "like the market in economics," an organized system with an identity extending over time, threatens a *reductio ad absurdum*, as Attfield well argues (1987: 21).[14]

---

ecosystems, unlike individual living creatures, are not truly autopoietic. Others (Singer 1979: 203f.; Regan 1983: 359; Feinberg 1974: 55f.) argue that such composite entities, even if autopoietic, have no morally considerable interests beyond those of the selves and sentients composing them. I consider here an argument to the effect that species and ecosystems are autopoietic and, therefore, worthy of moral respect.

[13] Rolston similarly describes (1988: 137ff.) species as "living processes." See, also, Fox 1990.

[14] Rolston is not troubled by this, I suspect, because he ends up relying on an appeal to natural creativity similar to that offered below.

Johnson responds to this threat by arguing (1991: 205) that species are distinguished by "an organic unity and self-identity on which [their] homeostatic feedback processes center." In this regard, species differ from merely teleotic entities such as waves (209):

> Like a wave moving over the water, a species is an ongoing process that is sequentially embodied in different bits of matter. Unlike a wave, however, a species has a cohesive self-identity that defines what is good for it. Some things contribute to the coherence, unity, and viability of a species, and some things detract. Unlike a wave, a species, when healthy, is a process that proceeds in a way serving to maintain its coherence, unity, and viability.

While this strikes me as true, it fails to lessen the disanalogy between our well-being and the good of species – a point holding all the more for ecosystems. The problem, once again, and even more so here than in the case of plants, is that the analogy with well-being is weak and, hence, moral significance minimal.[15]

Even if we allow that species and ecosystems have objectively determined goods of their own, there is no non-metaphorical sense in which these composite entities are alive, let alone live a life that goes for them better-or-worse. I conclude another foundation must be provided if we are to move beyond a kinship ethic. Moral extensionism has taken us beyond the campfire, into the wild. This expansion of moral awareness is not insignificant: no one takes wild nature seriously who does not take seriously the well-being of non-human selves and sentients. If, however, moral concern is to encompass species and, even, nature-as-a-whole, a more holistic account of moral standing has to be found, one that makes clear what is at stake, morally, in the good of species and ecosystems.

ENVISIONING A HOLISTIC ETHICS OF NATURE

Simply recognizing the moral standing of non-sentient beings, plants or species, would mark a fundamental departure from the now dominant, individual-centered ethos of traditional philosophical ethics.[16] Regan

---

[15] Even if, as Lovelock argues (1979), the Earth *qua* biosphere is a vast, all-encompassing organism, the moral relevance of this fact is limited due to the disanalogy between the Earth's good and that characteristic of selves and sentients. This does not mean the highly integrated, autopoietic-like character of the biosphere is morally irrelevant – only that we need to explicate its moral significance in a way that does not rely on an individualistic ethics of well-being.

[16] This point is made by Kenneth Goodpaster (1979: 28) and J. Baird Callicott (1989: 143). Each errs, however, in characterizing an individual-centered ethic as "egoistic," a stance rejected by Kant, Bentham, and virtually every traditional ethicist. See Annas 1993 for a thorough refutation of the claim that eudaemonaic theories, the most suspect in this regard, are egoistic.

and Singer, no less than Kant and Mill, adopt a view of moral concern that is focused on the good of individuals. They do so because this view makes good sense and, indeed, so we have claimed, is epistemically basic for the moral life: moral concern is rooted in an awareness that what we do matters to the well-being of individuals. That morality begins here, however, does not entail it must or ought end here. As Kenneth Goodpaster observes (1979: 32): "human persons may well be paradigms ... but paradigms provide clues and starting points – not stopping points." Citing the biosphere as an example, Goodpaster proceeds to argue that the "moral universe" includes "structures *inclusive* of persons respect for which is just as incumbent upon us" as respect for individuals. Recognizing this does not entail we must deny, *per absurdum*, the centrality of individual well-being for ethics.

Granting moral standing to "structures inclusive of persons" will not break the hold of ethical individualism, however, if we do so on grounds that are inherently individualistic, like appeals to autopoiesis. Any ethics that makes the having of a well-being essential for moral standing will be individualistic in that only individuals have a well-being of their own in a sense with which we can empathize. If we are to achieve a truly holistic ethic we will need a moral point of view that keys on something other than how well life is going from the inside-out. It is not enough that we grant moral standing to composite entities; we must do so for the right kind of reasons.

What will such reasons look like? An answer can be seen in the role natural processes and relations play in the well-being of selves and sentients. Even if the good of species and ecosystems does not constitute a well-being of their own, it does have a vital relation to the well-being of moral subjects. Further, crucially, this relation is not only instrumental but bears directly on the identity and, where applicable, self-awareness of the individuals by whom nature is composed. In this sense, a comprehensive ethics of nature depends on not only our view of wild nature but, no less, our own, true nature.

An awareness of this need for a transformed view of humanity appears in Aldo Leopold's epoch-making call for a holistic land ethic.[17] Leopold, arguing (1970: 238ff.) it is a mistake for ethics to focus all its attention on individuals, proposes (262), to the contrary, that "a thing is right when it tends to preserve the integrity, stability, and beauty of the biotic

---

[17] According to Wallace Stegner (1987: 233): "When [the] civilization [to come] assembles its Bible . . . *A Sand County Almanac* will belong in it, one of the prophetic books, the utterance of an American Isaiah."

community." As to what this "key-log" involves, Leopold says conflicting things. At times he claims (239) that "[t]he land ethic simply enlarges the boundaries of the community to include soils, waters, plants, and animals, or collectively: the land." Here, Leopold talks like an extensionist making a slight adjustment in his list of moral subjects. At other times, however, Leopold makes far more sweeping claims about our identity as human beings. In one Thoreau-like moment, he argues (240) that "a land ethic changes the role of *Homo sapiens* from conqueror of the land-community to plain member and citizen of it." Here, Leopold flags the role a transformed sense of self plays in the formation of a genuinely holistic ethic of nature.

The latter claim is more accurate. As Wendell Berry (1977: 51) puts it: "it is impossible to divorce the question of what we do from the question of where we are – or, rather, where we think we are." A determination of what we ought to do in any particular case will always reflect our under-lying sense of self, of where and who we are. The ethical imperative is bound up with the indicative of identify. Some idea of what this involves can be seen in Mark Sagoff's argument that in setting public policy we need to reckon with the cultural values which define our communities and, in so doing, shape our identity. In particular, Sagoff argues (1988: 141) that we, as Americans, ought to protect and preserve our natural environment in light of the extent America has been and continues to be defined by its relation to and historic abuse of wilderness.[18] "Our virtue as a people," Sagoff claims (141), "depends to a large extent on our benev-olence toward our natural environment." As to what this involves (142): "This kind of benevolence appreciates the character of things and allows objects their own integrity by restraining the interference of man. This is a reverence for all things on which we might base an acceptable envi-ronmental ethic: It respects nature enough to leave it alone." Whether or not this appeal to cultural values provides a sufficient basis for an environmental ethics, which I doubt, Sagoff's account illumines the role

---

[18] Sagoff stresses the oft-overlooked moral significance of our membership in "inclusive wholes," such as professions, communities, religions, and nations. Thus, he observes (1988: 121):

When you turn your attention to conditions in the workplace or in the environment, or when you consider the way wealth is distributed in society, you may feel responsible for the evil you see because you are a member of that society. You may be ashamed as an American, for example, for the racism in American society. You may have done nothing personally of which you are ashamed; shame, rather, touches what you are, not what you do; it touches you because you are a member of a profession, community, religion, or nation that practices discrimination.

I return to this crucial point in chapter six relative to the theme of corporate responsibility and, more broadly, irreducibly communal normative identities.

our sense of identity and, thereby, the holistic social entities to which we belong, play in an ethics of nature.[19]

Another illuminating and, in the end, more adequate account of the role values and identities play in environmental ethics is provided by Rolston, according to whom (1988: 341): "developing an ethics is a creative act, the writing of an appropriate chapter in an ongoing story, whether the 'writer' lives in culture or in nature."[20] While every "ethics should be rational," we must bear in mind that "rationality inhabits a historical system" (341f.). Thus, Rolston argues (342) we ought to protect the Grand Canyon not as "a representative canyonland" but because of its historical particularity, its meaning for us. Here Rolston echoes Sagoff's appeal to cultural value. Rolston differs from Sagoff, however, in his insistence that human identity as it relates to nature, our place in the great river of life, is a biological given with which we must come to moral terms. We live, along with other creatures, "in a historically objective world" (342f.; also 135f.; 177ff.): "Storied residence does not begin with humans ... The genome is a historical set but without awareness. Plants and animals are historical but do not know this subjectively." Correspondingly, it is not enough for Americans to recall the 400 or so years since America was colonized by Europeans nor, even, to recall the thousands of years native tribes inhabited the land; we must look beyond all this to the primordial struggles from which life – and we – arose. I want now, in the following two sections, to extract from this encompassing history the basis for a genuinely holistic ethics of nature.

THE INHERENT VALUE OF WILD NATURE

Nature-as-biosphere, the great river of life, has value for us because its history is our history, our identity. What remains unclear in Rolston's account of this value is the relation between history and moral concern.

---

[19] Clark puts the critical point well (1984a: 168): "though I have great sympathy for this approach, and think it one more flaw of far too much 'frigid philosophy' that this awareness has not been thought worthy of more philosophical comment, I must still ask whether such a culture is in the end worth remembering."

[20] Rolston (1988: 343) notes here the secondary role played by appeals to autopoiesis: "words such as homeostasis, conservation, preservation, stability – even species and ecosystem – are only penultimate in environmental ethics .... The ultimate word is *history*." For more on our "storied residence on earth," including characterizations of nature as the "living museum of our roots" and a "great river of life," see 341 ff. and, especially, 1986: 118–42 ("Values Gone Wild"). Here Rolston moves beyond limits imposed by an ethics of well-being, toward a truly holistic ethics of nature. Similar movement can be seen in Johnson 1991 and Fox 1990, both of whom stress the importance of a narrative-funded identity.

Until this is made clear, appeals to natural history fall into the same, morally peripheral category as appeals to natural beauty. What we want to know is not simply why we ought to care about wild nature; we want to know why the value it has for us makes it a direct object of moral concern. To see this we need to take a closer look at the inherent value of wild nature. We must see why wild nature, in mattering for us, matters in its own right.

Consider, in this regard, the construction, in Japan, of "Wild Blue Yokohama," a massive indoor, artificial beach."[21] Complete with sand made from concrete and rubber, simulated shipwrecks, plastic palm trees, and six-foot waves, the entire beach and bay, 60 yards wide at the shore and 100 yards deep, is situated inside a gigantic building, surrounded by a 380-yard artificial river, "a fake rain forest, water slides, a small outdoor pool, Jacuzzis and sunlamps." The builders of this and similar projects are calculating that many people, distressed by crowded highways, polluted seas, disappearing coastline, and "unpleasant and unpredictable elements like blowing sand, freezing winds, a torrid sun and insects," will welcome the opportunity to frolic in "the great indoors."

And so they do. One visitor to Wild Blue Yokohama, a man who lives "near a famous surfing beach outside Tokyo," explained: "I don't get dirty and I don't get suntanned." For him, like many, wild nature is troublesome. Surfing on artificial waves, skiing on artificial slopes, allows us to avoid discomforting aspects of nature, while, at the same time, reaping (for some) much the same benefit. Rather than taking pleasure in a pristine beach or ski slope, some find solace in the thought of a technologically tamed nature, free of jellyfish and hidden rocks. This view is not one I share. What reasons are there, though, for thinking it mistaken, morally or otherwise? On what basis are we to object when people find their pleasures in a "manufactured paradise," call on human ingenuity to escape "natural cycles of birth, growth, death, and decay"?[22] There are, of course, obvious (and not so obvious) problems having to do with access to public goods and resultant social injustice.[23] Are there, though,

---

[21] For more on this phenomenon, see "To Surf and Ski, the Japanese are Heading Indoors," *The New York Times*, Tuesday, June 15, 1993. Otherwise unattributed quotations in this and the following paragraph are taken from this article. Up-to-date information on Wild Blue Yokohama and other such facilities can be found on the Web, including plans to build in Anaheim, California, a 600,000-plus square foot "surf and ski" complex, with twelve-foot waves, shops, and restaurants.

[22] Berry (1977: 55f.) poses this question regarding the extensive reliance on technology throughout the modern world. I have learned much from his response regarding our true nature and good.

[23] Thomas Merton prophetically foresees a time "when people who cannot understand that rain is

reasons for distress that turn on a failure to appreciate the value of wild nature? By way of ferreting out one possibility, let me describe an experience I had some years ago backpacking with my father, a true devotee of wild nature, in the Sierra Nevada.

The day, a typically bright and sunny July day, had been spent walking twelve miles downstream from Simpson Meadow to Tehipite Dome, a place I had long wanted to visit. The Dome rises some 5,000 feet above the Middle Fork of the King's River, which at this point has carved out an almost equally deep canyon no more than a few hundred yards wide. After traversing a trail which kept disappearing under water, we arrived at Tehipite late in the afternoon, set up camp, and promptly went fishing. Not long after dinner, we were roused to action by the ominous sight of massive thunderheads rolling up the narrow canyon. Quickly huddling under what little protection we had, Pop and I proceeded to live through a harrowing experience, marked by enough rain to raise the river a foot and a half and, more significantly, enough lightning and thunder to convince us we were about to join our dinner in fried fish heaven. Eventually we crawled into our sleeping bags and settled down, prepared to ride or, perhaps, float out whatever the night might bring. Just as we were about to go to sleep, the clouds broke, not enough so we could see the stars or the full moon behind but enough so that the moon's light shone through and illuminated Tehipite Dome, of whose existence we had ceased to be aware. Suddenly there it was, moonlit, a marvelous, awe-invoking beauty, an embodiment in stone of the world of which we were now so much a part, a world of wonder and reality, a world that seemed in that moment eternal.[24]

That is not the kind of experience fathers and sons are likely to have in the Wild Blue Yokohama. Nor is it an experience I would trade for a life-time pass to any and all indoor paradises. Why is that? One obvious answer is that Wild Blue Yokohama, with its plastic trees and crushed concrete, lacks the awe-inspiring beauty of sugar pines and river-carved canyons: "nature constitutes a different and greater kind of order than anything that we, acting as one species alone, can create" (Worster 1993: 183). We need, though, to take care. Technology does not stand still.

---

a festival" will turn it into "a utility that they can plan and distribute for money": "they will sell you even your rain" (1966: 9). For more on social and moral problems relative to environmental degradation, see Northcott 1996: esp. 1–39, 257–327; also Attfield 1999.

[24] The experience reminds me, in retrospect, of a poem, "Oh, Lovely Rock," by Robinson Jeffers. See Devall and Sessions 1985: 103.

Consider another experience, more recent and not nearly so memorable but very much on target. This occurred while watching *Deep Space Nine*, a *Star Trek* spin-off. Among the characters in this television serial, which takes place on a space station near the entrance to an intergalactic wormhole many light years from Earth, is an African-American man, Captain Sisco. In addition to being a Star Fleet officer in command of the space station, the Captain is a single parent, a fact around which the pilot episode builds: it seems his eleven-year-old son, Jake, does not want to live on the space station, preferring instead the open skies and green fields of Earth. In one scene the Captain tries to persuade Jake he will enjoy life on the space station; their conversation takes place on a picturesque wooden bridge, on the edge of which Jake is sitting, fishing in a small stream. During it we can hear birds singing and see deer foraging among the trees lining the brook; Jake catches a fish and pulls it in. It is the kind of place any nature-lover can easily imagine a small boy having a difficult time leaving for the cold, dreary world of outer space. At last the captain persuades his son to give the space station a try and the two of them, gathering up their fishing equipment and the day's catch, walk off the bridge – at which point the captain nonchalantly remarks, "computer, end program," and the audience realizes to its surprise that the interaction has taken place in a small room on the space station. This room, the "Hollideck," creates a virtual reality so sophisticated that those inside cannot tell they are inside a computer-generated reality.[25]

Suppose now the experience shared by my father and me, that of seeing Tehipite Dome in the moonlight, took place on a Hollideck. What, if any difference would that make? To begin, there is no basis for distinguishing the two experiences in terms of beauty. There are no telltale signs of plastic trees or steel girders. Further, unlike the case with a Potemkin village, a front with no depth, there is no way here to look behind the scenery. Wherever we look, whatever we take apart, we find the same complexity and beauty we do in the real world. In short, wild nature no longer displays an order more complicated and marvelous than any we have been able to devise.

Does it follow that this virtual reality has the same inherent value as wild nature? By stipulation, no one, looking on, can tell one from the

---

[25] One episode of a sister program, *Star Trek: The Second Generation*, has characters attempting to gain access to the Hollideck to rescue compatriots from an errant program only to discover that their effort is taking place in the Hollideck, or so it seems. Since Hollideck worlds are indistinguishable from the worlds they model, the process of stacking can, in principle, go on indefinitely – a rich source of philosophical quandaries, akin to those portrayed in the movie *Total Recall*.

other.[26] To dismiss the Hollideck as a mere artifact is no more plausible than denying moral respect to androids on the same ground. It appears, then, so far as beauty and complexity go, that the Hollideck has as good a case for moral standing as wild nature. Still, there is something incredible about this. For one thing, there is no reason for distress when the Captain terminates the computer program. Clearly, though, there would be had Pop and I, calling on a mysterious power, terminated an ecosystem so as to end up, warm and dry, in bed at home. What is the morally relevant difference?

One obvious difference is that computer programs can be turned back on. Suppose, then, we stipulate that once a Hollideck program is terminated it cannot be recovered. Clearly, this gives a reason to pause before signing off. In the case of Tehipite Dome, though, we have an additional, more directly moral reason for hesitation. There, signing off will not only terminate a wonderfully unique program, it will result in the death of numerous living creatures, including many selves and sentients. Here is a source of inherent, moral value absent from the Hollideck.[27] Since we are attempting to find an inherent value in wild nature other than that of selves and sentients, let us remove, once again by stipulation, all selves and sentients from the Tehipite Dome ecosystem. Indeed, let us go further and remove all living creatures. All that remains, lying at the base of that giant, lifeless rock, is the primordial soup of organic compounds from which one day life and, with it, a vast flood of selves and sentients will emerge. Does a morally relevant difference remain?

Our earlier focus on beauty and complexity might suggest the edge now lies with the Hollideck. A moment's reflection, however, shows this is not the case. Reduced to its bare essentials, the inherent value of wild nature leaps forth. Unlike the Hollideck, wild nature is a life-creating, life-sustaining teleotic system, the womb of life from which we and our earth-born companions have emerged and apart from which we cannot survive, let alone flourish. The potential for this awesome process is present, long before the soaring beauty or mind-numbing complexity, in

---

[26] I include the clause "looking on" to address an interesting problem relative to the stipulated indistinguishability. Assuming we are dealing with holograms, not replicants, one way to tell if you are in the Hollideck is to "eat the fish" and see what happens to your hunger. To deal with this "disconnect," bodily functions need to be linked causally to the computer program, as they are in *Total Recall* and *The Matrix*.

[27] I assume that creatures appearing in Hollideck programs are *not* alive. If they are alive, as some episodes of *Star Trek: The Second Generation* suggest of a particular Hollideck figure, "Dr. Moriarity," the whole scenario changes. We would then be dealing with replicants, possessing parallel properties and moral status.

the first stirrings of that primordial soup, there prior to the coalescence of organic molecules into our most primitive ancestor, long before dinosaurs walked the earth, long before any of its offspring ever wondered about inherent value. It is *that* creative process to which the ever-changing, ageless wonder of Tehipite Dome bears witness.[28]

MOTHER NATURE

Wild nature has instrumental value of a kind and degree the Hollideck lacks. This makes wild nature not only a direct object of prudential concern but, no less, a vital, indirect object of moral concern relative to social, distributive justice. If wild nature is to possess moral standing in its own right, however, it must, in addition, have moral worth, inherent value of a morally relevant kind. Our dilemma, noted earlier, returns. Wild nature is not intentional or sentient in the manner true of paradigmatic moral subjects. Yet applicable values such as beauty and teleotic complexity are not clearly moral and, even if allowed, provide at most for peripheral significance. Morality, the moral point of view, is defined and, thus, delimited by concerns about well-being. This, in turn, appears to entail that only entities with a well-being of their own are direct objects of moral concern. Hence the interest in moral extensionism and subsequent arguments concerning autopoiesis.

It does not follow, however, from the fact that moral values are linked to concerns about well-being that only entities with a well-being of their own count as moral subjects. I want now to argue there is a morally constitutive property, "sentiosis," tied to concerns about well-being, yet not requiring, like sentience and intentionality, the living of a life that goes better-or-worse from the inside-out. Leopold points us in the right direction (1970: 253): "Land, then, is not merely soil; it is a fountain of energy flowing through a circuit of soils, plants, and animals ... a sustained circuit, like a slowly augmented revolving fund of life." Correspondingly, Rolston (1988: 221f.; also 197) describes nature as inherently

---

[28] Note that Tehipite Dome, far from being a bystander, is a vital element in the creative process: the organic soup requires inorganic ingredients and, no less, an inorganic bowl. Wild nature would not exist apart from the minerals and water, the lightning and thunder, that make the Earth an inhabitable planet. Like its kin in Yosemite and Zion, Tehipite Dome is a powerful symbol, a salient embodiment of the role inorganic substances – earth, water, air and fire – play in the creation of life. Even where destruction of such wonders does not threaten the integrity or stability of wild nature, it betrays a lack of sensitivity, a failure to take into account where and who we are – as Johnson observes (1991: 282ff.) regarding Ayer's Rock. For a probing, evocative reflection on our relation to fire, one of the basic inorganic elements of life, see Strohmaier 2001.

projective, creating, sustaining life in the face of powerful entropic forces to the contrary: "There flows this great river of life, strange and valuable because it flows (projects) uphill, negentropically from nonbeing to being, from nonlife to objective life and on to subjective life." What we most admire in nature and what most deserves respect, Rolston asserts (163) are "the vital productive processes . . . the lush life that ecosystems maintain." He adds (197):

Nature is a fountain of life, and the whole fountain – not just the life that issues from it – is of value. Nature is genesis. Genesis.

These images give a good sense, I believe, of what Schweitzer was getting at in characterizing life in terms of a will-to-live – the persistent blossoming of nature.

What makes this creative process a source of moral worth? We have already seen reason to doubt natural beauty alone can sustain the burden of moral concern. Nor will we get far in appealing to an analogy with the well-being of selves and sentients. Is there anything else? One possibility is to combine appeals to beauty, teleotic complexity, and antiquity. Nature, Donald Worster notes (1993: 183), is "a creative work that has been going on for billions of years." Similarly, David Ehrenfeld argues (1978: 207f.) that biotic communities and species "should be conserved because they exist and because this existence is itself but the present expression of a continuing historical process of immense antiquity and majesty." This claim, labeled "the Noah Principle" by Ehrenfeld, contains, no less than Schweitzer's ethic of reverence, a vital truth. We ought to honor the marvelous coming and going, the ebb and flow of life over countless generations. To capture what it is about this process that demands moral respect, however, we need to be more specific regarding its relation to paradigmatic moral concerns with well-being.

Imagine, in this regard, the existence of an anti-nature, on the planet Nearth. This world, let us assume, is indistinguishable from our own as regards age, teleotic complexity, and beauty. If a snapshot were taken, it would look very much like our own world. Further, it has come to be that way through an evolutionary process parallel to that we presume has occurred here. The only difference is that on Nearth the creative processes result in beings for whom the overwhelming reality of life is negative, woe upon woe. Take the worse case scenarios from our world and multiply them billions of times. While life on Earth often strays from heavenly bliss, life there, on Nearth, is unrelentingly hellish: nasty, brutish, and short. Those inclined to religious perspectives, like myself, may regard Nearth as the creation of a diabolical being, one that rejoices in misery.

It seems clear, however we fill in the details, that this anti-nature is not worthy of moral respect. Certainly, we ought not to disregard the suffering of its inhabitants in deference to its age, teleotic complexity, or diabolical beauty. Anyone who did so would not be taking the moral point of view seriously. This, in turn, tells us something important about the way our nature must be if it deserves moral respect.

One thing we presume in regarding nature as our metaphorical mother is its basic goodness. The world that we live in, the world that has come about through the creative process of nature, is a world whose positive features run deeper and count for more in the long run than its negativities. We associate the beauty and, more broadly, majesty of nature with its bounty, for us and all living creatures. The world of Nearth is fear-invoking, not gratitude-inducing and, correspondingly, awesome in a different sense than our nature, one not deserving of respect. Of course, some, among them John Stuart Mill, view this world as a kind of Nearth (1969: 28f.):

In sober truth, nearly all the things which men are hanged or imprisoned for doing to one another, are nature's everyday performances ... Nature impales men, breaks them as if on the wheel, casts them to be devoured by wild beasts, burns them to death, crushes them with stones like the first Christian martyr, starves them with hunger, freezes them with cold, poisons them by the quick or slow venom of her exaltations, and has hundreds of other hideous deaths in reserve such as the ingenious cruelty of a Nabis or a Domitian never surpassed.[29]

Schweitzer himself (cited in Johnson 1991: 137f.) remarks of wild nature: "when you read its pages like a book, it is horrible." What are those of us who perceive in wild nature a basic goodness to say in reply?

To begin, it must be allowed, as Rolston puts it in typically picturesque, compelling terms (1988: 239): "The world is not a jolly place, not a Walt Disney world, but one of struggling, somber beauty. The dying is the shadow side of the flourishing." Further, good and bad are frequently distributed in what appears an unfair manner. "Nature," J. Baird Callicott observes (1989: 43), "is not fair; it does not respect the rights

---

[29] Mill adds (1969: 30): "everything, in short, which the worst men commit either against life or property is perpetuated on a larger scale by natural agents." Whether one agrees or disagrees with Mill's view, it is crucial to see, one, that rapacious lions are not murderers nor marauding hyenas thieves and, two, that it does not follow from the fact we love, admire, and respect wild nature that we ought to transfer to human conduct patterns of behavior found there (nor that doing so would not be immoral). Rolston notes (1986: 40): "virtually none of us, except perhaps ethical mavericks like Nietzsche, will recommend that this pushing, kicking, and trampling be taken as a moral model for interhuman conduct." We return to this issue in chapter seven.

of individuals." At the same time, it must be allowed, as both Rolston and Callicott do, that good often comes along with bad. That the living die requires they first live; that we are disappointed by the absence of good flags our familiarity with and expectation of good. As to whether the "going up" outweighs the "coming down," is something about which people disagree. There is no proof this world is not a Nearth nor, counterwise, that it is a world we can respect and love for all its difficulties. Any plausible case for moral worth will, however, need to presume wild nature *is* a *fit* object of love and respect: "it is inconceivable to me that an ethical relation to land can exist without love, respect, and admiration for land, and a high regard for its value" (Leopold 1970: 261). Love, admiration, and respect go hand-in-hand.

This points to an additional presumption, implicit in that of goodness. We have no reason to love or respect nature, to think of her as a metaphorical mother, if the goodness we experience in nature is the product of a random process indifferent to the well-being of its creatures. An affirmation of goodness turns on the presumption wild nature is somehow, some way, inherently oriented toward our good and, more generally, the goods of well-being: the ways of nature, stochastic or not, must have a "prolife tendency" built into them (see Rolston 1988: 175). There is no way in which we can feel gratitude to, let alone love and admire, processes which are not oriented toward goods of well-being. In describing nature as sentiotic, then, I intend to say something about its deep *telos*, its proclivity, the end toward which it is oriented.

It would be nice, for various reasons, if we had a basis for affirming the moral worth of wild nature which avoided claims about inherent propensities and goodness.[30] Nor is it surprising, given the hard reality of nature, that Rolston, while stressing at times (1988: 172ff.) "positive creativity" and "prolife tendencies," ends up sounding at other times (144ff.) as if what we value morally about wild nature are its raw, generative power and resultant, unchecked movement through time and space, the bedrock of matter. Appeals to generativity alone, however, are no more successful in making a case for moral worth than appeals to beauty or autopoiesis: some generative processes, some unique stories, ought to be shut down.[31]

---

[30] Robyn Eckersley argues (1992: 59) that portraying nature as "essentially benevolent or benign" idealizes it, interpreting "nature selectively as something that is essentially harmonious, kindly, and benign (ignoring suffering, unpredictability and change)" and relying on "outmoded ecological notions (such as the 'balance of nature') that have little to do with the way nature in fact operates." I address this important concern in chapter three.

[31] Rolston allows (1988: 155) that in some cases our prima facie duty to not exterminate species can be overridden, as regards, for instance, the smallpox virus. (See Westra 194: 124.) My point

The basic problem here, as in the case of autopoiesis and beauty, is the absence of a constitutive link to paradigmatically moral goods of well-being. So far as I see, only the property of sentiosis can establish this link – which explains why appeals to sentiosis are so prevalent, if implicit, in the writings of those who call upon us to love and respect our wild mother. Invariably, however extensive the appeal to natural beauty, antiquity, teleotic complexity, so forth and so on, advocates of the wild invariably end up portraying wild nature as a fit object for admiration. This is not accidental.

The basic reason the creative process on Nearth lacks moral value is that its inner dynamic, its deep *telos*, is contrary to paradigmatic moral concerns about well-being. If our nature were that way, then, as Mill asserts, it would be fit only for conquest and transformation. We would owe that diabolical world no duty of care or preservation, whatever its antiquity, beauty, or teleotic complexity. Based on a proclivity, moral worth depends on moral goodness. This marks a vital difference between an ethics of well-being and an ethics of preservation. For an ethics of well-being, moral respect is based on the living of a life that goes better-or-worse. Accordingly, we are bound morally to respect all sentients and selves, good or evil. For an ethics of preservation, moral respect rests on a different kind of relation to well-being, one that keys on teleotic orientation, not vulnerability. Here, moral worth and goodness come together. Setting this link aside would leave us with affirmations less than moral.[32]

Affirming the basic, sentiotic goodness of wild nature does not require us to deny, *per absurdum*, the undeniable suffering and death that exists in this world. Nor need we deny that this world would be a better place were there fewer negativities. That is obvious. Nor need we presume that the hard reality of wild nature accords with its creation by an all-powerful, all-knowing, all-good deity. Affirming the sentiotic goodness of nature does not depend on a belief in God, let alone a theodicy. All that it requires is a belief that wild nature has an inherent proclivity to

is that we have no duty, prima facie or otherwise, to respect non-sentiotic processes or entities (other than selves or sentients). This does not entail, given our focus on nature-as-a-whole, we are free to (or, for that matter, ought not under some circumstances) destroy harmful aspects of wild nature, such as the smallpox virus. For a sense of the complexity involved, see the discussion of predation in chapter seven.

[32] And, correspondingly, the worship of an evil deity. The moral worth of God lies, fundamentally, in God's inherent goodness, his proclivity to love and justice – though there is also a sense, I argue in chapter five, in which God's life goes better-or-worse depending on how the lives of his creatures go for them.

well-being. This allows not only that wild nature lacks perfection but, also, that there exist elements within wild nature which work against its own deep *telos*. As to whether, all said and done, wild nature is "good" in the requisite sense remains a matter on which reasonable, well-informed people do and will continue to disagree.

In any case we need to distinguish the question as to whether wild nature is sentiotic from the more abstract question regarding the moral relevance of sentiosis. It is possible that our nature, our biosphere, is not sentiotic, either because it is somehow evil in its orientation or, more likely, that it lacks an orientation altogether. It would not follow that sentiosis is not a morally constitutive property. Let us, then, setting aside for a while the vital question of fact, inquire further as to what gives sentiotic processes moral worth. We have already identified two elements, purposefulness and goodness; together these generate an inherent value, independent of whatever instrumental or intrinsic value wild nature has for us. If wild nature is sentiotic, this inherent value is already there in the puddle of organic glop lying at the base of Tehipite Dome, long before its actualization in selves and sentients. This value consists in an inherent proclivity to create and sustain, over time, selves and sentients whose existence is, on the whole, good. This proclivity has, like beauty, value in and of itself. Exactly what gives this proclivity moral worth remains to be ferreted out, tucked away in the metaphor of motherhood.

To capture the moral worth of sentiotic realities, we must see not only their contribution to well-being but the unique relation in which they stand to the creatures, the selves and sentients, they create and sustain.[33] Edward Abbey touches on this point in his observation (1971: 190), "the love of wilderness is ... an expression of loyalty to the earth, the earth which bore us and sustains us, the only home we shall ever know, the only paradise we ever need – if only we had the eyes to see."[34] The theme of

---

33 Laura Westra's account of "biocentric holism" comes close to recognizing the source of moral worth, affirming "intrinsic value in wholes that are life-supporting" (1994: 124) and stressing (with reference to Rolston) the developmental character of natural processes (134ff.). She rejects (47), however, any appeal to (the contribution of) well-being, focusing on the autopoietic good of "integrity" (*qua* teleotic existence); this, in turn, leaves her facing the same problems as Rolston regarding our hypothetical planet Nearth. Peter Wenz, while recognizing the need to focus on what has value for well-being ends up, in his "Principle of Process-Harm," explicating this value in instrumental and intrinsic terms (1988: 302): "evolutionary processes are here valued not because they are natural but because they have produced results that we value." Our account, unlike these, focuses on the relation between sentiosis and the inherent, moral value of (individual) well-being.

34 Callicott remarks (1989: 262): "The land ethic seems almost parochial in extent and even tribal in nature because it restricts itself to local – that is, terrestrial – beings, and rests their moral

loyalty, so neglected in modern ethics, is vital for any would-be holistic ethic.

John Muir remarks (1954: 3), "when I was a boy in Scotland I was fond of everything that was wild, and all my life I've been growing fonder and fonder of wild places and wild creatures." Among the reasons Muir values nature is its "mystical ability to inspire and refresh" and, related thereto, the fact that nature, by virtue of its divine creation, was "an environment in which the totality of creation existed in undisturbed harmony" (Nash 1982: 128). For Muir, nature is self-evidently sublime, in its beauty and teleotic complexity. What makes Muir *fond* of nature, however, is another, less sublime, more sentimental reason having to do with kinship and commonality. He puts it this way (1954: 313):

Bears are made of the same dust as we, and breathe the same winds and drink of the same waters. A bear's days are warmed by the same sun, his dwellings are overdomed by the same blue sky, and his life turns and ebbs with heart-pulsings like ours, and was poured from the same First Fountain.

Bears come from the same divine source as humans (317):

From the dust of the earth, from the common elementary fund, the Creator has made *Homo sapiens*. From the same material he has made every other creature, however noxious and insignificant to us. They are earth-born companions and our fellow mortals.

In brief, Muir loves wild nature because it is the common home and fount of all earth-born creatures, wild and human.

This suggests a reason for being concerned about the survival and well-functioning of wild nature which is not applicable to the Hollideck, however sublime. We care about wild nature because it is our metaphorical mother, our one and only home, the place where our ancestors have lived and died – all the way back to Eden, all the way back to the first primitive, single-celled creature. This is our origin, our ground. No substitute, however perfect, can have the same meaning or value for us.

Arguing against the "restoration thesis," which claims that a loss of value in nature can be compensated for by a restoration of nature to its original condition, Robert Elliot (1986: 145) attributes his reluctance to agree to a valuing of "the original as an . . . object with a specific genesis

---

value on kinship and mutual dependency." See, also, Routley and Routley 1980. For comments on "earth-chauvinism" in relation to the obsession with outer space, see Ehrenfeld (1978: 120ff.) and Roszak (1972: 18).

and history."[35] Unpacked, this valuing refers to the deep particularity of nature, not its observable beauty or any other fungible property. Similarly, Muir valued Hatch Hetchy Valley not only for its beauty but, especially, its "primeval nature"; speaking of himself, Elliot explains (1986: 146): "I value the forest because it is of a specific kind, because there is a certain kind of causal history which explains its existence."[36]

Why does "the appeal that many find in areas of wilderness, in natural forests and wild rivers [depend] very much on the naturalness of such places" (Elliot 1986: 145)? If we are unable to tell the difference, why does it matter if we are dealing with the original rather than a perfect restoration or replication? Consider here the difference between Captain Sisco and his son, Jake, going home to spend Thanksgiving with relatives and a Hollideck visit with computer-generated duplicates. Clearly, Jake would have reason to be upset were he deceived in this matter, even supposing "the visit home" goes better with well-behaved, always appropriate holograms than it would have with unpredictable and rude relatives. We do not want to be deceived in such matters, even if life goes better within the deception. As Elliot Sober observes (1986: 189): "We love various people in our lives. If a molecule-for-molecule replica of a beloved person were created, you would not love that individual, but would continue to love the individual to whom you were historically related." That "our attachments are to objects and people as they really are, and not just to the experiences they facilitate," helps explain the difference in meaning and value between backpacking in the Sierras and spending time in the Hollideck.

In a moment I will argue that the special relation in which we stand to our wild nature gives it a special significance for us. The point I want to make here is more general and concerns the constitutive relation between any sentiotic process and the goods of well-being to which it gives rise. Sentiotic processes not only have inherent value by virtue of their proclivity to good, the good to which they give rise is inseparable from, part and parcel of, the process itself. As a result the good of a sentiotic

---

35 Elliot adds (1986: 149): "people who value wilderness do not do so merely because they like to soak up pretty scenery."

36 Elliot adds (1986: 146): "the castle by the Scottish loch is a very different kind of object, valuewise, from the exact replica in the appropriately shaped environment of some Disneyland of the future." Daniel Dennett makes a similar point (1978: 197): "*real* Chateau Latour has to have been made in a particular place, in a particular way, by particular people: an artificially concocted fluid indistinguishable to both chemists and connoisseurs from Chateau Latour would still not be *real* Chateau Latour." The same, Dennett observes (197), is not true of all things: "real vodka, on the other hand, can be made from just about anything, anywhere, by anybody."

process, its well-functioning, is constitutively related to the well-being of those creatures who not only owe their existence to it but are themselves living manifestations of its continuing proclivity. This constitutive intimacy makes the contribution of a sentiotic process to the well-being of its creations more than instrumental, in much the same way the good of a family is bound up with the good of its members. That is what gives moral force to Muir's fondness for earth-born companions and Schweitzer's reverence for all life: we are in this together, integral parts of the same, encompassing family of life. This family flows through time like a river, the great river of life; unlike the parts of a river, however, its many diverse parts are constitutively related, bound together, forever, by their common origin and, more fundamentally, nature. The same wild process, the same biotic proclivity, runs through, forms all. It follows, in light of their constitutive proclivity to the goods of well-being, that sentiotic entities have moral worth. Should we encounter sentiosis occurring on some other planet, one to which we stood in no special relation, it would demand moral respect, though not the same degree of care as our own, beloved Earth.

Just what the constitutive intimacy of sentiosis amounts to is not easy to say and I will not attempt to explicate it here, preferring to let its meaning unfold as we proceed. The point to see is that harming natural, sentiotic processes not only harms us indirectly, by diminishing resources on which we depend, but, also, *directly*, in a way analogous to that in which we are harmed by harm to loved ones with whom we are bound together in identity-defining, constitutive relations. The point is not, let me stress, that the unique relation in which we stand to our wild nature is a source of its moral worth, anymore than that in which we humans stand to one another is a source of our moral worth. If it were, the argument would not be generalizable. Where relationality plays a central role here, as in any ethics of preservation, is in the establishment of a constitutive link to the undeniably moral good of well-being. What this does is bring wild nature within our story, our narrative, and, more generally, make it visible from a moral point of view.[37]

A morality that fails to engage questions of individual and corporate identity has no reply to S.F Sapontzis' rhetorical question (1987: 244):

If we really could manufacture an environment that, for as far into the future as we could see, would have a greater excess of enjoyment and fulfillment over

[37] And reverse the process whereby "this poor, devitalized word 'nature' which we must use to speak of the non-human world has lost its force by coming to mean for us an objectified realm of miscellaneous physical things and events which is outside of and other than us" (Roszak 1972: 7).

distress and frustration than would the natural environment for all sentient beings involved, what would be wrong with preferring that manufactured environment over the natural one? Would it not be merely an expression of some sort of misanthropic prejudice to object, "But it wouldn't be natural!"?[38]

We see now, however, why naturalness matters all the way through. While taking sentiosis into account does not entail we ought never to opt for an artificial environment, it does reveal discomforting similarities between opting out of wild nature and opting out of reality in favor of an imaginary life on the Hollideck. We need to be aware of what is at stake in opting for holograms and plastic trees. The question, as Sagoff well sees (1988: 17; also 224), is not "what we *want*" or, even, "*believe in*; it is a question of what we *are.*"

We care about wild nature in part because of what it has done for us, instrumentally and intrinsically.[39] We also care, however, because it is an integral part of our shared identity, of what and who we are. Presuming that nature has moral worth, this relation justifies us in caring and, indeed, requires us to care about the integrity of those natural processes to which we are constitutively bound. We respect wild nature not simply or primarily for what it has done for us but, rather, because of its relation to us.[40] As a result, we owe our metaphorical mother not only moral respect but a constitutive duty of care. We ought to make a point of looking out for her good, as well as that of her offspring.

HUMANE HOLISM

Wild nature turns out to have moral worth in two, related senses. All selves and sentients are moral subjects by virtue of living a life that goes for them better-or-worse. Correspondingly, the encompassing, sentiotic processes of nature within which these individuals live and move and experience well-being, such as they do, are entitled to moral respect. Moral concern is rooted, in the first case, in an epistemically prior ethics

---

[38] According to Roderick Nash (1982: 388), Martin Krieger (1973) "presents good reasons for believing that, if culturally acceptable, there is nothing wrong with 'plastic trees'"; Nash proceeds to cite, in rebuttal, Tribe 1974. Tom Regan, in reply to Krieger, argues (1982c: 194ff.) that hedonistic utilitarianism is unable, given its lack of concern with the source of pleasures, to provide reasons for not preferring plastic trees so long as we get more pleasure from them.

[39] As Rolston observes (1988: 188): "When humans awaken to their presence in such a biosphere, finding themselves to be products of this process – whatever they make of their cultures and anthropocentric preferences, their duties to other humans or to individual animals and plants – they owe something to this beauty, integrity, and persistence in the biotic community."

[40] Rolston argues (1988: 342) that every ethic has twin foci, one nomothetic and recurrent, dealing with general patterns, the other idiographic and unique, focused on "historical particulars."

of well-being; here we come face to face with the demands of morality and, therewith, our own humanity. Moral concern is rooted, in the
second case, in a no less ontologically basic ethics of preservation; here
we honor the origin and ground of morality, the irreducibly communal
wellspring of individual well-being, wild and human. This gives rise to
our encompassing, programmatic ethic of humane holism.

Any comprehensive ethics of nature will have two focal points, one
engaging the well-being of individual selves and sentients, the other
focusing on the integrity of encompassing, communal wholes. That we
come to this conclusion is not new or startling; many other ethicists have
drawn a similar conclusion.[41] This is true not only of contemporary
environmental ethicists but the long tradition of Catholic social ethics,
which, following Thomas Aquinas' notion of the common good, centers
its account of the moral life on individuals-in-community.[42] What is new
(so far as I am aware) in humane holism is the manner in which it links
these two elements, accounting, thereby, for both the conceptual and
epistemic priority (for morality) of individual well-being and the moral
standing of composite, sentiotic realities lacking a well-being of their
own. This, in turn, allows us to see how ethics can be both individualistic
and holistic in its orientation. The two, an ethics of well-being and an
ethics of preservation, go hand-in-hand.

This, we argued, holds for not only an ethics of wild nature but no
less and thereby, an ethics of human nature. Humane holism serves, as
Johnson remarks of his account (1991: 230), "as a common foundation
for the ethics of our dealings with other humans, with nonhuman individuals, and with ecosystems and other environmental wholes." Where
we differ from Johnson, whose encompassing ethic also centers around
a notion of well-being, is in our explication of the relationship between
individualistic and holistic elements. Like Johnson (288), however, we
"offer no magic formula for determining, in each instance, the morally

---

[41] See, for instance, Rolston 1988, Callicott 1989, and Johnson 1991. Similarly, Don Marrietta
defends "a humanistic ethic that calls for a duty more inclusive than duty just to humans, or
even just to living things; it recognizes a duty to be responsible toward the non-living things
without which there would be no life" (1994: 5f.). While not engaging various questions central
to this endeavor, as regards, for instance, sentiosis, theistic naturalism, and normative identity,
Marrietta's "humanistic holism" parallels my account of humane holism in a number of other
respects, especially in the role attributed to world-views and inescapable moral disagreement, in
which regard Marrietta carries the discussion considerably further than I do.

[42] See, for instance, Maritain 1966, to which I owe a special debt. I attempt here, from the standpoint
of Christian ethics, to ecologize "natural law," which has traditionally affirmed a "constitutive
duty" to formative communities, yet remained largely indifferent to the encompassing, moral
community of creation.

best way to act toward those others of various sorts with whom or which we share the world," but, rather, an illuminating synthesis of moral concerns, one that does not claim to eliminate moral conflict, yet points us in the direction of its resolution – thereby empowering the moral life. As Johnson notes (230): "the important thing in our dealings with the rest of the world is not a specific set of moral rules but a wider understanding and a decent attitude."[43]

In Parts II and III, following the methodological reflections of chapter three, I will ask how humane holism can move toward moral determinacy, as it and every ethics must. Let me stress here, however, that my intent in this regard is more modest than that of historic ethical theories. Though I intend to show how moral reflection achieves determinacy, the philosophical ethic of humane holism remains programmatic; it does not claim at any point to provide moral closure. This is not accidental. Humane holism, recognizing the limits of moral reason and, no less, looking toward life in a pluralistic society, seeks to provide a shared framework for moral reflection among persons holding widely divergent views of nature, wild and human. In this regard, it aims, philosophically and politically, for a principled pragmatism, not a single, rationally compelling moral theory: the governing principles of humane holism remain indeterminate apart from incorporation in a particular cultural context.[44]

At the same time, humane holism presumes to know the bottom-line truth about the world in which we live and, especially, the basic norms in accord with which we ought to live: it is committed to a critical, scientific, and moral realism.[45] This appears in its claims regarding awareness and sentiosis and, even more strikingly, its three governing principles of necessity, decency, and deference. These are not presented as preferences or promising possibilities for political cooperation – though they are both – but, rather, across-the-board, moral constraints on human life. As such, they rely on truth-claims regarding inherent value and moral worth.

[43] See also in this regard Stone 1987, Wenz 1988, and Nash 1991. For a heroic but unsuccessful attempt to resolve conflicts through the use of five priority principles, see Taylor 1986: 256–313; Wenz 1988: 284–92, provides an illuminating critique.

[44] This makes me a "moral particularist" of a sort, though just what sort remains unclear, at least to me. For more on the many varieties of moral particularism and their relation to "epistemic holism," see Hooker and Little 2000.

[45] What makes this combination of relativism and realism possible is that in thinking our way *all the way* through the (sociological) fire (of contextualization), we find ourselves re-confronted by the same, objectively given, normatively laden concerns and world with which we began – as regards which see Berger 1970: 28–48.

Correspondingly, in setting aside historic claims to provide moral closure, humane holism does not give up on universally accessible, rationally compelling arguments; rather, it takes those arguments as far as they will go.[46]

---

[46] Humane holism turns out to be monistic in its central claims about the world and pluralistic in the way it allows these claims to be filled out and rendered determinate. As such, it addresses an on-going debate in environmental ethics between more traditional ethicists, such as Regan and Rolston, who persist in making claims about inherent value and the normative structure of reality, and ethicists, such as Norton, Stone, and Weston, who advocate a more pragmatic, pluralistic approach (Light and Katz 1996). I propose here, along the lines of Light 1996, an Aristotelian-like solution embracing both camps.

CHAPTER THREE

Ecological wisdom: a methodological interlude

UNRESOLVED QUESTIONS

Humane holism looks to integrate and clarify, not supplant our intuitions regarding the moral significance of wild nature.[1] These include: that it is wrong to inflict suffering on any creature without a good reason; that those non-human animals with whom we enter relations of reciprocity have a just claim to be treated fairly; that we ought to honor the good of all living creatures; that in situations of conflict human life and interests count for more, morally; that our own identity and well-being are bound up with that of the Earth and accordingly, we ought to cherish, not degrade wild nature. In so doing, humane holism aims to avoid one-sided moralisms. That questions remain is clear.

For one thing, there is the question of determinacy. Can humane holism move beyond indeterminate generalities of decency, deference, and necessity? If philosophical ethics cannot resolve the problem of comparative moral force, how are ethically serious people to find their way through the complex uncertainties of this world? By way of addressing this and related concerns, Parts II and III situate the programmatic principles of humane holism within an all-encompassing, faith-based perspective, theistic naturalism. What this involves will become clearer with time, though to start it is important to distinguish between a "scientific naturalism," centered on the denial anything exists other than what can, in principle, be discovered by way of scientific inquiry, and a much broader, less theoretically laden naturalism, defined by the belief that humans are "continuous with and at home in nature" (Kohák 1984: 7f.). Theistic naturalism is naturalistic in the second but not the first sense.[2]

---

[1] See Gutting (1999: 183ff.): "Limited or misleading as they may be, our intuitions remain an inevitable starting point for any intellectual activity" (185).

[2] Scientific naturalism, like religious faith, may assume an anti-naturalistic form in the second, ethically more fundamental sense. The deep ethical question is not the nature of nature, viewed as something out there, but, as Erazim Kohák puts it (1984: 8), "the place of the human in the

In particular, while seeking to incorporate what modern science tells us about the world in which we live, it relies on religious faith and cultural tradition to render determinate our understanding of nature and, thus, ascertain what nature requires of us, ethically speaking.

The complex path followed by humane holism in its quest for determinacy will become clear as we proceed. The most pressing question at this point concerns not determinacy but plausibility. While chapter one relies on claims about non-human animals almost everyone accepts, chapter two hinges on a claim – that nature is inherently purposeful – many have taken pains to deny. Do we, in reply, have reason to believe nature really is sentiotic? This is important since, as John O'Neill observes (1993: 201), "there is . . . a necessary relation between ethical concern for an object and true beliefs about it: proper concern for an object x presupposes the possession of a core set of true beliefs about x." Citing the example of a person who complains to her former lover, "you never really loved me; you loved someone else you mistook me for," O'Neill argues a similar complaint can be raised against those who hold "an anti-scientific, mythologized and personalized picture of the natural world: the natural world simply isn't the object of their concern." This is the question which I want to focus on here: are we, in portraying nature as sentiotic, turning our back on modern science?

To begin, let me allow, with Andrew Brennan (1988: 101f.), that "little biological or ecological credence" can be placed on the belief that living creatures have a natural movement toward fulfillment. Whether put in terms of a "struggle for survival" or "differential reproduction," modern evolutionary theory sets aside appeals to any purposefulness inherent in nature, providing instead "consequence-etiological explanations," allowing it to claim of any given factor "that it 'functions *as*' a purpose" without taking "the gratuitous risk involved in the unqualified assertion that it *is* purposeful" (Wright 1976: 96). The biological sciences are no less committed than the physical sciences to the elimination of "final causes."[3] This does not, by itself, entail that there is "no real reason to assume . . . evolution, over-all or in any particular case, has been either for better or for worse" (Simpson 1967: 240f.).[4] Nor does it imply the evolutionary

cosmos: whether we shall conceive of ourselves as integrally continuous with the world about us or as contingently thrown into it as strangers into an alien medium."

[3] Phillip Sloan claims (1985: 135ff.) Darwin shifts from viewing nature as a wise, selecting demiurge to an "inertial system." According to John Searle (1994: 51) "Darwin's major contribution was precisely to remove purpose and teleology from evolution, and substitute for it purely natural forms of selection." See also May 1992 and Ayala 1985.

[4] Robert Richards 1992 argues that Darwin, while denying purposefulness, viewed the evolutionary process as "progressive," resulting in ever more advanced forms of life.

process is "random," a claim countervened by the theory of natural selection. It does, however, support Elliot Sober's conclusion (1984: 105): "the defensible idea in the claim that mutation is random is simply that mutations do not occur *because* they would be beneficial." The modern science of nature finds no proclivity for either good or ill in nature.

It follows that the notion of sentiosis has no role to play in modern evolutionary theory. Does it follow that this notion has no role to play in our understanding of wild nature? Not a few have concluded it does. Thus, George Gaylord Simpson ends his oft-cited book, *The Meaning of Evolution* by claiming (1967: 345f.; see also 262, 293, and 311): "Man is the result of a purposeless and natural process that did not have him in mind ... [T]he universe apart from man or before his coming lacks and lacked any purpose or plan." If Simpson is correct, the ethic of humane holism collapses. Clearly, I do not believe he is. Why is that? Primarily because I disagree with the presumption shared by Simpson and others, among them Donald Worster (1985: 344), that "there is no other place to go [than modern science] for our ideas about nature."[5] In disagreeing, I do not challenge the above view of evolutionary theory, as if I had a superior theory, one with a place for sentiosis (or, for that matter, God). What I question are the implications Simpson draws from that account.

Here we need, before proceeding, to recognize the difference between "consistency" and "justification." No ethic *inconsistent* with the well-established results of modern science is viable. It is not necessary, however, in establishing the consistency of two beliefs to show that either can be derived from, or, *justified* in terms of the other. To see how this difference plays out with regard to sentiosis, I want to begin with the less contentious presumption of animal awareness. Seeing why we are justified in believing some non-human animals are conscious will make clear how and why some truths about the world in which we live never turn up in a scientific theory, even though they stare us in the face all the time.

THE CASE FOR ANIMAL AWARENESS

The commonsensical belief that non-human animals are selves and sentients has been affirmed by many scientists.[6] Recently, Donald Griffin,

---

5 Worster adds (1985: 344): "all the traditional rivals have been driven from the field." I argue below that science and religion are complementary forms of inquiry, not rivals.

6 Charles Darwin (1897: 66; 69) argues that "there is no fundamental difference between man and the higher mammals in their mental faculties ... The lower animals, like man, manifestly feel pleasure and pain, happiness and misery... [T]hat [they] are excited by the same emotions as ourselves is so well established it will not be necessary to weary the reader by many details."

an ethologist, has identified four lines of support for this belief: behavioral complexity, communication, physiology, and evolutionary history.[7] This evidence is extensive and compelling. After summarizing it, however, I will raise a question regarding its scientific lineage and significance. That, in turn, will flag a defining feature of scientific inquiry.

Griffin cites many examples of behavior complexity, ranging from the construction of insect nests, bowerbird bowers, and beaver dams to the use of stick-tools by termite-hunting chimps. That animals engage in such behavior – complex, versatile, end-oriented, adaptive – suggests some degree of awareness on their part.[8] This inference is supported by a second line of evidence involving a particular form of behavior, communication. Following Rosemary Rodd (1990: 77ff.) we can distinguish four categories: information transfer, expressions of emotion, the use of symbols, and language. In the first and, for us, least interesting case, information is conveyed involuntarily, as in the secretion of pheromones. In the second, information regarding an emotional state, for instance, anger, is conveyed by autonomic, unintended changes, as in facial appearance; that these changes parallel our own makes it reasonable to believe, that, for instance, dogs who snarl and cats who purr feel something akin to what we do when agitated or feeling-real-good (as regards which see Darwin 1965).

More disagreement exists regarding the second two categories of communication, the use of symbols and language, both of which require an intent to communicate. This achieves fullest form in language, "a flexible communication system theoretically capable of transferring detailed information about any novel situation and virtually infinitely modifiable" (Rodd 1990: 77). Showing that non-human animals possess a language in this sense would have great ramifications. For one thing, such creatures, being self-aware and possessing an agency akin to our own, would also possess capacity rights similar to our own. It is doubtful at this point that

---

Among the emotions mentioned by Darwin are suspicion, fear, courage, and timidity; speaking of elephants, he remarks, "they intentionally practice deceit and well know what they are about" (69).

[7] See Griffin 1981, 1984, 1992, and 2001; also Rodd 1990 and, for an overview of the mounting evidence, Page 1999.

[8] Donald Griffin notes the case of Clever Hans, a "performing horse" once believed to tap out answers to mathematical questions. After extensive investigation, Clever Hans was shown to be responding to subtle, unintentional signals from his human interrogators. While this "debunking" is commonly used to make a case against ascribing thought to animals, Griffin points out (1992: 25): "What has been almost totally overlooked is the real possibility that Clever Hans was consciously thinking something simple but directly relevant to his situation – perhaps something like: 'I must tap my foot when that man nods his head.'" Proficiency with numbers is not the only form of thought or intelligent behavior. See Weston 1994: 30f.

any non-human animals have such capacities. That the debate continues, however, lends credence to the belief that at least some non-humans use symbols (in at least a quasi-intentional manner) to communicate beliefs and desires.[9] The increasing number of rigorous, double-blind studies make it difficult to deny this (Page 1999: chapters 5–8). Not only do many animals express emotions in ways similar to humans, they communicate preferences, make requests, and, on occasion, express normatively laden views of us in much the same way we do of them.

The conclusion that these animals have an internal life akin to our own is strengthened by the fact that we, too, are animals and, more particularly, by the third and fourth lines of argument, appealing to physiology and evolutionary history. As Donald Griffin notes (1992: 4): "One reason to suggest that nonhuman animals do experience conscious thoughts is that the basic structure and functioning of neurons and synapses are quite similar, as far as we know, in all animals with organized central nervous systems." This is not surprising given our common evolutionary history: "The emergent property of consciousness confers an enormous advantage by allowing animals to select those actions that are most likely to get them what they want or to ward off what they fear" (Griffin 1992: 259). This evolutionary advantage supports the belief that non-human animals with a physiology similar to ours are aware of their surroundings. Where, as with apes, we find a closely linked evolutionary history and marked physiological similarity plus a social life akin to our own, this inference is even stronger.[10]

That, in brief, is the evidence Griffin and others amass in support of a belief in animal awareness. The extent and scope of this evidence make it initially difficult to understand why "most of the scientists who study animal behavior have had little or nothing to say about the feelings or

---

9 This claim raises complex philosophical issues we cannot explore here. Some, following a line of argument associated with Donald Davidson, have argued that only language-users possess beliefs and desires; see Frey 1980, Leahy 1994, and Carruthers 1992. This "linguistic Cartesianism" is unable, in my opinion, to account for either the way in which infants learn language or the continuing mental activity of adults who lose linguistic capacity due to senility or other factors. For a thorough, persuasive response, see DeGrazia 1996. Griffin (1992: 239ff.) discusses the issue in regard to two dueling American Philosophical Association presidential addresses: "Thoughtless Brutes" by Norman Malcolm, in 1973, and "Thoughtful Brutes" by Jonathan Bennett, in 1988.

10 Griffin, following N. K. Humphrey and A. Jolly, speculates (1984: 39) that "consciousness arose in primate evolution when societies developed to the stage where it became crucially important for each member of the group to understand the feelings, intentions, and thoughts of others." While this argument explains the initial appearance of awareness only if we (not implausibly) construe the preceding "feelings, intentions, and thoughts" behaviorally, it makes sense (in any case) of the need once awareness appears in a social context for the development of those forms of awareness and quasi-intentional behavior which distinguish mere selves from the merely sentient.

thoughts of the animals that interest them so keenly" (Griffin 1992: 6).
Griffin (1984: *v*), observing that "the conscious mental experiences of
animals ... was a central concern of both biologists and psychologists
during the half century following the Darwinian revolution," attributes
the change to animal scientists becoming convinced "there was no way
to distinguish automatic and unthinking responses from behavior involving conscious choice on the animal's part." He cites (1992: 8) J. F.
Wittenberger, an animal scientist, who argues (1981: 48) "we cannot assume that animals make conscious decisions because *we cannot monitor what
goes on inside their heads*." This straightforward observation calls attention
to two reasons scientists have avoided talk about animal awareness, one
involving inaccessibility, the other redundancy.

Let me begin with redundancy. While flexibility of behavior and social
cooperation clearly advance evolutionary fitness, this contribution can
be ascertained, scientifically, only when tied to observable patterns of behavior. The same holds true of awareness. So far as science is concerned
talk about what goes on inside the heads of animals, be it a matter of
thought or feeling, belief or desire, is beside the point unless it can be
grasped as an object of scientific study. Otherwise, such talk is redundant;
awareness becomes a mere "ghost in the machine."

Redundancy follows, scientifically speaking, from the fact that awareness is inherently subjective and, as such, directly engaged only from the
"inside-out." We cannot monitor what goes on inside another's mind.[11]
The difficulty is not simply that subjective states of awareness cannot be
directly observed. This is true of many things science talks about. The
problem is that subjective states cannot be characterized in a numerically
precise manner, one that enables claims involving them to be scientifically investigated. That is why they have no secure place in scientific
theories.

This problem will not go away if we argue that regarding non-human
animals as selves and sentients is the only way to make sense of the evidence amassed by Griffin and others. Even if true, this becomes from a
scientific point of view a confession of ignorance, the impetus for a research program aimed at finding a full-fledged scientific explanation.[12]
Toward this end, concerns about awareness disappear, replaced by

---

[11] We can, of course, contrary to Wittenberger's loose way of speaking, monitor what goes on inside
heads, relative to "event related potentials" and other brain-states.

[12] This point is directly relevant to recent attempts – see, for instance, Behe 1996 and Dembski
1998 – to argue that the complexity of living creatures cannot be accounted for by an end-
blind process of natural selection and, more positively, requires the postulation of "intelligent
design." Even if this is true, as I am inclined to believe (as indicated in chapter four), it cannot

re-defined, behavioral notions of belief and desire. Thus, no matter how much evidence we amass of thought or feeling, it invariably gets re-interpreted in terms of observable, quantifiable behavior: the facts are absorbed in an explanatory framework, one with no place for a non-quantifiable subjectivity.

The basic objection to talk about "animal awareness" is not factual but methodological. The case for reductive behaviorism rests on the logic of scientific inquiry, nothing less (or more).[13] What is the would-be defender of animal awareness to do? Clearly, it is not enough to gather more facts. Is it necessary, however, to re-conceptualize scientific inquiry in less quantitative, more sensitive, perhaps even value-laden terms?[14] I believe not. To see why, it will be useful to consider some reflections on the question of animal awareness by John Searle, a philosopher of mind.[15]

provide the basis for a *scientific* explanation, given the inherent, methodological constraints on scientific inquiry and explanation. Even if as compelling an argument existed for the existence of an "intelligent designer" as that for animal awareness, this divine designer would still, like subjectivity, have no rightful place in a scientific account of the world – no more than living creatures do in a surveyor's map.

[13] Griffin 2001, while informatively engaging philosophical and ethical issues (252–269), fails to distinguish, in its discussion of "testability" (272–274), between the issues of observability and quantifiability; it is the latter, not the former, which prevents scientists from monitoring what goes on inside the minds of animals (and, no less, humans). Given this problem, it can be expected that the developing discipline of "cognitive ethology," having acknowledged its debt to Griffin, will be re-conceived in more strictly quantitative (and, thus, non-subjective) terms; for an example, see Hauser 2000: 255ff. A parallel development, discussed below, occurred during the first half of the last century in the then emerging discipline of ecology.

[14] Thus, Robyn Eckersley (1992: 116): "It is surely not incongruous or regressive to suggest that a different and better science might result from a community of scientists who employ empirical-analytic modes of inquiry but who proceed on the bases of an ecocentric 'interest' in the world." And Sallie McFague (1993a: 94): "Scientists from other social locations (women as well as people of different racial, economic, and cultural backgrounds) could strengthen scientific objectivity by broadening its base, which would change what was considered important to research." While I agree society would benefit were scientists (along with lawyers, ministers, etc.) more representative of society-at-large and, the same by no means, sensitive to the value of nature, this would not by itself lead to a better (*qua* more objective) science and, indeed, as we see below, with regard to Arcadian ecology, and others have pointed out, with regard to well-known distortions of Soviet science, would likely result in a science captive to special interests. There is great value in a science that concentrates on the numbers.

[15] Searle, a scientific materialist, worries about the extent to which materialists, driven by "a terror of consciousness" (1994: 55), have succumbed to "an urge to get rid of mental phenomena at any cost" (49). He argues, to the contrary, that any account of reality leaving out consciousness and subjectivity will be unable to "account for our 'intuitions' about the mind" (52). This leads him, as a scientific materialist, to claim there exists a yet-to-be-discovered neurophysiological account of mental states. My own view, following Thomas Nagel (1986: 13–27), is that we not only lack such an account, we have no idea what it would look like. Accordingly, I argue in chapter four, contra Searle (100ff.), that the otherwise unexplained existence of consciousness provides a reason to believe that consciousness, awareness, is ontologically fundamental.

Allowing we lack direct access to the consciousness of dogs, Searle asserts (1994: 74) it is, nevertheless, "a well-attested empirical fact that dogs are conscious"; moreover, he adds, "it is attested by evidence that is quite compelling." How so? To begin, Searle calls our attention to complex behavioral and physiological similarities, the sort of evidence noted above. This leads him, however, to raise a more general, philosophical question regarding why, given our lack of direct access to "other minds," we believe in the consciousness of other humans. I (you) no more directly experience the minds of other humans than I (you) do non-humans. Why, then, do we all assume that what holds true of us holds true of our fellow humans? In short, it begins to look like belief in the awareness of other humans – and perhaps even ourselves – is no more credible than belief in the awareness of non-humans.[16]

Why are we so persuaded something is going on besides chemical reactions inside the heads of our fellow creatures? Why take our intuitions about subjectivity any more seriously than the historic belief in a geocentric universe? Searle suggests that before we play the skeptic's game, run off in search of evidence justifying our belief in other minds, we look closely at the nature and logic of this conviction, as regard which he notes (1994: 77): "except when doing philosophy, there really is no 'problem' about other minds, because we do not hold a 'hypothesis,' 'belief,' or 'supposition' that other people are conscious and that chairs, tables, computers and cars are not conscious." Unlike belief in a geocentric universe, belief in other minds is "constitutive of our relations to the consciousness of other people" (77), not least our ability to raise (with others) questions about consciousness itself. Skeptical doubts only appear "when elements of [this] Background are treated as if they were hypotheses that have to be justified" (77).[17]

Convictions about "other minds" are rooted in an irreducibly communal life, not philosophical or scientific arguments. It is this that persuades us solipsists have lost touch with reality. We do not have to wait for the latest edition of *Animal Physiology* or, even, the *Journal of Philosophy*. This does not imply empirical evidence is irrelevant; to the contrary,

---

[16] Correspondingly, some philosophers and scientists repudiate the "folk psychology" of subjective awareness for both humans and non-humans. See, for instance, Dennett 1978: 149–173, 267–285.

[17] Strictly speaking, Searle's notion of "the Background" encompasses only "capacities that are not themselves intentional" (1994: 175). I use it here loosely, in a way that implicitly encompasses not only non-intentional capacities but, also, what Searle refers to (176) as the "whole Network of other beliefs and desires." This poses no problem for the argument developed here and, so far as I can see, remains true to the main thrust of Searle's argument, given his own, sometimes inclusive usage (176f.) and references to "the work of the later Wittgenstein" (177).

our on-going experience of consciousness is critical to the rationality of our belief in its existence.[18] Similarly, the discovery that one's pet (or husband) is a hologram would eliminate a reason – organic properties – for believing him sentient like us. Thus, the evidence Griffin gathers is not irrelevant, even though modern science, strictly speaking, has no room for a subjective, non-quantifiable notion of awareness. What the evidence gathered does is provide strong *indirect* support by way of a comparison with our own, human awareness: once we see how similar the behavior and physiology of some non-humans are to our own, the case for believing they are not, like us, selves and sentients is undermined. Modern science supports, by analogy with ourselves, a claim it is not able to articulate in scientifically sanctioned terminology. There is nothing unusual or improper about this. Statistical analysis often supports (or undermines) beliefs which cannot be articulated, let alone justified in mathematical terms alone.

If we look to justify a belief in animal (or human) awareness in scientific terms alone, we will inevitably fail. Consciousness, our own or that of others, cannot be given the kind of characterization required by the logic of scientific inquiry. This methodological constraint is not enough, however, to make the skeptic's case as regards either animal awareness or other minds in general.[19] Our belief in animal and human awareness does not require justification by a scientific or philosophical theory.[20] Accordingly, the burden of proof remains, where it belongs, with the skeptic.

This does not mean our belief in animal or human awareness is beyond question. Even though these beliefs rest on a way of life we cannot imagine abandoning, in "a truth evidently given," this truth must be "tested

---

[18] It is necessary that Searle provide a characterization of "empirical experience" not dependent on universally accessible experience. He does so as follows (1994: 72):

> When people speak of empirical facts, they sometimes mean actual, contingent facts in the world as opposed to, say, facts of mathematics or facts of logic. But sometimes when people speak of empirical facts, they mean facts that are tested by third-person means, that is, by "empirical facts" and "empirical methods," they mean facts and methods that are accessible to all competent observers. Now this systematic ambiguity in the use of the word "empirical" suggests something that is certainly false: that all empirical facts, in the ontological sense of being facts in the world, are equally accessible epistemically to all competent observers. We know independently that this is false.

> I will call on this distinction in chapter four to defend, contra Searle, the rationality of belief in the existence of God.

[19] Michael Williams observes regarding skepticism in general (1996: 171): "the essential restriction on our evidence for beliefs about the world emerges . . . only as a methodological necessity, and this is far less than the sceptic needs." See, also, 357f. and, generally, Wittgenstein 1972.

[20] As Paul Holmer so often put it (in his inimitable way), "what do you need a theory for?"

and sustained in arguments"; such arguments, statistical, scientific, philosophical or whatever, provide reasons for calling dogmatic presumptions into question as well as "reasons for *not disbelieving* what we believe because we have seen" (Kohák 1984: 175). Accordingly, the indirect support provided by modern science for a belief in animal awareness is not insignificant – not least of all because that belief is open to question in a way belief in the subjective awareness of other humans is not. The evidence garnered by Griffin strongly supports our common presumption especially when we bear in mind the extent to which doubt regarding animal awareness springs from a lack of familiarity with non-humans[21] and/or, as Descartes allows, a desire for advantage.[22] In any case, whatever conclusion we come to regarding the mental life of non-humans, the fact that appeals to awareness have no role to play in scientific accounts of nature does not mean we lack good reason to believe in the awareness of our fellow animals – as my little friend Obie reminds me from time to time.

SCIENTIFIC INQUIRY

We cannot assess claims regarding what can or cannot be shown by way of scientific inquiry until we reach clarity regarding the nature of modern science. Here, we need to remember that the term "science" is used in at least three distinct senses. Sometimes the term "science" designates, simply, a disciplined form of systematic reflection, a *Wissenschaft*. Philosophy and theology, no less so than biology, are "sciences" in this broad, loosely defined sense. Clearly, if we are to grasp what is unique about modern science, we require a more restrictive definition. One possibility, found in a second common usage, is to limit our reference to disciplined inquiries that rely on *empirical* observation. Etienne Gilson notes (1984: 14) the term "science" was used in medieval times to signify the *ratio sensa*, or, "totality of rational explanations based on sensible experience." This form of explanation dates back to the Greeks and in its reliance on empirical observation obviously moves closer to the

---

[21] Larry Wright comments (1976: 146f.) on the difficulty people without pets have even conceiving the finely structured behavior attributed to pets by their owners; he attributes this "to the widespread human tendency to be prudently skeptical of the reliability of a subtle perceptual skill until one possesses it himself."

[22] "Thus my opinion [that (non-human) animals lack awareness] is not so much cruel to animals as indulgent to men . . . since it absolves them from the suspicion of crime when they eat or kill animals." So René Descartes, in a letter to Henry More, dated February 5, 1649 (in Regan and Singer [eds.] 1976: 66).

distinctive dynamic of modern science. At the same time, as its common name, "natural philosophy," suggests, this form of science remains closely tied to metaphysics and the quest for explanatory "first-principles."[23] By contrast, the inquiries and theories of modern science are empirical in a much narrower sense, one demanding the testing of hypotheses in controlled experiments and, therewith, explanation by appeal to observable, quantifiable regularities.[24] These strictures give rise to the methodologically constrained and, I will argue, inherently abstract nature of modern science.

It is no accident that modern science takes form in areas of inquiry, astronomy and physics, where the value of mathematization is evident. Though these sciences have grown and changed over the centuries, they continue to operate within terms laid down in their origin and most profoundly exemplified in the work of Newton, after whom it is not possible to overlook the existence of "a profound harmony between mathematics and the workings of the natural world" (Penrose 1992: 166).[25] Nature comes to be seen not as an inherently rational, mind-governed process but a vast spatio-temporal domain filled with quantifiable interactions governed by invariant laws oriented to no good or bad end.[26] That with time scientists adopt a more developmental, open-ended (*qua* statistical) view of these ordered processes leaves unchanged its basic, defining reliance on quantification and experimentation.[27] Indeed, with the disavowal of deistic dualism, an unstable half-way house, these

---

[23] Robert Collingwood observes (1960: 3): "Greek natural science was based on the principle that the world of nature is saturated or permeated by mind. Greek thinkers regarded the presence of mind in nature as the source of that regularity or orderliness in the natural world whose presence made a science of nature possible."

[24] Contrast in this regard the commonsensical, qualitative account of induced motion given by Aristotle with Galileo's counter-intuitive, quantitative, and experimentally verifiable appeal to inertia (Dijksterhuis 1961: 333–367).

[25] Dudley Shapere (1974: 138), commenting on the increasingly "mathematical treatment of nature" in Galileo, Kepler, and Descartes – to the point where mathematics is viewed as "both *necessary* and *sufficient* for a complete and precise account of physical nature" – concludes: "the importance of this shift cannot be overemphasized."

[26] As Richard Westfall observes (1992; 64f.): "During the scientific centuries scientists came to look upon the world in which we live in a way radically different from anything the world had ever known before . . . Nature was quantified; it was mechanized." See, also, Dijksterhuis 1961: 495–501.

[27] According to E. J. Dijksterhuis (1961: 500f.): "Neither the object of theoretical science nor its method was altered during the transition from classical to modern physics . . . In the present century functional thinking with its essentially mathematical mode of expression has not only been maintained, but has even come to dominate science." Westfall argues (1992: 64f.) that while the quantitative fabric woven by Newton "has been modified greatly in its details in the intervening three centuries, it is still with us, the very foundation of intellectual life in the West and increasingly in the whole world."

commitments become even clearer, as manifest in the struggle against appeals to divine intervention in the developing sciences of geology and biology. It comes to be seen that appeals to God, being neither quantifiable nor subject to experimental verification, have no role to play in modern scientific explanations.[28]

This has led some to conclude that God either does not exist or, existing, has no role to play in the natural world: nature as described by the natural and social sciences comes to include "all that has existed, does exist, or will exist in time" (Moore 1968: 40). While this leaves eternity for God (and Moorean ideals), it does not bode well for traditional theism or the belief that wild nature is sentiotic. I want now, with the intent of clearing a way forward, to generalize our observations regarding animal awareness. This will involve sketching a view of scientific inquiry that makes clear why it is not unreasonable to believe there are features of the natural world other than subjective awareness which have, like subjective awareness, no proper place in modern science.[29] Having done so, I will call on this view to illuminate the tension-filled history of one recently developed science, ecology.

The view I want to sketch traces its lineage to Alfred North Whitehead. Whitehead, a noted philosopher of science and co-author with Bertrand Russell of the *Principia Mathematica*, was concerned to reject the presumption that acceptance of a scientific cosmology commits one to "scientific materialism" and, thereby, the belief that nature is "senseless, value-less, purposeless" (1967: 17). In response, Whitehead argues that the dependence of scientific inquiries on mathematical devices like analytical geometry and infinitesimal calculus results in the abstract nature of these relations being "reflected in the order of nature under the guise of mathematically expressed laws of nature" (30). In brief, modern science, given its dependence on mathematical abstraction, invariably portrays the object of its study in correspondingly abstract terms: "scientific inquiry represents an abstraction from . . . the richness of the nature it seeks to know" (Gilkey 1993: 15). Those who, failing to recognize this, equate what scientific theories tell us about the world with the full, concrete reality of nature commit "the fallacy of misplaced concreteness" (Whitehead 1967: 50f.).

---

[28] As exemplified in LaPlace's reply to Napoleon upon being asked why he had not (in his account of celestial mechanics) appealed, like Newton, to the stabilizing intervention of God: "Sir, I have no need of that hypothesis." (See Dijksterhuis 1961: 490f.; also Brooke 1991: 148, 238–240.) The truth in LaPlace's reply consists in his progress relative to a scientific ideal, not a displacement of religious faith by scientific reason.

[29] This does not, by itself, provide reason to believe any such features exist. I turn to that task in Part II.

Whitehead does not mean to suggest science can or should be anything other than it is. In this he agrees with Oliver O'Donovan (1986: 48): the process of "self-conscious abstraction [by which science proceeds], in which the more obvious determinants of kind and end are forgotten in order that the object of investigation may be hypothetically included in other, less obvious classes ... is a perfectly legitimate stratagem of thought." No one could have identified the inverse square law of gravitation, let alone the existence of electro-magnetic fields, apart from a disciplined withdrawal from the cluttered, value-laden world of everyday experience. All Whitehead insists is that we take modern science for what it is, not a way of seeing the world-as-it-is *apart from* mathematical abstraction.

That modern science is inherently abstractive does not mean its "one-eyed reason" fails to describe the world-as-it-is, as suggested by Andreas Osiander in his preface to Copernicus' *De revolutionibus orbium coelestium*. There Osiander, looking to protect Copernicus, proposes the latter's heliocentric model be understood as a mathematical construct useful for finding our way around, not a description of reality. While this may be true of some scientific theories, most famously, quantum mechanics, it does not, I presume, hold true for scientific theories in general: the Earth really does go around the sun, not vice versa; the presence of oxygen, not phlogiston, explains combustion; matter is composed of atoms; the pongidae and hominidae have over time evolved from a common ancestor. Scientific theories and models succeed, as a rule, in characterizing the world-as-it-is.[30]

The belief that scientific theories are inherently abstract poses no problem for scientific realism. As every surveyor and architect knows, abstraction is consistent with realism. The maps surveyors prepare, like the blueprints of architects, depict places and things, relations, with numerical precision.[31] To confuse these necessarily abstract representations with the full reality of what they portray would, however, commit, in an

---

[30] Much has been written and many conflicting positions taken on this and related issues. I mean here to flag one plausible view of modern science, not stake out a determinate position in the philosophy of science. There are a variety of ways in which the general claims about abstraction and realism might be developed and defended. Let me note four: the "contextualist externalism" of Williams 1996, the pragmatic realism of Peirce (as developed in Ochs 1998), the "minimal foundationalism" and "alethic realism" of Alston 1989 and 1996, and the discipline-specific, anti-positivist, scientific realism of Miller 1987. That these diverse possibilities exist is not to say philosophical differences do not matter, only that we need not in every case resolve deep-lying theoretical disagreements before getting on with the issue at hand. For an informative overview and defense of the "critical realism" I presuppose as regards both scientific inquiry and theological reflection, see McGrath 1998: 140–164.

[31] I include both surveyors and architects for a reason. Modern science not only maps reality, it creates vast conceptual edifices in which we dwell intellectually. Polkinghorne observes, relative

especially blatant way, the fallacy of misplaced concreteness. Scientific theories depict nature in an analogous, numerically precise, inherently abstract manner. Accordingly, to suppose that the failure of something incapable of representation in such terms, be it God, awareness, or sentiosis, to appear in a scientific account of the world implies it is not there, misunderstands the disciplined withdrawal that makes modern science possible and, thereby, leaves open the possibility that science is "but a part, though an important one, of man's effort to understand himself, his culture, his universe" (Greene 1981: 8).

Modern science arrives at a true account of nature by way of mathematical constructs, constructs that trace vital regularities existing in nature. This process of abstraction not only enables scientific progress, it serves as an *ideal* for scientific inquiry. The true genius of Newton, as of Darwin, lies not in details open to revision, but the ability to envision and construct a quantifiable model useful to subsequent generations of scientists in their own pursuit of experimentally verifiable, quantitative regularities. That Newton falls short of this ideal in his invocation of divine assistance leaves room for Laplace to come closer to the scientific ideal, just as Darwin's blending theory of genetics leaves room for Mendel.[32] Science, like all forms of critical thought, serves a methodological ideal. Here it is instructive to consider the way in which young sciences, such as that of ecology in the first part of the last century, become full-fledged sciences.

THE END OF NATURE

In *Nature's Economy* (1985: *xi*), Donald Worster characterizes the history of ecology as "a struggle between rival views of the relationship between humans and nature: one view devoted to the discovery of intrinsic value and its preservation, the other to the creation of an instrumentalized world and its exploitation."[33] Though clearly preferring the former

to the cumulative nature of scientific inquiry (2000: 32): "Scientists are the map-makers of the physical world and, like all careful map-makers, their charts, though not complete in every detail, prove superposable."

[32] By contrast, the constructs of Freud have not found fruition, as he hoped, in a true science and, most likely, never will. This does not mean we cannot learn about human nature from Freud, only, if we can, that some truths – perhaps the most important – are not verifiable by way of scientific inquiry. Here it is worth bearing in mind Sir Arthur Eddington's warning, relative to his own concern as an astrophysicist with an ill-conceived reductionism, about "the fisherman with a two-inch mesh to his net, who concludes that all fish are at least two inches long" (Polkinghorne 2000: 198f.).

[33] Worster traces the first view, or, Arcadian, to the eighteenth-century English parson, Gilbert White; the second, or, Imperial, to the eighteenth-century Swedish botanist, Carl Linnaeus. For

ethically, Worster views the latter as truer to the logic of modern science. This contrast appears strikingly in the work of two scientists, Frederic Clements and A. G. Tansley, between whose conflicting views Aldo Leopold attempts to mediate in his "land ethic."[34]

Clements saw within nature an ideal, objectively determined line of development toward a "climax community." Every climate has its own, natural course of ecological succession. This patterning provides a criterion in terms of which we can assess our harmony with nature and, more generally, reflects the Arcadian belief in a natural harmony of nature disturbed only by human intervention.[35] This envisioned harmony serves "as a scientific check on man's aggrandizing growth," giving force to Thoreau's claim that "man must learn to accommodate himself to the natural order rather than seek to overwhelm and transform it" (Worster 1985: 241, 76).[36] This troubles Tansley, partly because it treats humans as "an intrusive, disruptive force in nature," but, more fundamentally, because it characterizes nature in teleological terms (Worster 1985: 239ff., 301ff). By contrast, Tansley seeks to purify the newly formed science of ecology by eliminating "all that was not subject to quantification and analysis," including "all those obscurities that had been part of its baggage at least since the Romantic period" (Worster 1985: 301). Toward this end, he introduces the overtly reductionistic, quantitative notion of an "ecosystem," focused on energy-exchange and aimed at supplanting talk about communities, climax or otherwise.[37] Worster elaborates (1985: 302):

Organisms indeed live in closely integrated units, Tansley agreed, but these can best be studied as physical systems, not "organic wholes." Using the ecosystem, all relations among organisms can be described in terms of the purely material exchange of energy and of such chemical substances as water, phosphorus, nitrogen, and other nutrients that are the constituents of "food." These are the

---

a parallel distinction between metaphysical and scientific, mathematical ecology, see Brennan 1988: 55ff.

34 Thereby, Worster notes (1985: 290), introducing "in the popular consciousness of ecology a fundamental and inescapable source of ambiguity and conflict." See also Rolston 1988: 16of.

35 This view is beautifully expressed by S. A. Forbes, a nineteenth-century predecessor of Clements: "There is a general consent that primeval nature, as in the uninhabited forest or the untilled plain, presents a settled harmony of interaction among organic groups which is in strong contrast with the many serious maladjustments of plants and animals found in countries occupied by man" (Brennan 1988: 46).

36 Worster notes (1985: 250): "usually where the climax [community] is ignored or discounted as an ideal, the only criterion left is the marketplace – the very standard that gave America the dirty thirties." Thoreau, according to Worster (1985: 76), is the person "most responsible for the development of the arcadian ethic into a modern ecological philosophy."

37 Worster notes (1993: 176) that from this perspective, "a cutover land can be seen as good ecologically as a forested one."

real bonds that hold the natural world together; they create a single unit made up of many smaller units – big and little ecosystems.

The goal is to bring "all nature – rocks and gases as well as biota – into a common ordering of material resources."

Tansley's vision dismisses qualitative notions of harmony and, in so doing, provides a powerful impetus to mathematical ecology. As he and, increasingly, other ecologists see it, the development of a truly scientific ecology requires a rejection of the emotional attachments and normative constraints so dominant among Arcadians: "the principle of objectivity demanded a cosmos stripped clean of all the emotional and spiritual qualities men and women theretofore had found in the natural world" (Worster 1985: 90).[38] Adopting a similar view, Andrew Brennan concludes (1988: 164): "Ecology furnishes us with no 'objective' account of the goods, the ends or the directions of biological communities or ecosystems. As species populations come and go, as whole species die out and others emerge, there is no natural pattern, no direction, no end to be served."[39] Like evolutionary theory, ecology comes to be formulated in overtly non-normative, quantitative terms. In this way, Tansley advances the inherently abstractive ideal of scientific inquiry and proves a truer disciple of Darwin than Clements.

It is not surprising that the science of biology, like those of physics and chemistry, is an inn with no room for normatively laden teleologies. This exclusion is methodological. Realizing this allows us to see that whether or not nature is sentiotic, the issue of purposefulness cannot be settled by modern biology. Thus, Jacques Monod's confident, endlessly reiterated declaration (1971: 172f.) that anyone accepting modern biology in its full significance must "wake to his total solititude," realize "that, like a gypsy, he lives on the boundary of an alien world . . . [a world] deaf to his music, just as indifferent to his hopes as to his sufferings or his crimes," epitomizes, with a smile or a sigh, the fallacy of misplaced concreteness.

---

[38] Worster adds (1985: 90):

> The world was not to be studied through love or sympathy – indeed, could not be, for it was widely subscribed to by scientists that nature had to be cleansed of sentiment and so deliberately made unappealing to human feelings. Such had been the Baconian mission from the first . . . Science was laying claim to nature, warning the pious to go elsewhere for their inspiration.

[39] See Brennan 1988: 101f. for criticism of Clements. Though arguing (163f.) that the failure of ecology to furnish us with any objective account of biological ends or goods makes "the prospects for any genuine environmental ethic appear poor," Brennan finds hope in "the ideas of self-realization and identification [with nature]"; he offers, in his final three chapters, insightful observations on the development of an "ecological humanism."

Here a defining presupposition of modern science is transformed into a basic principle of epistemology, making modern science the only form of knowledge about the universe: "the cornerstone of the scientific method is . . . the systematic denial that 'true' knowledge can be got at by interpreting phenomena in terms of final causes – that is to say, of 'purpose'" (Monod 1971: 21).[40] Whether or not Monod is correct regarding the ultimate nature of nature, his presumption that the indifference of ultimate reality has been established ignores the abstractive dynamic of scientific inquiry. To counter this, we must bear in mind that "the proposal to think reality without ends . . . is an artifice of thought" (O'Donovan 1986: 48f.), not a world-embracing philosophy or scientific discovery. Keeping this in mind, it becomes clear why evolutionary biology, though "shaping the dominant world view of the twentieth century," has "settled nothing in either philosophy or theology" (Greene 1961: 132). This is a mark of success, not failure.

FUZZY SCIENCE

While ethics needs to be naturalized, it cannot be scientized; to think it can misconstrues the nature of ethics and science.[41] The same holds for attempts to find ethical norms in evolutionary theories. Whatever regularities are appealed to, they all "demand the postulate that the trends of evolution or some particular one among these is ethically right and good" (Simpson 1967: 305).[42] An example of the problem this poses can be seen in Herbert Spencer's once influential, nineteenth-century ethic of Social Darwinism. Appealing to Darwin's theory of evolution, Spencer argues that the long-term well-being of humanity can be advanced by allowing the weak to die out, thereby strengthening the genetic pool and eliminating by natural selection the many miseries associated with physical and mental infirmity. Toward this end, Spencer advocates *laissez-faire* capitalism and rejects as misguided regulations and welfare programs proposed by social reformers, arguing these interfere with the upward, evolutionary movement of human life. Looking back it is easy to see, whether or not we agree with Spencer's political ethic, that his

---

[40] For more on Monod, see Hesse 1975: 123ff., noting the presence in Monod's argument of "*extra*-scientific assumptions" (126), and Midgley 1985: 75ff., arguing that Monod's picture of natural selection, in terms of "pure chance and pure necessity," is "a travesty" (81).

[41] For such an attempt, see Wilson 1975 and 1978. For a short, definitive critique, see Nagel 1980; also Greene 1981 and Midgley 1978 and 1985.

[42] Unfortunately, Simpson (1967: 288ff., 325, 347ff.; 319) violates his own strictures. For more on the tensions in Simpson's view and, therewith, scientific naturalism, see Greene 1981: 172ff.

social ethics depends on ethical presuppositions that are not part of evolutionary theory, even when that theory is cast, as Darwin did, in terms of a struggle for survival.

Attempts to make scientific inquiry settle ethical questions result in the distortion of ethics and, no less, the fuzzification of science. This happens when scientific naturalists claim the mantle of scientific certitude for their rejection of traditional religious faith no less than when scientific creationists attempt to formulate normatively laden religious conclusions in scientific terms. This error is easiest to see, of course, when we disagree with the conclusion reached. Thus, many modernist theologians and ethicists readily see the error committed by scientific creationism of the right – the kind engaged in by fundamentalists – yet remain blind to scientific creationism of the left – the kind so prevalent in contemporary eco-theology. Let me note three examples.

One way in which modern science has changed our view of human life and society involves the passage of time, especially the vast amount of time prior to the appearance of human beings. Thus, as the process theologian John Cobb (1992: 119f.) observes: "if we conceive the five billion years of the Earth's past as though recorded in ten volumes of five hundred pages each . . . it is not until . . . page 499 of the tenth volume [that] humankind appears. *The last two words on the last page* recount our story from the rise of civilization six thousand years ago until the present." While Cobb himself does not conclude that traditional beliefs regarding the unique value of human life are mistaken, it is easy to see why other ethicists have: how could we be so important if we show up so late, after so much has happened? It begins to look, unlike what people once believed, that "we are not at the center of things by any stretch of the imagination"; correspondingly, "the sense of our insignificance deepens when we see our place in an unimaginably old and immense universe" (McFague 1993a: 108).

Why, however, not conclude, to the contrary, that human life, given its extreme rarity, its formation by nature after countless eons of time, is like the rarest of jewels, worth more than all the rest of the universe combined? Someone finding a tiny diamond on an immense beach would not view it as insignificant just because there are vastly more grains of sand. Why should we not, likewise, value "the last two words" more than all the preceding? In short, nothing follows from a scientific chronology regarding the significance of human life. Believing our late and possibly brief sojourn has any normative significance depends on a non-scientific presupposition regarding the normative value of time, namely, that all time counts the same. Why not presume, to the contrary, that any time marked by human life has more value than any amount of time without it? There is no scientific case to be made one way or the other. The value we place on time, as on ourselves and nature in general, must come from elsewhere.

Here is another example. Having characterized ecology as "the study of how the earth works; in other words, the house rules of our home," Sallie McFague (1993a: 56f.), a Christian ethicist, cites the Second Law of Thermodynamics as an example. This Law, which holds (as McFague notes) that "entropy increases and available energy decreases in a closed system," is said to illustrate "the necessity for learning at least the rudiments of ecology and the kind of unity among all life-forms and their environments that emerges from an ecological perspective." This makes good sense in that we ought to pay attention to ecological consequences. It makes no sense, however, to describe the laws of thermodynamics or any scientific laws as "house rules," the reason being that all we do conforms to these invariant regularities. Clear-cutting old-growth forest for the hell of it complies with the laws of ecology no less than respectfully watching them grow. That devastation has the consequences it does is proof we cannot transgress ecological laws.[43] Ecological laws, like maps, only tell us what lies ahead, not the desirability or propriety of going where we choose. Even if we possessed a complete account of these laws, they would not tell us whether we should take the good of trees and spotted owls into account or live for a moment's pleasure.[44]

One last example, this involving interdependence. McFague, referring to "the common creation story" found in modern science, remarks (108): "From this story we learned that we are radically interrelated with and dependent on everything else in the universe and especially on our planet. We exist as individuals in a vast community of individuals within the ecosystem, each of which is related in intricate ways to all others in the community of life." This is basically true. Questions arise, however, when McFague elucidates the normative implications of this interdependence (108):

In this story we feel profoundly connected with all other forms of life, not in a romantic but realistic way. We are so connected, and hence we had better live as if we were. We feel deeply related, especially, to all other human beings, our

---

43 Even miracles, if they occur, obey the laws of nature, all of which include *ceteris paribus* clauses excluding overriding factors, such as an extended hand. If miracles occur, what they disrupt is the presumption that all causes can be captured on a scientific grid.

44 See Commoner 1971 for another example of this confusion. As Max Oelschlaeger notes (1994: 73), Commoner's four laws – everything is connected to everything else, everything goes somewhere, there is no free lunch, and nature knows best – while full of wisdom read as common-sense rules of thumb, lack normative content construed scientifically.

closest relatives, and realize that together we need to learn to live responsibly and appropriately in our common home.

Contrasting the common creation story told by modern science with the view of humanity prevalent in Western religion, McFague calls on us to "move beyond democracy to biocracy, seeing ourselves as one species among millions of other species on a planet that is our common home" (108f.); in support of this she claims that this "identification is not sentimental ... It is simply the truth about who we are according to the contemporary picture of reality." This, however, is false.[45] Causal interdependence says nothing about how we ought to identify with or treat other creatures, let alone ourselves.

Talk about the unity of life, scientifically speaking, is "a metaphor for the fact that all life is part of a complex ecological web" (Donald Regan 1986: 198). Community in this metaphorical sense involves none of the elements making for mutual care or respect, the sharing of burdens, emotional attachments, intentionally formed alliances, or, for that matter, moral significance of any sort. S. F. Sapontzis gets it right (1987: 266): "that plants and animals, including ourselves, need each other and other inorganic things like unpolluted water and air to survive does not make us a 'community' in a morally significant sense, and to try to stir up moral feelings by employing that term in discussing ecological issues is to equivocate and to substitute rhetoric for argument." That we are the interdependent products of a common evolutionary process neither compels us "to imagine and feel the suffering of others" nor, for that matter, to seek "mutually life-enhancing" forms of relationship. As Hegel makes clear, slaves and masters are no less – and probably more – interdependent than brothers and sisters.

The point, let me reiterate, is not that McFague or the many others who make similar claims are mistaken in thinking that our traditional self-centerness is mistaken, that we ought to pay attention to ecological consequences, or that we are part of an encompassing biotic community – all of which I believe true. The point, small but significant, is that such normatively laden claims are not to be found in the account given of nature by modern science, from which perspective there is no basis to choose between Spencer and Leopold. To suppose this an occasion for

---

[45] For similar confusions, see Simpson 1967: 281 and Leopold 1970: *xviii–xix*. It would be petty to contest this common way of speaking were not the point so crucial relative to science in general. As Robin Attfield observes (1994: 98): "What the facts of interdependence do is strengthen the argument from human and animal interests for the preservation of the system on which they depend ... [T]hey do not constitute an independent basis of obligation."

distress, as if morality had lost something, is misguided. While modern science has much to offer an ethics of nature, by way of information and inspiration, it can never provide a basis on which to construct a normatively laden account of our relation to nature, wild or human. That is not the kind of activity it is.

THINKING LIKE A MOUNTAIN

While every ethic needs to be consistent with what science tells us about the world, we must beware of fuzzy science and the beguiling illusion of a scientifically justified ethics. We must, in this regard, not expect too much out of science. This does not mean we are not advantaged, ethically, by modern science. Clearly we are. For one thing, science allows for a better understanding of what makes for well-being in individual cases as well as which kind of beings are selves and sentients. For another, evolutionary and ecological sciences reveal more clearly the ways and extent to which living creatures are causally related, thereby enhancing our understanding of biotic communities and their common good. In the end, where modern science counts most ethically is not with regard to theoretical foundations but the day-by-day, case-by-case pursuit of ethical goals.

Familiarity with the sciences of nature can also, of course, foster ethical insights and attitudes of a more sweeping character. Not all of these will be ones we can affirm, as Spencer's "Social Darwinism" well illustrates. Some people are misled, morally, by modern science.[46] It may even be, as suggested by the fallacy of misplaced concreteness, that the abstract character of scientific inquiry encourages a one-sided, reductionistic view of nature. John Muir remarks of Asa Gray, a renowed biologist and friend: "He is a most cordial lover of purity and truth, but the angular factiness of his pursuits has kept him at too cold a distance from the spirit world" (Cohen 1984: 39).[47] At the same time, however, it cannot be denied that the sciences of nature have led many, including Leopold and Muir himself, to a deeper ethical sensitivity and, therewith, valuable ethical insights. It may even be, as J. Baird Callicott (1989: 82) argues, that "the key to the emergence of a land ethic is, simply, universal ecological

---

[46] The modern eugenics movement, originating with the nineteenth-century British physician Sir Francis Galton and eventually playing a major role in Nazi racism, provides another, no less distressing example; see Blacker 1952.

[47] William Leiss (1974: 45–71, 145–165) argues that modern science instrumentalizes nature, turning it into an object of conquest and dominion; see, also, Marcuse 1964 and Tambiah 1990: 144ff.

literacy." In any case, we need, as ethicists, to do what we can to ensure the upside of familiarity outweighs the downside. Here it will prove helpful to take a brief look at the way ethics and science interact in the life and thought of Leopold.

To start, Leopold flags the role familiarity with biological science can play in heightening ethical sensitivity (1970: 117):

> We know now what was unknown to all the preceding caravan of generations: that men are only fellow-voyagers with other creatures in the odyssey of evolution. This new knowledge should have given us, by this time, a sense of kinship with fellow-creatures; a wish to live and let live; a sense of wonder over the magnitude and duration of the biotic enterprise.

What ends up moving Leopold to feel "a sense of kinship with fellow creatures" and, more generally, "think like a mountain," however, is not what he reads in scientific treatises but a transformative encounter with a dying wolf, shot by him and his companions (138):

> We reached the old wolf in time to watch a fierce green fire dying in her eyes. I realized then, and have know ever since, that there was something new to me in those eyes – something known only to her and to the mountain.[48]

Leopold comes to realize wolves are more than predators, just as he comes to see more generally that land is not a mere commodity, "merely soil," but "a fountain of energy flowing through a circuit of soils, plants, and animals" (*xix*; 258).[49] While these insights are closely related to scientific truths – one involving the mathematics of predator–prey relations; the other, measurable exchanges of energy within ecosystems – neither of these formulae fund Leopold's recognition that wolves and deer, all creatures and, even, the mountain on which they walk, are part of a community to which we humans belong and ought, as such, be used with love and respect. The latter may be denied, without contradiction, while affirming all the quantifiable truths of ecology.

---

[48] I ask what Leopold sees in the dying wolf's eyes – what it means to "think like a mountain" – in Part III. For a contrary view of Leopold, downplaying the role of such insights, see Bryan Norton 1996. Elsewhere, however, Norton remarks (1991: 253), "the linchpin of the modern environmental movement is the belief that the study of nature has [an] ecstatic aspect." Similarly, Worster (1985: 338, 344), citing as an example Joseph Wood Krutch's "quasi-religious conversion," notes "the ecology movement . . . often takes on the quality of a religious awakening." Both Worster and Norton envision nature-so-apprehended as a substitute for a no-longer-credible religious faith. This, in turn, suggests an alternative, non-theistic way the ethic of humane holism might be developed.

[49] Leopold's remarks occur in the context of criticizing what he erroneously labels "our Abrahamic concept of land." For a corrective account, see Brueggemann 1987.

Holmes Rolston captures the essential point by way of arguing for a greater, ethical appreciation of other species (1988: 344):

Neither science nor ethics can present an argument that either necessitates or justifies the existence of each (or any!) of the five million species with which we coinhabit Earth. But we can begin to sketch nesting sets of marvelous tales.

It is interesting in this regard to compare the rarely discussed, earlier sections of *A Sand County Almanac* with the better-known essays on the land ethic. My sense is that the latter simply make explicit what is already "demonstrated" in earlier ruminations on natural history, not by way of doing either science or ethics, but, more fundamentally, through the weaving of a narrative, the telling of stories about prairie seasons, dancing woodcocks, snow geese, and ourselves – the truth in the old wolf's eyes. These stories, more poetic than philosophical or scientific, enable us to see and make judgments regarding the myriad of living creatures that enrich our common history.[50] As Rolston observes (1981: 132):

We operate as impressed by our metaphors ... as well as by our calculations, whether those images are of the survival of the fittest, or the social contract, or lifeboat ethics, or the way of the cross. If seen as a symbol, [the evolutionary] river of life is no longer merely a metaphor, it is a truth that bears moral insight, because it helps us see more clearly how the life process is and how it ought to be.

These metaphors, images, and stories put flesh on the dry bones of scientific abstraction, which by itself "cannot teach us what we need most to know about nature, that is, how to value it" (Rolston 1986: 74). Since these insights cannot be justified in scientific terms, "we will have to accept them," Rolston says (1988: 344), "as good stories, perhaps to reform the stories by which we catch what is going on."[51]

[50] Here we need to pay close attention to not only natural science, strictly speaking, but "natural history writers" such as Muir, Abbey, Stegner, Nabham, Lopez, Dillard, so forth and so on. These writers quicken our awareness of a reality we are in danger of overlooking or having seen, forgetting, distracted by the rush of modern life and thought. See in this regard Stegner (1992: 207–213) for a profound reflection on Wendell Berry's contribution; my thanks to David Gleason for calling this book to my attention.

[51] Rosemary Ruether (1992: 58) calls for "scientist-poets who can retell the story ... of the cosmos and the earth's history, in a way that can call us to wonder, to reverence for life, and to the vision of humanity living in community with all its sister and brother beings." Two noteworthy examples are Teilhard de Chardin 1965 and Thomas Berry 1990. Berry's "new creation story," while prone like the "Christogenesis" of his great predecessor, Teilhard, to fuzzy science (see, for instance, 1990: 123–137), has quickened the ecological awareness of many. Dalton 1999, esp. 61–75, highlights Berry's expansion of Teilhard's anthropocentric focus to encompass the earth community as a whole. This parallels the account I develop in Parts II and III from a more traditionally theistic perspective.

Leopold's insights regarding our place in and responsibility to the encompassing web of life cannot be derived from the results of any scientific inquiry. Evolutionary and ecological theories can establish their validity no more than they can refute the story told about human society by Spencer. Are we to embrace Leopold's exhortation to think like a mountain or dismiss it as a dangerous, moral error, if not outright absurdity? Ought we opt for Spencer's brutal and allegedly benevolent struggle for survival or a society built on cooperation and mutual care? Modern science is unable to say, the reason being that our assessment of these competing images and metaphors depends in the final analysis on judgments of a sort, value-judgments, that have no place in its abstract, quantitative data and theories. Indeed, from the point of view of evolutionary and ecological science, Leopold's land ethic appears as a bolt out of the blue, a faith-based, charismatically compelling insight, not a testable hypothesis.

That Leopold's moral insights are not grounded scientifically is no more surprising than the inability of a topographical map to portray what would be lost or gained by damming the Middle Fork of the King's River; to anyone familiar with or caring about only the information contained on the map, it would make no difference one way or the other. The "ought" floats above, separated from the value-free "is."[52] What makes this epistemic gap so distressing to some (and helps explain the continuing effort to scientize ethics) is the apparent absence of a way to assess the moral adequacy of competing insights and stories with the confidence and resultant convergence of opinion characteristic of modern science. How are we to tell if Leopold is right or Spencer wrong? I want, in the next section, to comment on this frustration relative to the moral indeterminacy of Part I and, in so doing, set the stage for Parts II and III. Before going there, however, we need to take a closer look at the contribution science makes to Leopold's ethic. While it is true that no ethic can be justified in scientific terms, it is also true that science provides more relative to Leopold's ethic than inspiration.

Transformative moral insights, whatever their basis in faith or reason, do not occur in an epistemic vacuum. This holds for the realization that other creatures are looking back – interested in their own well-being,

---

[52] I qualify the "is" so as to indicate that I am not relying on the alleged impossibility of deriving an "ought" from an "is." Indeed, it is my view, as a theist and, thus, moral realist, that reality in its most fundamental form *is* value-laden. I do agree, however, with the claim and my analysis here depends on it, that it is not possible to derive an "ought" from the abstract, value-free "is" of modern science.

wondering what we are about – as it does for the realization that wild nature is worthy of respect in its own right. Earlier we saw how the compelling experience of other animals as selves draws support from the complexly interwoven fabric of everyday life; understood in this context scientific data and theories bolster the commonsensical belief that many non-human animals are creatures who, like us, care about what happens to them. We also noted in passing how science so appropriated allows us to refine common sense, understand other animals better than we did before the science of ethology appeared on the scene. The same, I want now to stress, holds for Leopold's transformative experience, an experience that takes place while he, a scientifically trained game manager, is carrying out his official duties. As such, Leopold knows well what the science of that time says about wolves and their prey; this knowledge of evolutionary and ecological relations plays a key role in his understanding of what it means to think like a mountain. Further, the moral insight to which he comes is closely associated with a scientific insight, subsequently verified, into the evolutionary history and ecological role of wolves. Thus, while no amount of scientific research could ever verify Leopold's ethic, that ethic flows from and finds itself indirectly supported, endorsed, by Leopold's scientific inquiries. "Here," as Rolston notes (1988: 231f.) with regard to environmental ethics in general, "an *ought* is not so much *derived* from an *is* as discovered simultaneously with it."

Rolston's remarks flag an epistemic relationship other than that of justification. This relation, "simultaneous discovery," consists, I suggest, in two interwoven elements, "inspiration" and "endorsement." We have been focusing, relative to moral insight, on the first: a familiarity with natural history can and does on occasion inspire a morally laden respect for wild nature. That is one reason many ethically serious people prefer to read novelists and nature-writers rather than moral philosophers: the former two are capable of fostering and sustaining moral insight in a way the latter commonly do not (and, indeed, sometimes discourage). It is the second element, however, that of endorsement, which proves more important in the long run. Here, critical thought pursues analysis and argument as far as it will go.

Endorsement occurs in the epistemic space between consistency and justification. In this, it resembles the indirect support that modern science gives to otherwise grounded beliefs such as that in animal awareness, beliefs which cannot, strictly speaking, even be formulated in scientific terms. Thus, Leopold's land ethic, while grounded (insofar as it can be grounded) in moral arguments of the sort found in Part I, is indirectly

supported, endorsed, by modern science in virtue of the way its normatively laden, non-scientific view of nature incorporates and illuminates,
humanly speaking, an evolutionary and ecological perspective on nature. Another example is provided by humane holism, which, as seen,
draws on Leopold's insights. Here, endorsement occurs through the assimilation (and filling out) of a philosophical ethic within a world-view,
theistic naturalism, that not only affirms but makes good sense, so I
argue throughout Parts II and III, of human life and, therewith, scientific inquiry. It is this relationship, endorsement, which ethically sensitive
fuzzifiers of science are searching for in claiming, mistakenly, that modern evolutionary and ecological theories show that we ought, in light
of our interconnectedness, to care about other creatures and nature-as-
a-whole. Their mistake lies in confusing the indirect support provided
by endorsement with the direct support, or, justification, of scientific
theories by scientific arguments.

While the difference between direct and indirect support may seem
inconsequential, as though the latter were only a weaker form of the
former, this is not so. For one thing, the possibility of direct support allows for not only justification but falsification; further, indirect support
may be quite strong, as proved the case with animal awareness. The
crucial difference is not strength but orientation, the kind and degree of
epistemic pressure brought to bear. The justification of a claim, A, by
another, epistemically more basic set of claims, B, limits the content of A
in accord with some encompassing logic; thus, scientific theories are required, by the logic of scientific inquiry, to not only stay close to the actual
evidence but, thereby, be formulated in terms that are open to scientific
assessment. This brings to bear a direct and, as it turns out, powerful
epistemic pressure; this, in turn, explains the degree of convergence in
scientific disciplines. Endorsement, on the other hand, while providing
more epistemic pressure than the demand for consistency, provides much
less than justification. In particular, while the scientific justification of a
claim precludes justification of its denial, it is not uncommon to find two
or more inconsistent, non-scientific claims endorsed by modern science.
Thus, both those who affirm and those who deny animal awareness find
indirect support for their views in modern science – albeit, to be sure, not
in the same features. Much the same, so I argue in chapter four, holds for
those who affirm and deny the existence of God; science cuts both ways.

There is nothing troubling in this looseness so long as we do not
confuse endorsement with justification. In particular, so far as other
minds and God are concerned, we need to bear in mind that (dis)belief
in either cannot be justified in scientific terms. So far as justification

goes, we must, in these cases, look elsewhere. That this is so does not render the epistemic pressure provided by way of endorsement trivial. Far from it, as I hope to have already made clear with regard to animal awareness and as I will argue at greater length in chapter four relative to theological reflection. There we will find that the incorporation of and resultant indirect support (*qua* endorsement) provided by scientific and other claims justified in non-theological terms plays a critical role in the development and, more fundamentally, reasonableness of religious faith. For the moment I want only to stress that Leopold's land ethic, the exhortation to think like a mountain, while incapable of explication or, thereby, justification in scientific terms, is, nevertheless, interwoven with and endorsed by scientific theories. Before, however, inquiring more (in Part III) about how this occurs and what it implies relative to humane holism, we need to step back and take a closer look at the underlying, no less complex relation between faith and reason.

FAITH AND REASON

The frightening thought, so far as moral convictions go, is that we cannot get around the element of subjectivity, that in the end it all comes down to what we see (or fail to see) in the wolf's eye. In part, I want to allow that this is so; there is no method, scientific or otherwise, that allows us to prove – establish beyond a reasonable doubt in universally accessible, rationally compelling terms – that a particular moral outlook is correct. In this sense, morality rests on faith in a way not true of mathematics, logic or, even, at its core, modern science – the affirmation of which serves as a measure of one's basic reasonableness.[53] Putting the contrast so starkly, however, proves misleading for two reasons. The first reason is that many ethicists, from Plato and Aristotle to Aquinas, Kant, Mill, and beyond, claim, explicitly and implicitly, that the unique validity of their own moral outlook can be shown by way of philosophical analysis and argument. Having noted this, I am going to assume here that these claims are mistaken.[54]

---

53 It is crucial here, of course, to allow for continuing debate within these disciplines as regards what actually is a well-established result – for instance, whether Fermat's Last Theorem has, indeed, been proven or, more contentiously, whether evolution proceeds by leaps and bounds. More generally, we must take care to distinguish between scientific theories and non-scientific presumption of the sort discussed above, relative to the underlying purposefulness of nature.

54 To argue this point in any detail is not possible. In any case, the possibility some future moral theory will succeed where others have failed cannot be ruled out in advance. Suffice it to note – an argument of sorts – that after twenty-five centuries of analysis and argument, philosophical ethicists disagree among themselves no less, if not more, than the combined religious and cultural traditions of humankind. For importantly different responses to this absence of convergence, see

A second, more important reason to hesitate before concluding that our diverse moral convictions rest on an act of faith is that appeals to faith threaten to obscure the role reason – analysis and argument – plays in the moral life. The problem lies in a common presumption, namely, that faith and reason are opposites and, more particularly, that any turn to faith results in a diminishment, if not altogether repudiation, of reason. I believe and undertake to show in Parts II and III that this common presumption is mistaken. Rightly understood, faith, rather than limiting reason, extends its domain, enables it to enlighten and serve humanity in ways it could never otherwise do. To see how this happens, however, requires a nuanced view of faith and reason, one that distinguishes commonly conflated meanings and elements. I want in this section to ferret these differences out by indicating how they are built into the structure of our overall argument and, especially, the respective roles played in that argument by Parts I, II, and III. Let me begin by looking back at Part I.

Part I approaches the problem of constructing an ethics of nature from the standpoint of philosophical ethics. This shows up in the issues it raises, the sources with which it dialogues, and the arguments it makes – all of which pursue an ideal set forth by Socrates in his quest for the truth about justice: universally accessible, rationally compelling arguments replace common appeals to religious beliefs and cultural tradition. That, like Socrates, I achieve only a relative success does not mean the net is not cast widely, aimed at our common humanity. Thus, where it is necessary to call on faith-based convictions, as in the presumption of animal awareness and sentiosis, I do so in a generic manner, allowing for a diversity of world-views and life-orientations.[55]

The generic character of philosophical ethics reflects its status as a branch of philosophy. Philosophy, though a "science" only in the first, broad sense (of a *Wissenschaft*), is committed like modern science to universally accessible reasons. Both are closely related in this regard to the disciplines and practices of mathematics. Mathematical calculations are paradigmatic instances of universally accessible, rationally compelling argument. Anyone who fails to see "two plus two equals four" denies the Pythagorean Theorem, or dismisses as nonsense the esoterics of

---

MacIntyre 1984, Williams 1985, Rorty 1989, and, for a useful overview of the larger debate, Gutting 1999.

[55] The goal in such cases is to achieve, by way of reflective equilibrium, an encompassing, reasonable pluralism. For more on this goal, see the account of "public reason" in Rawls 1993: xvi–xvii, 8, 24f., 28, 36f., 55ff., 97, 129, and 216f. Where I disagree with Rawls is on how far "public reason" can go, epistemically and politically; hence, the need for Parts II and III. For more on Rawls' project, see Fern 1987.

infinitesimal calculus forfeits the crown of rationality. The same holds for the disciplines and practices of logic. Not to see that *modus ponens* is a valid form of argument or that "affirming the consequent" is not, misses the boat so far as reason goes.

Allowing that there are many, important differences, I want to designate all forms of reflection that rely in principle on only universally accessible reasons instances of "generic reason." The disciplined commitment of these diverse forms of reflection to time- and place-invariant considerations allows them to become "academic disciplines," thereby, entitling them to a place in the "modern university."[56] Ideally, the modern university and its disciplines set aside particularities of religious faith and cultural tradition to provide a place where di-versity is subordinated to our common, uni-versal humanity and, more particularly, generic reason. This endeavor is of great value. We learn much regarding how the world functions by focusing attention on clearly delineated, repetitive features of experience – mathematical, logical, causal, epistemic, whatever – while holding at bay other, less disciplined factors.[57] In addition, the modern university provides a common meeting place for diverse cultures and religious faiths, a vital function in our increasingly diverse societies.[58]

---

[56] Hence, another term for generic reason is "academic reason." What makes for a "university" may, of course, like what makes for a "science," be understood in a broader or narrower sense. Hugh Goddard (2000: 99), for instance, characterizes the modern university, "going back to the establishment of Al-Azhar in Cairo in [969 C.E.]," as "a place of learning where students congregate to study a variety of subjects under a variety of teachers." Goddard contrasts this new practice with "earlier institutions of learning such as those of the ancient Greeks . . . centered on individual teachers." I adopt here a narrower characterization, centering – as that of modern science – on a defining ideal. In practice, of course, the modern university, like modern science, serves a plethora of sometimes conflicting ends.

[57] The scope of academic inquiry is, in principle, unlimited. All that is required for a form of generic reason are generically identifiable elements that behave in a regular, predictable manner. The status of some disciplines remains, of course, a matter of dispute. Are the "social sciences" scientific (in the sense true of biology)? Are they more closely akin to "natural philosophy"? To the humanities (such as history)? So forth and so on. Here it is important, as apparent in our discussion of ecology and diversification. Note, however, that on this characterization, theology – while open to study by academic disciplines (such as "religious studies") and, historically, an important part of the curriculum in many universities – cannot itself, given its reliance on the particularities of revelation, be an academic discipline.

[58] These gains, as apparent in our discussion of modern science, come at a price. All academic disciplines depend on a process of abstraction that focuses attention and, in the process, dismisses as irrelevant whatever fails to fit into its conceptual grid – as flagged in Eddington's image of the presumptuous fisherman. This does not mean academics must mistake the reality they dissect for the fuller, less disciplined reality in which we live; it does mean that this is a danger inherent in the academic life. One way to counter this danger is to provide a broad, liberal education; thus, Whitehead proposes the study of philosophy as a way to counter the "misplaced concreteness" induced by scientific inquiry. Another way, that adopted here, is to situate generic reason and, with it, the university, in the larger context of human life and faith.

My concern in Part I is with a particular academic discipline, philosophical ethics, and, in particular, its curiously interwoven compellingness and indeterminacy. No conclusion is more evident, morally speaking, than that the well-being of non-human selves and sentients counts morally; yet philosophical ethics is unable on its own to ascertain the comparative significance of these claims, tell us how much they count relative to our own or, even, each other. We are given a charge, yet left ignorant of the means to determine if it has been discharged satisfactorily. In this regard, Part I leaves us hanging, wanting, requiring more. This may, of course, be a consequence of my own failure, philosophically. As indicated above, I do not believe this is so, whatever other failures there may be. In any case, I have chosen to step back, put one foot outside the modern university, and ask what, if anything, the many diverse particularities of faith have to contribute, morally speaking.

That I choose this route reflects more general beliefs, in particular, as indicated, that faith and reason, far from being warring alternatives, cut to the truth only insofar as they work together.[59] Thus, in turning to faith, I affirm a "both-and," not an "either-or." To see how this both-and works, however, we need to draw two distinctions, one relative to reason, the other faith. This will allow us, in turn, to distinguish three modalities of moral reflection, correlated, respectively, with Parts I, II, and III.

The first distinction is implicit in our account of generic reason. The distinctiveness of generic reason, its relation to diverse, methodologically constrained disciplines, highlights its difference from an all-things-considered, "comprehensive reason." Comprehensive reason appears in numerous processes of reflection on which we rely in the everyday course of our lives. These all incorporate aspects of generic reason, apart from which they would not be reasonable. At the same time, however, they rely on faith-based considerations, beliefs, and values rooted in a diversity of religious faiths and cultural traditions. An example is provided by notions of "reasonable care" and, negatively put, "negligence." Apart from these notions, we would be unable to say when someone is at fault for accidentally harming another, that is, when they have acted "unreasonably." As legal treatises commonly point out, however, the standard of reasonableness laid down in such notions varies from one

---

[59] For more on the compatibility of faith and reason, especially as this bears on the alleged warfare between science and religion, see the informative overview in McGrath 1998: 1–35.

society, one community to another.[60] There are no determinate generic standards of reasonableness, the reason being that what people regard as reasonable depends on specific beliefs about human nature and good, beliefs which not only vary among but define different cultures.[61]

The ways in which we determine reasonableness of action and belief in the day-to-day course of our life depend on faith-based beliefs and values, convictions regarding ourselves and the world in which we live. Thus, ordinary legal reasoning provides a good example of comprehensive reason by contrast with a time- and place-invariant generic reason. This, in turn, allows us to explicate Pascal's seemingly paradoxical claim that the heart has reasons of which reason is unaware. There is no paradox so long as we bear in mind that comprehensive reason has culturally and religiously specific reasons incapable of formulation in rationally compelling, universally accessible terms. Forgetting about these reasons when thinking theoretically, as academics, is an instance of misplaced concreteness, a failure to remember we are guided by our hearts no less and no less wisely than our heads.

Putting it this way, with reference to hearts and heads is, of course, too loose. That is why, relative to "heads," I have just distinguished generic and comprehensive reason. I want now, relative to "hearts," to distinguish two irreducibly distinct kinds of faith, charismatic and constitutive. The basic distinction is this: charismatic faith affirms an insight or reality that, once seen, cannot be denied; constitutive faith, by contrast, affirms a perspective or practice, a way of life, that everyone (with the appropriate upbringing) takes for granted. I say more regarding what each amounts to in Parts II and III, respectively. Let me, though, expand briefly.

Charismatic faith centers around the perception of an object that is not clearly apprehended, yet in its mystery revelatory of what is taken to be the deep truth about reality, a truth so full of truth that it is terrifying

---

[60] John Fleming, a legal historian, observes (1985: 30):

> Since one of the most vaunted qualities of the "reasonable man" test, especially when applied by a jury, is that it permits the injection of a good dose of grass-root sentiment into the daily administration of the law by linking the legal standard of care to accepted community evaluations, much evidentiary weight perforce attaches to whether or not the defendant's conduct accorded with general practices for doing the particular kind of thing.

> For informative discussions of changing notions of reasonableness in nineteenth-century American law relative to property development, see Horwitz (1977: 37 ff.) and Hall (1989: 114 ff.).

[61] Generic standards of reasonableness, such as "don't cut off your nose to spite your face," serve as "rules of thumb," offering different advice in different cultures, as, for instance, relative to "dueling" in societies that place a high stake on personal honor compared to those that do not.

and fascinating at one and the same time, a *mysterium tremendum et fascinans* (Otto 1950). The classic examples of such experiences, like the visions of Isaiah, Ezekiel, and John the Revelator, are religious, though charismatically compelling experiences may be found in non-religious contexts, as in Leopold's encounter with the wolf or my awe-invoking experience of seeing Tehipite Dome in the moonlight. Whatever the object of charismatic faith, however, the glow of a nuclear reactor or Yahweh Himself, it is always perceived to be or to manifest a reality more real than that possessed by ordinary objects or seen on ordinary occasions. In such moments, the Really Real, the depth of reality, is (so it seems) uncovered, revealed.[62]

Part II calls on charismatic faith to assist in the search for a determinate ethics of nature. In so doing, it presumes we become aware of the bottom-line, normatively laden truth about nature, its deep, sentiotic *telos*, by way of charismatic encounter, moments of moral insight and conviction: the dry bones of generic reason are filled with marrow by the mysterious, life-giving Word of God. One danger this poses is that swept up in a chariot of fire, we succumb to (what might well be called) "the fallacy of misplaced ecstasy." Correspondingly, I will argue that in filling out, explicating, our charismatically grounded faith we need to recognize and respect the generic, rationally compelling analyses and arguments, scientific and philosophical, set forth in the academy. Accordingly, before offering a theological explication of my own, charismatic faith in chapter five, I consider, in chapter four, ways in which religious faith, rightly construed, incorporates and finds itself shaped by "all truth," academic and otherwise.

The real danger, however, is not that charismatic faith will abandon generic reason or, for that matter, vice versa. For every radical fideist and Enlightenment rationalist, there are a thousand more balanced minds and hearts. The real danger is that "faith and reason," God and Darwin, having found each other, will forget their common dependence on cultural traditions. Here it is important to see, as argued in chapter six, that generic reason and charismatic faith are both ideal in form and, as such, have a natural tendency to align themselves against the inherently conservative dynamic of constitutive faith, which aims above all to protect and preserve an irreducibly communal inertia, a shared way of

---

[62] Thereby enabling us to distinguish between appearance and reality. Though I focus here on discrete, overpowering instances of charismatic experience, it needs to be seen that experience in general has a charismatic dimension, the source of its compelling givenness and basic, irreducible epistemic authority.

life.[63] My claim to the contrary, developed in Part III, is that ascertaining the truth, moral and otherwise, depends on constitutive faith no less than generic reason or charismatic faith. It is culture that makes us who we are and apart from which we cannot ascertain, let alone be what we ought to be. Let me focus here, briefly, on the general shape of constitutive faith.

Constitutive faith is the epistemic authority accorded by the adherents of particular cultures to the presuppositions on which their common life depends. As such, objects of constitutive faith are never salient in the way that objects of charismatic faith are. Typically, objects of constitutive faith come to the fore only when there is a fading of faith; otherwise, we hardly ever notice them, let alone think to question them. This does not mean constitutive faith is underhanded, as though we would all be better off if these suppositions were exposed to the light of day. Sometimes this is true. More generally, the hiddenness of constitutive faith simply reflects the fact that *we* would never come to any conclusion, get anything done if *we* did not take some things for granted. In this regard, comprehensive reason requires not only analytic skills and uplifting vision but, no less, the presumptions and practices of ordinary, down-to-earth people, the proverbial man (and woman) in the Clapham omnibus.[64]

Every ethic, however ideal, depends for its determinacy on a (more-or-less coherent) constitutive tradition. This is true for religious ethics no less than its philosophical counterpart. The burning bush encountered by Moses is not a symbol of some rootless spirituality but a sign of Yahweh's

[63] The enduring, era-defining struggle of the last millennium has not been – as often claimed – between faith (religion) and reason (philosophy and modern science) but, rather, historic, cultural traditions (constitutive faith) and, on the one hand, and, on the other, charismatic faith and generic reason allied together in support of an imperialistic, centralizing and allegedly enlightened state, first, medieval, then, modern. This struggle reflects (not only the will of some to exploit others but even more importantly) a deep, ineliminable tension in human life. Accordingly, my goal is not to help one side or the other "win" but, rather, perpetuate the struggle, turn it into a self-reflective, socially productive "war by other means." Here, though less of a rationalist and more of a communitarian than he, I agree wholeheartedly with Alasdair MacIntyre's seminal observation (1984: 222): "A living tradition then is an historically extended, socially embodied argument, and an argument precisely in part about the goods which constitute that tradition."

[64] Charles Larmore (1996: 115), noting "the evident failure of the rationalist project of drawing fundamental moral obligations from a notion of practical reason as such," observes: "We can reason only in a context of given belief, which as such does not call for justification, but on the contrary gives us the means for considering possible changes of belief, a context that is ours in virtue of our place in history. Historical context is not something reason must transcend, but rather a condition of its possibility." Similarly, Samuel Fleischacker argues that "ethical traditions" and our faith therein make ethics possible and, with it, ethical universalism (1994: 20; 54); he concludes, parallel to what I am arguing here, that "from the moral point of view, cultures provide the prism by which we interpret and try to guide our history and sociology, not the other way around" (200f.).

continuing concern for the well-being of His people: "I am the God of your father, the God of Abraham, the God of Isaac and the God of Jacob" (Exodus 3: 6 [New Revised Standard Version (NRSV)]). Moses hears and lives out a culturally specific message of redemption. The same is true of Jesus and Mohammed. The Word of God never appears in a cultural void – not because God lacks the power to speak where he chooses but, simply, because, so I argue in Part III , no human beings exist in a cultural void.[65] It follows that the Word of God, like every word heard by a human ear, depends for its determinate content and, thereby, moral upshot on culturally rooted beliefs and values.[66]

By comparison with common-sense moralities, philosophical and religious ethics are invariably reactive, dependent for determinacy on a culturally embedded constitutive faith. This does not mean they lack moral authority. To the contrary. Since cultures depend for their legitimation on the recognized authority of philosophical and, especially, religious considerations, these possess prevailing authority relative to "the way things have always been done." That is why we characterize philosophical and religious ethics as ideal and, by contrast, common-sense morality as conservative. All three forms of reflection, however, are needed to find our way around in the world.[67] That is why we need, in conjunction with Parts I and II, a Part III.

---

[65] Affirming this claim makes my endeavor "postmodern" in at least two senses: (1) it "celebrates the multiplicity of local stories of truth without trying to reduce them all to the one, the universal," and (2) it preserves "differences through relation and dialogue" rather than isolation (Kepnes *et al.* 1998: 11). At the same time, however, it is important to see, relative to all three Parts, that this postmodern contextualization is tied to a critical common-sense realism, one that affirms the presumption that "local stories," cultural and religious, purport to tell *the* truth, and thus, end up disagreeing about what that truth is. Here I agree with "Dabru Emet," a recent Jewish statement encouraging dialogue between Christians and Jews (Frymer-Kensky *et al.* 2000), when, observing that "the humanly irreconcilable difference between Jews and Christians will not be settled until God redeems the entire world as promised in Scripture," it goes on to note that this does not mean Jews and Christians do not as theists have much in common nor much to gain from working together for justice and peace, each in their own way.

[66] This claim raises vital hermeneutical questions regarding the interpretation of sacred texts. Suffice it to note here that while agreeing with much George Lindbeck (1984) says regarding this task, I hold to the contrary that a "cultural-linguistic hermeneutic" not only allows but requires propositional and experiential-expressive elements – albeit, as Lindbeck argues, not in the exclusive manner many have thought.

[67] This reflects the dependence of comprehensive reason on three, distinct, individually necessary and jointly sufficient "sources," or, epistemic authorities: generic reason, charismatic experience, and constitutive tradition. This "epistemic trialectic" (not only calls to mind the "Anglican tripod" but, more importantly) proves fundamental to human thought and life. Each authority is essential and, correspondingly, poses, by itself, the risk of one-sidedness. Taking all three together will not, of course, eliminate risk, of which life is full. We can, however, minimize the risk and build on the promise of life by bearing in mind that every path to the truth is what it is and not another.

PART II

The wild god

CHAPTER FOUR

Religious faith

RELIGIOUS NATURALISM

Striking examples of religious naturalism occur in the "nature religions" of Amerindians and other tribal peoples. As Catherine Albanese observes (1990: 21 f.):

> For native North Americans the numinous world of nature beings was always very close, and the land itself expressed their presence. Indian peoples created religious geographies in which specific sites were inhabited by sacred powers and persons ... The sense of continuity with the sacred – and natural – world that was revealed in this language had its counterpart in a mythic sense of time, in which what we call history was conflated, for Amerindians, with events that had occurred outside of ordinary time.

Here, the well-being of individuals and society is seen to depend on their relation to sacred powers, beings, spaces, and times (23): "The material world was a holy place; and so harmony with nature beings and natural forms was the controlling ethic, reciprocity the recognized mode of interaction. Ritual functioned to restore a lost harmony, like a great balancing act bringing the people back to right relation with the world." Albanese concludes, "an ecological perspective came, for the most part, easily – if unselfconsciously – among traditional tribal peoples."[1]

What does it mean for the world to be "inhabited by sacred powers and persons"? Part of what it means is that the world in which tribal peoples live contains, so they believe, extraordinary, supernatural entities. Here, as the existence of ritual and its sacred objects indicates, a distinction is drawn between techniques for dealing with ordinary, everyday objects and more personalized forms of engagement required for spiritual powers, ones that honor their dignity and overlapping interests in the natural objects on which human life depends. Granting this, we must be careful

---

[1] Which is not to say they never acted foolishly, religiously or ecologically. See Regan 1982b and Callicott 1989: 203–219.

not to impose a contrast that reflects our own, modern mentality. For tribal peoples, there is an inherent continuity between the natural and the divine, earth and heaven.[2] Nature is personal all the way through. Correspondingly, adoption of a religious perspective on nature always involves more than the recognition of extraordinary entities.

Unlike merely extraordinary beings, beings with the capacity to do what we cannot, sacred entities stand in a special relation to the underlying purpose and meaning of existence and, therewith, human life.[3] That is what makes them worthy of *devotion*. Thus, Albanese remarks (1990: 6): "I understand religion as the way or ways that people orient themselves in the world with reference to both ordinary and extraordinary powers, meanings, and values."[4] Similarly, Wolfhart Pannenberg (1993: 74): "Religion . . . is concerned with the experience of the power that determines the reality of being as a whole, which transcends as such all special, isolatable and disposable powers and strengths." We cannot grasp the *religious* quality of a belief in sacred powers and persons until we see that the object of concern is Reality in its most fundamental, pervasive sense, never, simply, one more thing.

While historic religions all affirm the existence of realities denied by the non-religious, the true difference between religious and non-religious views does not consist in a list of entities, as though religious believers were especially inclined, like children, to believe in "things that go bump in the night,"[5] but, rather, a fundamental orientation toward life itself. Morris

---

[2] For an illuminating account of how nature is perceived in "archaic religions," see Langdon Gilkey 1993. Gilkey observes (102):

> To tribal and archaic religion, nature (to use Mircea Eliade's phrase) was not "natural" in the sense it is to us. That is, nature was not at all "desacralized," shorn of its sacred dimension and thus "on its own" and self-sufficient – and hence secular in its being and its processes. On the contrary, nature's power or powers and its life forces – in fact everything in nature – represented signs or symbols, vehicles, of a transcendent power and order: "hierophanies" of the sacred.

> Gilkey (109f.) links this awareness of the Sacred to "the certainty and confidence of an [inherently normative] order encompassing all experienced things." He explores the interweaving of sacred and natural in terms of "limit questions" involving power (79–94), life (95–107), order (109–130), and redemptive unity/meaning (131–141).

[3] Contrast in this regard traditional deities such as Thor or Zeus with the enigmatic, seemingly all-powerful figure "Q" in *Star Trek: the Second Generation*.

[4] Albanese follows Clifford Geertz' widely accepted definition: "a religion is (1) a system of symbols which acts to (2) establish powerful, pervasive, and long-lasting moods and motivations in men by (3) formulating conceptions of a general order of existence and (4) clothing these conceptions with such an aura of factuality that (5) the moods and motivations seem uniquely realistic" (1973: 90).

[5] This view of religion is dominant in nineteenth- and early twentieth-century attempts to provide a reductionistic, "natural history" of religious faith. For an informative history and critique of these attempts, see Evans-Pritchard 1965.

Berman captures the difference in his characterization of "enchanted worlds" (1981: 16):

The view of nature which predominated in the West down to the eve of the Scientific Revolution was that of an enchanted world. Rocks, trees, rivers, and clouds were all seen as wondrous, alive, and human beings felt at home in this environment. The cosmos, in short, was a place of *belonging*. A member of this cosmos was not an alienated observer of it but a direct participant in its drama. His personal destiny was bound up with its destiny, and this relationship gave meaning to his life.

To believe in a sacred reality is not simply (or, perhaps, even) to see "spirits" where others do not but, more fundamentally, to view reality as inherently purposeful, a cosmic drama in relation to which human beings find their own meaning and purpose.

This belief in a sacred cosmos need not and, indeed, rarely is conceived by tribal peoples in idyllic terms. Observing "the strange unity of life and death" found in archaic religion, Langdon Gilkey remarks (1993: 106): "Earth is thus the source of life and the fearful abode of death . . . Death and life are united in earth as they are in water, in moon, and in sun." On occasion, as appears to have been the case in Druidism, nature religions adopt a dark, terrifying view of nature (Powell 1958: 115ff.). As a rule, though, animists hold remarkably well-balanced views: nature, like life, is oriented toward the goods of well-being – albeit with a risk; care must be taken to stay in harmony with natural processes and, thereby, on the beneficent side of sacred powers and persons.[6]

What all such enchanted worlds have in common is a normative directionality and ultimate meaningfulness, a cosmic purposefulness that is not dependent on human beings or other, mere creatures for its existence but, rather, comes built into the very foundation of reality. It is this belief in a truly fundamental, inherently purposeful, sacred reality which differentiates religious views of the world from the (merely) magical or scientific.[7] Thus, as Odil Steck observes (1980: 100): "what [the biblical author] is looking for in the creation account is, in contrast [to scientific accounts of evolution], the elemental foundation and the ordained character of meaning and value, for the life of the individual and the world of life as a whole." This difference holds not only for the Bible but religious perspectives in general.

Not all religious perspectives, however, are *naturalistic* in the sense true of nature religions. Speaking of rituals performed in the "mystery

---

[6] The Navaho notion of *hozro*, or, harmony, offers an example; see Underhill 1965: 224ff.

[7] For more on the emerging differentiation of magic, science, and religion, see Tambiah 1990.

religions" of ancient Greece, George Hendry remarks (1980: 35) on their similarity to those found in nature religions:

[They] were elaborate procedures designed to bring the initiate into sympathetic rapport with the generative and regenerative powers of nature and to enable the person to participate in them . . . The secret imparted in the mysteries was the secret of life out of death, and the medium was the process of nature in which this secret is reenacted annually.

Here, though, we must take care. While it is likely many ordinary worshippers, reflecting the attitude characteristic of pre-Hellenic polytheism,[8] viewed "the mysteries" as a means to harmony with the value-laden, sacred-infused processes of nature, it is clear that others did not. In particular, there existed a literate, hermetic, and gnostic elite for whom participation in "the mysteries" was a means of escape from nature and eventual union with the divine in an immaterial, purely spiritual world. For the latter, the mystery religions are instances not of religious naturalism but, much to the contrary, its antithesis, a religious anti-naturalism.[9]

What makes a religion anti-naturalistic is the presence of a strongly negative attitude toward the material world. This stance presupposes, as a necessary condition, an ontological dualism: the Sacred is altogether other than and in no way dependent for its own reality or eternal well-being on the material world. By itself, this radical difference does not entail a negative attitude toward nature. Negativity appears in the way it is understood.[10] Three claims, in particular, stand out: (1) nature (*qua* materiality) is inherently evil; (2) human beings (or, commonly, some subset thereof) are essentially immaterial; (3) salvation involves release from the prison of materiality and, more positively, divinization, the realization of our true, incorporeal nature. Clearly, insofar as this otherworldly faith makes use of the vine, it will do so only for the inebriation, the escape, it

---

[8] "The plain man, then, in ancient Greece, lived in a world full of all manner of supernatural powers, great and small, friendly and unfriendly, and naturally tried to get and maintain right relations with them" (Rose 1959: 28). Though distinct from, this parallels the more evolved, naturalistic worship of earth-goddesses in Minoan and Mycenaean civilizations (47 ff.).

[9] For more on the mystery religions of late antiquity, including similarities and differences to Christianity, see Rose 1959 and Nilsson 1969, esp. 124–161. My intent here is to draw a contrast, not settle complex questions in the history of religion.

[10] This is an important point for the argument to come. I argue below, in chapter five, that traditional theism, while affirming a strong ontological dualism, is a form of religious naturalism. In particular, I show how and why its biblically grounded account of ontological dualism leads it to repudiate the following three claims, all integral to a religious anti-naturalism; the basic of this repudiation consists, in brief, in the constitutive binding of humanity to creation-at-large by the all-encompassing love of God.

brings. By contrast, religious naturalism detects inherent value in nature and natural processes: the wine is savored, the vine valued for what it is, not as a means to some other, alien world; nature itself, fermentation and all, is *the* place, the one and only place, where we encounter and live with sacred powers and persons.[11] Since this is an important point, let me give another example of the difference.

C. S. Lewis, in a sermon entitled "The Weight of Glory," tells us that attempts to find beauty and, with it, joy, in the natural world inevitably fail because the good we desire is not there but, rather, only comes through it. Lewis (cited in McGrath 1998: 209) says:

> These things – the beauty, the memory of our own past – are good images of what we really desire; but if they are mistaken for the thing itself they turn into dumb idols, breaking the hearts of their worshippers. For they are not the thing itself; they are only the scent of a flower we have not found, the echo of a tune we have not heard, news from a country we have not visited.

Lewis' remarks are interestingly ambiguous.[12] If Lewis is saying that we find our fulfillment in a place, a non-material, spiritual country, other than this place, nature, he is articulating an anti-naturalistic point of view. I believe to the contrary, as Alister McGrath's exposition (1998: 208f.) suggests, that Lewis is saying "the natural order beckons us onwards to discover its creator."[13] This, though, is perfectly congruent with Black Elk's claim that the Great Spirit is in and above all things and people (Brown 1971: xx). The same holds true of Calvin's reference to "this most glorious theater" of nature in which we have been placed by God, so long as it is allowed that we, unlike the unfortunates chained in Plato's

---

[11] For a good example of this attitude, see Black Elk's account of Sioux religion and ritual in Neihardt 1961 and Brown 1971.

[12] This reflects, in part, the influence on Christianity of otherworldly, anti-naturalistic faiths, as seen in the struggle against Gnostics and Manicheans and, more subtly, the continuing influence of Neoplatonism. More fundamentally still, it reflects tensions inherent in the life-encompassing stance of theism, as regards which see Santmire 1985. While anti-naturalistic faiths are, in my opinion, deeply flawed, it needs to be seen that this faith-orientation, like the four quasi-theisms discussed below, often affirms a vital, if one-sided truth. In particular, for all their denigration of this world, "otherworldly faiths," East and West, often enable persons to carry on and, even, affirm life in the face of otherwise overwhelming tragedy; for striking examples, see the accounts of religious conversion and mysticism in James 1961. This is the transformative truth Plato grasps (and my mother implicitly understood), the truth Aristotelians (and Episcopalians), in their more conventional moments, are always in danger of overlooking.

[13] This view is reinforced by the fact that Lewis includes among those natural things which are ultimately disappointing apart from God cultural artifacts such as books and music. In the end, Lewis, like Augustine, views the evil to be overcome as spiritual, that is, as sin, not material, as regards which both vigorously affirm, in historic Christian terms, a resurrection of the physical body.

cave, cannot and, indeed, have no reason to walk out of this theater, our one and only, eternal home.[14]

THEISM

Coming to believe in a sacred reality involves adopting an irreducibly personal interpretive framework in terms of which to see and make sense of the world and, therewith, our life. This perspective on reality assumes many forms, some more plausible than others. One problem with historic nature religions is that animism lacks the conceptual resources to explain what we have learned by way of scientific inquiry. This does not mean they have nothing of value to contribute. It may be, as Max Oelschlaeger persuasively argues (1994: 5, 224) that the underlying causes of our current ecological crisis can only be addressed from the standpoint of an "enchanted world." If we are to make progress in this regard, however, religious naturalism needs, as Oelschlaeger realizes, to find a more conceptually powerful form, one that can absorb the quantitative regularities of modern science while continuing to view nature as value-laden and purposeful all the way through.

Here, theism has much to offer. Theism involves the belief that Someone is there, looking back, listening in, Someone with something to say, Someone to whom it matters who you are and what you do. To understand traditional theism, however, we must see, as above, that this Someone is not only a uniquely powerful being but the be-all and end-all of existence, the essence of sacredness. Thus, as Steck observes (1980: 187), for the Israelites, "to be exposed to Yahweh is absolutely everything, to encounter him, to find meaningful existence solely in orientation toward him, in what he gives and what he takes away, in his reliably revealed activity and in the activity that is mysteriously unexplorable." To become aware of Yahweh's presence is to see reality in a different light: this God is personal and foundational, individual and ubiquitous, "out there"

---

[14] See Calvin 1960: 72 [I, 6. 2], 179 [I, 14.20], 341 [II, 6.1]. That we are placed here to "learn piety, and from it pass over to eternal life and perfect felicity" does not entail, anymore than the fact that "the sweetness of the divine generosity . . . whet[s] our hope and desire to seek after the full revelation of [God]" (715 [III, 9.3]), that the world in which God has placed us, the world of nature, is not an integral part of our relation to God. That Calvin, like Augustine, expresses on occasion an otherworldly point of view does not erode the deeply naturalistic, biblical tenor of his thought. The question as to what Christianity itself (or for that matter, Judaism or Islam) holds is, of course, essentially contestable, a matter for theological reflection and dispute, as seen below.

and "in here," highest of the high, yet the wellspring of subjectivity. To encounter this God is to find reality change from something we encounter to Someone who encounters us.

Theists believe God to be the most real of realities, the source of all power and value. Gregory of Nyssa captures this well when he says (1995: 405): "God is in His own nature all that which our mind can conceive of good; – rather, transcending all good that we can conceive or comprehend." "God," the recent *Catechism of the Catholic Church* (1994: 79) tells us, "is infinitely greater than all his works"; and adds (68), "God is eternal blessedness, undying life, unfading light." To stand before this One is to encounter *makom*, "the infinite, pure and primary place," and become transfixed by *makom kadosh*, the indwelling, Shekinah glory of God (Moltmann 1993: 153f.) – drawn forward by a mystery, overwhelmed by a power and value beyond comprehension.

Thus, God, like us, is a person, yet radically Other than us in modality of being. There is no limitation in or constraint on this One, the only One who can say truly, "I AM WHO I AM" (Exodus 3: 14 [NRSV]), God is the unlimited source of all limitation, a being who is no less the source of Being, a mystery beyond all others – but not, more mysterious still, an unfathomable or unknowable mystery. For in this God we encounter a holy power and will firmly on the side of all that is good, true, and right – and, thereby, life, even our own, particular life. "The holiness of God is the inaccessible center of his eternal mystery" (*Catechism* 1994: 673). God is not only all-powerful, God is love and, thereby, just: that "'all things are possible with God' does not mean his undetermined omnipotence; it means the determined power of his goodness" (Moltmann 1993: 168). We can count on the love and justice of God: "There is no 'dark side' to God – no side where he could also be conceived of as the destroyer of his creation and of his own being as Creator" (Moltmann 1993: 168). Evil is not an option for God, who cannot, unlike humans, war against the good of his eternal being.

The existence of similarities and differences between God and humans leads theists to adopt, relative to the characterization of God, an "analogical principle." The analogical principle tells us, simply put, that there exists between us and God a polarity of similarity and difference. Since it is important not to confuse this polarity with that involving immanence and transcendence, it will be helpful if we compare traditional biblical theism with some other views of the Sacred. I begin with two, overtly non-theistic faiths, religious scientism and karmic order, and, then, look more closely at four quasi-theistic faiths, polytheism, pantheism, deism, and emanationism.[15] This will help us understand what it means to believe not only in a sacred reality but, more specifically, God. Having done that we will reflect, in the remainder of this chapter, on the reasonableness of this belief.

The first view I want to note appears in Albert Einstein's claim to believe in a God like Spinoza's, "who shows himself in the orderly harmony of what exists, not in a God who concerns himself with the destinies and actions of human beings" (cited in Moltmann 1993: 194). On this view, the object of religious devotion is the world of nature described by modern science. This magnificent, orderly process is perceived to be awe-inspiring in its own right and, as such, worthy of respect, even worshipful adoration.[16] I will call this view "religious scientism." Whatever one thinks of it as an an explication of the Sacred, it is clearly, despite Einstein's use of the term "God," not theistic. Reality on this view lacks, in and of itself, any meaning or purpose.

This reason does not apply to our second, historically more important, non-theistic option, "karmic order." Here, as seen in the great Eastern traditions of Hinduism and Buddhism, the Sacred is understood, as in religious scientism, in terms of fundamental, all-encompassing laws. Unlike religious scientism, however, karmic order views these laws as value-laden, oriented toward justice and, more generally, spiritual realization. Reality on this view is not only meaningful but strongly teleological. At the same time this view, despite its affinities with theism, is overtly non-theistic.[17] Law-centered accounts, while not ruling out the existence of deities, ascribe at most derivative explanatory status to the nature and will of such beings. For theism, by contrast, reality at its most fundamental level is agential. One salient mark of this difference is the audacious claim, made by John Baker (1975: 90) and shared by

[15] This will show there are, relative to historic theism, anthropomorphic (polytheism) and non-anthropomorphic (pantheism) distortions of divine immanence as well as anthropomorphic (deism) and non-anthropomorphic (emanationism) distortions of divine transcendence. Historic theism attempts to keep these polarities in balance.

[16] For a sense of what this might involve, see James Gustafson (1981: 20; 26; 43–45; 97–99; 260–272; 274) and (1994: 13ff.; 45ff.; 72ff.). I agree with James A. Nash's claim (1991: 233f.) that Gustafson portrays God as "a nonconscious, nonmoral ordering process without intention, volition, or cognition." For a contrary, more orthodox reading of Gustafson, see Audi 1988.

[17] There are, it should be noted, quasi-theistic elements and off-shoots of this non-theistic option, for instance, Pure Land Buddhism, just as there are non-theistic elements and off-shoots of theism, for instance, the "death of God" movement. As one would expect (given the analogical principle) there is something of a "duck–rabbit" effect here. This helps pave the way for dialogue between Eastern and Western faiths and, therewith, adoption by non-theists of analogues to theistic naturalism, a possibility I do not explore here.

all theists, "that man is the nearest visible pointer to what God looks like."[18]

To be a theist in the traditional sense one must believe that reality, in its most fundamental aspect, is human-like. To this extent, the basic premise of theism is undeniably anthropomorphic; theism is committed to viewing reality in its most fundamental form as not only person-like but, all said and done, a person, God. Believing this is a necessary, though not a sufficient condition for being a theist. There are a number of quasi-theistic views, all of which view the fundamental reality as irreducibly personal, yet differ, in one way or another, from historic theism. Noting four such views will allow us to identify four other, defining features of traditional theism: unity, transcendence, immanence, and engagement.

The first quasi-theistic view with which I wish to contrast traditional theism is "polytheism." Polytheism, a form of faith found in many nature religions and common throughout the ancient world, affirms the existence of an irreducible plurality of gods, bound together by ties similar to those found in human societies. These gods exercise power over nature, even to the point of being a source of natural regularities. Here, as in theism, the most fundamental explanations are taken to involve the intentions and actions of human-like persons. Where (mono)theism differs, of course, is in its affirmation of divine unity: the Lord our God is One.[19] Rather than being caught up in the fragmentation and struggles of this world, God transcends conflict and divergence: "God alone remains one and the same in the contingent sequence of all occurrences" (Pannenberg 1993: 113). In this respect, theism insists on an idealized anthropomorphism: God is not only like us but, no less, radically Other.

This theme of Otherness, or, transcendence, is reinforced in the contrast between theism and a second personalistic counterpart, "pantheism." Unlike polytheism, pantheism ascribes an overarching unity to the Sacred. Pantheists, like theists, affirm that God is One. What distinguishes pantheism from theism is its assumption that God and world are integrally, inseparably united: there is no sense in which we can speak of God independent of God's relation to the world; thus, pantheists commonly speak of the world as God's body and, correspondingly,

---

[18] Baker cites Genesis 1: 26–27, claiming humans are made in God's image and after God's likeness, and Ezekiel 1: 26, describing God as having "the appearance of a man." The term "man" must, of course, be understood in a gender neutral sense, as it is by Baker.

[19] Polytheism, over time and with theological elaboration, tends to approach theism, as seen in the moving Stoic "Hymn to Zeus" (in Eliade 1977: 283–285). Counterwise, theists must take care not to forget, in pursuit of explanatory coherence, the distinctions and, from a finite perspective, tensions inherent in the Divine.

God as the World Spirit, or, Soul. By contrast, traditional theism affirms the independence and freedom of God, whose existence and well-being is denied to be in any way dependent on the world. God is a radically free, self-defining reality. Pantheism, in making God's relation to the world a part of God's own nature, fails to acknowledge the transcendent freedom and radical Otherness of God. That this is so does not mean theism denies the direct and immediate presence of God in the world. God, in the words of that paradigmatic theist, Augustine, (1955: 68 [3.6]), is "more inward to me than the most inward part of me; and higher than my highest reach."

Theists, like pantheists, believe God is intimately near. It is this aspect of nearness, the immanence of God, which leads them to reject a third quasi-theism, "deism." Deism comes to the fore in conjunction with the rise of modern science; as such, it marks an intermediate step in the development of modern, revisionist theism, of which I will speak shortly. Deism embodies an attempt on the part of would-be and, in some cases, once-were-theists to factor into account the newly discovered self-regulating quality of natural processes. It is hardly surprising, in light of these discoveries, that some come to think of nature as a giant mechanism and, correspondingly, God as a Supreme Clockmaker. This image is repudiated by traditional theism for two reasons. First, it establishes an inverse relation between the perfection of creation and the immediate presence of God: a well-made clock is capable, once set in motion, of running on its own; God, as conceived by deists, becomes a distant, originating cause. Second, where God does appear in immediate relation to the world, that presence comes to be mysterious, a "Humean miracle" marked by its inexplicability in scientific terms; God, so conceived, becomes a "God of the gaps," appearing only where modern science has no explanation to offer. Thus, faith comes to focus on a deity who, while sharing attributes with the God of theism, operates from afar, winding the cosmic clock from time to time, but remaining outside looking in. By contrast, theism not only denies nature an independent, self-sustaining reality, it affirms the existence of a God immediately, intimately involved with all of nature, a God who, in the words of Irenaeus (cited in Santmire 1985: 39) "containing all things, alone is uncontained."

For the theist, "nothing in creation is independent of nor identifiable with God" (Nash 1991: 96). It follows that theists cannot be deists or pantheists. Relative to the world of creation, God is immanent and transcendent. As to just what this complex relation involves, greater precision can be achieved by considering a fourth, quasi-theistic faith, "emanationism." Like pantheism, this Neoplatonic view assumes more-or-less theistic forms; in all cases, however, as McGrath observes (1994: 236):

> The image that dominates this approach . . . is that of light or heat radiating from the sun, or from a human source such as a fire. This image of creation . . . suggests that the creation of the world can be regarded as an overflowing of the creative energy of God. Just as light derives from the sun and reflects its nature, so the created order derives from God, and expresses the divine nature.

This model of the divine succeeds in capturing much that is missing in the previous three quasi-theisms: immanence, transcendence, and unity, along with a surpassing wonder and goodness – God is the Sun that lights and warms our way, making possible the many riches of nature. It is no wonder such imagery is commonly called upon by theists, including many early theologians of the Christian church. At the same time, however, as McGrath proceeds to note (236), "the idea of a personal God, expressing a personality both in the very act of creation and in the subsequent creation itself, is difficult to convey by this image." Portraying God as a cosmic radiator, however wonderful, results in an attenuated sense of personhood, leaving little if any room for personal interaction. As a result, emanationism violates the analogical principle; God turns out to be insufficiently like us, that is, for those mortified by such a comparison, insufficiently agential. This condition requires God be understood not only as near and far, immanent and transcendent, but, also, in a way that does not deny the human-like quality of divine actions.

Historic theism lives in a union of extremes. Its God, the God of the Bible, is Someone with whom it is possible to carry on an ordinary conversation, Someone who cares about the same kind of things we do – love, justice, and the good life. Indeed, the most amazing thing about the Bible may simply be the extent to which it portrays an on-going conversation between God and humankind. God likes to talk! Moreover, God listens and, even, adjusts his plans in accord with what we have to say.[20] What makes this so amazing is that this same God, the One with whom we talk, is the Supreme Lord and Ultimate Reality, the source of all power and value, holy and righteous beyond our imagination. This Yahweh is so much like us, yet totally, absolutely Other. He holds all things in the palm of his hand, yet in this world pursues justice and stands ever ready to comfort those who turn to him for solace.

---

[20] My favorite example is the conversation between Abraham and God in Genesis 18. What audacity (and faith): "Shall not the judge of all the earth do right?" That God takes Abraham seriously suggests he is fond not only of beetles, as Darwin suggested, but, no less, critics.

This mystery, this wonder, drives the theological quest for understanding. Who is this One who speaks to us in the storm, in the still of night, from the bush that burns, yet is not consumed? In answering this question, theists have much to learn from quasi-theists, who, after all, emphasize different elements of the deep tension within which a full-bodied theism lives. In this respect, pantheism and deism represent counterbalancing extremes relative to intimacy and independence, presence and absence – neither of which can be ignored by the theist. The same holds for polytheism and emanationism relative to spontaneity and systematic closure, diversity, and unity. There is no final resolution to this tension apart from the Eternal God himself, which is to say, no resolution that eliminates for us the mystery of his existence or, therewith, the challenge of his awe-inspiring, terrifying, yet captivating Presence. The wild God cannot be put in a strait-jacket, not even one "made in heaven."

What traditional theistic religions have done in response to this mystery and, more particularly, the need to maintain balance is to formulate over time a *regula fidei*, theological guidelines to a rightful understanding of the One who cannot be understood. Thus, we find in the early centuries of Christian faith a struggle to formulate "confessions" and "creeds" aimed at preserving the full mystery of faith, including the deep tension between likeness and radical difference. This occurs strikingly in relation to the distinctively Christian belief that Jesus is both human and divine and, therewith, belief in the Holy Trinity. Not surprisingly, there was and continues to be disagreement, sometimes deep-cutting, regarding how this balance is best struck. In any case, we remain theists only so long as we affirm the human-like intentionality and comprehensive scope of divine actions.

Let me put this in terms of two principles, one requiring a full, the other a real agency. The "full-agency principle" says that our account of the divine personhood must recognize and keep in balance aspects of transcendence and immanence, that is, it must affirm and clarify the presence and power of God in "the heights above" and "the depths within."[21] The "real-agency principle" requires in addition that our account recognize and keep in balance with an acknowledgment of the radical Otherness of God a genuine sense of agency, a sense in which God literally acts and, thereby, makes a difference in the world of nature.[22] The full- and real-agency principles specify defining conditions of historic theism.

---

[21] We might well label this "Augustine's principle" in light of his comprehensive vision of the divine, reference to which has already been made. Note that the full-agency principle is satisfied, in and of itself, by Neoplatonic emanationism; that is why theism also requires the real-agency principle.

[22] To say the sense of personhood involved is *literal* is not to deny that attribution of this sense to God is *analogical*, that is, done with an awareness of both anthropomorphic likeness and radical

THE REASONABLENESS OF FAITH

That the very thought of this God stirs many a heart cannot be denied. Before taking it as a given in our account of theistic naturalism, however, we need to inquire as to its reasonableness. We do not want our ethics of nature to rest on beliefs or values that are beyond the pale of reason. In addition, we need to raise the question of reasonableness by way of understanding what it means to adopt a *theistic* ethic of nature. This involves at core not only belief in the existence of God but, therewith, a way of thinking, reasoning about nature, wild and human. To see nature-as-creation one must think theologically and, thus, critically about the normatively laden relation between nature, God, and humanity.

That the world is a product of divine agency is by no means evident: "Every theology of nature interprets nature in the light of the self-revelation of the creative God ... The world does not disclose itself as God's creation just by itself" (Moltmann 1993: 53f.). We need, then, to ask what reason there is to believe such a thing. To some, of course, it appears obvious that theism is false. According to John Searle (1994: 90f.):

Our problem is not that somehow we have failed to come up with a convincing proof of the existence of God or that the hypothesis of an after life remains in serious doubt, it is rather that in our deepest reflections we cannot take such opinions seriously. When we encounter people who claim to believe such things, we may envy them the comfort and security they claim to derive from these beliefs, but at bottom we remain convinced that either they have not heard the news or they are in the grip of faith.

Searle queries, rhetorically (30): "do we not know from the discoveries of science that there is really nothing in the universe but physical particles and fields of force acting on physical particles?" If we do know this, there

Otherness. Traditional theism utilizes a sense of personhood which applies literally to both human beings and God. What this amounts to, analogically, is by no means evident, either in the case of God or human persons. A good sense of what is involved, however, is provided by William Alston's discussion of his own beliefs regarding the nature of God (1985: 197f.):

Moreover, I think of God as literally a "personal agent." By a "personal agent" I mean a being that acts in the light of knowledge to achieve purposes, a being whose actions express attitudes and are guided by standards and principles, a being that enters into communication and other forms of personal relations with other personal agents.

Alston continues, relative to our remarks regarding the analogical nature of this attribution (198):

In saying that God *literally* acts in the light of knowledge and purposes, I do not mean to imply that knowledge, intention, and other psychological states and processes are realized in God in the same way they are realized in human beings. What it is for God to intend something may be, and undoubtedly is, radically different from what it is for a human being to intend something.

Alston also notes here: "In taking God to be literally a personal agent my view is distinguished from pansymbolists like Paul Tillich and John Macquarrie."

is a serious problem with attempts to ground an ethics of nature in the will or nature of a sacred reality. One might as well look for support to elves and leprechauns.

Our account of what we do know by way of scientific inquiry suggests that Searle himself is in the grip of a faith he cannot deny. Science, like every other form of inquiry, can only grasp what it is prepared, methodologically, to see. In this sense, science has no more to say about God than geometry the reality of a three-dimensional universe. Pointing this out does not remove the critical bite from Searle's dismissive attitude. This rests on two presumptions. First, the presumption that there is no place left in our experience of nature for an encounter with the divine, that science has pre-empted faith: where in nature, wild or human, do we find God? Second, there is the concern, as George Gaylord Simpson puts it (1967: 274), that once faith enters the picture, "there are no limitations on flights of the imagination."[23] Does reason, once in the grip of faith, lose its grip, its ability to critically assess and sort out conflicting claims about the nature of reality? In response, theists need to say something about where in the world they find reason to believe in God and, therewith, how reason continues to function within the confines of religious faith.

What is the theist to say? To start, she needs to put the question about God in perspective, recalling that religious faith involves not only particular beliefs about the Sacred – that, for instance, the fundamental reality underlying all things is a divine person – but, more abstractly, an interpretive framework, a point of view regarding what *kind* of things exist. Theism is not simply a more-or-less reasonable position taken within a conceptually independent framework, as, for instance, believing in phlogiston within that of modern chemistry. Though the reasonableness of theism needs to be weighed relative to other possible views of the Sacred, we must begin by inquiring more generally regarding the general framework of faith: how reasonable is it to believe, as Jürgen Moltmann proclaims (1993: 103), that underlying all "it is not the elementary particles that are basic, as the mechanistic world view maintains, but the overriding harmony of the relations and of the self-transcending movements, in which the longing of the Spirit for a still unattained consummation finds

---

[23] Simpson is characterizing the debate between scientific "causalists" and, as he sees them, wishful thinking "vitalists" and "finalists." Warwick Fox (1990: 183f.) worries similarly that the "metaphysical richness of cosmic purpose ethics" makes them "far less parsimonious than other approaches and, hence, far more contentious" and, further, that "the unfalsifiable nature of the assumptions upon which cosmic purpose ethics rely" leaves them, as "most ecophilosophers" believe, "far less open to modification in the light of discussion and criticism than other intrinsic value theory approaches."

expression"? Is there reason to believe, in Erazim Kohák's audacious words (1984: 191, 195), that we dwell "in a nature which is God's poem, at the intersection of time and eternity" and, thus, that "any attempt to conceptualize nature as value-free – except as a special case theory for admittedly special purposes – is flawed from the start"?

While believers in a sacred reality need not "deny either the laws or the chain of cause and effect which pervade the cosmos" (Nasr 1981: 197),[24] they obviously hold a very different view of reality than that held by scientific naturalists such as Searle and Simpson. How, though, are we to tell if it is less or, possibly, more reasonable? Here it is useful to recall, from chapter three, Searle's argument that there is no need of evidence to support our belief in the reality of consciousness since (1994: 77): "we do not hold a 'hypothesis,' 'belief,' or 'supposition' that other people are conscious and that chairs, tables, computers and cars are not conscious. Rather, we have certain Background ways of behaving, certain Background capacities, and these are constitutive of our relations to the consciousness of other people." As to why some philosophers have erroneously demanded reasons for adopting this Background perspective, Searle perceptively observes that this happens "when elements of the Background are treated as if they were hypotheses that have to be justified." And this, it seems to me, is correct – not only about consciousness but, also, our belief in a sacred reality. In each case we are dealing, first and foremost, with an interpretive framework. Accordingly, it is a mistake to treat either belief as though it were analogous to a scientific hypothesis; it is not – nor should it be.

That this is so does not entail we have the same reasons for continuing to affirm a belief in the Sacred as we do consciousness. It makes sense to deny the first in a way it does not to deny the second. Why is that? Not, I think, that we find the notion of a sacred reality difficult to conceive. As Searle notes (1994: 99): "There is a sense ... in which we find subjectivity difficult to conceive ... Yet we all know that subjectivity exists." The difference, I suggest, lies in the fact that we cannot grasp what it means to accept or reject any interpretive framework apart from consciousness; in that sense, awareness is transcendental. While those who do not believe in a sacred reality may be foolish, not even a fool can

---

[24] Etienne Gilson (1984: 105) points out that Aristotle, the philosophical father of teleological finalism, "never denied that the mechanism of Empedocles was true, but [rather] reproached him with presenting it as a total explanation of reality in the order of living beings"; Gilson adds that while it is a rare mechanist who allows "that there may be teleology in nature," even rarer, "exceedingly rare – if they have ever existed – are those finalists who deny mechanism and its natural function in natural beings."

function apart from a presumption of consciousness. By contrast with our background belief in the latter, religious faith makes a more particularized, contentious difference in our lives. Accordingly, we need to inquire about the reasonableness of religious belief and, correspondingly, disbelief. In doing so, however, we must keep in mind that we are dealing not only with particular beliefs or hypotheses but basic, interpretive frameworks in terms of which we assess reasonableness in the first place. This holds true for scientific naturalists no less than it does for theists.

What if any reasons are there to adopt a religious perspective on nature? There are, I suggest, two general kinds of reasons, one concrete, the other abstract. The concrete reasons have to do with a believer's direct, charismatically compelling experience of the world: "the most basic trait of the world that confronts a dweller in the radical brackets of the forest clearing is that it is God's world, not 'man's,' and that here God is never far" (Kohák 1984: 182). While some such as Searle cannot see the presence of God in nature, others not only see but find themselves deeply moved by that presence. That, of course, is one, vital reason they believe. To grasp the force of this reason we must look at it not in terms of its ramifications for the truth or falsity of particular beliefs, say, regarding Pan or Yahweh, but, more abstractly, as the verification in experience of a general, religiously laden way of looking at the world. This verification is not a matter of controlled experimentation; rather, it "goes hand in hand with that direct experience of a spiritual presence which results from spiritual realization" (Nasr 1981: 201). Those who believe in a sacred reality do so, fundamentally, because they have undergone (what they take to be) life-enhancing experiences of the Sacred. Apart from this, no one would believe.

This charismatically compelling experience provides a reason for believing in the Sacred. As Kohák observes (1984: 5):

If there is no God, then nature is not a creation, lovingly crafted and evolved with purpose and value by its Creator. It can only be a cosmic accident, dead matter contingently propelled by blind force, ordered by efficient causality. In such a context, a moral subject, living his life in terms of value and purpose, would indeed be an anomaly, precariously rising above it in a moment of Promethean defiance only to sink again into the absurdity from which he rose. If God were dead, so would nature be – and humans could be no more than embattled strangers, doomed to defeat, as we have largely convinced ourselves we in fact are.[25]

---

[25] Accordingly, Kohák concludes (1984: 183): "no conceptual task is more urgent than that of recovering our awareness of the presence of God and of nature as His creation." See James

Correspondingly, Nasr criticizes scientific naturalism (1981: 210):

It has helped destroy in the name of scientific logic, but in reality as a result of a presumptuous extrapolation based on metaphysical ignorance, the reality of that vision of ultimate ends which gives significance to human life and which over the ages has had the most profound effect upon the behavior of man as an ethical being. It has also destroyed in the minds of those affected by scientism the grandeur of creation and the meaning of the sacrifice of primordial man. That is why this science has been so impervious to the amazing harmony that pervades the heavens and the earth.

In short, the experience of living in an "enchanted world," a place of belonging where personal and communal destinies matter all the way down, depends, not surprisingly, on the adoption of a religious point of view.

This is the single, most important, compelling reason why people have and continue to believe in the Sacred: that outlook on life makes a great, positive difference in their experience of themselves and the world in which they live. Coming to appreciate this requires us to look at life from the standpoint of a religious believer, to reckon with what they (claim to) see even if we cannot see it ourselves. Having done so, we may, of course, conclude like Searle that the comfort and security religious faith brings is a product of wishful thinking on the part of people unable to cope with life in a disenchanted world. This possibility puts the onus back on religious faith: what, if any reasons are there for taking these life-enhancing experiences for what they appear to be rather than signs of immaturity or, worse, mental illness?[26]

This question brings into play a second, more abstract but not insignificant kind of reason for adopting a religious perspective on nature. Some of these reasons undercut reasons for disbelief. The analysis of scientific inquiry offered in chapter three can be seen in this light; it undercuts the false presumption that modern science establishes the truth of scientific naturalism. Another line of reply addresses the dismissive insinuation of immaturity: so far as wish-fulfillment goes the shoe fits disbelievers

(1961: 124) on the frozen lake of a naturalism without God – "surrounded by cliffs over which there is no escape." See also, on the urgent need to counter this reductionism, Nasr 1996: 5f., 146; 222f.

[26] For a thorough discussion of this issue, see Alston 1991. Alston concludes (306):

Thus in order to answer the claim that one's putative experience of God is this-worldly only, one can appeal to the witness of others who are more advanced in the Christian life, to the revelation of God in His historical acts, and to general philosophical reasons for believing that God as construed in Christianity does exist and rules His creation.

as well as believers. The Sacred is a source of judgment and, therewith, insecurity no less than comfort and security. Accordingly, there is as much reason to think that those who disbelieve do so because they cannot face up to the hard reality of a world in which what we do matters all the way down as there is to think the same of those who believe. It is likely that not a few, troubled by the thought of eternity, have found relief in the sight of Nietzsche's lantern – swinging in the dark of night.[27]

More positively, religious believers can call on traditional arguments for the existence of God. Though typically formulated in overtly theistic terms, these provide, more generally, reasons for adopting a religious perspective on reality. These arguments do not, as some have mistakingly claimed, "prove" the existence of a sacred reality, an impossibility in any case so far as religious *faith* is concerned. Indeed, they are best seen not as attempts to convince those who do not already believe but, rather, as efforts to identify generally accessible features of the world in which religious believers experience the sustaining presence of a sacred reality. What makes these reasons in support of religious belief is that the features identified constitute "otherwise anomalies," aspects of our common experience that make good sense, arguably, only on the supposition reality, at rock-bottom, is sacred. Let me note three such appeals, known historically as the cosmological, teleological, and moral, or, anthropological, arguments.

The cosmological argument flags a relation between religious faith and the sheer givenness of existence. The claim, in short, is that existence itself, the existence of anything, makes little sense unless something exists necessarily, as a consequence of its own nature. If everything that is might not be, it seems not only possible but probable that at some time in the infinite past there was nothing; if so, however, unless something came out of nothing, nothing would exist now. Thus, the very contingency of this world, its ceaseless coming and going, lends credibility to the experience in nature of an unchanging, eternal reality. Of course, it may be, as David Hume suggests (1948: 176ff.), that the material world is eternal; similarly, it may be that the universe is sacred, that pantheism, not theism, is true.

---

[27] As Stanley Jaki (1978: 283) observes:

> That Creator and absolutes had no place in the vision presented in [Charles Darwin's *Origin of Species*] was a key to its tremendous popularity. The *Origin* supplied the already strong craving for the elimination of all metaphysics with a support which through its massive factuality appeared scientifically unassailable. The objective of that craving, as articulated mainly by Spencer for the second half of the century, was repose in the endless flux and reflux, a happy acceptance of the prospect that man and mankind were but bubbles on unfathomable deep and dark waves, bubbles free of eternal purpose and unburdened with eternal responsibilities.

None of these possibilities unduly trouble the argument at hand. All that is being claimed here, by theists and pantheists, is that it makes more sense than not to presume the reality which abides through time encompasses in its own existence a coming together of power and value.

The teleological argument flags a relation between religious faith and the marvelous order of our world. The claim, in short, is that this order is unlikely to have occurred on its own, apart from a directive intelligence. This argument, contrary to common belief, is strengthened, not weakened by the development of modern science. In part this is a matter of what science has been unable to explain. The mystery of consciousness, for instance, supports the belief that subjectivity is a fundamental aspect of reality.[28] On the other hand, the great success science has had in explaining the world calls attention to an even more mysterious, fecund order in nature.

> Even if the mechanisms offered by Darwinists old and new were a satisfactory explanation of the evolutionary record, a theist could still confidently press his claims. As the whole history of science shows, the more successful a scientific theory becomes, the more it prompts questions about its singular success in respect to a vast array of very singular phenomena and laws. (Jaki 1978: 283)[29]

Science cannot explain the order it discovers and, then, relies on in the explanations it gives.[30] One thing that would explain this, however, is the creative power of an inherently purposeful, order-generating, sacred reality.

The moral, or, anthropological, argument flags a relation between religious faith and the normatively laden experience of being human. The claim, in short, is that the "strong evaluation" characteristic of human life and society cannot be understood apart from the presumption that the authority of moral norms is rooted in the most fundamental structure of reality.[31] Those offering this argument need not deny that concerns with well-being make sense of morality as a human phenomenon. Religious believers have strong reason to believe that moral norms, far from being arbitrary, work to the good of nature, individually and collectively. The key here is not intelligibility but authority: the

---

[28] In addition: "There are a great many astonishing cases of mimicry, parasitism, and adaptations of organs, which to account for in terms of natural selection amounts to explaining miracles by magic" (Jaki 1978: 283). See Behe 1996 and Dembski 1998.

[29] Hence, ironically, "the more the Darwinists argue against purpose and design, the more support they provide to a theist fond of the argument from design" (Jaki 1978: 284).

[30] Gilkey (1993: 90) cites the "almost infinitely great" odds against the precise congruence of universal constants apart from which we would not be here to ponder the wonder of our existence.

[31] See Charles Taylor 1989, Part I, on the pivotal role "strong evaluation" plays in human life.

experienced, categorical authority of moral norms makes more sense given the existence of a sacred reality than it does in terms of a "hypothetical morality" rooted in concerns about well-being. Morality, as traditionally conceived, is not something we take up on a voluntary basis. Of course, it may be that we need to revise our view of morality. The fact, however, that belief in a sacred reality makes good sense of traditional morality and, more generally, the normatively laden shape of human life lends credibility to religious faith.

These three lines of reflection support the belief that life-enhancing, charismatically compelling religious experiences are what they appear to be, encounters with the sacred depth of nature. They do not, singularly or jointly, provide a proof; nor do they rule out reasons to the contrary, among them, the troubling reality of disorder and evil. Just as there are reasons to believe in God, so there are reasons to dis-believe. As to which way the balance of reasons leans, that is a matter of reasonable disagreement and charismatic conviction: in the end, arguments operative at this basic level tend to support what we are already convinced of on experiential, personal grounds. This does not mean arguments about reasonableness are unimportant; there are, after all, a limited number of plausible points of view. What it does mean is concerns about reasonableness play a role primarily in the development and shaping of those bottom-line faiths by which we live, not their initial acceptance. Here, we must come to terms with the given particularities and, at least for now, irreducible diversity of religious faiths.

THEOLOGICAL REFLECTION

Close reflection on the why and how of existence, relative to things such as contingency, order, and normativity, gives those who believe in a sacred reality reason to believe they are not for that reason alone deluded. Religious faith is not in the same category as belief in Santa Claus or the Easter Bunny. Those moved in their heart to believe are free to do so; those not so moved are free to believe as they are moved.[32] This much seems clear. Granted this, however, there remains a question as to how religious believers fill in the particularities of faith. Every historic religion goes beyond a general belief in the Sacred; historic theism even makes the audacious claim to not only know the inside-story of creation but to have spoken with the Person responsible. How are we to decide,

---

[32] "Dupery for dupery, what proof is there that dupery through hope is so much worse than dupery through fear" (James 1962: 58).

though, to opt for theism rather than karmic order or pantheism, for Christianity rather than Islam, for Canterbury rather than Rome? Does critical reason play a role in these vital decisions and, if so, what?

The answer, I suggest, is twofold. On the one hand, religious believers, theists and non-theists, Christians and non-Christians, Episcopalians and Catholics, have their own reasons for believing and, more broadly, living as they do; based on what they have seen and felt, the experiences by which their lives have been formed, these reasons may even be rationally compelling, as they appear to be for paradigmatic religious figures.[33] This, in turn, raises a question regarding the great variety of faiths and correspondingly variant reasons for faith. Are there any generic, rationally compelling reasons for going with theism rather than pantheism or Buddhism, Christianity rather than Judaism, Anglicanism rather than Catholicism? I do not believe there are, just as there are none for believing in a sacred reality or, counterwise, being a scientific naturalist. All said and done, we end up drinking from our own wells, sustained by "reasons of the heart" that cannot be articulated in universally accessible terms.[34]

That this is so does not mean generic reason has no role to play. As in the case of religious faith in general, there will be generally accessible arguments pro and con regarding particular contexts of faith. Arguments of this sort, though rarely providing for closure, are a common feature of life in a pluralistic society. Much more important, critical reason operates *within* contexts of faith, an integral part of the believer's quest to understand a Truth he cannot deny.[35] That a faith does not rest on generic, rationally compelling reasons of the sort relied on by scientists and mathematicians, does not mean critical, generic reason has no role

---

33 Presuming the stories of their lives are true, Moses, Peter, and Mohammed have compelling reasons for believing as they do – as do many of the individuals and communities whose stories are told in sacred texts. These stories identify the historic origin of particular faiths in transformative, charismatic experiences.

34 This is a good, not bad thing. The underdetermination of faith by reason does, of course, pose a problem insofar as our salvation and eternal destiny depend on getting "the right answer." This problem is one to which different religious faiths have different responses. I do not want to address these here, beyond noting that what makes this problem serious is not so much the downside as the upside: knowing the truth matters for human fulfillment insofar as deception and ignorance distract from the goodness of a life. Hence, it will not do to say that what people believe about the Sacred does not matter. At the same time, the problem can be addressed generally by allowing that non-culpable error need not result in the non-rectifiable lost of "hell" and, further, relative to "heaven," that opportunities to learn the full truth exist on the far side of death. In any case, theists can be assured, despite what some theists have said, that God will resolve the matter in a just and loving way. For a profound theological reflection on this issue, holding out the hope that all will be saved (eventually), see von Balthazar 1988, especially 218–221, quoting Edith Stein. See also, for a creative, literary approach, Lewis 1947.

35 For an insightful account of how this takes place and its relation to the internally nuanced structure of religious faith, see Christian 1987. See also Smart 1958.

to play in that faith. That religious faith plays the role it does in human life depends on its ability to incorporate what generic reason has to tell us about the world. Here, we encounter the discipline of theology and its three, interwoven branches, dogmatic, systematic, and imaginative theology. Let me expand briefly on each.

The first element, or, moment, in theological reflection is confessional. Historic theisms all rest on a belief in the self-revelation of God, as seen in the defining association of these faiths with sacred texts: to become a Muslim (Christian) (Jew) is, in part, to accept as a fundamental spiritual authority the Qur'ān (Bible) (Torah). These texts are viewed by those accepting their authority as divinely inspired sources of information about God and the world. In this sense, all theology witnesses to (confesses) the Truth of a particular tradition of faith and the charismatically compelling experiences and convictions, the beliefs and values, on which it rests. The task of identifying and articulating the core content of this revelatory tradition belongs to dogmatic theology. Toward this end, it formulates and defends, by appeal to the basic authorities of faith, various formal and informal creeds, amounting to a *regula fidei*, or, rule of faith. Believers, of course, differ regarding not only this rule, as seen in the existence of competing confessions during the Reformation era, but, also, the authorities to which appeal can be made, as in the disagreement among Catholics and Protestants over the Apocrypha and, more fundamentally, the "magisterium of Rome." In every faith, however, there exists a defining, dogmatic core.

Sometimes the process of reflection on this dogmatic core is understood, by believers and non-believers, in exclusively dogmatic terms, as if religious faith had no interest in what is known about the world on other, independent grounds.[36] I presume here, to the contrary, that religious faith can and ought to call on all truth in its quest for a rightful understanding of sacred revelation and, therewith, God. The task of incorporating this information into the dogmatic core of faith belongs to systematic theology, the aim of which is to formulate a faithful, comprehensive, and rationally coherent account of God and the world. In doing so, it has, naturally, a special interest in what is known generically, by way of academic reflection, and, more narrowly, scientific inquiry. Accordingly, a good example of the difference incorporation makes to the self-understanding of faith is provided by the significance of modern scientific theories of evolution for theological reflection on the account of creation given in Genesis. Can we accept the former without repudiating

---

[36] This delusion, "fideistic fundamentalism," is a spittin' cousin to "scientific positivism."

the latter? While the furor over creationism may suggest we cannot, such has never been the received view among theologians.

Thomas Aquinas, noting that the reference in Genesis, chapter one, to a firmament, or, great vault separating the waters above from those beneath supports, on its face, the Ionian doctrine that water is the primary component of all things, concludes that this cannot be the case. His reason? Since, Aquinas argues (1964: vol. x, 85 [I, Q. 68, a. 3]), "this theory can be shown to be false by solid arguments, it should not be maintained that it is the sense of this Scriptural text."[37] As to why the Bible speaks in the way it does, Aquinas attributes this to Moses' desire to put before the "ignorant people" with whom he was speaking "only such things as are apparent to sense"; calling on the best science and philosophy of his day, he argues

Everyone, no matter how unschooled, can perceive with his senses that earth and water are bodies. On the other hand, all do not recognize air as being a body – even some philosophers have held that air is nothing, and refer to something full of air as empty. Therefore, Moses makes express mention of water and earth but not air, in order to avoid introducing something the unlearned knew nothing about.[38]

The essential point lies not in Aquinas' explanation, which is time- and place-relative, but his confidence that what the Bible tells us about God and the world cannot conflict with what is known to be true on other, independent grounds. This leads him to adopt, as a hermeneutical rule, the presumption of harmony between divine revelation and truth in general. As a result he has no problem with the incorporation of material from other reputable sources in the interpretation of sacred Scripture.[39]

---

[37] Ernan McMullin (1985a: 20) refers to this as Aquinas' "accommodation principle." McGrath (1998: 122ff.) finds a similar accommodation in Calvin as regards Copernicus (by contrast with Luther) and notes its role in the development of modern science (as a methodological constraint on biblical literalism).

[38] Those who find questionable the presumption that Moses understood the process involved – which, I take it, would mean he had a different view of the matter than Aquinas – can easily distinguish between divine and human authorship. Given that God knows, there is no reason anyone affirming the inspiration or, even, infallibility of sacred Scripture need attribute such knowledge to the human authors (or redactors) involved.

[39] Edward Dowey (1994: 139), noting Calvin's rejection of a "naive intellectualistic Biblicism," cites a passage from his Commentary on Jeremiah in which Calvin claims, "astrology [by which he means what we would call 'astronomy'] may justly be called the alphabet of theology." The great Muslim philosopher and theologian, al-Ghazālī, writes similarly, a century and a half before Aquinas:

A grievous crime indeed against religion has been committed by the man who imagines that

Asked to comment on Darwin, Aquinas, remaining open to the possibility that God has created the world through an evolutionary process over vast periods of time, would most likely conclude the Bible has nothing much, if anything to say about dinosaurs – even though it tells us everything crucial about the underlying reality and value-laden processes whereby they and we come to be. In any case, this is the stance taken by Pope John Paul II in an address to the Pontifical Academy of Science (cited in Ayala 1985: 61):

The Bible itself speaks to us of the origin of the universe and its make-up, not in order to provide us with a scientific treatise but in order to state the correct relationships of man with God and with the universe. Sacred Scripture wishes simply to declare that the world was created by God, and in order to reach this truth it expresses itself in the terms of the cosmology in use at the time of the writer.[40]

Similarly, the Protestant theologian Pannenberg affirms (1993: 45):

The theological doctrine of creation should take the biblical narrative as a model in that it uses the best available knowledge of nature in its own time in order to describe the creative activity of God ... This model would not be followed if theology simply stuck to a standard of information about the world that became obsolete long ago by further progress of experience and methodical knowledge.

So long as we bear in mind methodological differences and resultant limitations, there is no reason why religious faith cannot call on scientific inquiry in its understanding of divine creation.[41]

Islam is defended by the denial of the mathematical sciences [among which he includes astronomy], seeing that there is nothing in revealed truth opposed to these sciences by way of either negation or affirmation, and nothing in these sciences opposed to the truths of religion. (Watt 1953: 34f.)

[40] The Bible, his Holiness continues, "does not wish to teach how the heavens were made but how one goes to heaven."

[41] Moltmann (1993: 33ff.), while criticizing "the theological retreat from cosmology," strongly rejects a return to cosmologies of the past, biblical, patristic, and medieval; he sees three stages in the history of the theological doctrine of creation: (1) the formation of a religious cosmology; (2) the emancipation of and separation from the sciences; and (3) the re-integration of science and theology. As regards the last stage, Moltmann, apropos our own claims, argues that theology reveals what science is unable to see, the inner longing and hope of creation (39f.), and, accordingly, that "it is only possible and meaningful to link the concept of evolution with the concept of creation if both concepts are de-ideologized and we keep them strictly for the sectors to which they were intended to apply" (195). For more on the interwined history of science and religion, see Brooke 1991; a good survey of theoretical issues can be found in Richardson and Wildman 1996.

The obvious advantage of this is that it allows theists to set aside false beliefs in their interpretation of the Bible and other sacred texts. That this has utility in the explication and defense of faith is made clear in Augustine's concern that non-Christians, hearing "a Christian, presumably giving the meaning of Holy Scripture, talking nonsense," will be unable to believe Holy Scripture "in matters concerning the resurrection of the dead, the hope of eternal life, and the kingdom of heaven, when they think [its] pages are full of falsehoods on facts which they themselves have learned from experience and the light of reason" (1982: 42f.). Augustine wants to avoid discrediting the Bible by loading it down with implausible claims. That this is so may, of course, suggest that what incorporation provides is not a method for the exercise of *critical* reason but, rather, a means to avoid the falsification of religious dogma. If this were so, religious faith would succumb to what Antony Flew characterized (1955: 97) as "the death by a thousand qualifications."

In fact, however, this proves no more true of theology and its method of incorporation than scientific inquiry, which commonly makes progress by backing away from questions it cannot and should not attempt to answer. Further, as Augustine's reference to "the resurrection of the dead" makes clear, his intent is not to avoid contention or, even, scandal but, rather, set aside superfluous and misleading claims. In this regard, he would readily agree with Pannenberg (1993: 48; see also 36, 75): "The theologian cannot in good conscience simply accept as exhaustive the description of nature given us by the natural scientist. There is more to nature than simply what the scientist, working within the confines of the established disciplines, has been able to report." If belief in a literal six-day creation in 4004 B.C.E is integral to the *regula fidei*, theism ought to go to the death defending it. That it should do so is not precluded by the method of incorporation, any more than a belief in the resurrection of the dead. Rather, it is a question of what we take, theologically, to be an integral part of theistic faith. Thus, while some have used this method wrongly to accommodate the "cultured despisers of religion," eliminating vital elements of faith in the process, that is not a consequence of the method, which aims only to refine the basic commitments and scandal of faith, not eviscerate it.

What makes this point less clear with regard to evolutionary theories than the common reliance by religious believers on other independent forms of inquiry, such as mathematics and linguistics, are the presumptions, one, that evolutionary theories entail the truth of scientific naturalism and, two, that respect for biblical authority requires a literalistic reading of Genesis. Neither of these presumptions, however, withstands scrutiny.

That we accept scientific and, more generally, academic inquiry on its own, inherently generic and thus, abstract terms does not mean we must accept the faith-based stance of scientific naturalism. Nor does it require that we deny a reliance on divine revelation is necessary to apprehend the bottom-line truth about nature. Pannenberg puts it this way (1993: 48): "Our task as theologians is to relate to the natural sciences as they actually exist. We cannot create our own sciences. Yet we must go beyond what the sciences provide and include our understanding of God if we are properly to understand nature." Rather than remaining tied to the primitive science of Genesis, we need to view the biblical cosmology and biology as means to the expression of theological claims regarding the creative activity of God. That we do does not settle on-going scientific debates; perhaps some biologist of the future will show Darwin was wrong. Nor does it tell us how we are to understand the creative activity of God. Does God actually talk with people? Does he intervene causally in the otherwise-course-of-events, work miracles to bring about desired ends? These and other questions regarding the manner and mode of divine activity are not settled by appeals to modern science or, more generally, the academy.

The point is not that what we know about the world in general has no bearing on our understanding of divine creativity or, more generally, God. Augustine for many years scornfully dismisses as mere superstition the numerous stories of miracles told with awe by ordinary Christians of his time. While affirming the occurrence of biblical miracles, such as the Resurrection of Jesus, Augustine believed the age of miracles had ceased and, accordingly, that it was a serious, religious error to expect or pray for them. Later in his life, after serving for many years as the Bishop of Hippo, Augustine comes to view miracles more positively, offering prayers for the ill and even compiling a record of contemporary miracles (Brown 1969: 413ff.). A theist all along, Augustine comes with time to change his view of God's creative activity in the world.

What changes Augustine's mind is not greater familiarity with the Bible. He knew about and accepted as true the miracle stories contained therein from at least the time of his conversion. More generally, he accepts, before and after the change, the same creeds and confessions of faith. Nor is his mind changed by anything he learns from the academy, with regard to which he retains throughout life an essentially Neoplatonic orientation, as seen in his view of divine and human love.

Augustine affirms before and after his change of mind regarding miracles the same basic view of the world set forth in his magisterial *City of God*. What induces change is that as bishop Augustine comes into contact with the lives, the needs and concerns, of ordinary, everyday Christians. This allows him to see and appreciate the role belief in miracles plays in the living out of their faith. Correspondingly, where he once saw only superstition, he now sees the power and love of God. His theology has been modified by the incorporation into a basically unchanging dogmatic and systematic framework of what he has seen with his own eyes, experienced in his own life.

Augustine's change of heart and mind illustrates the interplay of dogmatic and systematic theology with a third and all too often neglected branch of theology, the imaginative.[42] Here, theology seeks to capture and convey in a clear, compelling manner, through image and story, the underlying reality of divine presence. How are we to think of God and, more particularly, God's relation to the world in which we live? While dogmatic and systematic theology set more-or-less determinate parameters for imaginative theology, only the latter provides for closure relative to an otherwise unending series of reasons and arguments. Diverse, conflicting views of God and God's presence in the world can take into account not only the basic, dogmatic authorities of faith but, also, all that is known about the world by way of academic reflection. At this level, once the more-or-less obvious scofflaws are locked up, it really is argument all the way.[43] What gives the search for reflective equilibrium and, thereby, truth coherence is the vital role played by integrating images and stories, ruling models of the divine.

The inner rationality of religious faith consists not in its proof, with regard to either the general notion of a sacred reality or more particular theologies of the Sacred, but its openness to development, change, and growth by a process of critical, faithful reflection. In this process, the witness of sacred revelation and ecclesial tradition is filled out and refined by the incorporation of knowledge in general, under the guidance

---

[42] This is sometimes referred to as "fundamental theology." I prefer "imaginative theology" as a way of being overt about the role of creativity in faith and rooting out rationalistic pretense. Too much fundamental theology, traditional and modernist, ends up sounding like (poorly done) "religious philosophy." The term "imaginative" must not, however, be taken to signify "fanciful" or "imaginary." Rather, it refers to the faculty of imagination, a crucial and much neglected element in our comprehension of reality. The term "imagination," like "happiness," has been sadly hollowed out in modern times. On the eclipse of "figural interpretation" and, thereby, the alethic function of imagination in hermeneutics, see Frei 1974: 2ff., 25ff., 34, 220f., 267ff.; 282ff.

[43] Which surely says something important about human nature and good, a point I return to below relative to the role interminable conflict plays in creation.

of charismatically compelling images and stories, focal points for and recollections of charismatically compelling experiences of divine presence. This process is essentially contestable at every step; there are no non-defeasible authorities or claims on which we can rely to eliminate the risk or inevitable ambiguity of faith. That this is so means that critical reflection never comes to an end, not that it has no place. Consider, once again, the question of miracles.

Some readers may be persuaded Augustine got it right the first time round. Thus, some Reformers, concerned with what they saw as the superstitious excesses of Rome, came to believe, like the early Augustine, that miracles ceased after the apostolic era. Still other theologians dismiss miracles altogether. These "modernists" see belief in miracles as inconsistent with scientific inquiry and, more important, contrary to the transcendent dignity of God. As a result, modernist theology, in its imaginative mode, seeks to re-conceptualize the reality of God in ways which do not involve the notion of miracles, past, present or future.[44] This, of course, requires modernists to explain the historic belief in miracles and, more particularly, "de-mythologize" the biblical stories involving miracles, especially those like the Resurrection of Jesus that are part of the *regula fidei* (Bultmann 1958). In the final analysis, however, the appeal of modernist theology hinges not on its ability to resolve dogmatic or systematic concerns but, rather, like that of its traditional counterpart, the ability to capture and convey a vivid sense of the divine.[45]

Modernists theologians, understandably, view this process as an example of theological growth and refinement, of critical reason at work within contexts of faith. Those theists who continue to believe in a miracle-working God take a contrary view. In doing so, they need not repudiate critical reason or theological reflection. Much to the contrary, they can and do call upon critical reason to argue, one, that standard criticisms do not show what modernists presume and, two, that theism requires the historic notion of miracles in order to sustain its commitment to a personal, engaged deity. The upshot of this exchange,

[44] This re-conceptualization takes place along two, more-or-less intermingled lines of reflection. One, leading from Kant to Tillich, thinks of God as the fundamental, transcendental structure of existence, an ontological ground of morality and, more broadly, Being. The other, leading from Schleiermacher to Bultmann, thinks of God as the dynamic, phenomenological center of human experience. Process theology, the currently dominant form of modernism, seeks to integrate these two lines of development in a "bi-polar deity."

[45] That modernist theology has been able to do this reflects not only the changing socio-economic and technological context of faith but, more fundamentally, the largely peripheral role miracles play in traditional theism. For a good example, see Tillich 1952.

so far as dogmatic and systematic considerations are concerned, is a "Texas standoff." On one hand, the often arrogant modernist presumption that the historic belief in miracles has been shown beyond the pale of reason fails to stand up under close scrutiny.[46] Further, given the absence of any debilitating flaw in the historic notion of miracles, it is difficult to see why someone who believes God is not only an agent but the most fundamental reality there is, would want to deny God the power or will to intervene causally in the natural order, be it to float axe-heads or raise the dead. On the other hand, that a theology accepts the naturalistic principle does not mean, as many traditionalists have too readily assumed, that it must deny the personal involvement or agency of God.[47] Further, it must be allowed that the sporadic, haphazard occurrence of alleged miracles is not the sort of behavior one would expect in advance from a miracle-working God.[48] I conclude that there are no knock-down, rationally compelling reasons to affirm or deny the existence of miracles and, thus, neither

[46] In brief, Hume's claim that evidence in support of an alleged miracle will be overwhelmed by evidence to the contrary, in favor of uniformity, only holds if we view miracles as "surds," which traditional theism does not; for more, see Fern 1982. The further claim that belief in miracles is inconsistent with modern science overlooks the inherently abstractive, limited nature of scientific explanations; see chapter three above. As regards the alleged debasement of divine dignity, while some, such as Simon (Acts 8: 9–24), have viewed God in a debased way many others have not and, as we all know but some forget, you do not refute a position by pointing out absurdities in its most absurd interpretation. For an illuminating discussion and defense of the historic belief in miracles, see Swinburne 1970.

[47] Alston, having observed that "many people think, and I myself at one time thought, that the belief that God enters into active interaction with his creatures, a belief crucial to the Judeo-Christian tradition, requires us to suppose that God directly intervenes in the world, acting outside the course of nature," proceeds to argue to the contrary (1985: 213f.):

Just by virtue of creating and sustaining the natural order God is in as active contact with his creatures as one could wish. Merely by the use of natural causes God carries out his purposes and intentions with respect to creatures, and this surely counts as genuine action toward them. If God speaks to me, or guides me, or enlightens me by the use of natural causes, he is as surely in active contact with me as if he had produced the relevant effects by a direct fiat.

Alston's point is that God, as creator and sustainer of the world-as-a-whole, may engage us personally through the medium of natural causes taken as a whole, without being present in particular cases as a discrete, supernatural cause. It follows that theism does not require miracles to satisfy the full- or real-agency principles.

[48] This is the strongest objection to belief in miracles. Jesus raises it when he asks why, in the time of Elijah, none were cured other than Naaman the Syrian, angering worshipers at the local synagogue so much they attempt to throw him off a cliff (Luke 4: 16–30). While I have no answer to Jesus' question, it is worth noting that the problem posed by a sporadic occurrence of miracles is itself part of the larger problem of evil, or, divine absence. Why is the power and goodness of God not more apparent in the world he has made and lovingly sustains? This is a serious problem; I do not see, however, that a belief in miracles makes it worse or, counterwise, that a denial of miracles does anything to solve it.

traditional nor modernist theology has been shown untenable (in this respect).

Why, in light of this, has the question of miracles been such a focal point for theological controversy? The answer, I suggest, lies in imaginative, not dogmatic or systematic theology. The way theists view miracles makes a notable difference in the way they understand God and God's relation to the world.[49] Not only are the associated images and stories different, the sustaining wellsprings of faith differ, the way in which we envision the Christian life. Correspondingly, it is not surprising that traditionalists and modernists have a hard time understanding one another and, more particularly, tend to see the other as standing outside the parameters of a credible theism. In any case, my intent is not to settle this issue one way or the other.[50] Rather, it is to point out the important role played in theological reflection by imaginative theology and, therewith, to flag the way in which critical reason, operating within particular contexts of faith, provides not for a single, rationally certified convergence of religious faith, but, rather, for an on-going elucidation of the mysterious, irreducible givens of faith.

Those who think of God as a personally involved causal agent with miracle-working power will seek to understand God from that standpoint, calling on the resources of faith and reason. The same holds for those who view God in terms of transcendental structures or existential encounters and, accordingly, have no place in their theological endeavors for the historic notion of miracles. As to why theists opt for one model or the other, that remains a secret hidden in the mysteries of charismatic and, no less, constitutive faith. This does not mean we can throw up our hands and believe whatever we will. Faith continues to seek understanding, holding on to this, modifying that, sometimes setting aside once valued elements of faith – as we saw with regard to literalistic readings of the creation story. That a faith so engaged is willing and able to abandon once occupied ground is a mark of reasonableness – an ability to learn and grow in accord with directives of reason – not a lack of content or backbone. Accordingly, we ought in pursuing the Truth to concentrate on the credibility and development of our own faith, not prowl about

---

[49] I speak from personal experience, having been raised in a home and church where miracles were common fare and, later, spending many years in seminaries where the irrationality of such belief was taken (by many) for granted.

[50] Theistic naturalism, though overtly traditional in its affirmation of divine transcendence and human uniqueness, remains (unlike the author) neutral on the question of miracles.

like ravenous beasts eager to ridicule the faiths by which others live.[51] Critical reason does its best for us when focused on the particular faiths by which it and we live.

[51] This attitude is crucial to the strong, cultural and religious pluralism advocated in Part III. Note that it does not require us to (1) set aside a concern with the truth, (2) deny (what we take to be) the more-or-less unique truth of our own faith, or (3) cease criticizing (what we believe to be) error on the part of others (which, applied to others, would eliminate a prime resource in the critique of our own faith). As Nicholas Rescher well observes in defense of "perspectival pluralism" (1993: 105): "we have no choice but to see *our* truth as the *truth*"; see also 106ff., on the errors of "indifferentist relativism." What pluralism does require, alongside respect for the good-will and intelligence of others, is a focusing of concern on the reasonableness and truth of our own, deeply cherished faiths.

CHAPTER FIVE

Theistic naturalism

THE RADICAL OTHERNESS OF GOD

Traditional theism has been subjected to extensive criticism in the modern era, much focused on the notion of a miracle-working deity, regarded by modernists as antithetical to scientific inquiry and, more fundamentally, a proper understanding of God's relation to and *modus operandi* in the world-at-large. These concerns have led revisionist theologians to remove God from the causal nexus, thereby protecting, as they see it, the transcendent Otherness of God from anthropomorphic debasement. This critique is rejected by traditional theists, who argue, as seen in chapter four, that it fails on all counts and, more positively, that the transcendent Otherness of God demands an attribution of miracle-working power. Throughout this debate, until recently, both traditionalists and modernists have remained committed to the notion of transcendent Otherness, even though differing on what it involves.

Lately, however, some revisionists have begun to worry that the notion of radical Otherness introduces an alienating, morally dangerous dualism into our understanding of the relation between God and world.[1] The basic concern is that this notion privileges properties and entities, such as mind and men, associated with a radically Other God, while devaluing those, such as women and body, linked to the natural world.[2]

---

[1] For a concise statement of these concerns see Kaufman 2000.

[2] Concerns are expressed in this regard with a "monarchical model" of the divine, said by Sallie McFague (1993b: 91) to distance God from the world (since "royalty is 'untouchable'") and, moreover, to portray God as controlling the world "through domination and benevolence"; McFague also worries (1993a: 138f.) that this model raises "issues of human freedom and theodicy," while, by virtue of being "a political model," limiting its concern to human beings and, consequently, not only distant from but indifferent to the natural world. Jay McDaniel (1986: 200f.) criticizes that aspect of "the Christian mythical heritage" which makes the value of created entities dependent upon their relation to God, arguing:

Humans have thought of themselves as bare facts, devoid of value, until assigned worth by God. As Nietzsche pointed out, and as feminist theologians have increasingly insisted, this emphasis

This, in turn, is held responsible for historic abuses of devalued objects and persons, including the current ecological crisis. Accordingly, critics such as Dieter Hessel (1992a: 14), call for "a postmodern, non-dualistic way of viewing God's relation to the world – not as a spirit apart from matter but as spirit of matter, breath of all life, or presence throughout nature."[3] Acceptance of this ecological model is seen as not only theologically imperative but, also, as noted in chapter four, well grounded in modern scientific, evolutionary, and ecological theories of nature: "The model that comes to mind as we think about God and the world in the new creation story is not 'the king and his realm' but the 'universe as God's body'" (McFague 1993b: 95). So viewed, God becomes the dynamic, all-encompassing unity of existence, the creative font of possibility, and the total awareness of all that has been, is or will be, "a fellow-sufferer who understands," tied to the world, now and forever.

From the standpoint of religious naturalism, there is much to affirm in this "panentheism," not least its insistence that wild nature is an integral, indispensable element in our relation with God – a point I will argue below. Nevertheless, as a traditional theist, I have serious reservations. For one thing, the criticisms of radical Otherness motivating this change depend on distortions of traditional theism, as we see in this chapter. In addition, I worry that the proposed, panentheist model of God not only fails to solve the alleged problem of dualism but introduces theological problems of its own.[4] Be that as it may, however, my intent is not to

on obsequiousness before God has resulted in a slavish mentality that has thwarted wholesome self-affirmation. It has given rise to the oppressive idea that all goodness comes from God and all evil from the world.

See also McDaniel (1989: 115, 139), Hessel (1992a: 17), and McFague (1993a: 15, 21, 29, 156, 164f., 214 n. 13, 224 n. 29; 255 n. 29).

3 Similarly, McFague, in *The Body of God* (1993a: 96f.; also 38ff.), recommends an organic model that

pictures reality as composed of multitudes of embodied beings who presently inhabit a planet that has evolved over billions of years through a process of dynamic change marked by law and novelty into an intricate, diverse, complex, multileveled reality, all radically interrelated and interdependent ... The universe is a body, to use a poor analogy, from our own experience, but it is not a human body; rather, it is matter bodied forth seemingly infinitely, diversely, endlessly, yet internally as one.

4 As Jürgen Moltmann points out (1993: 78):

if [the world] is eternal and without any beginning like God himself, the process must itself be one of God's natures. And in this case we have to talk about "the divinization of the world." God and nature are fused into a unified world process, so that the theology of nature becomes a divinization of nature: God is turned into the comprehensive ordering factor in the flux of happening.

question panentheism but, rather, respond, as a traditional theist, to the questioning of my own faith.

To start I must allow that while I do not believe an anti-naturalistic, otherworldly stance follows from an affirmation of radical Otherness, there is no doubt but that some traditional theists have understood God and God's relation to the world in ways that ignore or, even, denigrate the value of wild nature.[5] In this regard traditional theists owe a debt of gratitude to panentheists, such as John Cobb, who have quickened their awareness of ecological and social issues too long ignored. Theists who continue affirming the radical Otherness of God need to show that traditional theism, far from being responsible for this neglect, supports concern for the well-being of all God's creatures and, therewith, the integrity of creation-as-a-whole.

I address this task here by sketching an account of creation, theistic naturalism, that portrays God as irreducibly personal, yet radically Other, eternal, infinite, altogether Holy. This account, though innovative in some respects, remains thoroughly traditional in its presumption of a fundamental, ontological, and normative divide between God and world. In formulating it, I draw primarily, though not exclusively, on Christian theologians, as reflects my own faith commitment and areas of study. It is important, however, to see that theistic naturalism is not a uniquely Christian account of God or creation. While those who are not Christians and, even, other Christians may want to modify the basic framework at points, it remains open to adoption by all theists, modernists included, with a correspondingly high view of divine transcendence.[6] This account views creation as a free, constitutive, eschatological act, self-limiting, vulnerable, trusting, and faithful. These diverse elements are held together

Unless this problem can be addressed, panentheism and, with it, process theology, threatens to collapse into a non-theistic form of faith, pantheism, karmic order, or, even, religious scientism. At the same time, attributing absolute and relative natures to God does not, the best I can see, eliminate the feared ontological and normative divide but, rather, replaces the substantive God-world, infinite–finite dualism of traditional theism with a post-Kantian formalism, a dualism of unchanging, absolute form and Heraclitean, relative substance.

[5] For more on the history of Christian attitudes toward nature, see Bratton 1993, Stoll 1997, and Fowler 1995. These provide examples of traditional theists who err in this regard as well as those, like St. Patrick, who side with the wild God. (For a fascinating, informative discussion of Celtic monasticism, see Bratton 1993: 182–216.)

[6] For somewhat similar projects see Keith Ward 1996 and David Burrell 1993. Ward draws on Christian, Jewish, Muslim, and Hindu traditions to formulate, in dialogue with modern cosmology, an account of "the Creator God" which is less traditional (and more "scientific") than that offered here. Burrell, congruent with our enterprise though from a more metaphysical point of view, explores conceptions of divine freedom operative in creation in the Jewish, Christian, and Muslim traditions.

by the governing image of a radically unconstrained Being speaking the world into existence out of love, a will to mutuality with the world created.

A FREE ACT

God, without any constraint whatsoever, freely creates the world. Such constraints as might have been imposed by a pre-existing reality are ruled out by the fact that God, unlike a Platonic demiurge, creates the world out of nothing: "In the beginning" – before there was anything other than God – "God created the heavens and the earth" (Genesis 1: 1 [NRSV]).[7] The act of creation is a *creatio ex nihilo* and, thus, radically free. This means there is no necessity, ontological or normative, in God's decision to create. That God creates is the result of a radically free decision; as C. E. Gunton observes (1992: 121): "it is of the essence of God's freedom-in-relatedness that he is not bound to create. He would still be God if he had not created this world or any other." In addition, there are no external constraints on what or how God creates; in that sense, the freedom of God is absolute.[8]

A CONSTITUTIVE ACT

God makes the world out of nothing, as he chooses. Theistic naturalism centers on this belief. Accordingly, much depends for theistic naturalism on how this radically free act is understood. Here it will prove helpful to consider two useful but ultimately inadequate models.[9] The first

---

[7] Moltmann (1993: 73) contrasts the Hebrew term *bara'* in verse one with the term *'asah*, used to describe the subsequent, shaping activity of God. Observing that the first term is "never used with the accusative of a material out of which something is to be made," he concludes: "The divine creativity has no conditions or premises. Creation is something absolutely new. It is neither actually nor potentially inherent or present in anything else." David Kelsey argues (1985: 186) that the doctrine of *creatio ex nihilo* is not clearly implied by Genesis 1, allows that it finds direct support in Romans 4: 17 and, possibly, Hebrew 11: 3, and concludes, as do panentheists, that it may cease to express the self-understanding of Christian faith. I show here that the case for such change has yet to be made.

[8] Such constraints as exist are internal, reflecting the eternal nature and antecedent will of God: "there is ... an irreducible duality between the freedom of God to act particularly in history and the generic ordering of the world which is reflected in morality" (O'Donovan 1986: 45). Since this ordering is internal, it does not interfere with the *arbitrium*, or, absolute freedom of God (33ff.), a point directly relevant to concerns regarding divine freedom raised by Plato in the *Euthyphro*.

[9] Alister McGrath (1994: 236ff. and 1998: 44ff.) distinguishes three basic models: emanation, construction, and artistic expression; of these three, he favors the third, as I will. McFague (1993a: 151ff.) also describes three models: production, procreation, and emanation; in accord with her claim that the world is "God's body," she favors a composite, procreation–emanation

model is that of fabrication, or, construction. On this view, God makes the world in the way a carpenter builds a house, the difference being that God, rather than having to call the lumber yard, provides his own material as needed. This model displays in a perspicuous manner the internally ordered nature of creation. The world is a structured reality, the order of which serves God's purpose – just as the internal ordering of a house serves the end of habitation. Irenaeus captures this point when he observes of God's creative activity (1995: 361):

> He himself, after a fashion which we can neither describe nor conceive, predestinating all things, formed them as He pleased, bestowing harmony on all things, and assigning them their own place, at the beginning of their creation. In this way he confirmed on spiritual things an invisible nature, supercelestial things a celestial, on angels an angelical, on animals an animal, on beings that swim a nature suited to the water, and on those that live on the land one fitted for the land – on all, in short, a nature suitable to the character of the life assigned them – while He formed all things that were made by His Word that never wearies.

As Irenaeus sees it, God is a master builder, one who designs and places what he makes in a mutually rewarding relationship to one another and, above all, himself.[10]

In a moment I want to note a difficulty with the fabrication model, one having to do with the pervasive, immediate presence of God throughout creation.[11] Before doing so, I need to note two points relative to the structure of creation. The first concerns a basic, over-all similarity between Creator and creation, the *analogia entis*. As Hans Urs von Balthazar observes (1992: 285):

> as to whether there should be a world or not . . . that is for God to *decide*. But *if* he decides to create a world, then . . . this decision can only take the form of the analogy of being, which is grounded in God's very "essence" itself. Created being must be by definition created, dependent, relative, nondivine, but *as* something created it cannot be utterly dissimilar to its Creator.

Since God is the sole source of being, whatever he creates must reflect his own being. This condition is satisfied in the fact that creation, in whole and in part, is good.

---

model. George Hendry (1980: 148ff.) distinguishes six models: generation, fabrication, formation, conflict, expression, and emanation; he argues that the fifth, expression, is closest to the biblical account and theologically most adequate. Moltmann (1993: 297–320) discusses various "symbols of the world" (and, therewith, images of creation).

[10] According to R. A. Markus (1954: 212; citing *Against the Heresies* 3.25), Irenaeus envisions "a single world full of God's glory and one God who contains it all and governs its history by his providence."

[11] This is a concern with which Irenaeus sympathizes, given his desire "to affirm the nearness of the hands of the Creator to all things" (Santmire 1985: 39; see 35–44 for more on Irenaeus).

The second point concerns one aspect of that goodness, namely, the revelation of God in creation to creation. That God conveys through creation an awareness of himself, has great implications for the way in which the world is structured. In particular, it requires that we think of the *analogia entis*, the analogy of being, as the internal ordering of creation. Accordingly, von Balthazar (285) defines nature as "that *minimum* that must be present in every possible situation where God wants to reveal himself to a creature." We see God in the world he has made, in the whole and in the details. This requires that *not* all aspects of creation manifest equally the being and glory of God. If they did, we would be unable to say God is one way rather than another, let alone that God is more like a person than a stone or sea urchin. Theism turns on the presumption that some aspects of creation reveal the nature and glory of God more fully and clearly than others.

That creation is internally structured, ordered in the way it is, reflects God's purpose in creating a world radically other than himself. Accordingly, thinking of creation as an intentional act of construction, a fabrication, has illustrative value. At the same time, however, this model can and historically has distorted the essential dynamic of creation. The central problem is well put by Augustine (1982: 117):

> For the power and might of the Creator, who rules and embraces all, makes every creature abide; and if this power ever ceased to govern creatures, their essences would pass away and all nature would perish. When a builder puts up a house and departs, his work remains in spite of the fact that he is no longer there. But the universe will pass away in the twinkling of an eye if God withdraws his ruling hand.

Thinking of creation as the building of a house or, as deists do, a cosmic clock, encourages the distinctively modern illusion of a "pure nature," a world capable of surviving and functioning on its own: nature and grace are separated into "two quasi-independent orders of reality" (Dupré 1993: 174).[12] In this regard, we need to see that creation is not only constructive of reality but, even more fundamentally, constitutive.

That nature has no place, no address, apart from the creative word of God, follows from the fact that God creates the world out of "nothing."[13]

---

[12] Louis Dupré argues (1993: 173) that "never never before the modern age did Christians consider a notion of extrinsic causality adequate to express the intimate, permanent presence of God to his creation." He sees (186ff.) the basis for a resolution to this problem in Nicholas of Cusa, who anticipates the pantheistic union of nature and grace in a single order of being. Theistic naturalism, while agreeing that bifurcating nature and grace is a serious theological error, envisions a more traditional solution, one Dupré believes precluded by our "passage to modernity."

[13] As Kelsey (1985: 176) notes: "To affirm that God 'creates' the world 'from nothing' is to claim that God is related to all that is not God in a continuously active 'productive' way."

God, the sole source of being and value, the one self-constituting reality, must be present, immanent in the world, sustaining it at all times and in all places. Thus, as Wolfhart Pannenberg (1993: 34) well puts it, "the act of creation did not take place only in the beginning. It occurs at every moment." If creation has occurred, it must continually re-occur as long as the world exists.[14] Here, it is helpful to engage a second model, generation, or, loosely put, procreation. Generative models avoid a division of reality into quasi-independent orders by stressing the growth-oriented, continuing function of divine grace in nature, the off-shoot of God's creative action. John Carmody puts it well (1983: 118): "At the center of any theology of creation I would find adequate is God's endowment of being. All that exists, inanimate and animate, non-human and human, depends directly on God, only exists or is real because of the divine largess." In this sense creation is analogous to an organic process, a living being, that remains alive and vital only because the creative power of God, the divine *energeia*, flows around, in and through its body. In God we live, move, and have our being.

The need for a *concursus divinus* has always been recognized by reflective theists. Irenaeus and Augustine provide two salient examples. Another, historically important example is provided by medieval scholasticism, as in Aquinas' observation (1964: vol. II, 113 [I, Q.8, a.1]) that God, the ultimate source of existence, must "exist intimately in everything" since the act of existing "is more intimately and profoundly interior to things than anything else, for everything . . . is potential when compared to existence." This way of putting it, in terms of potential and actuality, reflects the explication of divine properties in the language of metaphysical "first principles." The more organic, generative model favored by Carmody and panentheists in general balances this reductively abstract, formal view by rendering the presence of God more concrete and personal. The image of a mother giving birth is particularly nice: God births creation.[15] This allows us to conceive of creation as an all-encompassing personal relation, an analogy of love, or, *analogia relationis*.

---

[14] Thus, the basic question is never why God created the world but, rather, why God continues to sustain the world in existence. To see this is important not only because it ties the past to the present, but, even more so, because it ties the past and present to the future. Correspondingly, Pannenberg (1993: 72f.) argues we need to think of creation in the context of a "theology of nature," not as an isolated act in the past.

[15] Rick Richardson has suggested to me in conversation that the perfection and fullness of God's eternal, internally directed love leads God to love the world into being, as the love of a happily married couple leads them to create new life.

It is helpful, then, to pair the fabrication model with a generative, procreative model. The latter allows us to see that the internal ordering of creation, the *analogia entis*, is always a manifestation of and, thus, subordinate to the all-pervasive, constitutive presence of God in creation, the *analogia relationis*. What makes the generative model ultimately inadequate is that in overcoming the tendency of the fabrication model to bifurcate God and world, it too easily blurs the ontological and normative divide between God and world. Thus, however attractive this model may be to those prepared to view the world as God's body, it must, for traditional theists, be balanced by a stress on the radically contingent, fabricated nature of creation. So long as this tension is maintained, these two models give a relatively good sense of what it means to portray creation as a free, yet constitutive act. Later, I suggest a third model, one that integrates and preserves this tension. Before doing so, we need to take a closer look at the future-oriented nature of creation.

AN ESCHATOLOGICAL ACT

Creation needs to be understood as not only constitutive and continuing but, like a narrative, epigenetic and proleptic, a progressive unfolding of the divine will, a process "that is not completed already at its beginning but whose beginnings are already determined on the basis of the end" (Pannenberg 1993: 83). It is only in the future, in that which is coming-to-be, yet-not-yet, that we grasp the true nature of that which is. Creation, nature, is a future-looking, eschatological reality (Pannenberg 1993: 83): "If only the future will teach what is the significance of an event, then the 'essence' of an event or occurrence is never completely finished in the present. Only after the larger connection of occurrences to which an event belongs has been completed can the true essence of the individual event be recognized." The central point is not one of recognition but ontology: reality *is* eschatological; the ontological fullness of nature, the be-ing of finite being, lies in its future consummation.

The idea that creation is only complete, ontologically and normatively, at "the end of time" is a thoroughly biblical notion. As Bernard Anderson observes (1987: 110): "In the Bible creation opens toward the horizon of the future. Time rather than space, history rather than cosmology is the central concern . . . Creation and consummation, first things and last things, are inseparably joined together, like Siamese twins . . . [C]reation is an eschatological belief." One consequence is that the world we live in, the world-in-process-of-being-created, has an ambiguous nature to it, one which is and, yet, is not. It is the "yet-to-be," inherent in that which is, which gives nature normative depth and significance, sets an agenda for the future and, thereby, a natural law for human behavior: we are called to be in step with that which is coming to be, with that which is most real, the working out in creation of God's holy will.

Jürgen Moltmann (1993: 158) points out that biblical writers, unlike the Greeks, do not possess a single, unified term for the reality created by God but prefer, instead, to use the dual expression "heaven and earth." Of these two symbols, the second signifies "the sphere which is familiar and with which the human being has been entrusted"; the first, "the inner, relative transcendence of creation" (159, 174). Together these terms declare creation an *"ec-static* reality," a reality with "its unity, not in itself, but outside itself – in [God]" (163). Thus, Moltmann notes humans are given responsibility for *the earth*, not creation in general: we are called to tend and subdue the earth, to see that its manifest reality is in harmony with that "side of creation," heaven, "that is open to God." Creation exists in a state of dynamic tension. Only in the eschatological fulfillment of "the new creation" will the will of God be done on earth as in heaven (184).

This developmental element in an eschatological view of heaven and earth has a natural affinity for evolutionary theories of human nature and origins. Augustine, envisioning a gradual unfolding of creation over time, remarks (1982: 172): "God unfolds the generations which He laid up in creation when He founded it; and they would not be sent forth to run their course if He who made creatures ceased to exercise His provident rule over them." Thus, while viewing the "six days" of creation as timeless "stages in the angelic knowledge of creation" and, accordingly, believing "the creative action whereby all things came to be was instantaneous," Augustine likens the historical unfolding of creation to the maturation of a tree seed (1982: 175):

> In the seed, then, there was invisibly present all that would develop in time into a tree. And in this same way we must picture the world, when God made all things together, as having had all things together which were made in it and with it when day was made. This includes not only heaven with sun, moon and stars . . . [but] also the beings which water and earth produced in potency and in their causes before they came forth in the course of time as they have become known to us in the works which God even now produces.

Ernan McMullin, discussing these passages (1985a: 11–16), concludes (15) that despite striking differences between Augustine's notion of seed-principles and the Darwinian notion of natural selection, "there is some-thing to be said for situating Augustine at the head of the lineage not of evolutionary theory but of attempts to show how the notions of evolution and creation may fit together."

That creation is forward-looking and developmental raises a question regarding the extent to which nature is oriented toward and capable of achieving fulfillment in its own terms. Later, I will address this question relative to the vulnerability of nature and the subsequent necessity of soteriological grace. Before doing so, however, it is important to see that the temporally first and most persistent manifestation of grace is simply the immanence of God whereby all that is comes to be and remains in existence. In this sense, as argued above, there is and can be no "pure nature" untouched by grace. Since the *analogia relationis* subsumes and frames the *analogia entis*, nature apart from grace is nothing more than an abstraction, as in the quantifiable regularities and laws of modern sci-ence. Further, as argued above, the grace manifest in creation not only sustains, it orders nature, pointing it like an arrow at the source of its existence: "there is a transparency, meaning and even perfection of crea-turely imperfection" (Barth 1958: 382). Here we return to Moltmann's observations regarding the duality of heaven and earth: grace lies in the tension, not its elimination. As von Balthazar observes (1992: 124): "The nature of creation is its orientation to grace."

A CONVERSATIONAL ACT

Creation is an act in progress, a product whose reality is not only present but yet to come – a structure in the process of being built, a living creature in the process of maturation. What these images fail to capture adequately is the sense in which creation is already complete by the time it gets under way. What will be is what God has determined will be in the eternality of his being. Our future already exists in heaven. How, then, are we to think of this, the completeness of nature, without overlooking or denying the inherent incompleteness of nature? Is there another model on which we can call?

I propose to follow the example of Genesis and think of God as speak-ing the world into existence – only instead of explicating the act involved in terms of fabrication or generation – portray it in more literary terms as the telling of a story, the on-going, all-inclusive story of creation. God is not simply the Ground of our Being, the First Cause of Creation, but a divine Wordsmith, the Cosmic Poet, the Primal Storyteller. So viewed, creation differs from fabrication insofar as its product exists only in the telling; creation lives in the articulated intentionality, the life-giving breath, of God. This, in turn, differentiates it from procreation; there is nothing there apart from the flow of God's free, creative Word. Should God cease speaking, the world would vanish, gone in a word. We are confronted with something unique, God's narrative of nature and grace.

This model enables us to convey both the completeness and incompleteness of creation in a way that is normatively laden and irreducibly personal – all the way through. Thus, for instance, while we do not know in advance what the characters in Trollope's *Chronicles of Barsetshire* are going to do, we can take the natural history and culture of Barsetshire, the geography, architecture, economy, politics, family relations, social order, and such, as givens. Indeed, that we can is part of what makes Trollope such an engaging writer: he provides a rich context in which to place his characters. At the same time, there is no story until the Rev. Harding, his daughter Eleanor, the idealistic John Bold, and others, begin to interact in ways we cannot deduce from a mere familiarity with the background. The story, like each character, has a life of its own, a life that is complete only in the telling – and, even then, we are left with the prospect of more story, generations to come.[16]

To whom is the story of creation told? First of all, to God by God. God tells the story of creation to the only One capable of hearing and understanding it in its entirety. In this respect, God is like the Platonic Good: there is nothing more wonderful or interesting for him to do than listen to himself talk. What makes the biblical God, the God of Abraham, Isaac, and Jacob, different is that he takes pleasure in and responds to the reflection of his eternal Self in the mirror of creation, partaking not only of a Reality and Bliss that lies beyond our comprehension but, no less, the ups and downs, woes and weals of creaturely existence. This God is a participant in creation all the way through, the One who holds us in his hand so we can hear his story, listens in return as we tell ours, and, even, in the wondrous expanse of creation, allows us to hold him in return. Further, because God not only tells the story but hears and comprehends it, nothing is lost. From God to God in God.

The theist, I suggest, is best served by thinking of the world in terms of an encompassing narrative, a vast, sweeping historical saga told by

---

[16] Another advantage of this literary model is that normatively laden, personal relations, while incapable of being fabricated or grown, can be spoken into existence, as, for instance, marriage: "I now pronounce you, man and wife." This is of special interest to theistic naturalism, which views reality as an all-encompassing web of personal relations.

God, a story with no reality other than that found in the telling: it's God's story all the way.[17] In speaking the words of creation, God not only articulates a meaning, he gives substance to the referents of his discourse, the only substance they will or can ever have. So long as God speaks, the world continues. Apart from this address the world has no place or abiding reality. Thus, rather than creation being necessitated, logically *entailed*, by the bi-polar nature or overflowing goodness of God – as proclaimed by emanationists, pantheists, and panentheists – God, the author of our being, freely, under no constraint, *en-tells* the world, speaks it into existence, one word at a time.

That the world is nothing more than a divine speech act does not mean materiality is not real or in anyway "dream-like," as if we could somehow ignore the hard task of finding our way about in an externally given, objective reality. Here we must keep in mind the Otherness of God. God's speech, like God's thought, is only analogically similar to our own. For God there is no ontological divide between intention and reality, between what he says and what is, period. It is also important to keep in mind that the focus of our account is divine communication, conversation, not divine contemplation. It is God's speaking *to* and conversing *with* the world that gives the world a reality and, therewith, value of its own. Creation is not only God's story; it is God's audience. The ultimate aim of creation, like art, is communication.[18]

A SELF-LIMITING ACT

That God creates the world from nothing means the power and presence of God, the divine *energeia*, lies at the core of creation, in every place and every time. In this sense, creation resembles the Hollideck; shut off the program and you are left with nothing, an empty room. The difference, of course, is that reality really is God's story, his words, all the way, us included. This does not mean what we encounter is not real; indeed, it would not otherwise be real. Nor does it mean that we are not self-reflective, freely creative agents in our own right. God's world, our world, humanity included, is no illusion.

---

[17] Clifford Geertz (1973: 28f.) tells the story – slightly modified here – of an Englishman who, having been told by a Hindu that the world rests on the back of an elephant, proceeds to ask what the elephant rests on. When the Hindu replies, "a turtle," the Englishman repeats his original question, to which the Hindu replies, "another turtle." This goes on for a while, the Hindu replying to every question, "another turtle." The Englishman, growing amused, keeps repeating his question until finally the exasperated Hindu remarks, "You just don't get it, do you? It's turtles all the way."

[18] See Hendry 1980: 157. For more on God as conversationalist, see Wolterstorff 1995.

At the same time, there is a mystery, a puzzle, at the heart of creation. John Zizioulas puts it well (1993: 93): "How . . . can ultimate truth be linked up ontologically with creation and history in such a way that creation may keep its own distinct being, while God remains the ultimate truth of being?" Where is there room, how can there be room for anything else given the fullness of divine power and value? Will not God's abundance of being, God's richness of value, swallow up everything other than itself?

That creation has its being only in and through God means it is not sufficient to think of the world as a manifestation of God's creative will. We must also inquire as to the preparation of a space and time, a place within which the world can exist as other than God. Thus arises the question, so central to the kabbalistic doctrine of God, regarding the "nothing" out of which God creates the world. What is it? From whence does it come? It cannot be an "absolute nothingness," something other than the comprehensive reality of divine being; there is no outside void, no chaos, into which to place the world. The nothing from which creation comes must be a "relative nothingness," something that exists within God.

In order to create a world "outside" himself, the infinite God must have made room beforehand for a finitude in himself. It is only a withdrawal by God into himself that can free the space into which God can act creatively. The *nihil* for his *creatio ex nihilo* only comes into being because – and in as far as – the omnipotent and omnipresent God withdraws his presence and restricts his power. (Moltmann 1993: 86f.)[19]

God, as the kabbalist Isaac Luria makes clear in his development of the ancient Jewish doctrine of the Shekinah glory, only creates by virtue of a self-limitation on his awesomely, absolutely all-absorbing, utterly overwhelming reality. Before God can speak the world into existence, before God can tell the story of creation, he must call into being "a literally God-forsaken space" (Moltmann 1993: 87).

The self-limitation of God, the divine *zimsum*, is a condition for the extension of divine love outside the internal dynamic of God's eternal reality. It is only from within this opening that finite creatures can engage the love of God, can encounter the One who is like us, yet radically Other. That we *do* confront this love is, of course, not accidental. The relative nothingness in which we exist "outside God still remains *in* the God who has yielded up that 'outwards' in himself"; not even a "literally God-forsaken space" can exist apart from the absolute reality of God

[19] See Moltmann (1993: 74f.) for more on the critical distinction between *me on*, the relative negation of being (*nihil privativum*), and *ouk on*, the absolute negation of being (*nihil negativum*).

(Moltmann 1993: 89). What the self-limitation of God entails is that within this space, this relative void, the divine *pleroma*, the fullness of God cannot be comprehended in any moment of time or segment of space, not even the entire space–time continuum. Thus, God can be known therein not as God fully is but only *in part*: the power and value, the unified, all-encompassing goodness and glory of God is apprehended, always and ever under the order of creation, in a partial, fragmented manner. This limitation, in giving rise to the relative nothingness, the *me on*, constitutes the possibility of creation and, no less, a rent in the divine being, a separation and fragmentation apart from which the very act of creation makes no sense, has no reality.

Creation comes to be through the freely willed absence of God. This, in turn, imparts to creation an innate, fulfillment-oriented, eschatological dynamic. The deep Truth of nature, *natura naturans* and *natura naturata*, always lies beyond reach. In this sense, there is truth to the myth of divine sparks seeking return to the Godhead – only not the truth gnostics believe. The reflectivity that grasps in God the ultimate source and fulfillment of its fragmented nature remains, forever, fragmented and partial, dust of the earth. In this sense, the gnostic myth of return to eternal beatitude is deeply flawed: there is no other place for us to go, no other place for us to be.

Just as God can only create by keeping his distance, his *me on*, the world comes into being and continues to exist only so long as God remains present in his absence. Thus, creation finds its origin in "an immanent *tension* in God himself" (Moltmann 1993: 15). Moltmann elaborates (87): "creation is preceded by this self-movement on God's part, a movement which allows creation the space for its own being. God withdraws into himself in order to go out of himself. He 'creates' the preconditions for the existence of his creation by withdrawing his presence and his power." Creation requires a self-limitation on the part of God and, thus, an inherent risk, the vulnerability of creation.

One manifestation of this vulnerability is the element of chance and, therewith, unpredictability God builds into creation. Reflecting on recent developments in quantum mechanics, Christopher Peacocke says (1979: 95): "I see no reason why God should not allow the potentialities of his universe to be developed in all their ramifications through the operation of random events."[20] That chance plays a role in God's story,

---

[20] I agree, so long as the range of possibilities is delimited. Viewing chance as the "search radar of God, sweeping through all the possible targets available to its probing" (Peacocke 1979: 95), poses the danger of reducing God to a cosmic gambler, contrary to not only the quantum-anxious Einstein but the traditional belief in divine providence. While God may well leave some things

however, does not mean God must wait on chance to see how things will turn out. Nor does it mean that God gambles with the world or, worse, the good of selves and sentients. Whatever the odds, the world, top to bottom, side to side, always serves God's purposes, the end he has in mind.

A more interesting and important source of vulnerability and openness in creation lies in another category altogether, that of human freedom. Perhaps, just as God in creating the world limits himself ontologically, achieving presence through absence, God in creating humans limits himself gnoseologically, achieving intimacy through ignorance. How so? By allowing his creatures to surprise him. Perhaps, in addition to not knowing (or caring) which sub-atomic particle is going to decay next, God, more significantly by far, does not know (in some cases), yet cares (in all cases) what we are going to do prior to our doing it. Of course, God, knowing us better than we know ourselves, is not likely to be surprised. Still, why not allow that God, in the mystery of creation, leaves some of the details up to us, even allows us to surprise him now and then, for better and for worse.[21] Perhaps, God really did not know in advance when and how or, even, if Adam and Eve were to do what they did.[22] It is, after all, our story, too.

A VULNERABLE ACT

By rendering God near and distant, the order of nature, the *analogia entis*, generates possibility, not merely chance. This structure and resultant, relative openness exists by virtue of a tension between divine immanence,

up to chance – perhaps, even, the particularities of evolution – the basic directionality, the *telos*, of nature has been locked in by grace from the start. Accordingly, it is misleading to compare the creativity of God with the spontaneous, morally indifferent play, *līlā*, of the Hindu deity Shiva (Peacocke 1979: 106ff.). While God delights in, even plays with creation (Job 41: 5), the spontaneity God manifests is always disciplined, like the anger of God, by God's overriding commitment to the good of creation.

[21] John Polkinghorne (2000: 127) speculates that along with a self-limitation of divine omnipotence "creation might also imply a kenosis of omniscience in that an evolving world of true becoming is one in which even the Creator does not yet know the future, for the future is not yet there to be known." For more on the question of divine foreknowledge and its ramifications for human freedom, see Fischer 1989.

[22] I have discovered, as a fledgling fictionist, that characters, once given a character of their own, tend to surprise even their creator. Hendry observes (1980: 157), relative to a literary model of creation: "The novelist creates his characters, but the better he is at doing this, the more the characters tend to acquire identities of their own and to work out their own destinies. The writer who makes his characters act like puppets that he dangles on a string is an inferior artist." The possibility this is true of us relative to the divine author of our being adds a special meaning to prayer, petitionary and otherwise: perhaps God really does listen and, sometimes, responds, miraculously enough.

manifest in a continuing will to relation, and transcendence, manifest in a no less loving cloaking of the divine Glory. God, the master of indirection, "has revealed himself by veiling himself, in disguises as it were; that is, in a way fundamentally different and dissimilar to the way objects confined to this world are given to us" (von Balthazar 1992: 49). While always there for us, God is never, can never be there in the straightforward manner of other, natural objects. It follows that created beings contain at their core an element of privation; Jaki puts it well (1978: 292): "A genuinely created thing is always specified by boundary conditions, the signs of its limited perfections. A perfectly unlimited being cannot be created, for such a being is God himself." Imperfection is an inherent feature of creation: "if all were perfect, would not all be God?" (Gendler 1993).

Here, we confront another and existentially more troubling side to the self-limitation of God in creation. The love of God for creation is manifest, by necessity, in an inherently incomplete and risky manner: throughout creation, God appears ever and only in his own, horrifying shadow. While there is no dark side to God, "no side where he could also be conceived of as the destroyer of his creation and of his own being as Creator" (Moltmann 1993:168), it is also true that in this world, under the order of creation, the enlightening presence of God is inseparable from the shadow of his presence.[23] This shadow serves, as Douglas John Hall notes (1986: 5) in regard to his own Christian faith, as a wake-up call for faith: "darkness entered into, darkness realized, is the point of departure for all profound expressions of Christian hope." More profoundly still, the shadow of creation is a precondition for any relation between divine and created beings, however harmonious. Recognizing this is a vital part of the humility fitting to our relation with God and, no less, one another.

What must be avoided is the historically common presumption that the barrier to God's full presence is "matter," the hard and dense, recalcitrant stuff within which our aspiring "spirits" find themselves imprisoned. On this presumption, the path to follow is that of "a heavenly eros," a turning away from the material world to pursue a more divine, spiritual reality. Just such a view leads Origen (1979; cited in Santmire 1985: 52) to exhort his fellow Christians: "If you do not wish to fall in the wilderness, but

---

[23] See Exodus 33: 12–23 (NRSV): "You cannot see my face; for no one shall see me and live." Note that this follows verse 11, which tells us, flat-out, that Yahweh spoke with Moses "face to face, as a man talks to his friend." One way to understand this obviously intentional tension, a tension recurrent throughout the Bible, is as the mark of a relation combining intense, joyful intimacy with agonizing absence, at one and the same time: the bush that burns yet is not consumed, the life that rises from its own ashes, the ignorance that is knowledge, the presence in absence.

to have attained the promised land of the fathers, you should have no portion in the land nor should you have anything in common with the earth. Let your portion be only with the Lord, and you will never fail."[24] Faith for Origen is a matter of the soul's journey back to God, its escape from an essentially alien, material world. This imagery and the presumption from which it springs, though recurrent in Western thought and theology, is deeply contrary to the account of creation given here and, more fundamentally, in the Bible.[25]

While it is essential to the logic of theism, as embodied in the *analogia entis*, that some aspects of creation are more god-like than others, any attempt to separate the components of creation, placing those that are spiritual on God's side of the divide and consigning those that are (merely) material to some lesser status, is confounded by the radical transcendence of God to *all* aspects of creation, humanity included. That we are analogically more similar to God than a stone does not entail we are ontologically closer to God than stones or, more generally, that our being is of another sort, ontologically, than that of stones, mere materiality. We, too, are dust – all the way through. Our intellectual and moral capacities are the capacities of thoroughly physical beings, so limited in their nature and exercise relative to God that rather than bring us closer to God they place us, as sinners, at a further remove from God than the rest of creation (see Isaiah 64: 6; Romans 3: 10–12). Even apart from the distancing of sin, however, God remains radically Other than humans and stones. We do not remove the difference between finite and infinite by stripping properties away so as to leave a rarified, weightless rendition of the former. Much to the contrary, the more personal aspects of creation only model the divine analogically by virtue of their place in creation-as-a-whole. We encounter the living reality of God in the fullness of creation.[26]

The world, materiality and all, points us in the direction of God. At the same time the world, in part and in whole, hides the full reality of God from us and, in so doing, introduces the risk of not only partiality but evil. Here lies the true vulnerability of creation. The first hint of this

[24] Origen's exhortation illustrates the metaphor of ascent and, therewith, the spiritual motif in Christian theology (see H. Paul Santmire 1985: 49ff.). Santmire's seminal study contrasts the otherworldly perspective of this motif (and metaphor) with the ecological motif and its formative metaphors of fecundity and migration to a good land (13–29).

[25] Failure to see this constitutes the Colossian Error spoken of in Colossians 2: 16–23; for which see Hall (1986:77): "There is evidence in the author's injunctions against this *philosophia* that it conceived of the world in basically dualistic terms: matter is evil, spirit is good."

[26] See, for instance, Romans 12 and Ephesians 4 on the unity of the Body. I develop this point at length in Part III relative to "the body of humanity."

appears in the necessarily imperfect nature of creation. By itself this is not evil, lacking moral significance. It gains moral significance and, therewith, becomes evil at the point where awareness appears. Apart from a capacity to experience and regret (in however limited a way) the absence of good, there would be only imperfection. Once selves and sentients arrive, bringing with them limitations on the good of well-being, evil becomes an inescapable part of God's story. This "natural evil" is inevitable in any world containing finite selves and sentients.[27]

That God creates requires a decision, not only a decision to create but, therewith, a decision that the limitation and loss is worth the gain, finitely speaking. This does not require that the world be free from evil. Not even God can create a world of finite selves and sentients free from natural evil. It does require that the world be a good world, a world in which the good outweighs the bad, the kind of world it is better exists than not. Creation has a price, for God and for us. That we pay that price is a condition of our existence. We would not be here to enjoy or regret it did God not give nature its own nature, allow it room, space, and time, in which to grow and develop in accord with its own laws and ways, its own constitutive, inherently limited dynamic.

Natural evil and, with it, conflicting, frustrated interests are part and parcel of our world, integral to its goodness. This is not true of evil freely chosen, or, *moral evil*. That moral evil appears in creation requires not only moral agency but, therewith, culpable wrongdoing, a rebellion against God. It takes not only Adam and Eve but sin to actualize "the limitations and potential dangers inherent in creaturehood, if creation is left to itself" (Zizioulas 1993: 101f.). Here we must take care not to confuse the constitutive reality of finitude with the tragic reality of sin. The introduction of sin, rebellion against God, generates a new tension, one that goes beyond that inherent in the relation of finite and infinite.

Thus, while it is true, as Claus Westermann notes (1974: 89), that the biblical account of creation and, more generally, the Old Testament as a whole contains no developed concept of original sin, it does not follow, as he goes on to suggest, that Adam and Eve are not portrayed from the

---

[27] That natural evil is the consequence of an ontological necessity inherent in the project of creation provides a partial answer, rooted in faith, to those who, viewing the extent of imperfections, the sickness, ill fortune, earthquakes, storms, distress, and death, conclude the world must, at best, be "the work only of some dependent inferior Deity . . . the object of derision to his superiors" (Hume 1948: 169). Disenchantment is set up by the Leibnizian supposition that God, being perfect in all respects, would necessarily create "the best of all possible worlds." There is, however, no such world: the very perfection of God requires the imperfection of creation, the ever-present, ever-evolving possibility of a brighter future. This held true in Eden, as, so I expect, it will in heaven. That it does is a good thing, integral to the dynamic of human well-being.

very beginning of their creation, prior to their disobedience, as complete, responsible individuals, capable of living as their Creator intends. Here it is important to see, contrary to what many have presumed, that the story does not tell us that there was no conflict or, even, natural evil in Eden prior to the appearance of sin: the presence of the clever serpent and, especially, the way in which he approaches Eve indicate just the opposite. In this regard, Westermann captures an important, often overlooked truth when he points out (72) that, though "created good . . . it is of the very essence of man, inseparable from his nature, that he is defective." This follows not simply from the fact that humans are finite and, thus, imperfect but, more particularly, from the basic, reflective awareness of creatures with the capacity to act as they choose (for no other reason than that they so choose): "From his beginning man appears in a state of conflict: God has given him his being, yet he can set himself up against God. Man is only man in the midst of this conflict" (72f.). This conflict and, with it, the possibility of sin are inherent features of human life, made fruitful for good only through the acquisition of moral and intellectual virtue, that is, a settled propensity to live and think as morality and right reason require.

It does not follow, as Westermann's remarks suggest (94f.), that human beings are incomplete apart from sin and the sense of shame, the awareness of imperfection, that it brings.[28] To think it does conflates "temptation," which does have "something positive to offer" – and would not otherwise appear in Eden as part of God's good creation – and sin, which promises only dissolution, expulsion from the presence of God. Though sin clearly gives "man an insight which he did not have before" (94), this insight relative to nudity and, more fundamentally, our natural innocence – the idea of using deception as a cloak, like the clever serpent – proves destructive in the extreme and is only brought to a good end by the prevailing grace of God. Further, that God continues to take Adam and Eve seriously after their rebellion (and develops, thereby, a new, more indirect mode of relation) does not imply, as Westermann suggests (97), that Adam and Eve are not taken seriously prior to their sin.

---

[28] Westermann is not alone in seeing a link between sin and the realization of a full humanity. Paul Ramsey remarks (1950: 263): "reason and intelligence as we know them empirically in man came into existence only as a consequence of the Fall." While rejecting this claim, theistic naturalism does go further in this direction, relative to the place of conflict and natural evil in creation, than some theists may be comfortable with. Accordingly, my intent here is to draw a sharp line between finitude (conflict and natural evil) and sin (rebellion and moral evil), however conceived – *not*, I stress, to commit theistic naturalists, Christian or otherwise, to a doctrine of original sin, though that is a belief I myself, as an Episcopalian saved by grace, affirm.

If it did, it could hardly be true, as Westermann rightly affirms earlier (91), that: "The command in the Creation narrative ... is an act of confidence in man in his relationship to God. It takes him seriously as man who can decide in freedom and it opens to him the possibility of loyalty." Whether this account is literally true or, more generally, whether any humans have actually lived in a sinless, Edenic state, the crucial point remains: unlike the natural conflict and evil inherent in the creation of selves and sentients, neither sin nor moral evil is an integral part of God's good creation.

The possibility of moral evil is the most serious and, indeed, only real risk God takes in creation. By creating selves with the freedom to rebel, God renders creation vulnerable to wills other than his own. He gives creation its own voice, allows it to tell its own story. Free to imagine themselves gods, free to transform dominion into bondage, humanity and, with it, all of nature are set up for a fall from grace, from the reality of their own being. The obvious question is why God runs such a risk, the risk of creating creatures with the power to turn natural into moral evil.

A LOVING ACT

Why does God take the risk? The answer, I suggest, lies in three, progressively more revealing reasons. The first and most comprehensive reason is that creation abounds to the glory of God. Chapter four of the Westminster Confession of Faith puts it this way (Schaff 1996: 611): "It pleased God the Father, Son, and Holy Ghost, for the manifestation of the glory of his eternal power, wisdom, and goodness, in the beginning, to create or make of nothing the world, and all things therein, whether visible or invisible, in the space of six days, and all very good."[29] God creates the world because it abounds to his glory. This does not imply that there is any sense in which the being or perfection of God stands in need of or, for that matter, is capable of augmentation. As Jonathan Edwards put it (1989: 420):

The notion of God's creating the world in order to receive anything properly from the creature, is not only contrary to the nature of God, but inconsistent with the notion of creation; which implies a being's receiving its existence, and all that belongs to its being, out of nothing. And this implies the most perfect, absolute and universal derivation and dependence.

[29] The Westminster Confession was first issued in 1647 and has come to constitute a more-or-less definite position within the Reformed Tradition.

To some, this may not appear a good or even morally acceptable reason for God to run the risk of creation – as if God were an egoist obsessed with his own greatness. Such a view fails to take into account the radical Otherness of God and, especially, the fact that God's glory encompasses all desirable ends. Hence, there is nothing suspect in God doing all that God does for the sake of his all-encompassing glory. That this is so, however, leaves appeals to divine glory devoid of explanatory force: they do not allow us to see why God does one worthy thing rather than another.

A more determinate and explanatory useful reason why God runs the risk of creation appears in one central aspect of divine glory, the goodness of God. "Cantata Domino," issued by the Council of Florence in 1441, gives this explanation for the act of creation (cited in Kelsey 1985: 192f.):

Most strongly [the Church] believes, professes, and declares that the one true God, Father, Son and Holy Spirit, is the creator of all things visible and invisible, who, when He wished, out of His goodness created all creatures, spiritual as well as corporal; good, indeed, since they were made by the highest good, but changeable, since they were from nothing, and it asserts that nature is not evil, since all nature, in so far as it is nature, is good.[30]

A similar theme appears earlier in Augustine (1984: 455[XI, 23]), who identifies "this good and simple explanation for the creation of the world, namely, that it is the nature of a good God to create good things" and, later, in Calvin, according to whom (cited in Stewart 1983: 9f.) "there was no other cause why He should make all things, neither can He be moved by any other reason to conserve them, than for His only goodness." It is the goodness of creation that renders the world a theatre of divine glory.

A still more specific and explanatory useful reason, one that goes deeper into the arena of motivation, is love: "the creative process ... is an act of love, and its creatures are products of love and recipients of ongoing love" (Nash 1991: 95).[31] This love is attested throughout sacred Scripture, as, for instance, Psalms 136: 3–9 (NRSV):

---

[30] The remark, "all nature, in so far as it is nature, is good," captures the essential difference between the created reality, or, *telos*, of nature and its current, fallen *ecos* (appearance).

[31] Juliana of Norwich, a fourteenth-century English mystic, remarks (1977: 88) that in one of her visions:

[our Lord] showed me a little thing, the size of a hazelnut, lying in the palm of my hand ... I thought "What can this be?" My question was answered in general terms in this fashion: "It is everything that is made." I marveled how this could be, for it seemed to me that it might suddenly fall into nothingness, it was so small. An answer for this was given for my understanding. "It lasts, and ever shall last, because God loves it. And in this fashion all things have their being by the grace of God."

> O give thanks to the Lord of lords,
>   for his steadfast love endures forever;
> who alone does great wonders,
>   for his steadfast love endures forever;
> who by his understanding made the heavens,
>   for his steadfast love endures forever;
> who spread out the earth on the waters,
>   for his steadfast love endures forever;
> who made the great lights,
>   for his steadfast love endures forever;
> the sun to rule over the day,
>   for his steadfast love endures forever;
> the moon and stars to rule over the night,
>   for his steadfast love endures forever.[32]

This reason points us back toward the essentially free character of creation; as Moltmann observes (1993: 75f.):

God's freedom is . . . love, which means the self-communication of the good. If God creates the world out of freedom, then he creates it out of love. Creation is not the demonstration of his boundless power; it is the communication of his love, which knows neither premises nor preconditions . . . [C]reation was called into being out of the inner love which the eternal God himself *is*.

This claim lies at the heart of theistic naturalism, though with regard to it we must take special care, for love is no one thing; everything hinges on the way God's love is understood. Toward this end let me offer, all too briefly, seven points.

First, it cannot plausibly be denied that the love manifest in creation is, in part, sacrificial. Like us, God pays a price. The initial manifestation of this price lies in the divine *zimsum*, the self-limitation of God essential for the very appearance of a finite reality. A second manifestation occurs in the risk God runs in creating the derivative freedom of humanity; divine love sustains the real possibility of its rejection. Finally and most often noted, God sacrifices in the provision of a soteriological grace over

---

Similarly, Abraham Heschel, contrasting the God of philosophers with that of the Bible, stresses the centrality of "divine pathos": "At the heart of the prophetic affirmation is the certainty that God is concerned about the world" (1962: 259).

[32] This steadfast love encompasses all of creation, not just humanity. Note, however, that Psalms 136 continues by offering praise to God for deliverance from Egypt, thereby involving the Creator in the quest for social justice. A similar dynamic appears in Psalms 19, where the praise of creation passes immediately to praise of "the law of the Lord." In both cases, as throughout the Bible, there is a natural transition from the marvelous ordering of creation to the rightful ordering of human life and society.

and above that manifest in creation. In all this and more, God freely takes upon himself the burden of creation.[33]

Second, the love manifest in creation is just as clearly not primarily sacrificial. The sacrifice God makes in creation, out of love, is a price God pays *for love*, the love that moves him to create in the first place. Hence, the love that drives creation cannot itself be sacrificial. Creation is not for the sake of sacrifice; sacrifice is for the sake of creation.

Third, it cannot plausibly be denied that the love manifest in creation is, in part, an erotic, attractive love. Like us, God finds pleasure in creation, a point with regard to which the Bible is abundantly clear. God sees that what he made is good (Psalms 1: 31). God rejoices in the marvelous works of creation (Psalms 104: 31). While this facet of divine love may be wrongly elevated, as it has by some due to Neoplatonic influences, that is no reason to deny the pivotal role it plays; that *eros* cannot account for the entirety of divine love, does not mean it is not a vital component in that love.

Fourth, the love manifest in creation is just as clearly not primarily erotic. The value-laden attractiveness of creation is itself a product of and, hence, cannot be a reason for divine love. God not only sees that creation is good and, then, takes delight in it, God makes creation good, bestows on it the value, all the value it has.[34] Hence, the love that drives God's creative activity cannot be primarily erotic in form.

Fifth, the love manifest in creation is constitutive of creation. That this is so follows naturally from our account of creation as storytelling and the further assumption that God is motivated to tell the story by love. Zizioulas puts the upshot well (1993: 97): "neither the *logoi* of things nor the *logos* of God are conceivable apart from the dynamical movement of love. The substratum of existence is not being but love . . . If [God] ceases to love what exists, nothing will be. Being depends on love." Here we see the underlying significance, ontologically, of the *analogia relationis*. God does not create the world and, then, love it, erotically or sacrificially. God loves the world into being. There is no source of being or value other than the constitutive, creative love of God.

---

[33] For more on the suffering of God see Fiddes 1988. Fiddes, who stresses the comprehensive nature of divine love – encompassing not only sacrificial but erotic and relational elements – argues that the transcendence of God "cannot be an otherness beyond suffering, but must be an otherness in suffering" (142). As to how this is possible, Fiddes observes (106), "I believe we can conceive of a blend of triumph and tragedy in God in his experience of suffering, as we can also think of a future which is certain and yet also unknown." Doing so is crucial to avoiding the anti-biblical notion of divine immutability and, therewith, a rightful understanding of divine transcendence.

[34] See Singer 1984: 3–22, for more on the distinction between "appraisal" and "bestowal."

Sixth, the love manifest in creation must, therefore, be all-encompassing. God's creative, constitutive love embraces all the world, in whole and in part, beginning to end. In this sense, it is like the intent behind a vast, historical novel, manifest more fully and clearly in some scenes, some chapters, than others, yet present in every passing paragraph, every punctuation mark and, no less, every empty space, every pregnant silence.

Seventh, the love manifest in creation embodies God's will to relation. God creates the world by bringing it within the inner, relational truth of his own being, the unending, self-sustaining love of "*communion* in itself."[35] It is the will to relation that forms the substance and *telos* of creation. Moreover, the relation sought is not abstractly metaphysical but concretely personal and, thus, communal: "in perceiving the world as creation, the human being discerns and enters into a community of creation" (Moltmann 1993: 70). God's will to form and be part of this community is the deepest rationale for creation: "creation is thus seen as a self-emptying by God, a risk which he incurs lovingly and willingly for the opportunity of the greater good of freely responsive man coming to be within the created world" (Peacocke 1979: 199).[36]

A TRUSTING ACT

The point and danger of creation is well illustrated by that aspect of the Genesis account which tells us that having created humans and placed them in the Garden of Eden, God comes down to enjoy the evening breeze with his talking animals. What makes this puzzling, at least to a theistic naturalist, is not that God comes down to enjoy the cool of evening; that is what one expects from a wild God. What is puzzling, given the stakes involved, is that God leaves his humans alone during the heat of day, alone with that cosmic trickster, the serpent, intent on

[35] Zizioulas (1993: 93f.) attributes this view to St. Maximus the Confessor, the first to develop fully the eucharistic theology of Ignatius and Irenaeus. Paulos Gregorios (1978: 63) attributes a similar view to Gregory of Nyssa, according to whom "matter . . . is God's will, his energy, made palpable to our senses." Gregorios adds (63), capturing a central commitment of Eastern Orthodoxy: "While [God's] *ousia* remains transcendent, his *energeia* is the whole principle of existence – the immanent existence – giving, constitutive, teleological principle of the universe." I am much indebted here to Albert Outler, who in his teaching of theology stressed the contribution of the East, especially as regards the co-equal work of the Holy Spirit. He understood and helped me appreciate the theological roots and spiritual depth of my Pentecostal heritage.

[36] Peacocke, though leaving too much to chance in my opinion, has much of value to say regarding the conflict and, therewith, natural evil inherent in creation. See Page 1996 for a similar difficulty and contribution.

playing games with these already puffed-up, divinely designated rulers-of-the-garden. Why does God allow the ironic twist in creation to have its way with his brains-of-clay fools-in-the-garden? Why does he not hang around or, at least, send an angel or two to keep the serpent in line?

The answer, I suggest, is love: God grants creation its own, creative freedom for the sake of a love, a mutuality, that cannot exist apart from genuine freedom and risk. It is not enough to have created creatures with whom he can talk, creatures capable of grasping creation and, analogically, himself in thought, God must give these creatures and, thereby, creation, the nature he has so lovingly made, the capacity to choose their own future, to form and act for reasons, ends, and goals, of their own. Having done so, God steps back, into the shadow of creation, hiding himself in the clouds, allowing for the free exercise of creaturely freedom, the constitution in action of human nature and good, individually and communally, in action. Having placed the future of creation in its own reflective awareness, God waits for the free reciprocity of his continuing, sustaining love – then, as now.

Something subtle is going on here. God is conjuring up the possibility of love: "we have distance for the sake of nearness, autonomy for the sake of exchange and love, irreducible otherness for the sake of genuine union" (von Balthazar 1992: 126). For the first time, God assumes a true risk: this rabbit will not come out of the hat until it chooses of its own free will. The *analogia relationis* becomes fully, irreducibly personal; creation assumes a life, a will, of its own. From now on, the Truth of creation can only be grasped proleptically – in the living-out of a mutuality "too profuse to be caught in the net of any finite concept" (von Balthazar 1992: 251). The wonder of freedom coming to freedom in love, the yet-not-yet, vulnerable, trusting unity of difference.

Creation depends for its completion on a mutuality of trust. Nature, having come to awareness, must trust its Creator. The Creator, in turn, must trust the freedom of his created nature. It is in this trust, the covenant of love, that creation finds its true fulfillment. That it does, however, depends on a logically prior mutuality of freedom. Both parties must be free to reject the other, to walk away from the relationship; otherwise it would not be truly, fully personal. On God's side, this freedom consists in the continuing creation of the world from nothing; the existence of the world depends on the free, unconstrained choice of God, the divine will to mutuality. On our side, this freedom consists in the capacity to live in harmony with God and, thus, our own created nature for no other reason than that this is what we choose, in the mystery of freedom, to do and be.

Thus, the internal dynamic of divine love, its longing for a full reciprocity of love, leads to the presence within nature of a vulnerability not inherent in the concept of finitude. It is not enough for God to love the world into being. For love to exist between God and creation, it is necessary that the world love God in return. The story he tells, the reality he creates, must be reciprocated. That creation has this freedom makes possible its fulfillment and, at the same time, poses a threat to its integrity. Our failure to love God in return is, at core, a rebellion against our true being, the eschatological fulfillment of nature, wild and human.

A FAITHFUL ACT

With the appearance of creaturely freedom a new vulnerability is introduced into creation, one that goes beyond the risk inherent in finitude itself. Along with the possibility of loving relation with God, there arises the possibility of willful rebellion. In actualizing this possibility, humans freely turn nature, their own nature and good, against itself. This twisting of creation must be carefully distinguished from the division and conflict inherent in creation and, therewith, human nature. While God, in remaining faithful to creation, turns sin to our advantage, it is a mistake to believe that humanity is dependent on sin for the realization of its created nature. Sin stands to human freedom like creation stands to divine freedom; in neither case do we find an explanation which goes behind the uncoerced exercise of a free will. Just as there is no explanation for creation other than the freely manifest goodness of God, so there is no explanation for sin other than our willful perversion of human nature. Adam and Eve eat the apple because they want, like us, to do what they please, when, where, and how they please.[37]

In so doing, humans do not, as they think, do it their own way but, rather, act contrary to their own, true way, the grace of God manifest in nature, wild and human. This grace appears to humans, as free, reflective agents, not only ontologically, as it does to all created entities,

---

[37] Though we need not concern ourselves with the details, I would argue that moral evil enters the world *in force* not when Adam and Eve eat the forbidden fruit, that is, with the appearance of *moral error*, but, rather, with the appearance of *moral arrogance* – when having erred, they refuse to admit their error and, instead, hide from God, clinging to the aspiration to be "as gods." Like Saul and unlike David, they refuse to accept the reality of their sin, admit the necessity of living by grace. In that "hiding," the *me on* essential to creation takes the form of an impending *ouk on*, an absolute nothingness defining and, thereby, negating humanity.

but, also, gnoseologically, as an awareness of the normatively laden order, "the natural law," of creation. This innate sense of "the good, true, and right" orients human life and society toward mutuality with God and, therewith, the mutually rewarding, conflictual harmony of creation. That this awareness appears in human beings is not incidental but an integral part of human freedom; its orientation takes the place for humans of what is written, without chance of deviance, in the instinctual nature of other creatures.

That humans have a reflective awareness of the ought embedded in creation is essential to human freedom and responsibility. That this awareness lacks power to compel conformity is also essential to human freedom and responsibility. If moral norms had power to match their authority, the result would not be, as Butler supposes (1950: 41), that morality would rule the world; rather, it would be that human freedom and, therewith, morality ceased to exist. We find in the feebleness of human conscience, an epistemological manifestation of the divine *zimsum* relative to creation-as-a-whole. Not only is it necessary that nature reside in a literally God-forsaken space, God must maintain an epistemic distance from humanity to protect the possibility of freely reciprocated love. That this is so does not require that God keep humanity "in the dark," only that he stay in the shadows, behind a veil, to ensure that his rejection remains a real possibility. Thus, the good, true, and right appear not only fragmented and conflicting but vaguely and uncertainly, as "through a glass, darkly."[38]

Thus, the grace manifest in creation assumes for human beings both an ontological and gnoseological form – leaving humanity with no excuse. When this grace proves insufficient to prevent sin, the created, teleotic harmony of heaven and earth is broken. This, in turn, threatens to transform the relative nothingness of nature into an absolute nothingness. Humanity claims divinity, the right and ability to make creation, wild and human, a mirror of its own glory.[39] Rather than accept the nature and name provided for them, Adam and Eve set aside the *telos* of nature and aspire to become self-constituting realities, gods in their own right. The result is quite different. Once introduced, sin cascades, making it ever more difficult for humanity to grasp the normatively laden

---

[38] See 1 Corinthians 13: 12 (King James Version). The mystery here parallels that found in Exodus 33.

[39] Hence the force of God's questions to Job: "Where were you, where was humanity when I laid the foundations of creation?" (See Job 38–41.) Here we see why a theistic ethics of nature can never be anthropo*centric* in its fundamental orientation.

law of its nature, a reality now hidden behind the false promise of God's vacuous enemy, the *ouk on* of Satan.[40]

God, in response, must either abandon the project of creation or involve himself in the story of creation in a new and redemptive manner. The decision is clear: in creating humans God has already committed himself to go the extra mile.[41] God not only keeps his part of the covenant of creation, his faithfulness extends to the provision of a new covenant, grounded in "soteriological grace." Parallel to the two modalities of constitutive grace, ontological and gnoseological, this soteriological grace assumes a dual form. First, it reconciles humanity to God in the face of sin, pulling creation back from the brink of absolute nothingness. Second, it redeems humanity by providing a path back to God and the fellowship of Eden. Together, constitutive and soteriological grace form the alpha and omega of creation, assuring that the faithfulness of God will not be frustrated. Here, we find the basis for a "new heaven and earth," a renewing of creation that honors and respects the old by bringing it to eschatological fulfillment.

Here, too, of course, we encounter the great diversity of theistic faiths. These faiths offer conflicting, if overlapping answers to the recurrent question of sinful humanity, "what must we do to be saved from the threat of absolute nothingness, the *ouk on*?" Each understands the redemptive grace of God differently and there is no reason to doubt that it makes a difference which faith we call our own.[42] Theistic naturalism, setting

---

[40] The concept of Satan is not incidental to theism and repays careful thought, as regards which see Forsyth 1987. Satan, from the perspective of traditional theism, is a derivative entity, not a co-eternal chaos – on which point see the illuminating discussion in Anderson 1987: 160ff. Milton's image of satanic beings lurking defiantly in hell is, thus, terribly misleading. "Satanic beings" lack substance and, thus, individuality. Rightly understood, they are merely [!] horrifying negations which vanish with the light. Thus, it makes no sense to think of Satan as "redeemed." There is nothing to redeem, only the would-be, yet-never-can-be annulment of God's good creation.

[41] In that sense, Christianly put, while "the cross" is not implied by creation, the creation of humanity can only occur in the shadow of God's reconciling, redemptive love. See Gunton 1992: 93ff.

[42] That we are unable to resolve these differences by way of reasoned argument is a matter for concern but, by no means, despair. Here, it is worth bearing in mind some remarks of Charles Larmore (1996: 216), reflecting on the existence of ineliminable, reasonable disagreement about human nature and good:

that our vision of the good life is the object of reasonable disagreement does not entail that we should withdraw our allegiance to it or regard it as henceforth a mere article of faith. On the contrary, we may still have good reasons to affirm it, based on our experience and reflection. We should remember only that such reasons are not likely to be acceptable to other people who are equally reasonable but have a different history of experience and reflection – just as their basis for their different conceptions of life will not win our assent ... People's grounds for belief aside this concern, affirms from a more generic position that whatever path we follow, the grace imparted has as its goal not the supplanting but, rather, re-enforcing of the covenant made in and with all creation. The story of creation, like the grace manifest in creation, coheres all the way through, start to finish. Thus, while "the world" – as an embodiment of humanity's sinful nature – must and will be overcome by soteriological grace, this involves no repudiation of the world-as-created.[43] The second, derivative covenant concerns humanity's sinful nature, a consequence of the Fall. The first, constitutive covenant encompasses humanity's created nature.

Soteriological grace carries the story of creation forward, in the face of human sin, by introducing both a reconciling, re-constitutive moment and a redemptive, end-oriented moment. Here we find the fullest out-work and ultimate triumph of that divine love which creates and sustains the world at its very core. Here, too, we find the deepest meaning of the divine *zimsum*, that act of humility wherewith the self-constituting, radically Other Creator embraces a mutuality of love with a finite reality. In grace we know that the *analogia relationis*, God's purpose in creation, will not, cannot, be denied. On this all theists agree, thanks be to God.

and action draw upon their different background convictions . . . Reasonable people may thus have good reason to believe in the visions that divide them; they would simply be foolish not to expect that a careful and informed discussion would keep them in disagreement.

While Larmore himself (41 ff.) regards modern society as "beyond religion," "for cosmological and moral purposes" (44), and, further, offers insightful, though not fatal criticisms of ethical holism (Larmore 1987 and 1996), his view of moral reason, as that of Williams 1985, helps overcome rationalistic prejudices against both religious faith and cultural tradition.

43 Murphy distinguishes three senses of "the world" found in the Bible (1989: 15f.): the world of sin and death, the entire human family, and the immense reality of creation. We are particularly concerned here to distinguish between the first and third senses.

PART III

The body of humanity

CHAPTER SIX

Human nature and good

THE BODY OF HUMANITY

Theistic naturalism understands the love of God manifest in nature as a quest for mutuality, the unity of difference. Here we are reminded of Calvin's bold assertion (1960: 58 [I, 5.5]): "it can be said reverently, provided that it proceeds from a reverent mind, that nature is God."[1] Calvin's intent is not to deny the Otherness of God but, rather, portray nature as the outworking in time and space of divine creativity. This, in turn, gives theists strong reason to treat nature, wild and human, with respect. What remains to be settled are the moral particulars and, more broadly, our place in nature-as-a-whole. I explore this issue in two, progressively more inclusive steps.

In this chapter, the focus is on humanity and, especially, the *imago Dei*, the image of God impressed on and borne by human beings. This, I argue, sets us apart, gives us a special responsibility and authority: we cannot fade into the crowd; we are not just one more species. That this is so contains relative to creation-as-a-whole a promise and a threat – for it is in humanity that not only the image of God but, therewith, the relative nothingness, the *me on*, of creation is most clearly manifest. Human beings are the most vulnerable aspect of creation, the linchpin of success and failure. In our will and well-being hangs the fate of nature. Accordingly, we need to inquire more closely regarding human nature and good.

Addressing this question is not only crucial theologically but, no less, ethically. We cannot otherwise determine what our "necessity" justifies nor, thereby, what decency and deference require of us. In theistic naturalism we discover a governing orientation, one that defines human good in terms of our relation with God. It remains to characterize that good

[1] Edward Dowey (1994: 67) notes that for Calvin: "The *ordo naturae* is simply *the orderliness or constancy of God's will within nature.*" It follows that nature, for Calvin as for theistic naturalism, is "both a concept of being and a concept of a norm" (66; citing Brunner 1946: 37) and, further, that "human society is part of the order of nature" (67).

in a more precise, down-to-earth way. What does the good of mutuality with God involve? How are we to understand, here and now, the end for which we were created?

I argue, relative to that end, that humanity – past, present, and future – constitutes a normative whole: we stand together, one and all, before God. This commonality and the special relation to which it gives rise provides a basis for the recognition of distinctively human (status) rights and, therewith, the moral priority of human interests and life. At the same time, however, our commonality is invariably particularized: we cannot grasp what it is to be a human being nor, therewith, live a truly good, fully human life apart from culturally based particularities. The species-encompassing, corporate unity of humanity is internally diverse. One consequence is that what makes for our well-being and, therewith, a morally reasonable use of wild nature is always, to some extent, culturally relative. It is only in the irreducibly diverse particulars of human life that we find a resolution to the problem of moral indeterminacy.

Recognizing this point, relative to human necessity, illumines concerns regarding the other two principles, decency and deference. I engage these in the final chapter, where I argue the diverse and sometimes conflicting interests flagged by all three principles are elements in an all-encompassing, constitutive whole, the great fellowship of creation and extended body of humanity. We are bound together not only corporately and communally but, also, naturally. Only here, in the conflictual harmony of nature-as-a-whole, do we come to understand rightly the dominion of humanity in creation. We need to begin, though, by asking how this responsibility is acquired.

SPEAKING FOR GOD

What does it mean to say human beings are made in the image of God? It is natural to think of this similarity in terms of properties, capacities, that set us apart, make us more god-like than other creatures. Obvious candidates include attributes such as rationality, freedom, and moral agency, traits at the core of theism and its qualified anthropomorphism. In this sense, the claim humans image God by virtue of their substantial, species-defining properties follows from the analogical principle. We are more like God than creatures lacking these properties. It does not follow from this, however, that the *imago Dei*, God's special mark on humanity, consists in this similarity. The *analogia entis* on which our substantive similarity to God rests is a manifestation of and subordinate to the *analogia relationis*. This deeper reality requires us to view human uniqueness in terms of our *relationship* with God (Moltmann 1993: 232f.). This, in turn, shifts attention from our distinctive endowment, to "our unique calling to be in responsible relationship with God, with each other, and with the rest of creation" (Wilkinson 1991: 285).

Some sense of what this relationship involves is provided by Odil Steck, who observes (1980: 102f.) that the designation "image of . . ." served in biblical times as "a titular and functional term, rooted in declarations about kingship"; hence, to designate someone "the image of God" was to convey to him the authority "to represent God to whatever lives beside him in the earthly and horizontal region of creation." To be created in God's image is, thus, not simply or primarily to be god-like, analogically, but, rather, to be set "in an especially close relationship to God" and, in particular, given the task of representing God in creation (Bratton 1986: 62f.; also Gunton 1992: 102f.). Insofar as humans are defined by this relationship, it cannot be evaded or destroyed, not even by human sin: the *imago Dei* and, with it, "the dignity of human beings is unforfeitable, irrelinquishable and indestructible, thanks to the abiding presence of God" (Moltmann 1993: 233). We are constituted by a task, a task like that given to Jonah, from which we are unable to escape, however hard we try, however many times we fail.[2]

This task, an inherently ethical task, has a psychological and social dimension. The latter will be our central concern, relative to both the collective identity of humanity and nature-as-a-whole. In this sense we need to view individual humans as parts of a much larger, corporate whole, not as "images of God" in their own right. Here, reliance on a psychological model can be misleading. By way of explicating our collective, God-given responsibility, however, the psychological, or, personal analogy, proves indispensable for two reasons, one having to do with pre-conditions of the *imago*, the other its exercise.[3]

While it is true a substantialist account of the *imago Dei* fails to grasp the underlying dynamic of creation – in which regard "the only significant theological difference between humans and animals lies in a unique

---

[2] "From a metaphysical point of view the rebellion of man against Heaven is itself proof of man's being made 'in the image of God', to use the traditional formulation" (Nasr 1981: 195).

[3] While agreeing with Jürgen Moltmann's claim that we ought to view the *imago Dei* in terms of a "social analogy," I do not agree with his apparent conclusion (1993: 229ff.) that in doing so we must reject the "psychological analogy." The problem with Augustine's utilization of the psychological analogy and the source of its "far reaching and tragic consequences" for Western theology lies not in the psychological analogy *per se* but, rather, as Moltmann's own observations indicate, in Augustine's portrayal of the *imago Dei* in terms of a soul governing the body and, by extension, world. The psychological analogy is not tied to a substantialist view of the *imago Dei*.

purpose given to humans by God" (Hauerwas and Berkman 1993: 64) – it is also true this purpose presupposes the requisite capacities and, further, that these capacities, so far as we know, are given only to humans. Adam alone is able to name the animals. It follows humanity is not one species among equals and, thus, a relational view of the *imago Dei*, no less than a substantialist, requires the attribution of unique, morally significant properties. What makes a relational account superior is not a denial of human uniqueness but the tieing of our essential nature and, thereby, fulfillment to the all-encompassing mutuality of creation. So viewed, a relational account blocks the assumption that human uniqueness, our analogical similarity to God, isolates us from the cares and concerns of other creatures, transforming them into mere means for our ends. It does so not by denying what is obvious, our differences from them, but, rather, putting our unique capacities in a larger perspective, one defined by our purpose and place in the on-going dynamic of creation.

This normatively laden role requires us, in turn, to draw a moral distinction between "image" and "likeness." Consider in this regard Paul Ramsey's account of the *imago*, offered as an alternative to the historically dominant substantialist model (1950: 255):

The image of God is rather to be understood as a relationship *within which* man sometimes stands, whenever like a mirror he obediently reflects God's will in his life and actions ... The *mirror* itself is not the image; the mirror images; God's image is *in* the mirror. The image of God, according to this view, consists of man's *position* before God, or, rather, the image of God is reflected in man because of his position before him.

On this account, the *imago Dei* only exists when humans are obedient to the will of God; as such, it is *not* a constitutive part of human nature, not a task given to human beings insofar as they are human, but a relation that may be destroyed by sin. On the surface, this account clashes with that given above; there, representation cannot be gotten around, no matter how much our life gets out of focus. On closer inspection, however, the two views turn out mutually illuminating: the constitutive, ethically laden *task* of humanity only makes sense supposing we can fail relative to that task. It is the fact that we bear the responsibility and dignity of speaking for God, that makes it so troubling when we fail to speak as he has spoken.

Consider how this matter gets worked out in Karl Barth's account of the *imago Dei*. Barth, a strong advocate of a relational model, argues (1958: 185) that "the analogy between God and man ... is simply the mutual existence of the I and the Thou in confrontation. This is first constitutive for God, and then for man created by God. To remove it is tantamount to removing the divine from God as well as the human from man."[4] Despite our being *"ordained* to be the covenant partner of God," however, we "are not created the covenant-partners of God but *to be* His covenant-partners" (1960: 320f.; italics added). Whether we achieve our proper end depends, as is true of no other creature, on our free affirmation of that end (Barth 1960: 184):

> While the animals and all the creatures around him praise God the Creator in their manner, by being as God has made them, by remaining true to the law and function of their being, man, if he withdraws from his own determination that God should be glorified in him, represents a void in the divine creation and is an utter failure in his own sphere.

We are called, accordingly, not to bear the image of God – which we cannot avoid – but, rather, bear it faithfully, mirror God in creation. In this sense, as Douglas John Hall observes (1986: 108; citing Kierkegaard 1946: 52): "Kierkegaard rightly summarized the whole discussion of the *imago Dei* when he wrote: '. . . we can resemble God only in loving.'"

That human beings may succeed or fail in this task means they may be more-or-less successful in fulfilling the underlying *telos* and good of human life. The notion of an *imago Dei* is inherently meritarian, part and parcel of the fact humans, unlike others, are held responsible for the life they live. This cannot be avoided by setting aside the substantialist illusion nor, erroneously, eliminating the historic distinction between image and likeness. That it cannot is no cause for concern so long as our evaluations, like the *analogia entis* in general, are kept in perspective. The enemy is not evaluation or comparative merit, any more than it is reason; we want to encourage and reward excellence of every sort. Neither human life nor human society makes any sense apart from evaluative hierarchies.[5] Problems arise not from a recognition of difference or, even, failure but, rather, from a failure to keep differences in perspective and, in particular, understand in our heart of hearts that not only are we all failures in one way or another but, more fundamentally, that the radical Otherness of God relativizes earthly hierarchies, subsuming them within the infinite depth of divine love.

---

4 "Basically and comprehensively, therefore, to be a man is to be with God. . . . To be in sin, in godlessness, is a mode of being contrary to our humanity" (Barth 1960: 135f.).
5 Hall fails to appreciate the extent to which hierarchical orderings and meritarian evaluations are essential and good features of human life – despite their common and distressing abuse. See Fern (1993: 25f. and 35ff.) and, more generally, Sher 1987.

Here it is important to see that the *imago Dei* is not only relational but collective: "If we see man in and for himself, and therefore without his fellows, we do not see him at all" (Barth 1960: 226; also 273, 278; 280). Since humanity only exists "in the encounter of I and Thou," its basic form is not found in individual humans but our "fellow-humanity" (285).[6] Likewise, John Zizioulas (1993: 105) holds "a person cannot be imagined in himself but only within his relationships"; though each is responsible for him- or herself, no person stands alone, not even before God (107): "A human being left to himself cannot be a person . . . The only way for a true person to exist is for being and communion to coincide."[7] Jürgen Moltmann (1993: 216; also 241, 246), calling on distinctively Christian imagery, argues that "human beings are *imago trinitatis* and only correspond to the triune God when they are united with one another" (see also Gunton 1992: 101). It follows, as Charles Murphy puts it (1989: 117), that "life in communion and solidarity with others is the divine model for all earthy existence."[8]

The notion of an inherently relational, communal *imago*, for all its neglect, has deep roots in traditional theism. Claus Westermann observes (1974: 56): "man in the Creation narratives is a collective. Creation in the image of God is not concerned with an individual, but with mankind, the species man . . . Mankind is created to stand before God."[9] This holds true not only of the Creation narratives. Throughout, the Bible deals with human beings as parts of collective, communal entities. Accordingly, we must beware of overly individualistic accounts of salvation, allowing as we do that each of us is really and truly our brother's (and sister's) keeper. A good sense of what this dependency involves, positively and negatively,

[6] Barth (1960: 250ff.) characterizes "fellow-humanity" in terms of (1) the manner in which "one man looks the other in the eye," (2) "mutual speech and hearing," (3) the rendering of "mutual assistance in the act of being," and (4) the doing of all these things "on both sides with gladness." According to Barth (286), the most fundamental form of fellow-humanity, "the only structural differentiation in which [we exist]," is that of men and women. I argue, by contrast, that human beings are more fundamentally differentiated in communal and, thereby, cultural terms: every human, male and female, is inherently incomplete, biologically. Barth's resistance to this point is understandable given the demonic distortion it assumes in the form of National Socialism, as regards which it is imperative to see that the role cultural particularization plays in human life precludes neither normative commonality nor, therewith, the constraint of cultural norms by universal human rights.

[7] Zizioulas (1993: 105) views death as a consequence of "this individualization of nature to which the whole cosmos is subjected." My inclination is to see death as a natural feature of life, an essential passageway to life eternal.

[8] Murphy (1989: 117) attributes the view that "the image of God in humanity is a social one," to His Holiness, John Paul II, citing the Papal Encyclical *Sollicitudo rei socialis*, December 30, 1987, no. 29.

[9] See Westermann (1974: 56ff.) for an informative history of biblical exegesis on this issue.

can be seen in the seemingly archaic notion of "corporate responsibility." I want to comment on and defend this notion in the next section; in doing so I will introduce an irreducibly communal sense of human, normative identity. This, in turn, will prepare the way for an exploration of the role constitutive, cultural traditions play in human life and morality.

HUMAN NATURE

I propose to build our discussion around two biblical stories, both distressing for the way they call seemingly innocent persons to account for the actions of others.[10] The first story involves a man named "Achan," a most unwise thief (Joshua 7). Achan, contrary to the command of God, takes from the wreckage of Jericho, "a goodly Babylonish garment, and two hundred shekels of silver, and a wedge of gold of fifty shekels weight." As a result, God brings about a military disaster and promises to do worse unless, as he puts it to Joshua, "you destroy the accursed from among you"; lots are cast and Achan, his guilt confirmed by a confession, is taken, along with "his sons, and his daughters, and his oxen, and his asses, and his sheep, and his tent, and all that he had," to the valley of Achor, where he and the others are stoned to death, after which "the Lord turned from the fierceness of his anger."

Another similarly distressing instance occurs in the story of a severe famine in Israel during the reign of King David (II Samuel 21: 1–9). David inquires of the Lord regarding the cause and, rather conveniently, discovers that it is a result of the previous king, Saul, having unjustly slain some Gibeonites. Having been told by the Gibeonites that atonement can be made only if they are allowed to hang seven of Saul's sons, David, with the approval of God, delivers them to the Gibeonites and they are hanged in the first days of the barley harvest. Atonement having been made, God lifts the famine he has imposed on the land.

In both cases we have morally questionable behavior attributed to God. This, in turn, raises a question regarding the historical accuracy of the stories: would God really do that? Leaving aside these and related questions, I want to focus on the moral issue posed by holding apparently innocent parties responsible for the behavior of others. Can we make sense of this, morally? Other biblical passages appear to repudiate thoroughly such a notion. According to Mosaic law (Deuteronomy 24:16): "the fathers shall not be put to death for the children, neither

---

[10] All biblical quotations in this section are from the King James Version.

shall the children be put to death for the fathers; every man shall be put to death for his own sin." Similarly, Ezekiel 18: 1–4 informs us:

The word of the Lord came unto me again, saying, "What mean you, that you use this proverb concerning the land of Israel, saying, The fathers have eaten sour grapes, and the children's teeth are set on edge?" "As I live," saith the Lord God, "you shall not have occasion any more to use this proverb in Israel. Behold, all souls are mine: as the soul of the father, so also the soul of the son is mine; the soul that sinneth, it shall die."

The tension between these two sets of passages is commonly explained by attributing those affirming individual responsibility to a subsequent, more developed stage: the Israelites come to see that each person is responsible for what he does, not the deeds of another.[11] While I see no need to deny that some such realization occurred, I want to argue the two sets of passages are not, as commonly assumed, inconsistent and, further, that the centrality of individual responsibility for ethics does not rule out a suitably nuanced notion of corporate responsibility.

Supposing we ask ourselves what is troubling about the stories of Achan and Saul's seven sons, the basic idea is simple: it is not fair that someone be punished for what someone else did. This line of argument is prima facie persuasive and, indeed, forms a bedrock of any just criminal law. The apparent absence of concern with this basic principle renders these stories problematic. It does not, however, show the presumed notion of corporate responsibility is inherently flawed. Indeed, it is an accepted principle of tort and criminal law that in some circumstances persons are responsible for the actions of others. One such situation involves the notion of *respondeat superior*, affirming the responsibility of a "master" for the actions of his "servant"; this is a matter of "delegated authority."[12] A second situation involves "joint endeavors" and the dispersion among partners of responsibility for the actions of one another.[13] Our participation in arrangements of these sorts makes us accountable for the actions of other individuals.

What differentiates these situations from the biblical stories is the presence of a "moral trigger," an initiating act, be it the hiring of an

---

[11] This insight would parallel that of the Greek Achilles, who, Homer tells us, is brought to see the importance for moral judgment (and punishment) of intentionality.

[12] If you, acting for me under power of attorney, sell my house, I am bound, legally and morally. Likewise, if you pay someone to kill another, you are as guilty of murder as the killer.

[13] As in the case of business partnerships, by contrast with the law of corporations. Another example is provided by "felony murder," whereby a person only incidentally involved in the death of another can be held responsible for that death.

agent or willing participation in a joint endeavor. No such trigger exists in the biblical stories.[14] Achan's family, like Saul's sons, just happen to be related to the wrong people. Might a morally relevant link exist in such cases? Finding it will require us to take a closer look at the different ways in which one individual can be related to and, thereby, affect others for better or worse. What we find is not only a greater vulnerability to the actions of others but, also, a pivotal and often overlooked reason why the same Bible that consigns Achan's family and Saul's sons to death displays a strong and abiding concern for those who are poor and socially marginalized.

First and most obviously, we can be affected *extrinsically*, subject to a harm or benefit that does not depend on anything we do and, further, can be described independent of our relation to the one who harms or benefits us. A good example is provided by the following rabbinic story:

Rabbi Simeon bar Yohai taught: There is a story about men who were sitting on a ship, one of them lifted up a borer and began boring a hole beneath his seat. His companions said to him: "What are you sitting and doing?" He replied to them: "What concern is it of yours, am I not drilling under my seat?" They said to him: "But the water will come up and flood the ship for all of us."[15]

Here, the harm to which the borer's companions are exposed is extrinsic and, as such, might have been caused by the passing of a meteorite.

Second, we can be affected *intrinsically*, subject to a harm or benefit that can be described independent of our relation to the one who harms or benefits us, as true of extrinsic affects, but which, unlike extrinsic affects, depends on what we do. A striking example is provided, positively, by the process of moral education; another, negatively, by that of moral corruption; still others by the situations, presented above, of *respondeat superior* and joint endeavors. Here, the affect is dependent on what we do, be this an initiating "moral trigger" or a subsequent "moral upshot." In the case of intrinsic affects, our willing involvement generates personal responsibility.

Third, we can be affected *constitutively*, subject to a harm or benefit that, like extrinsic but unlike intrinsic affects, does not depend on anything we do but cannot, unlike both extrinsic and intrinsic affects, be described independently of our relation to the one who harms or benefits

---

[14] We might, of course, presume that such a trigger exists but that would make our task too easy and the corresponding notion of corporate responsibility too weak.

[15] This story appears in Kaminsky 1995b, which opened my eyes on a number of related concerns; see also Kaminsky 1995a.

us. Constitutive affects occur only in forms of association that have a "common good," a good that cannot be defined apart from the relation: thus, the distinctive good of marriage, as that of political community, cannot be characterized in extrinsic or intrinsic terms. In such contexts, the upshot of actions by one may be transferred to others independent of anything they do; this transfer takes place automatically, across a web of constitutive relations. Let me give an example.

When Tryal Pore, a resident of seventeenth-century Massachusetts, begs forgiveness of fellow colonists for her act of fornication, she acknowledges that like Achan she has called the wrath of God down on the community (Morgan 1966: 10). In thinking of God's wrath, however, she has in mind not primarily extrinsic and intrinsic harms, like bad weather and moral corruption, which the Puritans in good biblical tradition commonly attribute to the wrath of God, but, rather, first and foremost, the wounding of Christ's body, the violation of her community's constitutive covenant with God and one another. This is troubling to her and her fellow colonists whatever other effects it has because it breaks the morally limed bond of love uniting them with one another and, above all, God. What she does, what each of them do, affects the others immediately, constitutively, by virtue of its significance for their common, communal identity. Simply by virtue of being what they are, they become responsible for and vulnerable to the actions of others.

That we can make sense, morally, of this now uncommon notion of a shared, communal identity and resultant responsibility is seen in our own society's requirement that wartime reparations be paid by Germans and Japanese who were not personally responsible for the war or crimes committed therein. A similar presumption appears in the claim that African-Americans ought to be compensated for the evil of slavery – or native peoples for the dispossession of their ancestors by colonizing Europeans. In such cases, some individuals are required to compensate others for harms done by individuals to individuals none of whom are any longer alive. Even if we presume, as clearly appears to be the case in general, that these harms and benefits have been passed down the line, generationally, we still must presume that the moral responsibility to rectify these wrongs is transferred to persons who were not only not involved but not even alive at the time they occurred.[16] In short, the only

---

[16] In addition, by virtue of treating the people involved as members of groups, not as discrete individuals, we dismiss numerous complicating factors – such as the historical fact that some blacks were involved in the slave trade and, even, slaveholders while many whites were not and, even, some so strongly opposed to slavery they died to eradicate it.

way we can make sense, morally, of these "group reparations" is to treat the individuals involved as members of trans-generational communal entities wherein responsibility for the actions of some are shared by all. And this makes perfectly good sense – in some cases.[17] Paul Taylor (1986: 263, 304ff.) even argues, persuasively to me, that humans ought to make restitution to other species for the destruction of natural habitat.[18]

That the notion of communally shared responsibility is applied wrongly at times does not mean it makes no sense. Thus, that the penalty imposed on Achan's family and Saul's sons was, it appears, excessive does not mean those involved did not bear some measure of responsibility for what their kin did – any more than the fact, if it is a fact, that capital punishment is wrong means it is wrong to punish murderers. Perhaps the family of Achan should have taken part in an act of public contrition; perhaps the sons of Saul ought to have paid reparations to the tribe their father unjustly harmed. Accepting this would not mean we must reject the idea of individual responsibility or, even, deny its centrality for ethics. Neither corporate nor individual responsibility by itself captures the full truth about human life and community. The latter assures us, from a theistic point of view, that the relation of individuals to God is not ultimately vulnerable to the actions of others.[19] This does not entail, as the former implies, that with regard to the communal good of relationship with God and one another we are not ultimately dependent, as in marriage, on the actions of others, regardless of what we do.[20] That this is so makes us vulnerable to the faults of others and gives each of us reason to keep an eye on how others are doing, morally and otherwise.

The displeasure with which we moderns tend to view such "holy watching" must be counterbalanced by what we lack in attentiveness to the well-being of others. Achan and Saul's families are done in by the same strong sense of community which moves biblical prophets to protest

[17] Everything depends on the cohesiveness of the groups involved and the specificity of harms done. Thus, it makes more sense to require reparations be paid to the Oglala Sioux for broken treaty agreements by the U.S. government (and, thereby, the American people in general) than it does to require reparations be paid to women (in general) by men (in general) for the historic abuse of women by men. The issue is similar to that found in "class action suits." For more on this issue, and the topic of corporate responsibility in general, see May 1987.

[18] This moral requirement is reflected, in part, in the legal requirement developers of ecologically sensitive areas, such as wetlands, set aside and/or restore other, similar habitats.

[19] Note that Ezekiel 18 and Deuteronomy 24 are composed near or during the time of exile and, as such, reflect a radical change in cultural context.

[20] Note the role played by the earlier stories of Joshua 7 and II Samuel 21 in the formation of a religious and cultural identity.

the failure of society to treat justly those members of the community who are poor and vulnerable. Their point is not simply that wealthy individuals have failed to do as they ought but, more fundamentally, that *the community*, represented by unholy kings, has failed to act properly. Here, the ascription of individual responsibility undermines social unity: not only are we no longer responsible for what our brother does, we are no longer our brother's keeper.[21] At this level, the recognition of corporate responsibility, a responsibility shared by all members of the community, is an integral part of the thick relationality which enables us to call on some to sacrifice their life and goods for the sake of others.

We encounter here the much neglected notion of an irreducibly communal normative identity. The "normative identity" of an entity makes possible the attribution to it of evaluative terms: *that* painting is beautiful; *that* tree is doing better since the rain; *that* dog was naughty; *that* person owes *me* ten dollars. What can be meaningfully attributed to an object depends on the kind of normative identity it has; it makes no sense to claim a tree or dog owes you money.[22] Likewise, what can be truthfully attributed to an object depends on that object's normative identity: we must succeed in capturing the right "that." To the extent we fail to perceive the normative identity of an entity, we are normatively blind, unable to find our way around in normative space.

The above notion of normative identity is distinct from that of personal identity, a necessary but not sufficient condition for the normative continuity of persons.[23] Consider, for instance, "brainwashing." Here, a normative discontinuity impedes the attribution of responsibility: "it wasn't me that did it."[24] A similar discontinuity appears in some cases of mental illness; hence, the plea of "temporary insanity." By far the most important departure of normative and personal identity, however, occurs with regard to corporate responsibility and, more generally, irreducibly

---

[21] Think in this regard of practices used in the military to generate *esprit de corps*: when one person messes up (does well), everyone pays (benefits); one for all, all for one – no bodies left behind.

[22] Though a trust fund set up for the tree or dog might. The normative identity of teleotic objects follows their objectively determined good. In the case of selves and sentients this amounts to a well-being of their own. In the case of persons, it involves a full set of moral relations.

[23] This parallels the relation between physical and personal identity: physical identity (material continuity) is a necessary but not sufficient condition of personal identity. The dead body of Josephine is not Josephine.

[24] Put on trial for her participation in a bank robbery while a captive of the SLA, Patty Hearst does not deny that it was she, physically and personally, holding the gun. What she claims is that she was not herself, normatively speaking, and, thus, that she, herself, should not be held responsible for what she did. Note the difference between this and claiming that her body had actually been taken over by another person.

communal, shared normative identities. In such cases the normative identity of individuals embraces more than their personal identity; this is what makes them responsible for the actions of others with whom they share a common normative identity. Responsibility flows freely along lines of constitutive relationship. That it does is an often overlooked but vital part of human nature and good. I want now to say a brief word about how this takes place.

CULTURE-AS-NATURE

Constitutive relationships and the common goods to which they give rise involve more-or-less structured, communal processes that shape the normative identity of those individuals who are integral parts of and components in them.[25] These processes, or, traditions, can be viewed, like natural processes in general, piece-by-piece, as *tradita*, or holistically, as *traditio*. Unlike wild natural processes, however, it is necessary to distinguish between an *etic*, external perspective, and an *emic*, internal perspective. The first is that of an onlooker, say, an anthropologist; the second is that of a participant and adherent.[26] In this sense every tradition has, like selves and sentients, an inside-out; for traditions, however, this inside-out is perspectival, not experiential. Every tradition has a point-of-view, an *ethos*, that defines its identity and shapes its unfolding over time. Adoption of this *ethos* is part of what makes one an adherent of a given tradition. No tradition would exist apart from its affirmation by adherents; it is this which gives rise to an inside-out, emic perspective.

What does it mean to affirm a tradition? At core it means to adopt as one's own a given, more-or-less determinate, more-or-less comprehensive pattern of behavior, an established way of doing and seeing things – it means, in short, to accept as authoritative a set of communally instantiated beliefs and values. Where this authority is non-derivative, we encounter constitutive, cultural traditions; these give substance to life-encompassing, essentially self-sustaining, communal forms of life. Where the authority is derivative, we encounter (merely) formative traditions.[27] These traditions are non-comprehensive and, thus,

---

[25] I am indebted in this and the following three sections to a wide range of sources, including Berger 1969, Berger and Luckmann 1967, Eliot 1968, Erikson 1962 and 1963, Fleischacker 1994, Niebuhr 1951, Shils 1981 and 1982, and Wittgenstein 1958.

[26] The same individual may, of course, adopt both an emic and etic perspective, as reflective persons commonly do.

[27] There are, I suggest, four pivotal kinds of (merely) formative traditions, two instrumental – the political and the economic – and two ideal – the academic and the religious.

dependent on a cultural *ethos* for essential skills – linguistic, conceptual, and practical.[28] The authority of formative traditions is grounded, independently, in an idealized reflection, academic and/or religious. Thus, in a formative tradition, it is always possible (in principle) to give the justifying rationale for an established practice. This allows for the externalization and rationalization of formative traditions in ways not true of constitutive, cultural traditions, which explains why some have thought it desirable and possible to view culture in (merely) formative terms, as a "social compact" or the instantiation of a divinely given law.[29]

Constitutive, cultural traditions are most easily conceived as linguistic communities. While this is not without considerable ambiguity of its own, it is a good starting point for the simple but profound reason that individual humans come to be the selves they are in and through their acquisition of a language, which is to say, by virtue of their participation in a linguistic community. Our culture is embedded in the way we talk and, correspondingly, think. Were cultures to be sealed hermetically, they would be differentiated linguistically, as holds true of primitive tribes and premodern civilizations in general. More recently, with the rapid onset of globalization, cultural isolation and diversity are disappearing, their place being taken, at least on the surface, by a common commercial culture and an increasingly dominant language, English. This change, while extremely important in many regards, does not alter the relation between culture and language. Nor, for that matter, does the distinction between socially undifferentiated and strongly unified tribal cultures and the more loosely unified, vocationally specialized, and socially stratified national cultures (of so-called civilized societies).[30]

We are ready now to formulate the thesis of sociality. This thesis holds that the human self is a product of interaction with significant others in a normatively structured, cultural context. Apart from this interaction,

---

[28] This is one reason formative traditions appear later in the development of selfhood than constitutive, cultural traditions. It is also why adherence to formative traditions is more typically dependent on a voluntary exercise of will.

[29] The distinction between constitutive and formative traditions is complicated by, one, the presupposition of constitutive elements by the latter and, two, the incorporation of formative elements by the former (for purposes of legitimation and transformation). What differentiates these two kinds of tradition is not their content, which in many cases overlaps, but their mode of justification, the epistemic authorities on which they rely.

[30] Among other things, the latter are distinguished by the appearance of relatively independent, well-defined formative traditions, instrumental and ideal. The resultant "structural pluralism" inevitably leads to weaker social ties and a need for the official, force-backed legitimations, subtle and not so subtle, so evident in the modern nation state. For more on the historical complexities involved in attempts to define "culture," see Fleischacker 1994: 115–148.

human individuals would not acquire the linguistic and, more broadly, relational capacities essential for human life and society. In this regard, human beings, unlike social insects, such as ants and bees, are underdetermined by their genetic heritage. Like our fellow social mammals, such as wolves and chimpanzees, we depend on a process of socialization, only much more so, amounting in our case to "enculturation."[31] This complex process occurs, simply put, in three stages, each corresponding to one dimension of a three-dimensional cultural *ethos*; I designate these stages/dimensions, the ecotic, the alethic, and the teleotic.[32] Together they generate and sustain the communal, normative identity of persons.

In the first, ecotic stage, the human child has her behavior shaped (molded) to conform in broad outline to that expected in her particular cultural context. Hopis are raised as Hopis; Bostonians as Bostonians. As a result of this process, the child is gradually transformed from a "howlin', smilin' bundle" of biologically given needs and impulses into a recognizably social creature, a "miniature adult." This transformation is marked by a gradual introduction to and participation in social activities; it is symbolized by changes in dress and accompanied by the development of linguistic skills.

Structurally, this change presupposes the ecotic dimension of a cultural *ethos*. This, simply put, is the normatively governed pattern of behavior that distinguishes one society from another. This "ecotic patterning" consists in not only externally observable behavior, the phenotype of society, but, therewith, a shared set of beliefs and values, the underlying, significance-laden genotype of society. It is this culturally authoritative, normatively laden patterning that embodies the epistemic authority of constitutive, cultural traditions, as argued below. To grasp the full meaning and force of this ascription, however, it is necessary to see that the ecotic dimension acquires ethotic force, becomes an *ethos*, only in relation to the remaining two dimensions.

In the second, alethic stage of development, the child becomes reflective and, especially important, acquires a sense of right and wrong, a conscience and, with it, a morality, namely, the morality of (what amounts

---

[31] It follows – a point of great interest relative to the current globalization/commercialization of human culture – that human life and society, no matter how well positioned materially, cannot survive apart from coherent constituting cultures: neither man nor woman can live by bread alone.

[32] These stages and dimensions are "rational reconstructions" and, as such, deliberate simplifications of an extremely complex, layered process. In reality, the stages and dimensions are intermingled, as seen in Erik Erikson's eight-stage epigenetic model of development (1963: 189–274).

in her culture to) common-sense. The child also acquires at this time a developing curiosity about how things work and, more generally, a need to find what "reality" lies behind "the appearances," where, for instance, the food we eat comes from – and where it goes once the toilet is flushed, so forth and so on. Here the child develops a capacity to distinguish truth from falsehood, both by virtue of a new ability to think critically and, equally important, absorb a fund of basic, culturally embodied knowledge. In the process, children learn from significant others "the where and why" of established practices, beliefs, and values, coming as they do to affirm their culture from an emic, inside-out, point of view.

Structurally, this change presupposes the alethic dimension of a cultural *ethos*. The alethic dimension, unlike the ecotic, is inherently evaluative; as such, it distinguishes across-the-board between appearance and reality. This links the alethic to the linguistic and, more narrowly, propositional elements of society, the truth-claims on which it rests. The resultant processes of critical reflection allow culture to transcend limitations present in its ecotic patterning, thereby transforming the (merely) ecotic into a normatively laden *ethos*. Guided by charismatic faith and generic reason, shaped by the goal of reflective equilibrium, the alethic dimension functions like a compass needle, pointing beyond the cultural tradition it legitimatizes, giving normative depth to otherwise meaningless patterns of behavior.

In the third, teleotic stage, the child comes to acquire a particularized identity, a sense of her place in the culture and, therewith, world-at-large. This process is complex, involving all elements and aspects of human life, including, among others, the social (class), the religious (church), the familial (marriage), and the vocational (career). Here the child becomes an initiated member of society, with all the responsibilities and privileges of an adult occupying her particular place and role in society. The successful completion of this process positions an individual for the living of what amounts in that culture to a distinctively human life.[33] Here, we call on skills and dispositions acquired earlier to address difficulties and, hopefully, live what amounts, for us, here and now, to a good life.[34]

Structurally, this change presupposes the teleotic dimension of a cultural *ethos*. This sets the particularized end, or *telos*, of human life and,

---

[33] Typically it is possible during this stage to address some, though not all deficiencies relative to the first two stages. Historically, human cultures, like wild nature, have relied heavily on redundancy, a wisdom lost in the foolish efficiencies of modern society.

[34] For eons, this process was completed early which, in turn, allowed for procreation while individuals were young and vigorous, a process expedited by the relative simplicity of life. In modern, socially differentiated and technologically advanced societies we find, by contrast, an extended, frequently stormy "adolescence."

thereby, the underlying dynamic for the first two stages and dimensions, which apart from it lack a particular, cultural identity. The ecotic dimension, as a patterning, remains open to a variety of interpretive possibilities. The range of *viable* possibilities is determined by the alethic dimension, which evaluates possible trajectories of meaning in terms of their worth and likelihood of realization. Neither of these, however, provides for a determinate trajectory and, thereby, a normative continuity between past and future.[35] Here, a stance must be taken, a choice made as to who we are, individually and collectively, past, present and future.[36] It is only with this constitutive affirmation, in the interwoven narrative unity of self and other, that a particularized human nature and good appears.

HUMAN GOOD

The thesis of sociality is a socio-psychological hypothesis regarding the origin and structure of human selves. While there are serious questions regarding the details and, surely therewith, the above, oversimplified account, the thesis is not, in general, contentious. I want now to make some contentious claims regarding the normative upshot of this constitutive process.[37] These have to do with the scope of moral concerns, the sources of moral authority and the nature of human good. Let me begin with the last.

An interest in what makes for human good is not incidental but central to an ethics of nature. One reason is that our well-being is no less natural than that of other creatures: culture itself is a natural phenomenon. Hence, any ethics of nature that aspires to completeness must concern itself with not only wild but human nature. Another reason is that we cannot ascertain what use we are justified in making of wild nature unless we know what makes for human well-being and, thereby, what necessity

---

35 Borrowing freely from Aristotle, we can say: the ecotic dimension provides the "material cause" of a cultural tradition, the basic stuff, the "sociality" of which human societies are made. The alethic dimension, being ideal and evaluative, constitutes the "formal cause"; it gives normative shape and direction to the raw material of human life. The teleotic dimension, being projective, constitutes the "final cause," the particularized end for which a culture exists and, thereby, gives it a determinate identity. The efficient cause operative in this process is, throughout, love and, more specifically, a proleptic, constitutive love. Humanity, like God, only derivatively so, loves itself into existence, in whole and in part.

36 This choice is not – let me stress – unconditional; its parameters are set by the ecotic and alethic. That we can and must choose, does not mean we can choose to be anything, individually or collectively. Human lives and, more fundamentally, cultures differ in the range and kind of "live possibilities" they provide.

37 For more on the normative implications of human sociality, see the close analysis and illuminating argument in Gilbert 1989 and 1996 and, also, Kekes 1989 and 1993.

does and does not justify. There is little point in knowing that wild nature counts morally if we are unable to determine how much it counts, when and where, in comparison to our own morally significant interests and lives. Still another, more positive reason is that a knowledge of human good is required to see the role constitutive relations play in human society and, therewith, that "care for the natural world is constitutive of a flourishing human life" (O'Neill 1993: 24).

What makes for human well-being? I purpose to defend four theses – the feel-good, do-well, do-good, and be-content theses – and identify three conditions – continuity, truth, and community. To begin, it is evident that the well-being of sentient creatures cannot be understood apart from the "felt quality" of their lives. We take pleasure in the satisfaction of our desires, displeasure in their frustration – be this a first-order desire for pecan pie or a higher-order desire for the will-power to stay on our diet. What counts here, relative to satisfaction, is how we feel from the inside-out – the pain, the joy, the hope, the despair – in short, our subjective, mental state, or, loosely put, "happiness."[38] The "happenings" and "havings" which contribute (or take away from) our happiness matter a great deal. No one can live a truly good, fully human life who is not, in general, satisfied with her life from the inside-out, who finds herself to be really, truly unhappy. I will refer to this as "the feel-good thesis."

The feel-good thesis conveys an important truth about human well-being: how we feel matters. At the same time, as the various qualifiers indicate, it is not enough, so far as well-being goes, to feel good here and now. We must also, at the least, take into account how this positive state unfolds over time, subjectively and objectively. For one thing, for the satisfaction of desire to make us really, truly happy we must not be distracted by the thought of impending disaster; however fine, the last meal of a condemned man rarely makes for happiness. More positively, deprivation itself may intensify the value of a future good, be it by way of contrast, deferred gratification, or the associated thrill of accomplishment. At all these levels, of course, we may be forced to choose between conflicting desires, be it with regard to pecan pie or the kind of job we hold. It follows that satisfaction, "feeling good," cannot be conceived in a straightforward, linear fashion.

Even if we could understand satisfaction in a one-dimensional way, however, it would be an error to equate a person's happiness at any

---

[38] I use the term "happiness" in the modern, narrow, subjective sense. My use of the term "well-being" corresponds to the older, broader usage, as in Aristotle's *eudaemonia*; see Annas 1993: 43–46.

particular time with their well-being. The reason, simply put, is that well-being concerns the larger scope of life; that a manic-depressive is ecstatic does not mean his life is going well. Thus, Aristotle, citing the example of Croesus, advises us to judge no one's life good until they are dead. Well-being requires more than a momentary state of feeling good: to be in a state of well-being it is necessary that a person not only be "happy," in some requisite sense, but, no less, secure relative to that happiness.[39] We can summarize this "condition of continuity" as follows: to be in a state of well-being a person must be in "good health," not about to fall off the wall and splatter, like a smiling, careless Humpty Dumpty. As to whether someone is in a secure position, that depends on the facts, not (simply) on how she feels.

Together the feel-good thesis and the condition of continuity identify necessary and minimal conditions for well-being. Are they sufficient? Does secure, continuing happiness make for well-being? I want to argue that it does not. For one thing, we need to reckon with the possibility of ignorance and deception; what if our state of mind, our continuing happiness, depends on not knowing the truth about ourselves? Does it matter so far as well-being is concerned? Consider the following example, posed by Peter Carruthers (1992: 78):

Suppose that Kurt is married to Philippa, and wants very much that Philippa should be faithful to him. Philippa, however, has other ideas, and carries on a love affair with another man without Kurt discovering. Suppose that nothing in Philippa's relationship with Kurt ever suffers as a result – so far as Kurt is concerned, things are just as they would have been if Philippa had in fact been faithful to him throughout. Is Kurt harmed by Philippa's infidelity, merely because his desire that she should be faithful to him is objectively frustrated, and despite the fact it is subjectively satisfied?

Carruthers concludes that he is not and, hence, that his well-being has not suffered as a result of Philippa's deception. My view, to the contrary, is that Kurt, though unaware of it, has suffered a genuine harm. His life is worse than it might have been had he not been deceived in a matter of such importance.

What makes it seem plausible to deny that Kurt has "suffered" a harm is that we associate *suffering* with a felt quality; in this sense, Kurt clearly

---

39 William Galston remarks (1980: 69): "The presence [of the totality of what appears good] must be secure and enduring; we are not satisfied if what appears good is (or is felt to be) in danger of being removed from us. Second, what appears good when absent must continue to appear good when present."

does not suffer a loss. How is he harmed? It is necessary here to distinguish "hurts" and "deprivations." The paradigmatic example of a hurt is pain, physical and mental. Since pain causes a decreased quality of life (in that respect), we can readily see that harm has occurred and, accordingly, empathize with the individual harmed. The issue is more complicated as regards deprivations. Deprivations, though often involving a strong sense of loss where awareness is present, do not hurt at all when, like Kurt, we are unaware of them. That deprivations may cause serious loss, however, is clear, even where awareness is absent. Regan (1983: 97) cites the example of "a bright young woman . . . reduced to the condition of a contented imbecile by painless injections of debilitating drugs." Though there is no point at which the young woman suffers or, for that matter, has any awareness of her loss, it is impossible to deny she has been harmed.[40]

Suppose, though, as in Robert Nozick's "experience machine,"[41] someone has consented to the treatment in hope of finding relief for a deep-seated psychic distress or, more positively, becoming a delusional yet experientially delighted participant in her own, custom-designed virtual reality.[42] She is perfectly happy and, per hypothesis, will remain so. How, then, even supposing we would not prefer that sort of life, can we deny that she is living what for her amounts to a truly good, fully human life? Not only is there no overt suffering, there need be no deprivation, experientially; we can program in any life we want.[43] Why does it matter that the person is lying inert, her life and mind sustained by a machine? What is the loss relative to well-being?

Responding to a similar question, Peter Wenz (1988: 282) argues that few people would trade real life for such a state. According to Wenz, "This is because (most) people value more than just good experiences. They value good experiences which are *not delusional*, that is, which relate to a reality external to the human mind the way that waking experiences (presumably) do and dream experiences do not. For such people, myself

---

[40] One can generalize this to a concern with the invidious effects of sexism and, more generally, all social orders which form people in ways which make it difficult, if not impossible for them to realize their full potential.

[41] The experience machine is a device which enables one to design her own "virtual reality" and, then, "plug in." We presume that the machine is flawless and will not, by error or malice, result in experiences other than those programmed. The catch is that once plugged in you cannot be unplugged and, thus, will spend the rest of your life in a state of radical delusion, convinced you are an active participant with others in some objective world, while in reality you are lying on a slab, attached to a machine. See Nozick 1974: 42–45.

[42] Imagine the machine has been programmed to allow one to experience (what one takes to be) the beatific vision, a state of perfect, eternal harmony with God.

[43] In this respect the experience machine is analogous to the Hollideck.

included, experience is not the sole measure of good." On this view, which I share, knowing the truth becomes a condition of well-being, at least insofar as not knowing it changes the basic meaning and significance of our life. This condition is commonly called on in objections to religious faith, the claim being that it is better for humans to face the hard reality of life without God than to find comfort and, even, happiness in the false belief that God is there, caring for us, working to see that our needs are met. If this is so, it surely follows that those who plug into the experience machine suffer serious loss. Correspondingly, there is good reason to believe Kurt is harmed by Philippa's adultery even if and precisely because he remains unaware of the truth about his and her life together.[44]

Recognizing the condition of truth is vital not only in its own right but, also and especially, because it shows we care about "what we do and are" not only because of the way it makes us feel but, also and fundamentally, because we care about what we do and are in their own right, really and truly.[45] That we do requires us to supplement the feel-good thesis with two others, one focused on power *qua* efficacy of action, the other on value *qua* worthiness of life. I call these, respectively, the "do-well" and "do-good" theses. The first tells us that our capacity to achieve, really and truly, the ends we pursue matters to well-being; this is not simply a matter of the satisfaction we get from so doing but, more fundamentally, the skill and power we manifest in the process. The second thesis says the same as regards the quality and excellence of the ends we pursue and, therewith, the life we live: success in the pursuit of meaningless or evil ends, however happy it makes one, does not make for well-being.

That we must take into account, along with "happenings" and "havings," "doings" and "be-ings," reflects the distinctive nature of human life.[46] The living of a truly good, fully human life will reflect the

---

[44] In some cases this loss might be justified by the horrible cost of knowing the truth. In one *Star Trek* episode, a severely injured starship captain chooses to remain with aliens and continue living out the pleasant delusion they have created for him rather than return to a life of sheer, useless misery. Such cases, far from undermining the condition of truth, support it by showing how extreme the cost must be before we are willing to opt for delusion.

[45] Thus, experiences induced by the experience machine lack value relative to the real thing in precisely the same way as those on the Hollideck. The reward we get from "doing X" and "being Y" invariably depends on the value we ascribe to "doing X" and "being Y" in their own right, independent of the pleasure they actually bring – as argued by Joseph Butler (1950: 12ff.) in his justly famous refutation of "psychological hedonism." For informative critiques of the appeal to preference satisfaction in cost-benefit analysis, see O'Neill 1993: 44–122 and Sagoff 1988: 99–123.

[46] Note that the first two involve "extrinsic affects," the second two, "intrinsic affects." In a moment I will call on the notions of community and contentment to introduce "constitutive affects."

entirety of human nature, of who and what we are all the way through. Our well-being, as self-reflective agents, cannot consist solely in what happens to us. If it did, there would be no qualitative difference between the well-being of humans and that of merely sentient creatures. To the contrary, as Aristotle saw, the good of each creature must reflect the distinctive shape and form of that creature's life. Thus, human well-being must involve the characteristically human excellences, the source of our pride and, no less, shame.[47]

This points beyond continuity and truth to a third condition of well-being, community. That our efficacy and worthiness matter in their own right suggests that what is most troubling about the experience machine is not its reliance on deception but the absence therein of genuine personal relations.[48] Clearly, the case for plugging into the experience machine is strengthened insofar as the delusion created is, *à la* Durkheim, genuinely communal. In such a case we would have to presume that the illusion shared allows *us* to recognize "who is who" and, moreover, know enough about ourselves and the world in which we live so that the relations formed are real.[49] If those with whom we come into contact are nothing more than projections, if they have no possibly recalcitrant reality of their own, we have not entered into a world of personal relations. Nor, thereby, will it be a world in which we can achieve anything real, worthy or not. Insofar, then, as we value genuine social relations, view them and the kind of things they make possible as indispensable parts of our well-being, we are forced, so long as we accept the truth condition, to accept that of community.

How important is community to human well-being? To begin, the range of satisfactions, doings and be-ings characteristic of what is normally taken to be a truly good, fully human life only makes sense for a life involved in communal, constitutive relations. The goods of parenting and citizenship, for instance, require community for their realization. While we can get by with "mere association" in some cases, tennis partners and such, attempting to do so across the board results in a diminished life: the "highs" are lower, the "achievements" less. In some cases, of course, the cost associated with constitutive relationality may be so high

---

[47] Hence the force of John Stuart Mill's observation: better Socrates dissatisfied than a pig satisfied – though I would argue in this regard that the well-being of Mill's pig, a mere self, depends on more than what happens to it, albeit not to the same extent or in the same way as human well-being.

[48] Correspondingly, Philippa's deception, like that of Tyral Pore, is troubling primarily because of the constitutive harm it does to a special relation.

[49] This, in turn, makes it difficult, relative to personal relations, to imagine a world more delusional than our own.

that we are better off avoiding "the ties that bind" – as a person dying of cancer and in horrible pain may be advised to opt for mind-numbing, delusion-creating drugs. Such a truncated life is, however, far from ideal. What would it mean if the best we could do was to live alone, free from all attachments? Would that not be the greatest slavery, the worst life of all?[50]

It is difficult to see how anyone, given the social conditions of human life, could live a truly good, fully human life apart from irreducibly communal, constitutive goods such as friendship, family and civil society. A life devoid of such attachments is not likely to be happy, successful, or worthy of praise; indeed, little if any is left of human life apart from thick relationships of this sort. Mutuality not only makes for intense, lasting happiness, it is the single most important background condition for meaningful, worthy endeavors. What pleasure, what success – however great – is not rendered bittersweet by the absence of someone special to share it with? What pleasure, what success – however small or trivial – is not enriched by true love?[51] In brief, a life apart from the good of community, no matter how angelic in other terms, is not a truly good, fully human life.

All else being equal, thick community increases the value of what goes to make a human life meaningful and good. In addition, community plays a vital role relative to what might well be called the capstone of well-being, contentment. The importance of this element becomes clear once we realize "satisfactions," "doings," and "be-ings" not only contribute to well-being but, in so doing, pose a threat. This is most apparent with regard to the element of satisfaction: no matter how graced we are it is inevitable that we will eventually want something we do not have, a good that lies beyond our grasp. Since we cannot have all that we might have, we must, if we are to be happy, be content at some point with what we have. Otherwise we will be like a person eating fine chocolates who can only think of the pieces she has yet to eat.

A similar problem arises with regard to the other elements of well-being. At some point we have to accept the risk of life and, correspondingly, the limited security we have. Similarly, unless we fall prey to the error of thinking we "know it all," we have to live with the inevitability of ignorance and error. Contentment, at core, is a matter of humility, not humility in the false sense of abject servility or, counterwise, modest

---

[50] As Faust, that archetypical modern, comes to realize near the end of his life.

[51] "Better a dish of herbs when love is there than a fattened ox and hatred to go with it" (Proverbs 15: 17 [NRSV]).

magnanimity, but, rather, a willingness and ability to accept and affirm the reality of and, therewith, limitations inherent in our finitude: not for us the life of a god. This proves especially important relative to the elements of efficacy and worthiness. We are so constituted, in a sea of difference and conflict, that it is impossible ever to do as well or as good as we might and ought. This means, no matter how hard we try, we must inevitably confront our limitations and failure. It follows that for what efficacy and worthiness we have to make a contribution to our well-being, we must either remain blind to our deficiencies or, at some point, come to accept and affirm, be content with, our lives as they are.[52] I will designate this the "be-content" thesis.

People who are not content remain unhappy come what may, even when things are going well.[53] What makes people content is to some extent an unfathomable mystery. At the same time, there is a clear relation between the ability to accept and affirm oneself and one's acceptance and affirmation, in community, by "significant others." Here we see both the danger and indispensable value of constitutive bonds relative not only, abstractly speaking, to normative identity but, more concretely, the pursuit of well-being. Contentment comes to us by way of the contentment those to whom we are constitutively bound feel with themselves and us.[54] Typically this occurs through a process of nurturing; sometimes it occurs, miracle-like, through life-transforming religious experiences, thereby stilling not only the restless heart but enabling persons to overcome tragedy. Here, I want only to stress the vital role constitutive community, divine and human, plays in fostering contentment and, thereby, human good.

---

[52] A classic example occurs in the case of Martin Luther, who is unable to affirm his life despite success in achieving ordination and, even, because of it. He falls into what for his colleagues is a puzzling state of global distress. With time, Luther finds relief in a strong sense of God's affirmation – via the Pauline doctrine of justification by grace through faith (Erikson 1962). Another, less happy example is that of Captain Ahab, the vengefully determined, paradigmatically discontent, would-be conqueror of nature – wild and human – in Herman Melville's great novel, *Moby Dick*.

[53] Hence the frustration expressed in the Rolling Stones' rock-and-roll classic, "I can't get no satisfaction." I take it what they mean to be saying, insofar as they mean to be saying anything, is not that they never get what they desire – like a young man unable to get a date – but, more complexly, that they find no value, no meaning, no contentment, in the pleasure they so freely get: the good times are empty. It is contentment – like the "fourth man" spoken of in Daniel 3, the one with "the appearance of a god" – which keeps the other three elements – satisfactions, doings, and beings – from being burned up in the consuming fire of life.

[54] Contrasting "ego integrity" – "the acceptance of one's one and only life cycle" – with a state of "despair" – "signified by the fear of death" – Erikson concludes (1963: 269): "healthy children will not fear life if their parents have integrity enough not to fear death."

MORAL RESPECT AND NORMATIVE AUTHORITY

The constitutive, cultural traditions by virtue of which we come to be the particular individuals we are play a vital role in human life, providing not only for overlapping normative identities but, therewith, mutual concern and responsibility. We are who and what we are in relation with others. This, in turn, has sweeping implications for human well-being: for better or worse, we stand together. Later, drawing on theistic naturalism, I will argue that this applies not only to particular "communities of nurture" but, more comprehensively, humanity-as-a-whole and, beyond that, nature-as-a-whole. This, in turn, will prove crucial to our explication, in chapter seven, of humane holism. Before going there, however, I want to argue – returning to the line of argument introduced in chapter two – that constitutive communities deserve moral respect insofar as they are sentiotic and, further, that historic cultural traditions possess a non-derivative normative and, more broadly, epistemic authority.

Consider, in this regard, the moral institution of promising. Clearly, this structured practice is entitled to moral respect in that the keeping of promises is required, *ceteris paribus*, by the moral law. In addition, however, the practice of promising is not only instrumental to but a constitutive element in distinctively human forms of relationship and good. Nothing like a human life could exist apart from this practice. Thus, it has inherent value and deserves moral respect for the same sort of reasons natural, sentiotic processes do.

A similar argument applies to social institutions such as the family and state and, even more fundamentally, the constitutive, cultural traditions that sustain them. Like the practice of promising these not only make possible uniquely valuable human goods, they are constitutive parts of those goods, as of human life in general. That we might, for instance, raise children in orphanages or otherwise apart from the family, does not mean that we would not, in giving up on the family, lose a constitutively valuable part of *human* life. The same holds with regard to the state and its often maligned political process; while we might be governed by benevolent aliens to better affect than we currently are by ourselves, this change of affairs would eviscerate *the good of humanity*, reducing us to the status of well-cared-for animals. An even greater loss would occur were culture, *cultura culturans*, to disappear: cultural formation is as crucial to our life as the air we breathe, the food we eat. Were it not for this process, enculturation, there would be no human nature or good.

The argument from sentiosis is especially important as regards fundamental social institutions and, more generally, culture. The reason, in short, is that it ties these processes to the moral law. While this link is inherent in practices such as promising or the doing of justice, there is no inherent reason why institutions such as families and states or, more generally, cultures must be moral. Indeed, it is clear that they typically fall short in this regard. This, in turn, indicates why it is not enough to claim that family, state or culture are "orders of creation" – though, in a sense, it follows from theistic naturalism that they are. The problem is not simply that such arguments will persuade only those persons who share the requisite religious faith but, more fundamentally, that they fail to make clear the critique of "disorder" inherent in these "created orders." By appealing to their sentiotic nature, however, we make clear that such processes deserve moral respect only because and to the extent they generate and sustain goods of well-being. This, while not requiring, *per absurdum*, that families and cultures be perfect to deserve respect, builds into affirmation an impetus for self-correction. We also and not incidentally allow that there is no single, divinely mandated form of family, state or culture – just as there is no single, divinely mandated form of biotic community. [55]

Cultural processes, like natural processes in general, possess moral worth by virtue of their constitutive role in the realization of moral values (relative to well-being), not as a consequence of their living a life that goes better-or-worse from the inside-out. As a result whatever duties of preservation we have to them must be nuanced in light of their actual contribution to moral values. It is the failure to see this which opens the door for the morally unnuanced, objectionable stance of "cultural fascism," in which an overriding right of preservation is attributed to social entities on the basis of blood ties or other, constitutive relations among adherents.[56] The line of argument developed here, though affirming a duty of preservation in regard to cultural processes, is directly contrary to this and the tribalistic communitarianism found among fascists in general. While "special relations," blood-based and otherwise, play an important role in any well-thought-out ethics of nature, these

---

[55] Charles Taylor argues (1994: 72f.) that all cultures are entitled to a "presumption of equal worth" and "almost certain" on close inspection to deserve "our admiration and respect." The argument here, though perhaps going further than Taylor would, supports this conclusion and, in particular, provides a response to Taylor's critics (see Gutmann 1994: 9f., 78ff., 150f.; 156), especially Jürgen Habermas, who argues (1994: 128ff.), contrary to what I claim here, that "the ecological perspective on species conservation cannot be transferred to cultures."

[56] Such distortions parallel attempts to ground moral standing in species membership.

relations are always subordinated to universally applicable moral norms. Thus, *status quo* conservatism, focused on a mere preservation of what is, regardless of its moral propriety, turns out to be inconsistent with not only moral respect but, more fundamentally, the inherent value of those social entities that are entitled to moral respect.

Bearing this important point in mind, I want now to argue that constitutive, cultural traditions not only deserve moral respect but, in addition, possess a non-derivative, normative and epistemic authority. This appears most immediately in the understanding of our own, particularized (human) nature and good: we cannot grasp our life as a determinate project apart from the particularizing beliefs and values embedded in a more-or-less determinate, more-or-less coherent cultural *ethos*. Let me unpack this argument in three steps.

The first step is implicit in our discussion of human nature. We come to be selves by a process of enculturation. This involves not only the ecotic patterning of behavior and thought but, also, the adoption of an emic, insider's perspective on this patterning and, therewith, appropriation of a cultural *ethos*. We are "social selves." This *ethos* provides the shared, normative background for the various activities and judgments which go to make up a livable, distinctly human way of life. In this sense, every person comes to be a reflective, critical self by virtue of accepting at some point the common-sense morality of some constitutive community of nurture; it is that patterning which not only enables us to first make sense of life but, more fundamentally, become judgment-making selves. Thus, every cultural *ethos* has for its adherents a prima facie normative and epistemic authority; that it does is part and parcel of the process whereby we come to be reflective, critically engaged selves.

The second step is also implicit in our discussion of human nature; it becomes explicit in our discussion of moral respect. Every cultural *ethos* contains not only an ecotic patterning but an inherently ideal alethic dimension, actualized by way of religious and academic reflection. This dimension not only provides for the legitimation of an *ethos* but, also, creates – in the very process of legitimation – a critical awareness and, with it, an internally motivated impetus to reform, a movement in more ideal directions. It follows that in accepting the normative and epistemic authority of a cultural *ethos*, we by no means issue it a blank check. This point is extremely important; in particular, it provides a barrier to fascistic distortions of cultural authority.

The third and most crucial step is implicit in our discussion of faith and reason, in chapter three, and teleotic particularity, above. Apart from normative determinacy provided by the latter, an otherwise abstract morality would allow us no determinate grip on the world or ourselves. Put otherwise, the abstractness of human nature and good apart from cultural determination means that reliance on a cultural *ethos* cannot finally be avoided: no matter how far we go with generic reason and / or charismatic faith, we can never achieve normative determinacy apart from the particularities, the givens, of some cultural *ethos*. It follows that the normative and epistemic authority of a cultural *ethos* is, for its adherents, non-derivative and fundamental.

The qualifying phrase "for its adherents" is crucial. I am not claiming that any particular cultural *ethos* has authority, like the moral law, for human beings in general, as though we were bound not only to respect but adopt as our own every cultural tradition. This is hardly possible, given that cultures are distinguished by a wide diversity of inconsistent behaviors, beliefs, and values. Rather, constitutive, cultural traditions, while deserving respect from all, have *authority* only for those persons constituted selves by and in their affirmation of them. The difference is analogous to that between respecting the political and legal order of a state in which one does not reside – as a good-producing order the good of which is constitutively related to that of its citizens – and obeying the authorities that exist in, and the respective laws of, one's own state, even where one believes they ought to be changed for the better.[57] It is the fact that these norms are constitutive of our own normatively laden nature and good which makes their affirmation as authoritative a matter of self-realization and autonomy, not heteronomy.[58] Not surprisingly, the attribution of non-derivative authority to cultural traditions is linked to the recognition of irreducibly communal normative identities.

WHY CULTURE MATTERS TO AN ETHICS OF NATURE

We have already noted a variety of reasons why an ethics of (wild) nature needs to be concerned with the ins and outs of human culture. One of these concerns the naturalness of human life and society: culture is

---

[57] Obedience to the law has its limits in either case. Hence, the call on occasion for civil disobedience and armed resistance to tyranny. The authority of law is exclusionary, not absolute.

[58] I use Kantian terminology, though clearly Kant would not agree. What makes for the difference is my belief that the moral law is unable to direct us apart from its incorporation within cultural givens. In making this claim, I challenge the individualistic presuppositions of Enlightenment rationalism and its positivistic god-children. There is, of course, an analogy here with Rousseau's argument for "positive freedom" and, correspondingly, the Pauline notion of "Christian liberty," that liberty wherewith Christ has made us free to live in harmony with God and, thus, our true self.

the form nature assumes in creating humanity from inorganic molecules, dust of the earth.[59] We can understand neither human nature nor human good apart from the constitutive, cultural *ethos* in and by which they come to exist. Unlike other animals, humans have no set nature apart from culture. This has great significance for what "necessity" justifies in our use of (wild) nature and, positively, the manner in which we conceive of that good toward which we are oriented by nature and, therewith, culture. In particular, it allows us to see that human well-being is irreducibly communal, bound up with the kind of life we live in community.[60]

This point, this perspective, has great significance for the ethics of nature. In particular, it allows us to avoid an overly individualistic, reductionistic view of human well-being, the kind commonly relied on in economically driven, cost-benefit analyses, where concerns count only insofar as they can be given a monetary value – as if a person's (nation's) well-being were to be measured solely by the size of her (its) bank account. This perspective also comes into play in determining what is and is not a morally reasonable use of nature. We cannot begin to answer that question until we grasp the range of goods vital to human well-being and, thereby, the kind of decisions – and trade-offs – that must be made in the living of a truly good, fully human life; there are no cost-free, painless answers.[61]

I want, in chapter seven, to explore some of the trade-offs and costs involved in a common and, from a theistic point of view, puzzling feature of nature, namely, predation, that of wild beasts and, no less, our own (less civilized version). Before doing so, though, I need to note three other ways in which culture matters to an ethics of nature. Each raises an issue, as above, which we will explore in the final chapter. These involve, respectively, the shape and dynamic of a holistic ethic, the role

---

[59] Thinking the ethics of nature can avoid the question of human nature and good is like thinking we can restore Yellowstone to a state of nature without the "injuns." See Chase 1987: 105ff.

[60] Thus, Socrates, though not eager to die, reasons it would be contrary to his true interests to circumvent the sentence of death imposed on him by his fellow Athenians. These interests involve, importantly, not only an obligation to obey the law but, also, the opportunity, by willingly, cheerfully going to his death, to bring his life's work to a dramatic, narratively brilliant end – thereby helping his disciples grasp the point of his life. Socrates knows himself, all of himself, and, thus, realizes what is at stake when he drinks the hemlock; he is no fool.

[61] For a probing, cross-cultural engagement with this issue relative to water usage in the arid Southwest, see Bowden 1977. Both Thomas Berry (1990; see Dalton 1999: 7–32) and Wendell Berry (1977) are especially sensitive to the role of culture in addressing ecological concerns. David Ehrenfeld perceptively observes (1993: 183; original in italics): "the ultimate success of all our efforts to stop ruining nature will depend on a revision of the way we use the world in our everyday living when we are not thinking about conservation."

played in an ethics of nature by communal identity, and the implications of cultural relativity for moral reflection.

First, our understanding of ethical holism in relation to wild nature is advanced by an awareness of the form taken by a holistic *social* ethic. To begin, the argument for moral respect is the same in both cases: the processes involved are not only instrumental to but constitutive of well-being. This, in turn, allows us to see that adopting a holistic ethic of nature (culture) involves taking up a stance within nature (culture), viewing nature (culture) from the inside-out. It is not enough to show that nature (culture) is a direct object of moral concern, be this by appeal to beauty, autopoiesis, whatever. Adopting a holistic ethic of nature (culture) involves viewing nature (culture) as a constitutive, communal, way of being in the world. Further, the normative authority of nature (culture) must, accordingly, be understood in terms of deference to our own, extended, constitutive identity, not to an external, heteronomous authority. This means, for one thing, that deference to the ways of wild nature cannot be explicated in terms of an invariant order, be this the value-indifferent "laws of nature" or the normatively laden "natural law"; rather, it must be understood in terms of a dynamic, all-encompassing "ecological harmony."

While ecological holists need not be cultural conservatives or vice versa, the affinity is natural and strong, provided each is rightly understood. In this regard, it appears that much of the resistance to a genuinely holistic ethics of nature stems not from a disregard of nature but resistance to its corollary, a holistic ethics of human nature. Granting moral standing to irreducibly social entities such as family, state, and community runs counter to the modern presumption we are free to associate with whomever and define our relationships in any way we please. Constitutive, irreducibly communal bonds limit that freedom and, so it seems from the standpoint of a normative individualism, threaten human well-being. Hence, the eagerness to replace the authority of culture with that of merely formative traditions. By contrast, ecological wisdom directs us to modify culture and wild nature where a higher morality requires, aiming as we do at the deep *telos* of nature, all the while humbly deferring to our constitutive nature, common and diverse. An inability to honor our parents, our cultural history, is part and parcel of our inability to honor our natural history.

Second, as regards the role played in an ethics of nature by communal identity, constitutive, cultural traditions provide the base for a self-transcending process of self-discovery, a means by which to expand normative identity beyond its naturally, culturally constrained scope. Ideality, academic and religious, enables us to conceive and affirm our constitutive relation to humanity and, beyond that, nature-as-a-whole. We have taken the first step in this chapter, engaging the comprehensively human body of humanity. So far as academic reflection goes, this involves the development of an etic perspective on human culture – nature and good – that applies across the board to all cultures and humans: we see that there is a commonality of causal factors and relations. The move from here to constitutive normative unity is taken by charismatic faith as in our account of the *imago Dei*, the common, collective task of humanity. This, in turn, has many critical consequences, among them: (1) a belief in human normative equality and universal human rights; (2) an acceptance of our responsibility for wrongs committed against wild nature by past generations of humans; and (3) an obligation to take into account and fairly provide for the well-being of future generations, human and non-human.

We take the next step in chapter seven, arguing, relative to the nature-encompassing, extended body of humanity, that every human being is constitutively related to the entire bio-sphere. In this sense, we are one and all forever earthbound. The argument for this perspective on humanity encompasses, as above, two tasks. The first of these involves the assimilation of a scientific, evolutionary, and ecological account of nature, wild and human; this abstract but comprehensive, etic perspective allows us to see that there exists, across the board, a commonality of causal factors and relations. The second, ethically critical task, requires the development of an inside-out, faith-based, emic perspective; it is here that we perceive the normatively-laden, constitutive unity of nature-as-a-whole. Theistic naturalism engages these interwoven tasks in its account of "the fellowship of creation," that glorious end for which God continues to tell the story of creation. This, in turn, has many important consequences, among them, the belief that there exists a deep harmony between the interests of humanity and those of wild nature: we are all in this together.

Third, as flagged in chapter three, filling out the ethic of humane holism as we have depends on various, more-or-less contentious methodological presuppositions. One involves adoption of a holistic point of view on the moral life: we take into account not only the discrete good of individuals but, also, what builds up and sustains our common, constitutive relations, the many, diverse "bodies of humanity." Another, related presumption involves the significance of our normative identity: the ethical imperative flows from the indicative of identity. Still a third, on which I want now to comment briefly, involves the authority of cultural traditions and, therewith, the possibly disturbing fact of cultural relativity.

The attribution of basic normative and epistemic authority to constitutive, cultural traditions introduces an undeniable element of relativity into moral reflection. This appears at two points of special note for an ethics of nature. First, *we* are inevitably, literally, in our particularity, cultural constructs, the product of a more-or-less particular, more-or-less coherent cultural *ethos*. It follows that there is no such thing as a determinate, universal human nature and good. Human commonality is inescapably abstract. Second, while wild nature is not a cultural construct in the same, literal sense – it was there, in whole and in part, before human culture came on the scene – the concepts by which we conceive that reality, like every reality, are culturally relative, dependent on numerous historical contingencies.[62] Later, in chapter seven, we will have to ask how in light of this relativity wild nature can be our teacher (relative to deference). Here, I offer a few quick observations relative to the discussion in this chapter.

To begin, the fact that human nature and good are invariably indeterminate apart from cultural formation does not mean there are no objective limitations on what culture can make of human beings. These limitations are inherent in culture not only by way of its own history (*qua* ecotic patterning) and resultant normative inertia but, more fundamentally, the alethic dimension, by way of generic reason and charismatic experience. So viewed, cultural relativity is not only consistent with but presupposes a causal and normative realism. That we must at some point rely on cultural givens does not mean anything goes: the world tames cultural presumption, so long as we remain open to the directives of reason and experience. In this sense, culture, no matter how creative, is a check-written-on-reality: "our view of the world is fundamentally a bet, a function of hunches about reality measured against interests in it" (Fleischacker 1994: 39). Hence, while real, cultural relativity is not, rightly understood, vicious.[63]

---

[62] For an informative study of ways in which culture influences our perception of nature and, therewith, environmental issues, see Milton 1996. A number of ethnographic case studies are collected in Descola and Palsson 1996.

[63] It is difficult to imagine a theist (of any sort) denying ontological realism or epistemic objectivity (relative to either "facts" or "values"). Certainly I do not. What I argue is that these are consistent, up to a point, with cultural relativism and ethical creativity. Keeping our feet on the ground does not require nailing them to the floor.

At the same time, cultural relativity is real and must be taken into account. Apart from the ecotic patterning and ethotic depth of culture we could not, as individuals, make sense of the world or, therewith, achieve closure in our lives. In this sense, every culture is a transcendental condition of human language and thought, though, unlike Kantian transcendentals, neither a priori nor universal. It follows that we can never come to know the world or God, as they are, apart from cultural presumption, the stories and ways of thinking we learned at mother's knee – however many experiments we run or scriptures we read. This, in turn, has not insignificant implications for the way we ought to live.

One thing it implies is that we ought to pay close attention to our own beliefs and values. In particular, we need to ascertain which of these rest on our affiliation with and affirmation of a shared, constitutive way of life.[64] This is important as regards legitimation and, more comprehensively, the unifying narrative, the story, of our life. Our goal here ought not to be the elimination of cultural particularity but, rather, a critical faithfulness to ourselves and that culture, which is to say, those people, by whom we have been given the gift of particularity and, therewith, life. The danger, especially great in modern, pluralistic societies such as our own, is that, lacking self-awareness, we will give way to anomy or alienation; both states, dissolution and false rigidity, contribute to and reflect the increasingly weak cultural processes of modernity.[65]

Another and less apparent implication is that we ought to value the diversity of cultures. That this is so may seem odd, given that relativity and diversity together result in a conflict of beliefs and values which cannot be overcome by way of critical reflection, academic or religious. That we ought, however, follows from this very fact: it is only in the play of

[64] Though there is necessarily an element of free affirmation here – we choose to be one kind of person rather than another – it is crucial not to confuse this fundamental choice with (mere) life-style choices, to live one way rather than another. The latter always occur within a cultural context – and are to be found not only in our society but every society, a natural outworking of the teleotic dimension and closely linked to the existence of diverse personalities. The former always involves deep-cutting, fundamental beliefs and values we cannot deny; free affirmation, so far as cultural affiliation is concerned, appears in our decision to act and live in accord with what we find ourselves *to be* and which, alternatively, we would have to resist, curse, or pray for deliverance from.

[65] This weakening of culture is a product of many factors, including, most notably, one, the false presumption that it is possible to replace "cultural prejudices," "folklore," and "popular superstitions" with a rationally and/or charismatically compelling point of view, and, two, the socio-political dominance of a trans-cultural merchant-class and with it the commodification of culture: the real gets defined in monetary terms and, therewith, value reduced to preference-satisfaction (by fungible goods).

life, the course of history, that cultures are tested: their measure is that of a life well lived.[66] This means that we ought to respect cultures that have stood the test of time, which is to say, in effect, every historic culture; such cultures, for all their failings, will have great value by virtue of providing for meaningful, personally and communally rewarding lives.[67] In this sense, cultural diversity is directly analogous to biotic diversity: each culture, like each species, embodies a unique way of being in the world, a wisdom that can be known and preserved in no other form. What Rolston says of species can be applied to cultures as well: it is not *form* as mere morphology but the *formative* process that humans ought to preserve; to kill a culture is to shut down a unique story.[68] Destroying cultures is not only contrary to the respect they are entitled to, as sentiotic processes, it is foolish in the extreme, eliminating the hard-won richness of human life and putting all our eggs, culturally speaking, in increasingly few, narrowly defined, and poorly made baskets.[69]

---

[66] We ought, in short, to take the advice of Gamaliel (Acts 5: 33–40). That only time will tell what is of God, does not, of course, mean there are not limits on what we ought to tolerate here and now; in some cases, morality will not allow us to adopt a wait-and-see, live-and-let-live attitude – though where morally possible that is precisely what we ought to do. Lao Tzu (1963: 78), writing from a non-theistic perspective, captures the underlying dynamic: "As a thing the way is shadowy, indistinct ... Yet within it is an essence. This essence is quite genuine and within it is something that can be tested ... It serves as a means for inspecting the fathers of the multitude."

[67] See Chief Justice Burger's opinion (for the United States Supreme Court) in *Wisconsin v. Yoder*, 406 U.S. 205 (1972).

[68] Adapted from Rolston 1988: 137; 145.

[69] These modern cultures (and the one, global commercial culture toward which the world appears heading) are adapted to life under conditions created and sustained by modern technology – which is not surprising. This makes them, under those conditions, more efficient and powerful than traditional cultures. The question remains as to whether modern cultures can stand the test of time, which is to say, provide for genuine well-being and, in the process, sustain the ecological and social conditions of their survival – not, like a virus, kill the host on which they feed, done in by their own power and a false sense of well-being.

CHAPTER SEVEN

The fellowship of creation

THE BIG HUG

Theistic naturalism gives those who share its formative faith reason to believe that wild nature is sentiotic. In this, as in other respects, it supports humane holism. At the same time, theistic naturalism is committed to a qualified anthropomorphism: though radically Other, God is a person, like us. It follows that reality at its core is not only analogous to human life but more like human life than any other part of nature, the most striking example of which lies in the analogy of love: humans bear witness to God in a unique way. One risk inherent in this similarity is that it will lead to a theanthropocentric disregard of wild nature, as appears in Augustine's oft-cited claim to care only for God and the human soul and Karl Barth's account of the *analogia relationis*.

Consider the latter. Barth, though viewing the *imago Dei* as communal and placing human life "within the context of creation as a whole" (1960: 286), often portrays this context as little more than background for our interaction with God: "creation sets the stage for the covenant of grace" (1958: 44).[1] Since only humans are the covenant-partners of God (1960: 359), creation apart from humanity – despite repeated exhortations to kindness and wise use[2] – is relegated to the status of a dispensable framework, becoming, in the words of H. Paul Santmire

---

[1] Thus, following the previously cited remark (chapter four) regarding the "transparency" and "perfection of creaturely imperfection," Barth continues (1958: 382): "This is not intrinsic to it. It has gained this perfection from the fact that God in His Son has for our sakes appointed it His own vesture and nature." See, also, Barth 1961a: 41ff. Hans Urs Von Balthazar (1992: 121; citing Barth 1958: 94–228 and 228–329) argues that the duality of nature and grace for Barth "can be nicely expressed in the pregnant formula: creation (that is, the order of nature) is the external ground of the Covenant; and the Covenant (that is, the order of the Incarnation and redemption) is the internal ground of creation."

[2] Barth not only expresses interest in the place of non-humans in creation – addressing it at 374f., 394f.; 407; 417; 521, and 523 in volume III.2 (1960) alone – but displays genuine concern for non-human animals – as in his claim that we are justified in killing them only "under the pressure of necessity" (1961b: 354).

(1985: 155), "mainly . . . an object of manipulation, over against which God stands in his majestic dissimilarity."

Examples such as the above help explain the eagerness of "ecological theologies" to deny both the radical Otherness of God and the allegedly god-like nature and witness of human life. In response, theistic naturalism agrees that historic theism has too often failed to capture the organic unity of creation: "for many of the churchly, the life of the spirit is reduced to a dull preoccupation with getting to Heaven" (Berry 1977: 108).[3] This, however, is not the consequence of believing in an irreducibly personal, radically Other God but, rather, a failure to grasp the implications of that belief and, especially, as argued in Part II, to see that the ontological divide between God and world requires the *analogia relationis* to encompass the entirety of creation (Moltmann 1993: 61ff., 81f.). Accordingly, rather than proclaim the world "the Body of God," as panentheists, theistic naturalism looks at creation as a unified whole sustained by divine love and, in so doing, proclaims the world the extended body of humanity: "man is not a being isolated from the rest of creation; by his very nature he is bound up with the whole of creation" (Lossky 1973: 110). We are not only spokespersons for God, *imago Dei*; we are no less and therewith, spokespersons before God for creation, *imago mundi*, in whole and in part (Moltmann 1993: 186). As a result, "in his way to union with God, man in no way leaves creatures aside, but gathers together in his love the whole cosmos disordered by sin, that it may at last be transfigured by grace" (Lossky 1973: 111). Nature, creation itself, is the extended, encompassing body of humanity.

We do not just happen to be here, as though we might be some place else; we exist, one and all, "in an integral relation to the universe of things, plants, and animals" (Gregorios 1978: 64). Gary Snyder, a non-theist, puts it well (cited in Sale 1991: 181): "We are all natives here, and this is our only sacred spot." This view is biblical to the core (Wilkinson 1991: 284): "The Hebrew word used [in Genesis 1 and 2] for 'earth' is *adamah*, and the Hebrew word for 'man' is *Adam*. What the words and the whole account suggest, then, is [that] . . . whatever else we are, humans are also *earth*; we share our nature with its soil, its plants, its animals." For all its concern with the relation between humans and God, the Bible, Odil Steck notes (1980: 149f.), "grasps nature and man throughout . . . [as] a total cohesion . . . directed from the very beginning to a given,

---

[3] Berry continues: "this separation of the soul from the body and from the world is no disease of the fringe, no aberration, but a fracture that runs through the mentality of institutional religion like a geologic fault."

overriding divine order of significance that is neither confined to man, nor takes place simply for his sake, but extends to all living things."[4] As a result, "it is foolish to see God and nature as alternative poles placed so that if man turns towards one he must turn his back on the other" (Gregorios 1978: 84). To the contrary, the loving, sustaining embrace of God encompasses all that is or ever will be. Accordingly, we affirm an all-embracing, "big hug" theory of creation.[5]

While "the universe would be incomplete without man ... it would also be incomplete," as John Muir (cited in Fox 1985: 53) observes, "without the smallest transmicroscopic creature that dwells beyond our conceitful eyes and knowledge." Creation is a continuing totality; hence, we can be confident that no element, no aspect of creation is insignificant. This holds true in three distinct senses, each integral to the creative love of God.

The first sense is that found in the theological doctrine of *vestigia Dei*, or, "the signs of God."[6] This is beautifully put by Ernesto Cardenal (1974: 24; cited in Moltmann 1993: 63f.): "God's signature is on the whole of nature. All creatures are love letters from God to us." Likewise, a thirteenth-century Carmelite text, *Ignea Sagitta*, affirms (Montefiore 1975: 49): "All our sisters, the creatures, who in solitude charm our eyes or our ears, give us rest and comfort. In silence they give forth their beauty like a song, encouraging our soul to praise the wonderful Creator." Calvin put it thus (cited in Santmire 1985: 247): "after the world had been created, man was placed in it as a theatre, that he, beholding above him and beneath him wonderful works of God might reverently adore their author." Just such an experience is conveyed in the following report by Jonathan Edwards (cited in McGrath 1994: 237): "as I was walking there and looking up into the sky and clouds, there came into my mind so sweet a sense of the glorious majesty and grace of God that I know not how to express." Like Puritans in general, Edwards sees the glorious presence of God in nature.

In addition, theistic naturalism affirms a deep ontological continuity: the being of humanity embodies that of the universe, as microcosm

---

4 So viewed, the Bible becomes not a means for "the freeing of the spirit from the world" but, as Berry (1977: 109) claims, "the handbook of their interaction." That the Bible records a history of salvation (*heilsgeschichte*) focused on humans is what one would expect given that we are, one, the only animals who can read and, two, responsible for the mess soteriological grace aims to correct.

5 It is interesting to contrast the ambience and import of this normatively laden image with that conveyed by the "big bang" theory of creation.

6 This doctrine is paralleled by the Islamic notion of *āyāt*, or, "signs," for which see Cupitt 1975: 163f.

to macrocosm. Paulos Gregorios (1978: 64ff.) attributes to Gregory of Nyssa "the noble Christian conception that humanity, in a conscious self-offering, lifts the whole created universe up to God." Likewise, the "cosmic exemplarism" of Bonaventura affirms that "man embodies and brings with him all levels of creation, so that the material world participates in his ascent to God" (Bowman 1975: 195).[7] Muir also expresses such a view (cited in Austin 1987: 24f.), arguing that man, "who has flowed down through other forms of being and absorbed and assimilated portions of them into himself, [is] a microcosm most richly Divine because most richly terrestrial, just as a river becomes rich by flowing on and through varied climes and rocks, through many mountains and vales, constantly appropriating portions to itself, rising higher in the scale of rivers as it grows rich in the absorption of the soils and smaller streams." Theistic naturalism readily agrees: humanity is "a microcosm in which all previous creatures are to be found again" (Moltmann 1993: 186).

Thinking of nature and humanity as macrocosm and microcosm is important relative to the *analogia entis* and, therewith, the place of humanity in creation. At the same time, living creatures are not only part of our metaphysical being nor, simply, "love letters" from God to us, they themselves are the objects of and in their own way responsive to the love of God. Like us they see and feel, hear and smell, taste the wonder of God in creation: "all things affirm Thee in living; the bird in the air, both the hawk and the finch; the beast on the earth, both the wolf and the lamb; the worm in the soil and the worm in the belly" (Eliot 1935: 86). Every creature, the Qur'ān informs us, "knows its own [mode of] prayer and psalm. And Allah is aware of what they do" (Surah 24: 41); Allah, al-Ghazālī elaborates, "knows [even] the creeping of a black ant upon the rough rock in the dark night" (cited in Cragg 1975: 14).[8] That most unorthodox of theists, William Blake, put it ever so eloquently (1987: 64):

> The Bleat, the Bark, Bellow and Roar
> Are Waves that Beat on Heaven's Shore.

---

[7] See Pierre Teilhard de Chardin 1965 (on "Christogenesis") and Santmire 2000: 46–60 (for an ecologically sensitive, theologically engaging reformulation of the above).

[8] Al-Hafiz B. A. Masri notes (1986: 172) that in the Qur'ān and Hadīth all species are viewed as "communities in their own right and not merely in relation to humankind or its values." Further, "the Quran uses the same arabic word *Wahi* for God's revelation to all his prophets, including Prophet Muhammad, as well as to the bee" (175). Masri concludes with the following Hadīth of the Holy Prophet Muhammad: "Whoever is kind to the creatures of God, is kind to himself" (195).

Similarly, we are told in Genesis that God blesses the animals (1: 21–22) and provides them with food (1: 30), even that he forms covenants with all living creatures and, like an ancient Leopold, the earth itself (9: 9–17). What we find on every hand is that God seeks and finds mutuality with his creatures, soaring high in the air with seagulls and turkey vultures, crawling in the hot sand with snakes and lizards, bounding with pronghorn antelope, osmosing with tiny ferns and mighty sequoias, even occasionally reflecting on the mysteries of life with a puzzled human or two.[9]

We must take care to remember, as Jürgen Moltmann (1993: 186; 190) points out (and Muir would surely agree), that the human being is but "a creature in the fellowship of creation" and, thus, "must neither disappear into the community of creation, nor . . . be detached from that community." It follows that we can never find fulfillment in this world or that to come, apart from the entirety of nature, *natura naturans* and *natura naturata*. Thus, while it may appear absurd to some to imagine dogs and cats, oaks and sycamores, spawning salmon and fungi, in heaven, theistic naturalism cannot imagine otherwise. Would we not lose our souls, our identity and purpose, in a world made barren by their absence?[10] What might God provide that would compensate us for such a loss? Counterwise, what might we provide God with to make up for his loss? Will he not grieve even more than we for the mighty Leviathan, the weeping beech, the pesky mosquito? In any case, it is hard to see why God, having created and loved the whole thing, would decide one day to drop everything but us into the well of oblivion.

The really interesting question, for theistic naturalism, is whether, as John Wesley proclaimed in his sermon on "The General Deliverance," non-human animals will, like us, be resurrected from the dead.[11] There are at least two reasons for believing that they will: first, compensation for the pains of existence and, second, fulfillment of their created potential for good. The basic idea in the first case is that every life must be

---

[9] Hildegard of Bingen puts it well (in a translation by Gabriele Uhlein; cited in McDonagh 1990: 174): "As the Creator loves His creation so creation loves the Creator. Creation, of course, was fashioned to be adorned, to be showered, to be gifted with the love of the Creator. The entire world has been embraced by this kiss."

[10] See Gary Kowalski (1991: 101): "the lives of animals are woven into our very being – closer than our own breathing." Aldo Leopold, arguing for the preservation of native fauna, remarks in a similar vein (1970: 277): "relegating grizzlies to Alaska is about like relegating happiness to heaven; one may never get there."

[11] See Linzey and Regan 1988: 101–103. Many theists have shared this belief, among them Samuel Clarke, an eighteenth-century theologian, who "told an acquaintance that he thought it possible that the souls of brutes would eventually be resurrected and lodged in Mars, Saturn or some other planet" (Thomas 1983: 139). Ward (1982: 202) argues that "immortality for animals as well as humans is a necessary condition for any acceptable theodicy." See Linzey 1995: 100f.

such that it is, on the whole, worth living; otherwise God, being good, would not have brought it about. The basic idea in the second is that God will not allow the potential for goodness inherent in creation to be frustrated; hence, every creature must live a good life after its kind. These considerations give reason to believe, given the hard reality of life in this world, that at least some non-human animals will be restored to life in the world to come, though here we need to take care. It does not follow that this holds true for living creatures in general nor that any non-humans will live forever in the sense true of human beings.

For one thing, the above reasons apply, so far as individual well-being is concerned, only to selves and sentients. Though I am fond of the pine tree growing outside my bedroom window, so fond I have resisted pressure to cut it down, I have no reason to expect it will have an opportunity on the other side to become the truly magnificent tree it might have, were it not for its unfortunate location. The reason is not that it lacks a potential for good; all living things, being teleotic, have an objectively determined good-of-their-own. Nor is it that God does not particularly care for trees: the trees of the Lord are full of sap (Psalms 104: 16 [King James]). The reason is that trees, lacking a well-being-of-their-own, are not normative individuals: there is nothing it is like to be a tree nor, more particularly, one tree rather than another. Thus, while I expect to find *pinus nigra* in heaven, I do not expect to find my stunted little pine there nor, for that matter, any of the other trees whose beauty and persistence I admire.[12]

The case is different with selves and sentients, though here we must also take care. For one thing, criteria of individuality are difficult to apply in the case of (merely) sentient beings and it may be best to think of such entities as "supra-organisms," or, composite entities; in such a case, normative individuality might be distributed over a population of animals or, even, an entire species. For another thing, even if life-after-death is required to address harms or develop potential, it may be that *immortality* is neither required nor appropriate in the case of non-humans. The reason, in brief, is that for non-human (mere) selves a truly good, full life is a life in which they live, grow old, and die according to their kind; their life has a natural end inextricably linked to its physical processes.

---

[12] H. Paul Santmire (2000: 68–73) expands Martin Buber's distinction between I–thou and I–it experiences to include a third category of experience, the "I–Ens": "In encountering the Ens, I am captivated by its openness to the infinite, by its openness to a dimension that lies behind and permeates its givenness, its spontaneity, and its beauty" (72). This allows him to "salute the maple tree in [his] front yard as a member of [his] own extended family" (73), while preserving the distinctiveness of personal relations. This, in turn, dovetails nicely with our distinction between an ethics of well-being and one focused on sentiotic process.

What makes for a difference in the case of humans is not the presence of a non-material soul but the fact that our physical processes issue in self-awareness and, thus, have no natural end: our capacity to learn and grow is unlimited; hence the case for an unending future. It may be, then, that insofar as non-human selves and sentients appear in the life-to-come, it will only be, as individuals, for a limited period of time, until they, too, are able to live a good life after their own kind. As for the details, everything depends on the story God is telling, much of which must remain now and forever hidden, beyond our capacity to understand. What we do know is that our life there, as here, will be enriched by the full repertoire of creation.

HUMAN DOMINION AND THE FELLOWSHIP OF CREATION

It follows from the constitutive unity of creation that all living creatures stand in a special relation to one another. This relation consists not only in the fact that they "are made of the same dust as we, and breathe the same winds and drink of the same waters" (Muir 1954: 313); nor, as Muir puts it elsewhere (cited in Fox 1985: 52), that they, like us, "fill the place assigned them by the great Creator of us all."[13] More central still, our lives, their lives, the places we fill, are parts of an integrated whole; "they are earth-born companions and our fellow-mortals" (Muir 1954: 317). All living things, Muir tells us (323), "alike pass on and away under the law of death and love. Yet all are our brothers and they enjoy life as we do, share Heaven's blessings with us, die and are buried in hallowed ground, come with us out of eternity and return into eternity." Their life, their well-being, is integral to our own. Thus, as Moltmann puts it (1993: 186), we "can only exist in community with all other created beings and . . . only understand [ourselves] in that community."

Why have so many learned, otherwise faithful theists failed to see this, asserting to the contrary, like Aquinas (1964: vol. XXXVIII, 21 [II–II, Q. 64, a.1]), that "God has ordained . . . the conservation of the life of plants and animals, not for their own sake, but for the sake of man"? Why does it not occur to them, as Muir puts it (1954: 317), "that Nature's object in making animals and plants might possibly be first of all the happiness

---

[13] Muir continues, speaking of alligators: "Fierce and cruel they appear to us, but beautiful in the eyes of God . . . How narrow we selfish, conceited creatures are in our sympathies! how blind to the rights of all the rest of creation!" For more on Muir's belief that alligators and snakes are "part of God's family" and cared for with the same "tenderness and love as is bestowed on angels in heaven and saints on earth," see Strong 1988: 90.

of each one of them, not the creation of all for the happiness of one"? The problem here is not cruelty or a disregard of natural limitations; like Barth, theists in general call for kindness to animals and a wise, sustainable use of wild nature. The difficulty lies in a constricted view of divine love and human good. Why is such a view so common? One reason, I suspect, is that many who hold it, along with many who rightly deny it, wrongly surmise that affirming the love of God for wild nature is inconsistent with a belief in human uniqueness and dominion. This is mistaken. That we are unique in bearing the *imago Dei* and, as a result, exercise dominion over the rest of creation does not entail that God has created the world for our sake alone or, even, that God cares more about us than other creatures.

How can theanthropocentrism be overcome without giving up on the claim that human beings stand in a special relation to God and nature? The makings of an answer can be found in the response of Maimonides, a medieval rabbi, physician and philosopher, to claims such as the following (Bleich 1986: 106):

Thus, the Gemara, *Berakhot* 6b, reports: R. Eleazar said, "The Holy One, blessed be He, declared, 'The whole world in its entirety was not created other than on behalf of this [human species].'" Even more explicit is the statement of R. Simeon ben Eleazar, Kiddushin 82b, declaring " . . . they [animals] were not created other than to serve me."

While allowing that God has, indeed, made the world for the benefit of humans, Maimonides (1963: 452) denies that "all the beings exist for the sake of the existence of man. On the contrary," he adds, "all the other beings too have been intended for their own sake." Maimonides' point, as I understand it, is that creatures serving the good of humanity have, as well, their own created good – or, as J. David Bleich puts it (1986: 106), more formally: "there is no contradiction in acknowledging that service to other species is the instrumental purpose of some creatures while still affirming their own existence as the final cause of those creatures."[14]

---

[14] Maimonides' discussion is not entirely clear on these matters. Thus, he remarks at one point (1963: 454) that "plants were brought into existence only for the sake of the animals, for these must of necessity be nourished" (while explicitly denying that "the stars . . . exist for our sake"). He also claims, relative to the opening verses of the Torah, that "all the other beings [than man] too have been intended for their own sake and not for the sake of something else" (452). These tensions can, however, be removed by implicit qualifications so that the deeper point toward which Maimonides is working stands out, as regards which he offers a revealing example (454; italics added):

As far as what is reached by the good that is always coming is concerned, it may seem that what receives the benefit is the final end of the thing that caused its good and its liberality to overflow toward it. Thus an individual from among the people of a city might think that the final end of

All creatures, Maimonides affirms with marvelous ecological sense, are made for their own sake *and* that of others.

Maimonides' distinction and the integrated totality toward which it points reveals that a hierarchical ordering of creation toward the greater glory of God is congruent with the well ordering and, therewith, good of its parts.[15] Theistic naturalism, in its recognition and subordination of the *analogia entis* to the *analogia relationis*, adopts precisely this point of view. As a result, it has no trouble affirming both the universal fellowship of creation and the hierarchical reality of human dominion. As Loren Wilkinson puts it (1991: 283):

humans do have a unique place in creation and a unique responsibly to all of it. But such passages as [Psalms 104 and Job 38–39] make plain that the goodness of creation does not depend on people. Its purpose is not merely to fuel the engines of human progress; it is also to provide water for the thirsty trees, crags for the goats, and open sky for the south-flying hawks.

The good experienced in creation is not limited to human beings. Indeed, if modern evolutionary theories are correct, God must have spent a lot of time sporting with Leviathan, flying on the wing with pterodactyls, and rolling dung with Darwin's beatles before he got around to bringing humans on the scene. I see no reason to think he was just biding his time.

Human beings are uniquely unique. While every creature, every species, is unique in its own way, humans stand out, as Muir observes (cited in Austin 1987: 25), being "most richly Divine because most richly terrestrial." What makes us most richly terrestrial, however, is not, as Muir's imagery of the river suggests, our evolutionary history. Rather, it is that we and we alone of all creatures are able to comprehend the whole

the ruler consists in safeguarding his house at night against robbers. *And this is true from a certain point of view.*

Here, Maimonides recognizes both the interdependent good of created things and the possibility that there exists, relative to this good as a whole, more particular ends, "from a certain point of view." An error common to much "eco-theology" is that in calling attention to the first point, it presumptively dismisses the second (relative to human uniqueness).

[15] This commonsensical, thoroughly biblical integration of end (Platonic) and function (Aristotelian) oriented teleologies flags a way to free the systematic theology of that other great medieval integrationist, Thomas Aquinas, from its bondage to an otherworldly rationalism and, thereby, realize the moral potential inherent in its highly perceptive account of the common good and justice. This integration allows us to see, in turn, that it is not true, as Gary Gutting claims (1999: 126), that "Christianity requires a choice between God and creatures as our ultimate end" – nor, as James Rachels claims (1990: 99ff.), that Darwinism forces theists to abandon "the idea that humans are made in God's image and enjoy a special place in his creation." The good of our unique relation to God only comes to focus in a right relation to the good of those creatures, wild and human, to whom we are bound by the constitutive love of God.

of nature intentionally, to conceive of ourselves and others in relation to nature-as-a-whole and, therewith, God. Thus, while all of creation exists for the good of every creature, humans alone are capable of becoming aware of that and, accordingly, reflectively mourning the loss of another: "For one species to mourn the death of another is a new thing under the sun" (Leopold 1970: 117). This forms an important feature of creation-as-a-whole and its relation to God.

Apart from the self-transcending freedom of humans, creation would be unable to achieve a free and full mutuality of love with its Creator: "man alone can contemplate and offer the action of the created world to God" (Peacocke 1979: 295f.). It follows that "man's ordering-to-flourish as [the] ruler [of creation] is a necessary condition for the rest of creation to fulfil its own ordering" (O'Donovan 1986: 38). Just as nature proves the extended body of humanity, so humanity proves the means, the will and arms, whereby nature returns the loving embrace of God.[16]

That we have this capacity places us in a special relation not only to God but nature. For one thing, as Barth so quaintly puts it (1960: 78):

Real man cannot merge into his environment. He cannot surrender to it and be assimilated into it. If he did, or even if he could, he would cease to be real man. He is this creature, and as such he is not another, or a mere component part of a total creaturely reality. Although he belongs to the latter, he is marked off in specific ways from his fellow-creature.[17]

Another thing it means is that "man has responsibility because it is to man and man alone that the meaning of the whole of creation has been made known" (Steck 1980: 200).[18] This responsibility encompasses the right and charge of dominion: "man cannot be man and cease ruling over nature" (Baer 1971: 47). Like every creature humans naturally, properly exercise control over their environment, transforming it in accord with

---

[16] I cannot help but think here of the characters in J. R. R. Tolkien's fabulous fantasy, *The Lord of the Rings*, especially old Tom Bombadil and Goldberry, the river-daughter (1965: 167–189).

[17] The same holds, of course, for "real women"; Barth's usage is generic. For informative comments on this passage, see Rolston 1988: 332f., arguing that humans "are not to be free *from* their environment but to be free *in* their environment."

[18] Gregorios remarks (1978: 85), from a more specifically Christian perspective: "Humanity has a special vocation as the priest of creation, as the mediator through whom God manifests himself to creation and redeems it." Masri observes (1986: 176):

The real criterion of man's superiority in Islamic thought lies in his spiritual vocation, called *Taquwah* in the Quran. This spiritual power bestows on humans a greater measure of balance between their conscious and unconscious minds, thus enabling them to make the best use of their freedom. They are considered the best of God's creation only because of this difference. Without the proper exercise of this power, our superiority would be groundless.

their wishes and needs. The crucial difference is that humans can do so consciously, with an eye to the good of creation and therewith, all living creatures. Herein lies the basis of our rightful and inherent dominion: we are "the place where the process [of nature] transcends itself and becomes aware of itself" (Moltmann 1993: 328).[19]

This dominion, as pointed out numerous times and ignored even more, "does not give man the right of autonomous and autocratic disposal . . . for his own self-chosen purposes, detached from God" (Steck 1980: 105; see O'Donovan 1986: 52). The seal of dominion inherent in the *imago Dei* cannot be severed from the duty to speak for God and, thereby, display his love for all of nature, in whole and in part. Correspondingly, the moral priority of human life and interests, as affirmed in chapter one, does *not* rest on an appeal to dominion but, rather, the special relation in which all and only humans stand to one another – and, thus, on our naturalness, the fact that we, like all creatures, have been set on earth to pursue and enjoy well-being. Dominion enters the picture by virtue of our unique ability to grasp and speak for creation as a whole.

Neither the dominion nor moral priority of human beings rests on a greater love of God for humanity. If this were so, a question would arise as to why God created such a world in the first place. Paul Taylor, presuming this is what theists believe, puts the challenge this way (1986: 142):

If we were to take the standpoint of an animal or plant, God would *not* be considered to be loving, merciful, or just in making it an inferior being and giving humans dominion over it . . . At the very least this down-grading of animals and plants by their Creator would cast doubt on the supposed absolute perfection of His love for all His creatures.

Taylor has a valid point: it would be objectionably partial for God to create two selves of unequal strength and, then, allow the stronger to bully the weaker. What would be the point of doing that other than a desire to benefit the stronger at the expense of the weaker? Rightly understood, however, theism provides no such sanction, requiring of humans that we speak for God in nature and, thereby, linking our well-being to the good of creation.

It follows that human dominion needs to be viewed positively, as the task to which we are called from the beginning: "[Eden] is a land

---

[19] Quoting T. Runyon (1971: 42). Moltmann also notes Julian Huxley's characterization of humanity as "evolution become conscious of itself." Here, we must beware of false humility, remembering that sin comes in the form of not only pride but sloth, for an illuminating discussion of which see Outka 1992: 48–60.

which needs tilling and care" (Westermann 1974: 81).[20] Thus, Wilkinson (1991: 307f.) "We have concluded, based on scripture, that humans have been given dominion over nature and that they are to use that dominion to serve nature and humanity. Such service is the will of him who charged us with dominion: its purpose is to preserve, enhance, and glorify the creation, and in so doing, to glorify the Creator." By way of explicating this service, however, we need to avoid two common errors regarding the kind of love involved. The first and most general lies in the heroic temptation to construe this love in sacrificial terms.

Theistic naturalism views the love of God manifest in creation and, thus, the love to which we are called as first and foremost mutual, not sacrificial.[21] While a willingness to sacrifice one's own, particular interests is inherent in the notion of a rightful dominion, humanity is not asked by God to disregard its own well-being. Nor should we; our good – no less or more so than that of other creatures – is an integral part of creation's good. What God calls on us to do is pursue our true, created good, that is, seek happiness and, more broadly, well-being "in obedient enjoyment of the world, sharing what can be shared, delighting in the dance of time" (Clark 1984: *viii*). So viewed, the task of caring for creation becomes not punishment endured or sacrifice offered for the sake of a life to come but a life in which we delight, an ever-new well-spring of good. That we give priority in the living of this life to our interests is not wrong but perfectly natural, the way God intended – so long as we keep in mind our true interests.

The good life is a life of service. We need in explicating this life, however, to take care regarding a second and even more common error, embodied in the imagery of stewardship.[22] While the notion of stewardship has much to recommend it as regards integrity and diligence, the debilitating problem is that what makes stewards "stewards" in the first place is their responsibility for managing another person's *property*. Hence, use of this imagery presupposes that God, having created the world,

---

[20] Claus Westermann adds, congruent with our account of well-being in chapter six: "The idea of a Paradise which is a perpetual state of bliss is quite foreign to the Old Testament ... Work is regarded as an essential part of man's state ... A life without work would not be a complete life; it would be an existence quite unworthy of man" (1974: 81).

[21] See James A. Nash (1991: 152ff.), identifying seven dimensions of love: beneficence, other-esteem, receptivity, humility, understanding, communion, and justice. Nash calls communion "the consummation of love," the end to which creation is directed: "communion not only wants the loved ones to be in their distinctiveness; it wants them to be *our* loved ones in fully reconciled relationships" (159).

[22] Here I disagree, atypically, with Nash, who dismisses (1991: 107f.) objections to the stewardship model as "verbal squabbles." See also Wilkinson 1991: 308 and Katz 1997: 206–210.

owns it – as in the following line of argument, taken from Moltmann (1993: 30f.): "Interpreting the world as God's creation means precisely *not* viewing it as the world of human beings, and taking possession of it accordingly. If the world is God's creation, then it remains his property and cannot be claimed by men and women. It can only be accepted as a loan and administered as a trust."[23] There are three basic problems with such claims. One is that they presuppose a dubious account of property rights. That parents make babies does not mean they own them; nor would this change if they made them, miraculously, out of nothing. A second, even more fundamental problem, is that this imagery distorts God's relation to the world. While God retains an absolute prerogative over the existence of all things and might, therefore, at some point bring the world to an end, the eternal nature of God and, thus, point of creation establishes an inherently personal relation between God and the world, ruling out of court any construal of the world as God's property. No one, God included, can *own* someone with whom she enters a relationship of mutual love. Hence, a third problem: to think of ourselves as stewards of the world for God distorts our relation to the world and creatures over which we have been given dominion, as if they were chattels for which we will have to give account on the day of reckoning. That is not the kind of account we will be required to give.

How are we to think of our responsibility if not in terms of stewardship? Interestingly, once the misleading terminology is set aside, illuminating answers appear in many of those, such as Nash, Moltmann, and Wilkinson, calling on us to be good stewards. Thus, Eric Katz finds in Jewish tradition an orientation, centered on three elements, gratitude, mercy, and respect, that illustrates and illumines well our own appeal to necessity, decency, and deference.

The first element, gratitude, sets an attitude toward nature, one that subordinates our prerogative in the use of nature to the underlying purpose of creation, which is to say, God's relation to the world he has created. "The earth is the Lord's, and the fullness thereof; the world and those who dwell therein" (Psalms 24: 1 [King James version]).[24] It follows that in using natural objects for our good we are not to view them as mere instrumentalities but, rather, beings whose well-being matters to not only themselves but God: "All the objects of the material world are as

[23] This passage is *not* representative of Moltmann's position, which stresses the sabbath feast and, therewith, the fellowship of creation (see Moltmann 1993: 276ff.).

[24] Katz (1997: 208) takes this to support a theocentric world-view and the imagery of stewardship. I agree with the first claim and, by way of explicating that, disagree with the second.

sacred as the entities of heaven, for they are all the creation of God, and belong to him" (Katz 1997: 209). That is why we ought never to make use of the world without first asking God's permission and, then, offering to God thanksgiving, reciting a blessing. For all the world belongs to God, not as property, but integral parts of the divine story. The creatures and processes on which we rely for our well-being are embraced by God no less than we. To ask God's permission and render God thanks is to recognize that our prerogatives are always and ever subordinated to his ends, the all-encompassing fellowship of creation. Correspondingly, theistic naturalism, in affirming the principle of necessity, subordinates our necessity, our well-being, to our true nature and, therewith, the deep *telos* of nature, the end for which God created the world.

This, in turn, requires that we show to God's world mercy and respect. The first requirement is embodied in the fundamental principle of Jewish thought known as *tza'ar ba'alei chayim*, or, "the pain of living creatures" (Katz 1997: 212). This, Katz informs us, while not ruling out the use of non-human animals for food, "requires a concern for the well-being of all living beings" and, therewith, "compassion for animal suffering." We must treat all creatures decently.

The second requirement is captured by the principle of *bal tashchit*, or, "do not destroy" (213). This principle, enshrined in the Mosaic prohibition against cutting down food trees when besieging a city (Deuteronomy 20: 19–20), aims "to maintain respect for God's creation" (215). Other examples occur in the provisions for sabbatical and jubilee years (Leviticus 25: 1–13), allowing the land and animals to rest every seventh and, additionally, fiftieth year. The motivating concern here, Katz argues, is not economic or even, more broadly, social but the incomparable wonder of God's creation, dramatically affirmed in God's response (Job 38–41) to the questioning Job (Katz 1997: 215f.). The upshot is, as Katz observes (217): "Natural objects are valued, and cannot be destroyed, because they belong to God. They are sacred, not in themselves, but because of God's creative process." Thus, we defer, with "a sense of awe, wonder, and responsibility," to a theocentric nature (218).

TOWARD A THEISTIC ETHICS OF NATURE

We saw in Part II that theistic naturalism supports the belief that wild nature is sentiotic. We see now that theistic naturalism in its normatively laden account of created order provides support for the three basic principles of humane holism: necessity, decency, and deference. That it does, situates our questions regarding what God requires of us as the embodied self-awareness of his creative will. In particular, we come to see that necessity, decency, and deference are woven from the same cloth, diverse angles of approach to the same divinely appointed end. At the same time, however, we are left with a theoretical and practical conundrum: what are we to do, how are we live with the deep tensions inherent in creation? These tensions run through all of nature, appearing not only in our relation to wild nature, *natura naturata* and *natura naturans*, but, no less, family and friends, community and nation, humanity itself. While theistic naturalism puts these many tensions in perspective, holding out hope of their harmonious resolution, it does not tell us what we are to do here and now. Nor should it. Just as there are no obvious or easy answers to the social and ecological crises of our time, so there are no pre-ordained answers. The task with which we are confronted calls for not only a channeling of divine love and justice but, no less, genuine creativity.[25]

That there are no pre-ordained answers does not mean there are no wrong answers nor, correspondingly, that we ought not to do all we can to lessen the risk of going astray. As regards what can be done, I have sought to model that in the text, showing at various points what philosophical ethics and scientific inquiry can (and cannot) contribute, how religious faith can clarify (and distort) the basic orientation of life, and how our perspective on life and morality is inevitably shaped (for better and for worse) by our cultural heritage. The latter is especially important in light of its pervasive, oft-ignored influence. We do not approach life or ethics as normative nomads. To the contrary, we are bound to our fellow humans and creation-as-a-whole by enculturation and, thus, conditions of well-being inherent in the natural order of creation. We stand, ponder, and create in relation.

My hope is to have cleared the way for a more fully developed theistic ethic of nature. As to what that endeavor might look like, I want to conclude our explorations by reflecting briefly on two questions regarding predation, one hypothetical, the other pressing and real. Engaging the first, involving predation in the wild, will allow me to say something regarding the independent status of deference as a norm relative to decency. Engaging the second, involving human predation, will allow me to

---

[25] "No single mode of social organization is likely to provide a unique way of delivering the goals of ecological thought. No single blueprint will do, what is needed is a 'greenprint,' a strategic orientation which acknowledges the complexity and uncertainty of the changing relationships between society and nature" (Smith 1998: 82).

reflect more closely on the significance of culture for our understanding of human necessity.

PREDATION IN THE WILD

Suppose it were possible, using a wonder drug, to reduce the reproductive rate of prey animals and eliminate the predatory behavior of predators while sustaining resultant populations on a diet of carrion and plant material. Should we do it? At first glance it may seem we should – for humane reasons. Reflecting on the possibility of transforming nature into a pleasure garden, Stephen Clark notes the appeal (1984: 166):

> No-one really likes to struggle for life, and if the wilderness were wholly tamed [animals] would be spared that struggle. So returns Paradise . . . If it were true that everyone would be better off in this situation, and if we really did have the power to bring it about equitably . . . why then perhaps we should transform the earth into a pleasure garden.

Clark proceeds (166ff.), as his "if's" suggest, to question the gains realized in such a transformation.

For one thing, Clark doubts the extent once wild animals can count on human beings: "the fate of our domestic beasts and such park animals as now exist does not encourage any optimism about the way we would treat them." Even assuming good will, there is still the problem of good judgment: "once we have taken on the role of arbiter and lord [how, precisely,] shall we decide their disputes?" There is no reason to believe we possess the knowledge, let alone goodness and constancy of will required to successfully run their lives. Further, even if we assume good will and good sense, "what will happen when our civilization falls – as fall it will – to such poor creatures as have been stripped of their ability to find their own way in the world?" If we plan to change nature so radically, we need to think not only about the first day in paradise but the long run, the thousands and, hopefully, millions of years to come. What will we do when the drugs run out? Who, Clark asks, will save the beasts when they are no longer wild and self-sufficient?

That we so readily assume human reason in the guise of modern technology can radically transform nature for the better is more than a little interesting in light of the fact, as David Ehrenfeld notes (1978: 5, 92), this faith has produced "a viciously inhuman world." Ehrenfeld argues (126) in response that those who believe that we are able to create a struggle-free, toil-less utopia ignore constraints on the knowledge and power of humans, among them the inability "to work everything out for the best simultaneously"; this, he argues, is why "evolution has proven more reliable than our substitutes for it."

Evolution is slow and wasteful, but it has resulted in an infinity of working, flexible compromises, whose success is constantly tested by life itself. Evolution is in large measure cumulative, and has been running three billion years longer than our current efforts. Our most glittering improvements over Nature are too often a fool's solution to a problem that has been isolated from context, a transient, local maximization that is bound to be followed by mostly undesirable counter-adjustments throughout the system.

We need to be careful lest in our quest to transform nature we end up with a Wild Blue Yokohama (see Monsma 1986 and, especially, Postman 1993).

Whatever we decide with regard to the hypothetical wonder drug, its postulation raises an important question regarding our argument for the moral worth of wild nature-as-a-whole. That argument appeals to the allegedly sentiotic quality of nature, its inherent orientation toward well-being, and concludes we ought to defer to that *telos*, the constitutive relation of nature to goods of well-being, not its awesome beauty or value-free, quantitative regularities. It follows that we cannot specify the object of our deference in non-moral terms; the sentiotic *telos* of nature is morally laden all the way through. Does this, however, transform deference into a front for decency, holism for humaneness? So construed, deference to the ways of nature would be rooted in a concern for well-being combined with an awareness of human limitation, not something done out of respect for wild nature in its own right.

In responding to this question, we must at some point address the underlying epistemic issue: how do we know what is and is not natural in the world-we-encounter? Where are the normatively laden natural processes to which we are to defer? I engage these issues directly in the next section, asking what Leopold learns in learning to "think like a mountain." Here, I approach them more indirectly, arguing the hypothesized transformation is morally wrong, independent of any problems in its realization. In so arguing, however, it is important to bear in mind that decency and deference are no more independent of one another, normatively, than individuals and the communities of which they are constitutive parts. What we need show is not that holistic objects of deference can be identified independent of concerns about well-being but, rather, that the natural processes to which we defer are integral to our understanding of well-being and, thus, decency. Hence, the importance of our irreducibly communal account of human well-being in chapter six. What we require here is an account of how wild nature plays a similar, constitutive role in the well-being of wild creatures.

The fundamental problem with transforming wild nature in the manner proposed can be seen by supposing it possible to use our hypothetical wonder drug on humans; indeed, suppose that not only are rates of procreation lowered and aggressive, predatory behavior eliminated but that human health improves and contentment levels go sky high. Should we do it? Tempting as it may be, the answer is clearly no. Humans have a right to live their own life, to succeed or fail on their own terms. It is wrong to preempt that responsibility and right by giving them a chemical lobotomy, however much they smile afterwards. Those seriously tempted by such a "final solution" have little, if any understanding of human nature and good.

Somewhat the same – though not exactly the same – holds for non-human selves and sentients; they, too, ought to be allowed to live the lives to which they are suited by their nature. That they ought to follows not only by way of whatever individual rights they have relative to their own, self-defining nature but, more broadly, from our constitutive duty to that nature by virtue of which all earth creatures, human and non-human, are what they are. To transform non-human animals in the way proposed would not only change their lives, it would end their lives. Were predation to be eliminated from the behavioral repertoire of lions, wolves, and other predators, they would cease to be the creatures they are. Similarly, rabbits, antelopes, and other prey animals would cease, as individuals and as species, to be the animals they are apart from a vulnerability to predation. Wild creatures can only be preserved *in situ*, in the wild (Rolston 1988: 153f.).

The naturing of nature, *natura naturans*, is played out through conflict and struggle, life and death. To conceive of wild nature apart from predator and prey, we would have to reject evolutionary theory or, accepting it, deny that the process by which nature has come to be what it is, is constitutive of its identity. The first option is not viable; evolutionary theories are so interwoven with the sciences of nature they cannot be set aside without repudiating biological science. The second option, which denies predation is part of the normatively laden identity of wild nature whatever its current, ecotic significance, remains open given the distinction between *ecos* and *telos*. I want to argue in reply that this view fails to probe deep enough into the identity and subsequent good of wild nature. I do so in three steps, exploring, first, humane concerns, second, an eschatological vision, and, third, the place of suffering and death in a finite world.

Some, like John Stuart Mill, adopt the hard-nosed Darwinian view of wild nature as "a kind of hellish jungle where only the fittest survive, and these but barely" (Rolston 1986: 40).[26] If this is our view, we will hardly agree wild nature is sentiotic, let alone deserves moral respect. Here, though, awareness of competition, suffering, and death needs to be balanced by a recognition of more communal and irenic aspects of nature: most animals, most of the time, enjoy their interwoven lives. Granting this does not remove a concern with predation; perhaps wild creatures would enjoy life even more were it not for this dark prospect. In weighing this possibility, however, we need to keep in mind two things. First, as Clark observes (1984: 166), "it seems quite likely that all animal organisms are so constructed as to *require* a struggle, and problems surmounted in a worthy purpose." It is the necessity to struggle, the threat of suffering and death, that adds an edge to their life, keeps them alert, ready, and fit. Many people, knowing the danger it involves, would readily choose the life of a wild antelope to that of a well-fed domestic sheep.[27] Second, we must beware of a false sentimentality regarding the up- and down-side of non-human life. The lives of wild animals are different from our own, as from each other. While they, like us, have an interest in their own good and, counterwise, avoiding harm, these matters do not carry the same meaning, the same upshot for them as for us. For one thing, death is less of an evil for those who cannot see it coming and for whom it does not cut short reflectively affirmed projects and plans; similarly, where wild animals suffer physical harm or meet frustration in attempts to find food or reproduce, we must neither deny nor anthropomorphize their loses.

The above cautions do not show predation is part of God's good creation. What they do is minimize the likelihood of unthinking, knee-jerk conclusions to the contrary. The issue itself, however, remains. By way of addressing it theists will want to consider not only modern science and their own experience but, also, theological reflection and, especially, sacred revelation. Here, we encounter what some have viewed as a virtual proof predation is not part of God's good creation, Isaiah's vision of the peaceable kingdom (Isaiah 65: 25 [NRSV]): "The wolf and the lamb shall feed together, the lion shall eat straw like an ox but the serpent – its food shall be dust! They shall not hurt or destroy on all my holy mountain,

---

[26] This is not Rolston's view; he refers to it as "the Darwinian paradigm of nature."
[27] See, here, the anthropomorphic but ecologically sound account of an otter's life in Williamson 1990.

says the Lord."[28] Given this, one might wonder how anyone who regards the Bible as divinely inspired, as I do, can view predation as a natural, good feature of creation: if it will not be present in the restoration of creation, it must be an imposition, a distortion, not something to which we ought to show moral deference. In response, I want to argue that Isaiah's vision, like eschatological visions in general, conveys truths about the future in figurative, culturally relative terms. That it cannot be read literally becomes apparent once the larger context is taken into account.

What we find are images that make little sense when understood literally. For one thing, we are told earlier (Isaiah 60: 19–20 [NRSV]) that in that time "the sun shall no longer be your light by day, nor for brightness shall the moon give light to you by night . . . Your sun shall no more go down, or your moon withdraw itself."[29] Once, however, we take into account the reason Isaiah gives – "for the Lord will be your everlasting light, and the days of thy mourning shall be ended" – there is clearly no need to think Isaiah is saying there will be no day or night, no sun or moon, in that time. Similarly, there is no reason to think Isaiah is claiming serpents in that time will literally eat dust – as he says right after telling us lions will eat straw and wolves lie down with lambs.

Why does Isaiah make these metaphorical references? Why not? The analogy between God and light is clear. As for the imagery of dust-eating serpents, that is taken directly from the story of the Fall (Genesis 3: 14) and used to make a point about faithfulness: in that time temptation will be cast under our feet, a thing of contempt. Likewise, the oxymoronic image of wolves and lions hanging around with lambs and oxen makes a point about life in that time relative to a major source of frustration for sheep-herding, agrarian people: they need not worry wild beasts will come by night to destroy their livelihood.[30] Isaiah is not envisioning a giant nature-park where animals are free to run and play, do their own thing – other than eat one another.

[28] See Isaiah 11: 1–9 for a parallel passage.
[29] Similar imagery appears in John's description of the New Jerusalem (Revelations 21: 22–25 [NRSV]):

I saw no temple in the city, for its temple is the Lord God the Almighty and the Lamb. And the city has no need of sun or moon to shine on it, for the glory of God is its light, and its lamp is the Lamb. The nations will walk by its light, and the kings of the earth will bring their glory into it. Its gates will never be shut by day – and there will be no night there.

This follows an account of the city stressing the use of precious jewels in its construction.
[30] Thus, the curse pronounced earlier (Isaiah 56: 9–10 [NRSV]): "All you wild animals, all you wild animals in the forest, come to devour! Israel's sentinels are blind, they are all without knowledge; they are all silent dogs that cannot bark; dreaming, lying down, loving to slumber."

For one thing, Isaiah envisions the continuation of animal sacrifices (Isaiah 60: 7 [New American Bible]): "All the flocks of Kedar shall be gathered for you, the rams of Nebaioth shall be your sacrifices; They will be acceptable offerings on my altar, and I will enhance the splendor of my house." It is the welfare of humans with which Isaiah is most concerned. Here is how he describes the world to come prior to his reference to wolves and lambs (Isaiah 65: 19–24 [NRSV]):

I will rejoice in Jerusalem, and delight in my people; no more shall the sound of weeping be heard in it, or the cry of distress. No more shall there be in it an infant that lives but a few days, or an old person who does not live out a lifetime; for one who dies at a hundred years will be considered a youth and one who falls short of a hundred will be considered accursed. They shall build houses and inhabit them; they shall plant vineyards and eat their fruit. They shall not build and another inhabit; they shall not plant and another eat; for like the days of a tree shall the days of my people be, and my chosen shall long enjoy the work of their hands. They shall not labor in vain , or bear children for calamity; for they shall be offspring blessed by the Lord – and their descendants as well. Before they call I will answer, while they are yet speaking I will hear.

This is not a world without death or the use and killing of animals for human purposes. It is a time when people reap the fruits of their labor, die after long and fruitful lives, with many healthy children and grandchildren, a time when beasts and humans live as they were intended.[31]

I conclude that Isaiah's vision of the peaceable kingdom does not show that predation is not part of God's good creation. It is not concerned with that issue. Does it follow the Bible or, more broadly, theistic naturalism has nothing to say regarding the hard reality of predation? Not at all. We need, however, to get beyond "proof-texting" and reflect theologically. Here it is interesting to note an analogy with the question of social order. Theists have long argued about the state and its place in the order of creation. Some, like Augustine, are post-lapsarians, believing that political authority and the state only appear after the Fall, as a means of controlling sin. Others, like Aquinas, are pre-lapsarians, viewing the state and political authority as integral parts of human nature and good. Briefly examining this historic argument will make clear

---

[31] By contrast, the author of Revelations, writing in a time and place dominated by the imperial power and wealth of Rome, fills the world to come with things which would turn even an emperor green with envy. Both are making a point, in terms they and the people to whom they are writing understand, about the ultimate triumph of God. God's will *will* be done on earth as in heaven. Visions of paradise, our own included, are inevitably culturally laden. How else is paradise to be envisioned?

why theistic naturalism supports a pre-lapsarian view of the state and predation.

The argument for a pre-lapsarian view of the state depends on distinguishing the state's role as a restraint on and punisher of moral evil from its role as a forum for deliberation and decision. That the former function will have no place in a sinless society does not imply that political authority and, thereby, the state is not required as a means whereby the common identity and collective will of a truly, fully human, deliberative society can be formed. Indeed, the only alternative to this is to presume differences and deliberation are not inherent to human life. That finite creatures see the world from different points of view, however, and have as a result conflicting views and interests is part and parcel of our inherently finite nature and good. This point was reiterated in chapter six relative to the constitutively communal shape of human nature and good: it is difficult to see what would be left of our humanity in a world without real deliberation and real decision. Thus, as dismal as the thought may be, given the sad reality of politics in our own time, there must have been in Eden, as there will be in heaven, not only a state but, along with it, a political process.[32]

Disagreement and conflict – a war of ideas – is an inherent feature of human society. This alone, of course, does not entail that predation is integral to creation. What would an argument to that effect look like? To begin, it need not deny the genuine losses associated with predation nor, for that matter, claim predation is integral to every possible good world, as it clearly is not. What it will argue is that predation, as an integral part of *this* world, contributes to *its* goodness by serving the end of mutuality with God and one another: adversity – conflict and struggle – turn out, ironically, to foster bonds of love. Can such an argument be made?

We begin with the presumption, defended in chapter five, that a world of finite selves and sentients is impossible apart from the discomforting presence of natural evil. Going further requires us to ask whether such a world will contain not only natural evil but, more specifically, suffering and death. The case for suffering is straightforward: while natural evil exists without suffering, in the form of deprivation, numerous higher-order

---

[32] More needs to be said regarding the historic debate. For one thing, Augustine views violence as a defining feature of the state and, thus, never has in mind the peaceful, deliberative process in terms of which Aquinas defines the state. This, clearly, reflects differences in their cultural context. Still, all said and done, Aquinas makes a great advance in his account of the state and, more broadly, justice, one that re-orients theology in a distinctively communal, biblical direction. See Markus 1970: 197–210 (Appendix A) and 211–230 (Appendix B).

goods depend on the presence of hurt-inducing harms.[33] What, then, about death? While not a logical necessity, the introduction of death need not involve a disproportionately greater degree of suffering and, further, may contribute to higher-order goods, most obviously, procreation and parenting, neither of which make much sense in a world without death. Difficulties involved in the application of this reasoning to humans can be met by arguing, one, that death is not natural for humans, unlike other animals, or, two, my preference, that death prior to the Fall had for humans a different, less frightening significance. In any case, however we view human death, there is no reason, morally or theologically, to deny it is a natural and good part of life for wild creatures in general.

The question then becomes whether a good and loving God would create a world with not only suffering and death but suffering and death by way of predation. I see no reason why not – even allowing that some forms of predation are more suspect than others. Meeting one's end in a lion's mouth or hawk's talons need not be worse than meeting one's end through starvation, disease, or, simply, old age. Bearing in mind that humans have disrupted ecological patterns and introduced misery and woe which, otherwise, would not have existed, it is reasonable to conclude that predation, like politics, is part of God's own, good plan for creation. This conclusion is supported by the faith-based intuition that neither wild predators nor their prey would be the creatures they were created to be apart from a nature occasionally red in tooth and claw.[34]

HUMAN PREDATION

That the use of other animals for food – human predation – is justified under some conditions follows directly from the principle of necessity. The starving men in the lifeboat did nothing immoral in killing and

---

[33] It does not follow that the extent of suffering in this world is inevitable or justified. That in this world suffering and death overwhelm the goods to which they would contribute under more benign circumstances is the result of sin, not integral to created order; hence the need for a "general deliverance."

[34] Aquinas concludes (1964: vol. XIII 125 [I, Q. 96, a. 1]): "For man's sin did not so change the nature of animals, that those whose nature it is now to eat other animals, like lions and hawks, would then have lived on a vegetable diet." Similarly, Basil (1995: 92) finds in nature, predation included, "a wise and marvelous order" and notes (105) that God omitting nothing necessary, gave "to carnivorous animals . . . pointed teeth which their nature requires for their support." Others have taken Genesis 1: 29–30 and 9:3 to indicate, in conjunction with Isaiah's vision, that not only Adam and Eve – on which there is general agreement – but all creatures were vegetarians prior to the Fall and, even, free from suffering and death; thus, Wesley envisions "no heat or cold, no storm or tempest, but one perennial spring" (cited in Linzey and Regan 1988: 103). See, also, Linzey 1995: 129.

eating the sea turtle. At the same time there would be something morally troubling if the non-human animal killed and eaten was a dolphin the men befriended after it saved their lives, keeping them afloat until they reached the lifeboat.[35] Our relation to wild nature is morally limed. "Et tu, fishy" arguments, holding we are justified in eating other animals by virtue of their eating one another,[36] are undermined by the fact that many of the animals we eat (other than fish) are herbivores and, more fundamentally, the unique nature of human life. Unlike non-human predators, we are capable of reflectively ordering our behavior in accord with moral norms, including those of decency and deference.

Here, relative to human predation, we come face to face with the physiological fact that humans, unlike wild predators, do not have "pointed teeth," which is to say, are not dependent for their survival on the consumption of animal flesh. We can easily live, as many people have and do, on a virtually total, if not altogether vegetarian diet. This, in turn, leads us to ask whether we ought to abandon the practice of using other animals for food, doing so only on those occasions when it is necessary for survival. Before engaging this question, however, as we will in the final section, I want to address a more focused, purer form of predation, that of "nature hunting," asking whether it is the kind of

[35] Alfred Guillaume (1956: 54) tells the following story, taken from the life of Muhaammad:

A woman barely escaped with her life from some raiders by galloping off on one of the prophet's own camels. After recounting the story of the raid she said: "I vowed to sacrifice the camel to God if he saved me by her." The prophet smiled and replied: "That's a poor reward! God saved you by her, and then you want to kill her! Leave the animal alone, for anyhow it is my property; and go home with God's blessing."

[36] Benjamin Franklin (2001: 41 f.) tells the following, possibly tongue-in-cheek story – meant, it appears, to illustrate the vicissitudes of human reason. The story takes place on a fishing boat becalmed off Block Island and begins with Franklin noting that he had previously "stuck to my resolution of not eating animals food" – viewing, "with my master, Tyson, the taking of every fish as a kind of unprovoked murder, since none of them had or ever could do us any injury that might justify the slaughter." Franklin continues:

All this seemed very reasonable. But I had formerly been a great lover of fish and, when this came hot of the frying-pan, it smelt admirably well. I balanced some time between principle and inclination, till I recollected that, when the fish were opened, I saw smaller fish taken out of their stomachs; then, thought I, "if you eat one another, I don't see why we mayn't eat you." So I din'd upon cod very heartily, and continued to eat with other people, returning only now and then occasionally to a vegetable diet.

Franklin concludes, a point Augustine and Luther would have well appreciated: "So convenient a thing to be a *reasonable creature*, since it enables one to find or make a reason for every thing one has a mind to do." It is especially important in this regard, given the argument to come, to bear in mind the social context of Franklin's reasoning. This is, no less, a story about Franklin's relation to his master, Tyson, and the larger community of which they were a part.

activity in which a theistic naturalist and, more generally, someone who takes seriously the ethic of humane holism will engage.[37]

Nature hunters hunt despite the fact that they do not need the meat. In this sense they resemble sport, or, recreation hunters, hunters who hunt for the thrill, the fun of it. Unlike the latter, however, nature hunters value the meat of game animals and, where possible, make a point of using it for food.[38] More fundamentally, nature hunters differ from both meat and recreation hunters in the value they place on the hunt itself. Thus, Ortega y Gasset (1986: 110f.; cited in Kellert 1996: 72), a nature hunter, observes that he "does not hunt in order to kill [but] kills in order to have hunted." The point of the hunt becomes immersion in wild nature. As to what this involves and why it comes only by way of predatory behavior, Ortega y Gasset is once again helpful (1986: 119; cited in Kellert 1996: 71):

When one is [nature] hunting, the air has another, more exquisite feel as it glides over the skin or enters the lungs; the rocks acquire a more expressive physiognomy, and the vegetation becomes loaded with meaning. All this is due to the fact that the [nature] hunter, while he advances or waits crouching, feels tied through the earth to the animal he pursues.

In this way one comes to experience, according to nature hunters, a transformative awareness of and appreciation for the prey and, therewith, our own inherent naturalness.

What makes nature hunting of such interest, theoretically, to theistic naturalism is that it defends the practice of hunting not as a hard necessity but positive ideal, part and parcel of a life lived in harmony with (the deep *telos* of) nature. This returns us to the question of epistemic access: how do we determine the true, normatively laden nature of nature, wild and human? We have argued that this knowledge cannot be grasped by a rationally compelling generic reason, by way of an inherently quantitative, abstractive scientific inquiry or the programmatic commonalities

---

[37] Stephen Kellert (1996: 65–77) distinguishes nature hunters (from meat and recreation hunters) by their "deep participatory involvement" in and "vivid appreciation and awareness" of natural processes and ecological relationships. He does so in the course of exploring nine different values found in (and resultant relations to) wild nature: utilitarian, naturalistic, ecologistic-scientific, aesthetic, symbolic, dominionistic, humanistic, moralistic, and negativistic. Kellert's discussion of these differing stances, while not settling moral issues regarding propriety and priority, discourages one-sided views of our relation to wild nature. For more on these values in relation to "biophilia," see Kellert 1997.

[38] The "where possible" must be construed broadly to allow for the killing of predators, such as bear and cougar, which are as a rule not eaten, and "trophy hunting," a border-line pursuit on which nature-hunters differ.

affirmed by a philosophical ethics. While both of these contribute much to our understanding of nature, they cannot provide a determinate account of what makes for harmony with nature or, therewith, well-being. In this regard we are forced to rely on faith-based convictions, convictions rooted in charismatic insight and cultural givenness. Consider Leopold's defense of nature hunting.

We saw in chapter three the importance for Aldo Leopold's land ethic of his transformative encounter with the dying wolf. In that encounter and others like it, with dancing woodcocks and plaintive geese, Leopold learns "to think like a mountain." This involves coming to see that wolves are not only predators but vital parts of a larger, ecological community, contributors to the evolutionary and individual well-being of their prey. In addition, Leopold recognizes the contribution this network makes to our own well-being (1970: 240): "a land ethic changes the role of *Homo sapiens* from conqueror of the land-community to plain member and citizen of it." Thus, "thinking like a mountain" involves not only recognizing the mutually beneficial roles of wolves and deer but, also, finding our own place in the encompassing community of life. This image of interwoven lives provides Leopold with a governing orientation, an ethical ideal. This ideal, while tempering his "trigger-itch," fuels Leopold's "congenital hunting fever" (183f.; 233).

The wrong Leopold sees, looking into the eyes of the dying wolf, is a wrong against the biotic community, not this individual or her scattered pups. Similarly, witnessing the aesthetically moving "sky dance" of the woodcock moves Leopold not to give up hunting these "game birds" but, rather, limit his take to "be sure that, come April, there be no dearth of dancers in the sunset sky" (36). The most remarkable example involves geese, for which Leopold feels obvious affection.[39] Noting the appearance during spring of large numbers of "singles – lone geese that do much flying about and much talking" – Leopold remarks (22): "One is apt to impute a disconsolate tone to their honkings, and to jump to the conclusion that they are broken-hearted widowers, or mothers hunting lost children." After a quantitative, scientific study, he concludes this initial impression is correct, leaving him (22) "free to grieve with and for the lone honkers." That he grieves does not, however, weaken his

---

[39] This affection leads him at two separate points in the text to sum up the wonder and mystery of wild nature by a reference to geese. In the first case, commenting on the value of remaining ignorant regarding some aspects of animal behavior, he remarks, regarding the odd preference of geese for prairie-corn (1970: 22): "What a dull world if we knew all about geese!" Commenting on the sad degradation of nature, Leopold sounds his most disconsolate note, asking (233), "what if there be no more goose music?"

passion for goose hunting or lessen his efforts to instill the same passion in his sons (232f.).

This passion is not an aberration in Leopold's general ethic. To the contrary, hunting, rightly practiced, serves for Leopold as an expression of that ethic. He tells us (230): "Poets sing and hunters scale the mountains primarily for one and the same reason – the thrill to beauty. Critics write and hunters outwit their game primarily for one and the same reason – to reduce that beauty to possession." Who but the hunter, Leopold asks (230), "so thrills to the sight of living beauty that he will endure hunger and thirst and cold to feed his eye upon it?" Correspondingly, Leopold disapproves of those hunters who lack appreciation or concern for the integrity, beauty, and stability of wild nature: rightly done, hunting builds the kind of character required by a land ethic.[40] Far from being an incidental recreation or, even, a mere struggle for sustenance, hunting is for Leopold, as for Rolston (1988: 91), "a *sacrament* of the fundamental, mandatory seeking and taking possession of value that characterizes an ecosystem and from which no culture ever escapes."

For Leopold, predation, hunting, is integral to humanity's place in nature. His charismatically compelling encounters with wild animals, as a result of which he dramatically changes some beliefs, reinforce and refine this conviction. Others, of course, experience hunting differently. I recall a student, taught to hunt by his father, telling me with reference to Leopold's experience with the dying wolf of his own experience looking into the eye of a deer he had shot before ending its life. Rather than finding in that act solidarity with nature, he found only senseless brutality and has since become active in the animal liberation movement.[41] While he tried to appreciate Leopold's point of view, it puzzled him, as it does me, how individuals so thrilled by the sight of "living beauty" could exert so much effort to leave it dead and ugly – or that Leopold could grieve for the lone honkers, yet continue to shoot them and their kin, be it part of a sacramental bonding with wild nature or not.

[40] Leopold asks (1970: 232):

What is the effect of hunting and fishing on character as compared with other outdoor sports? . . . [T]here are two points about hunting that deserve special emphasis. One is that the ethics of sportsmanship is not a fixed code, but must be formulated and practiced by the individual, with no referee but the Almighty. The other is that hunting generally involves the handling of dogs and horses, and the lack of this experience is one of the most serious defects of our gasoline-driven civilization.

[41] I recollect a similar experience, as a young boy, watching my father and an older cousin shoot a large grey squirrel, the point of which escapes me to this day.

Three things in particular make it difficult for me to affirm the ideality of human predation. The first, as stressed above, is that our physiology differs from that of wild predators. Not only do we not have long teeth, but our intestines, like those of sheep, are folded over and exceptionally long, evolved for the consumption of vegetative material, not animal flesh. Second, taking morality seriously ought to make us look to build up and support all life, rejoice in its flourishing, not look to destroy the creatures or processes in which life is embodied. This is even more evident if, as humane holists, we ground the moral worth of natural processes in their sentiotic proclivity to foster the goods of well-being for selves and sentients in general. Third and for me, as a theistic naturalist, decisive, there is the responsibility inherent in human dominion, the responsibility of speaking for God on earth. Is it not unseemly, if not unjust, for the divinely delegated judges of the whole earth to kill and consume creatures whose good they have been charged with advancing? If it is necessary to call down fire from heaven, we ought to do so hesitantly and in a way that causes the least harm possible, not make fire-throwing an integral part of our well-being (see Genesis 18: 17–33). Yahweh is not Zeus or Thor.

Accordingly, it seems to me we ought, like Augustine advises the Christian ruler, to work and pray to be delivered from our hard "necessities." At the same time, however, while persuaded by the above considerations to affirm a contrary, more irenic ideal of harmony with nature, one with no place for nature hunting, I am concerned, for reasons I want now to flag, that this dismissal of Leopold's ideal is too quick and easy. Though unable to regard nature hunting as an integral or, even, valuable part of a life lived in harmony with nature, it does appear to me on reflection that we lack the compelling reasons for rejecting it we have with regard to the natural oxymoron of "vegetarian predators." Let me, then, develop an argument against myself.

To begin, we need to realize the extent to which opinions regarding human predation are culturally laden, bound up with the way in which we live day-by-day. This link is evident in statistical correlations between cultural location and attitudes toward hunting (Kellert 1996: 69):

The proportion of Americans who hunt ... has been steadily declining for a quarter of a century while the ranks of those opposed or indifferent to the activity have swelled. This change signifies a fundamental shift in the cultural context of hunting in America. Hunting participation historically depended on recruitment from a rural-based, extended-family network, as fathers, grandfathers, and other male role models socialized young boys from one generation to another, often within stable territorial boundaries. The decline of rural living, the disintegration of the extended family, the increasing transience and mobility of Americans – all have altered the social conditions at the core of hunting's continuity and succession.

The strong correlation here, similar to what one finds in the case of religious affiliation, makes it impossible to deny that culture makes a difference relative to not only the range of our experience but, more significantly, the actual content of our charismatically sanctioned convictions.

The lessons we learn from nature (and God) are always cast in a language we understand, given form and content by our normative and, thereby, cultural context – past, present and, especially, future. In this sense, neither cultural relativity nor the risk of existential commitment can be escaped any more and, indeed, less so than our physical skin. We are what we are – what we were and what we choose to be – not another thing. This does not mean the nature we experience is a mere product of thought, any more than it means we can make six the square root of twenty-five or "denying the antecedent" a valid form of argument. It simply means there are no culture- and, thereby, commitment-free, Archimedean points of view from which we can evaluate our life or that of others, as regards hunting or anything else. Every determinate moral judgment rests on, bears the weight of constitutive commitments. This is part and parcel of our existence, of being who and what we are.

The question is not how to escape these limitations; we cannot nor should we aim to – for in the end they are no more constraints than the ground on which we walk: as Lewis put it (1947: 91), if you see through everything, you see nothing at all. The question is how to take into account, learn from an awareness of the role cultural and social factors play in our understanding of morality. Doing so will not resolve deep-seated moral disagreements; it will make us less prone to the self-righteous indignation Jesus warned against (Matthew 7: 1–5), the kind quick to condemn others, yet unable to grasp its own shortcomings. This is especially important when criticizing culturally embedded practices such as hunting (and anti-hunting). Even if our criticisms are on target, we will not understand why they (we) believe and act as they (we) do until we see how their (our) beliefs and actions are intertwined with their (our) on-going, irreducibly communal lives.

That is the first thought that made me hesitate before writing off Leopold's defense of nature hunting as a mere rationalization. A second involved the realization, inherent in Leopold's defense, that human predation, though too often done in a morally atrocious way, may be done in ways that display genuine concern for the well-being of prey animals.[42] Thus, Rolston (1988: 61) proposes that Leopold's ecological constraints on hunting be supplemented with a "homologous principle," requiring that the suffering caused by humans (in the course of hunting or whatever) be no more than or, at least, comparable to that suffered in the ordinary course of a wild animal's life. This limitation is especially important given the argument that wild predation is not inconsistent with the basic goodness of nature: hunters who abide by the homologous principle become, in terms of impact, natural predators, part of a sentiotic process entitled, so I have argued, to moral respect. While this does not by itself resolve questions about the moral propriety of human predation, given our distinct nature and good, it does, not insignificantly, address concerns about animal suffering.[43]

In this regard, it needs to be remembered, a third thought, that hunters have, as a matter of historic fact, contributed to the preservation of ecosystems and, therewith, the well-being of wild animals, the classic example being that of wetlands and wild ducks (see Reiger 1986 and Belanger 1988). The preservation of wetlands owes much to the license fees and lobbying of hunters. We may, of course, hold out for preservation without hunters, believing that there is no difference in the killing of humans and non-humans or, more plausibly, that non-human selves, game animals included, have a capacity-based right to life. Whatever we decide, however, we ought not, even in the case of oppressed humans, start wars of liberation unless there is a reasonable chance of making things better, not worse. And in this regard it seems clear that ducks, given a vote, would opt for wetlands and hunters rather than no hunters and no wetlands. They have, after all, been dealing with predators from time immemorial.

Expanding on the above, possible trade-off raises a question regarding the extent to which our civilization and, therewith, our lives depend on the harming of wild nature, in whole and in part. Finn Lynge argues

---

[42] See Linzey 1995: chapter 7, for a critical but ultimately appreciative discussion of "the conscientious Christian hunter."

[43] It also calls attention to a deep tension in humane holism and, therewith, theistic naturalism. This tension appears not only in the affirmation of decency and deference as co-equal principles but, also and more fundamentally, the hiddenness of God, the shadow of creation. While it would be more tidy conceptually to dispense with one or the other principle, worship a God thoroughly like us, domesticated, or thoroughly unlike us, beyond good and evil, the tension-filled reality of life suggests we are wise to accept both principles and worship a God who is like us, yet radically Other.

(1992) in this regard that Westerners pushing an anti-fur, don't-eat-seal-or-whale agenda are guilty of cultural imperialism against "the old hunting ethos" of native peoples. We find here, he asserts (35), "a struggle between cultures, wherein one – earnestly and with a great deal of self-righteousness – believes itself to have a natural authority to dictate how things ought to be." In response, Lynge asks (93): "What is one to think of a society where people talk about the liberation of animals while – as a precondition for this exercise – destroying the living conditions for animals far and wide?" While this telling question hardly settles the debate – for one thing, we may wonder whether societies that use snowmobiles and high-powered rifles to take game have not already abandoned the old hunting ethos (especially if done as a way of gaining access to world-markets) – it raises a valid concern regarding cultural imperialism.[44] It is troubling when "outsiders," using technology and time accorded them by a society grossly abusive of wild nature, attack a culture-based way of life which, even if not ideal, causes far less harm to wild nature, in whole and in part.

Even if we eliminate the gross ecological and social excesses of modernity, we will still be left with a way of life and needs, from electricity-generation to road-building, that cause far more harm to wild nature, in whole and in part, than hunting by native peoples and individual nature hunters combined.[45] This raises a question of bad faith when we embrace modernity, reformed or not, yet criticize hunters for harming non-human animals when this is not necessary for their survival. What would it require for *us* not to do so? Ought we give up electric lights and internal combustion engines, artifacts without which people lived for millennia? Ought we go further, give up printed books and horse-drawn carriages, adopt the life-style of fourteenth-century Native Americans?

---

44 One we ought not to dismiss out of hand, as Andrew Linzey (1995: 189) apparently does. For more on this critical issue, see Garner 1993: 151–180, especially 165–168 on "eco-imperialism," and, also, Wenz 1996: esp. 118–148. Note that the laudatory fact that critics do not participate in activities to which they object, such as fur-wearing and meat-eating, does not answer Lynge's question.

45 A good example is provided by non-human animals who thrive in human-created environments, deer, coyotes, beavers, raccoons, rats, so forth and so on. The population of these animals increases rapidly, posing serious problems for them and us, unless controlled by externally imposed means, as regards which it appears there are often no more humane or less detrimental ways of doing so than direct (or indirect) killing. Consenting to this weakens the case against allowing hunters to assume the role of natural predators, requiring us to treat pest control, like executions, as an activity suitable only for the state. While this may be the case, we need to take care less we wink and frown simultaneously at what turns out, from the prey's point of view, to be the same activity. See Dizard 1999 for a close study of debates over the control of deer in the Quabbin, a large reservoir northwest of Boston.

Would that suffice? Where do we stop? How lightly are we required to tread?

Here it is worth nothing that the principle of necessity, as affirmed by humane holism and, by extension, theistic naturalism, focuses on well-being, not bare survival. Obviously, this opens the door for activities that are not, as a rule, required for our survival. It also, of course, opens the door to contention: what is essential for our well-being? The account of well-being given in chapter six helps us get hold of this question by identifying the kind of things which matter to well-being. It does not tell us, however, or pretend to tell us how we are advised to live here and now. That, like "reasonable care," only gets settled with requisite determinacy by the faith-based convictions, religious and cultural, which give individuals and communities a determinate identity.

That, in brief, is why differences in charismatic experience and cultural context matter so much – and, more particularly, give rise to and sustain different views of well-being and, therewith, nature hunting. Thus, for me, unlike Leopold, nature hunting is not part of an ideal human life, a life lived in harmony with wild nature. This does not mean I am unable to hear and appreciate the contrary ideal, as I hope comes across in the above exploration of reasons for agreeing with Leopold – reasons that lead me to qualify and refine, though not repudiate long-standing convictions. As to why I take these reasons seriously, I owe a special debt to those students who made an effort to enlighten me, show me why they saw the matter differently. In the end, dialogue, encounter, is more important for understanding and appreciating others than an ability to think like a lawyer.

I recall in particular one after-class conversation with a forestry student who was also an avid duck hunter. Having already engaged in class the arguments about hunting, pro and con, there was little we could say to each other in that regard. What he did was share with me his experience as a duck hunter. Not surprising, what he said was more-or-less what Leopold says. Hunting was for him a form of communion with nature: planning the trip, getting up early, spending the day in the woods with his dog, relying on one another for a common goal, all highly rewarding whether or not they got a bird, an allure made all the greater by the fact that he had, as a boy, hunted ducks with his father. What made the difference for me between reading Leopold's account and talking with him face-to-face was that I could see the truth of what he said in his eyes, sense the conviction in his voice, witness the way he related to his dog, could tell, in short, that duck hunting really was for him part of a quest for harmony with nature, not a rationalization for cruelty.

I still cannot agree that shooting ducks or any other non-human animals is part of a truly good, fully human life – even if it proves necessary on occasion, relative to our and/or their well-being, to shoulder the responsibility of dominion and bring their life to an end. In doing so we ought to act with regret, realizing that our true dominion and well-being lies in providing as best we can for the earth and our earth-born companions, not pretending to be lions and tigers. At the same time, conversations such as the above have given me a feel, more than analysis and argument, for why a good person and lover of wild nature might do such a thing. Now, when I come across hunters in the fall, I try to remember my friend and wish them a good day – though not success.

THE POLITICS OF NATURE

Our response to the question of human predation depends not only on what we see in the old wolf's eye but, even more, our own, reflected in the mirror of self-understanding. The fact no one can get around is that equally sincere, intelligent, and well-informed people come away from these encounters with divergent convictions regarding the normatively laden reality of nature, wild and human. This, in turn, the absence of a rationally compelling resolution, may lead some to believe we are left at the end of the day with no more than conflicting preferences, the values we happen to affirm. I have tried to show throughout that this is *not* the case. Faith and reason work together to illuminate the life we live all the way through – as regards which it matters greatly how we talk and argue with one another about the things on which we cannot agree. Even if the reasons we give do not persuade others, they help clarify the shape and scope of our own, faith-based convictions, making it possible for us to live and work together.

The convictions and values by which we live are situated, made compelling, given power, by the way they interact with the cultural ethos in which we live and the on-going, internally differentiated dynamic of our thought, our comprehensive reason. This enables us to grasp our beliefs and values reflectively, talk to others about them, find out what they believe and why. The last is critical. We do not confront others as black-boxes. We can talk and reason together, even learn from those with whom we disagree, as I have tried to show those troubled by hunting can learn from hunters. The same, of course, holds in reverse. Just as the former need to realize that not all hunters are atavistic cavemen, so the latter need to see that not all who object to hunting do so because they seek to impose "the anti-natural prophylactic ethos of comfort and soft pleasure" (Callicott 1989: 34) or because, "in utter disharmony with the way the world is made" (Rolston 1988: 91; also 80f.), they refuse to kill any animals at all.

Until we take the step of engaging our fellow, disturbingly obtuse humans in dialogue we cannot understand them or, no less, ourselves. Engaging in dialogue, of course, presupposes the good will and intelligence of those with whom we disagree; we will get nowhere unless we allow for an honest, informed disagreement. And this, it seems to me, we must. For every Luther refusing to bend his knee before a faith not his own, for every liberationist fighting to free wild nature from its chains of bondage, there is a no less principled Sir Thomas More willing to die for the faith Luther rejects, a lumber company executive trying her best to see stockholders make a profit and the forest preserved for tomorrow. This does not mean the executive is right any more than it means the liberationist is right. As an Episcopalian I have my doubts about both Luther and More, theologically speaking. I am sure, however, it is worth my while to listen closely to what they have to say. Of course, I prefer they not bring their respective armies along, which in turn points us toward the need for a viable politics of nature.

Though we simply must get along, we cannot simply get along, if by that one means leave others free to do their own thing, be this a matter of clubbing baby seals, clear-cutting rain-forests, subjecting young girls to clitoridectomies, or leaving doctors free to perform partial-birth abortions. Sometimes we have to draw a line in the sand. My point here, in stressing the vital role faith plays in deciding where to draw that line and the need to try and understand those with whom we disagree, is *not* to deny the need to draw lines *nor* settle the hard question as to when and where we ought to draw these lines. Rather, it is to help us do so in a reasonable, well-informed, moral way – not a way that eliminates the risk of getting it wrong but, rather, increases the odds of our getting it right and, not insignificantly, makes it easier for all creatures to live with the errors we are bound to make. Finding a way to do this is the fundamental problem of our time.

I have no solution to offer, not least one that can be given in the few pages remaining. I would, however, like to offer three suggestions, flag three things we need to do in pursuing a politics that respects nature, wild and human. All of these follow from the argument bringing us to this point. In the course of expanding on the third, I will re-engage, as an example, the issue of vegetarianism, raised at the start of the last section. First, we need to affirm an overtly faith-based, cultural and religious pluralism. This will require us to reject the illusion that there exists a single, rationally compelling solution to our normatively laden concerns. Neither a reductionistic, deceptively precise cost-benefit-analysis nor an allegedly neutral "public reason," dependent for determinateness on hidden presumptions and cultural biases, can provide a uniquely rational consensus.[46] In addition, we must resist the more realistic temptation of a *de jure* or, as now emerging, *de facto* cultural hegemony. This follows from the principle of deference and, no less, the interest we all have in a culturally rich world. The current movement toward a single, global culture, rooted in international commerce, is destroying artistic, religious, and social traditions of great value, leaving us with a one-dimensional, deeply impoverished understanding of our own well-being.[47]

While affirming an overtly faith-based, cultural and religious pluralism runs the risk of balkanization and strife, religious and cultural wars, this danger will not be overcome by spurious claims of commonality nor the cultural hegemony such claims mask – barring the use of totalitarian force and propaganda, such as now appears, distressingly, on every hand. To avoid this sad fate, the death of humanity, we must find a way to live with bottom-line, conflict-inducing religious and cultural diversity. Recognizing the extent to which these disagreements are rooted in individual and communal faith provides a basis for hope, not despair. That generic

[46] For developed criticisms of the former see Sagoff 1988 and O'Neill 1993. For a critical discussion of "public reason" (and, therewith, Jürgen Harbermas and John Rawls, the two philosophers most associated with this notion), see Nicholas Rescher 1993, defending a strong, pragmatic pluralism of the sort advocated here. See also Fern 1987 and, more generally, Benjamin Barber 1984.

[47] Finding a way to counter this movement will require hard thinking and determinate action on economic, legal, and political fronts. Economically, a way must be found to ensure the market advances or, at least, does not harm the good of nature, wild and human. As to whether this requires sweeping transformations of the sort proposed in Schumacher 1973 and Daly 1980 or the more limited changes proposed in Chertow and Esty 1997, I will not speculate. For a good example of the kind of legal thinking required, see the discussion of land-use policy in Caldwell and Shrader-Frechette 1993. The most fundamental question, of course, involves political structures, on which economic and legal reforms depend. A political structure that takes cultural and religious diversity seriously will need to be "federal," that is, combine limited but effective central governments with a dispersion of day-to-day power – as envisioned by both the Articles of Confederation and the subsequent United States Constitution. I mention both to highlight the existence of disagreement and, correspondingly, the need for creative thinking. For a start in this regard, I recommend, on a theoretical level, Walzer 1994, Taylor 1994, Audi and Wolterstorff 1997 and Gutting 1999, and, on a more practical level, Morehouse 1989, Bryan and McClaughry 1989, and Dobbs and Ober 1996. Terrie 1993, Terrie 1994, and Graham 1984 provide instructive cultural and political histories of attempts to integrate people and wilderness in the Adirondack Park region of New York State.

reason underdetermines human life and morality allows us to set aside the rationalistic presumption that those who dare disagree with us are either correct or, more likely (at least in your [my?] case), less virtuous, well-informed, and intelligent. That our life-forming convictions rest at crucial points on faith allows for ineliminable differences of opinion among equally virtuous, well-informed and intelligent persons, without collapsing our differing convictions regarding the deep truth of reality into mere preferences. Thus, what might have been a curse turns out to be a blessing, fostering epistemic humility, mutual understanding, and forbearance.

Second, we need to engage our own convictions critically, in a manner similar to that adopted here. In particular, we need to do three things: (1) subject beliefs and values to philosophical, scientific, and, more generally, academic scrutiny, taking generic reason as far as it goes while allowing that there will be strong and occasionally significant disagreement regarding how far this is and what it shows; (2) attempt to ascertain which of our beliefs and values rest on non-universalizable, charismatically compelling convictions, seeking as we do to understand and order our governing faith theologically, incorporating and making sense of all truth; and (3) ask seriously who we are and, therewith, to whom and what we are committed with regard to the overarching shape and dynamic of our life, allowing as we do the ideality of generic reason and charismatic faith to engage critically and shape for the better the constitutive ground upon which we walk. This thought- and life-encompassing task constitutes the conceptual side of a reflective self-understanding. Just what it involves and how it is carried out, with regard to recognized epistemic authorities, will vary from one individual, one culture to another. All I presume here, based on my own, reflective faith, is that if done thoroughly and honestly, it will end in a morally nuanced position, revealing not only differences but constructive commonalities with the reflective faith of others. In the end we not only disagree about much, we agree about much, by way of reason and faith.

Third, we need to form broad, political coalitions to pursue our common good, locally, nationally, and globally. Doing so will require us to balance a hard-nosed, fact-based realism and a hope-inducing, vision-driven idealism. Let me begin with the first.

Realism is needed in not only assessing possibilities relative to change, as in the case of anti-hunters and wetlands, but, also and especially, characterizing the goals we seek. Building broad coalitions will depend on identifying and stressing risks that are objects of concern and apparent to many, not a few. Consider the following argument for adopting, as individuals and a society, an essentially vegetarian diet.

This argument has three prongs.[48] The first prong focuses on the way literally billions of animals are treated, every year, on "factory farms," the claim being, relative to decency, that no one who cares about the well-being of non-human animals can approve of these practices. The second prong focuses, relative to deference, on the widespread ecological deterioration produced by waste from these facilities, the use of chemicals in farming, and, in general, the overuse of natural resources, land and water, to grow enough grain to feed such a vast number of food-animals, the consequence of our eating high on the food chain. The third prong focuses, relative to both decency and deference, on threats to human health (due to meat toxicity, diseases of affluence, the extensive use of antibiotics on overstressed food-animals, etc.) and, more broadly, socio-political instability (induced by developing conflicts over dwindling resources). The argument concludes that we ought to take immediate steps, individually and corporately, to radically reduce our use of animals for food, adopting a largely vegetarian diet.

Each prong of this argument is subject to dispute; contention abounds. What makes the argument so strong is its comprehensive, non-absolutist character. Even if things are not as bad as claimed on any one of the three fronts, the overall situation remains bad enough that strong reasons to the contrary are required to justify continuing down the path of modern agribusiness.[49] Should special conditions relative to individual health or, for entire peoples, geographic location necessitate extensive use of animal products, the argument does not preclude this. Indeed, the argument does not ask anyone to become a vegetarian, readily allowing for occasional meat-eating, be this special, ceremonial occasions or mere impulse. All the argument seeks is to significantly reduce the use of animal products.

If persuasive, this argument gives ethical vegetarians and nature hunters, family farmers and animal liberationists, deep ecologists and eco-humanists, Christians, Jews, Muslims, Hindus, Buddhists, traditional theists and panentheists, socialists and capitalists, atheists and animists, so forth and so on, compelling reason to come together and work

---

[48] For more on the general argument see Hill 1996 and Fox 1999. On the treatment of animals, see Mason and Singer 1980, Singer 1985, and Rifkin 1992. On ecological problems and associated dangers to human health, see Fox 1986.

[49] Thus, Martin Lewis, though highly critical of "radical environmentalism," concludes (1992: 145): "the need to adopt a less carnivorous diet is paramount."

closely with people of whose ways they strongly disapprove to reduce the widespread, non-sustainable and increasing use of non-human animals for food. Bringing this broad coalition into existence will require a sustained effort to educate people regarding risks and wrongs involved in the way our society now feeds itself. It will also require, however, and it is with this point I want to bring our discussion to an end, the formulation of positive, hope-inducing visions of the future. The primary reason coalitions like the above seem so unlikely, despite the obvious risk and wrong of continuing doing what we are doing, is the difficulty people in general have in imagining and affirming a world so changed.[50]

Consider the extent to which our sense of well-being is tied to what we eat. In part, this is a matter of gustatory delight – which explains why people historically have been willing to pay so much and even fight wars to obtain spices we take for granted. More fundamentally, the significance of food for well-being is cultural and social (Berry 1977 and Telfer 1996). Jeremy Rifkin observes (1992: 63) regarding the consumption of beef in nineteenth-century England:

Eating fatty beef served as an initiation rite for aspiring Englishmen. The taste for fat was synonymous with the taste for opulence, for power and privilege, for the values that made these island people the feared and envied rulers of the world. Marbled beef brought the bourgeoisie and later the working class into the colonial fold. By consuming the fatty flesh of the bovine, these other classes signaled their willingness to take part in the colonial regime. This modern-day baptism of beef aligned the classes in common pursuit.

To understand the appeal of meat-eating we need to appreciate the role particular kinds of food play in fostering community and, with it, contentment. Hot dogs at the ballpark, turkey at Thanksgiving, corned beef on St. Patrick's Day – all these symbolize, even embody community. Not to participate is, prima facie, an insult, no less in New York than the forests of Borneo. It follows that not only is there tremendous social pressure to participate but, also, even deeper, that people in general understand and experience well-being in terms of what they eat.

For society-at-large to turn even essentially vegetarian would require

---

[50] Following a close analysis of attempts to build a broad-based coalition to save "the northern forest," David Dobbs and Richard Ober argue that success in this regard requires a rejection of "the conservation movement's fundamental belief" in centralized, top-down, science-driven solutions and, positively, the adoption of realistic agendas, "granting primacy to local influence, ideas, and interests" (1996: 319–343).

a massive change in self-understanding, individually and socially. Once again, Rifkin hits the nail on the head (1992: 4f.):

The elimination of beef from the human diet [would signal] an anthropological turning point in the history of human consciousness. By moving beyond the beef culture we force a new covenant for humanity, one based on protecting the health of the biosphere, providing sustenance for our fellow human beings, and caring for the welfare of the other creatures with whom we share the earth.

What advocates of vegetarianism tend to overlook, understandably, being that they tend to be vegetarians, is the extent proposals for the abandonment of meat-based foods threaten the general sense of well-being on which every society depends. This not only gives rise to cultural inertia, it provides a prima facie legitimation for continuing to eat "as we always have." We cannot simply smash the world to bits and reshape it nearer to the heart's desire.

It does not follow that overcoming cultural inertia in this regard is not in our collective interest. It does follow that a case for change will need to do more than stress the risk involved in going on as we are. The reason, in brief, is that our response to risk depends not only on "the bare statistics" but, more so, how we view possible losses and gains relative to our own well-being and that of those about whom we care. We are willing to run extreme risks rather than give up practices and objects closely tied to our sense of well-being.[51] People in general refuse to give up meat not because they are particularly stupid or selfish but because meat-eating is so tied to their sense of well-being they cannot envision living in (or leaving to their children) a world in which that good is absent.

Consider in this regard the extent to which vegetarianism is dismissed as not only kooky but "unnatural." The dominant images in Western society of lives lived in harmony with nature are those of noble savages and family farmers.[52] Try to imagine living either life as a vegetarian. The upshot? We grow up envisioning harmony with nature, from the smell of bacon in the morning to the thrill of a successful buffalo hunt, in ways contrary to the practices and ethos of vegetarianism. Hence, advocacy of vegetarianism or, even, an essentially vegetarian diet, comes across as a call to turn our back on wild nature, opt for a different, less

[51] Thus, we elect politicians who tell us the future will be ever bright, while turning out of office those who call on us to give up our overheated houses and gas-guzzling SUVs. This is dumb, all things considered, but not nearly so irrational as one might think on first thought.

[52] Thus, in Ernest Callenbach's widely read deep ecology novel, *Ecotopia*, the goal of Ecotopians, living "in balance with nature," involves hunting deer with bows and arrows (1975: 18f., 36ff.).

natural way of life than that of cowboys and mountain men. If people shaped by these ideals are to eat lower on the food chain, veggie burgers rather than hamburgers, they will need to see how what they value most in wild nature, be this rooster reveille or goose music, is preserved in a less carnivorous world. Otherwise they will not change, no matter how great the risk.[53]

If a broad-based change in diet is to occur it will only come about, barring an overwhelming catastrophe, by way of a realistic appraisal of the risk we all run in not changing, and, in addition, hope-inducing, culturally specific visions of the future. In this regard we need, in working for change, to stress not only what we have in common but, also, our ineliminable differences. We do not live in generic worlds. We live in the culturally specific commitments and charismatically funded convictions that make us the particular persons we are.[54] Accordingly we require multiple, overlapping, yet irreducibly diverse and conflicting visions of the future. A large part of the problem in moving forward is that we assume people who agree about immediate problems (and the socio-political structures needed to address them) must share the same vision of a good life. This is self-defeating. What we need to and can do is get together and plug the holes in our common lifeboat, even as we continue to argue about where the boat is going, all the while resisting the impulse to throw overboard those with whom we disagree. Doing so will require a shared, realistic sense of what is required to keep the boat afloat – drawn from our common humanity – and, no less, a plethora of individually and culturally diverse, faith-based legitimations, motivating visions of the end for which God created the world, disagreements and all.[55]

We need in working together in common fields for common goals

---

[53] It is interesting here to note the transition from Ehrenfeld 1978, stressing the danger of overconfidence in our ability to deal with risk, to Ehrenfeld 1993, calling for a transformative vision of life in the new millennium. Both books can be read with profit, yet the first remains incomplete, politically, without the second. As another wise book indicates, "the lure of gold [is our] ticket home" (Jackson 1996: 118). Wes Jackson's story of the homesick slave, who lies to his Spanish captors about the presence of gold in his native Kansas, illustrates, of course, not only the extent to which change depends on the hope of something valued but, also, the need for a prudent vision if we are not to end up disappointed or, like the slave, dead – as regards which these three books provide invaluable counsel.

[54] Hence, the importance of culturally and religiously specific comprehensive guides-to-life of the sort so common in nineteenth-century America – as, for instance, Child 1972 and Beecher and Stowe 1869, the multiple editions of which enabled real women and men to create a new "traditional American family" in response to a changing socio-economic reality.

[55] Hence, the political error in portraying traditional theism, the culturally dominant form of faith for Christians, Jews, and Muslims, as inherently hostile to ecological and social concerns. This is especially unfortunate, since unnecessary: traditional theism is deeply committed to the good of nature, wild and human.

to pause every now and then and drink deep from our own wells. The resultant divergence of expectations and hopes, the persistent and some-times troubling intractability of human nature, rather than undermining our commonality and good, is an integral part of it, being nothing other than the sentiotic flowering of wild nature. Who would want a meadow with only one kind of flower? Certainly not God.

* * * * * * *

O God, enlarge within us the sense of fellowship with all living things, our brothers, the animals, to whom thou gavest the earth as their home in common with us. We remember with shame that in the past we have exercised the high dominion of man with ruthless cruelty, so that the voice of the earth, which should have gone up to thee in song, has been a groan of travail. May we realize that they live not for us alone but for themselves and for thee and that they love the sweetness of life. (St. Basil the Great)[56]

[56] Cited in McDonagh 1990: 167.

Bibliography

Note: The first date given is that of the edition used. Where this differs significantly from the date of origin, the latter is given in square brackets following the work cited; where this is unknown, the author's dates of birth and death are given in square brackets at the end of the entry.

Abbey, Edward 1971, *Desert Solitaire: A Season in the Wilderness*, New York: Ballantine Books.

Adams, Carol J. (ed.) 1993, *Ecofeminism and the Sacred*, New York: Continuum.

Aiken, William 1984, "Ethical Issues in Agriculture," in Regan (ed.), 247–288.

Albanese, Catherine L. 1990, *Nature Religion in America: From the Algonkian Indians to the New Age*, Chicago: University of Chicago Press.

Alston, William P. 1985, "God's Action in the World," in McMullen (ed.), 197–220.

1989, *Epistemic Justification: Essays in the Theory of Knowledge*, Ithaca, NY: Cornell University Press.

1991, *Perceiving God: The Epistemology of Religious Experience*, Ithaca, NY: Cornell University Press.

1996, *A Realist Conception of Truth*, Ithaca, NY: Cornell University Press.

Anderson, Bernard W. 1987, *Creation Versus Chaos: The Reinterpretation of Mythical Symbolism in the Bible*, Philadelphia: Fortress Press.

Annas, Julia 1993, *The Morality of Happiness*, Oxford: Oxford University Press.

Aquinas, Thomas 1964, *Summa Theologica* [1265–1273], Blackfriars edition (63 vols.), executive editor, Thomas Gilby, New York: McGraw-Hill.

1975, *On the Truth of the Christian Faith (Summa Contra Gentiles)* [1261–1264], trans. A. Pegis, J. F. Anderson, V. Bourke, and C. O'Neil, 5 vols., Notre Dame, IN: University of Notre Dame Press.

Attfield, Robin 1983, *The Ethics of Environmental Concern*, New York: Columbia University Press.

1986, "The Good of Trees," in VanDeVeer and Pierce (eds.), 96–105; originally published in *The Journal of Value Inquiry* 15 (1981): 35–54.

1987, *A Theory of Value and Obligation*, London: Croom Helm.

1991, *The Ethics of Environmental Concern*, 2nd edn., Athens: University of Georgia Press.

1994, *Environmental Philosophy*, Aldershot: Avebury.

1999, *The Ethics of the Global Environment*, Edinburgh: Edinburgh University Press.

Audi, Robert 1988, "Theology, Science and Ethics in Gustafson's Theocentric Vision," in Beckley (ed.), 159–185.

Audi, Robert and Wolterstorff, Nicholas 1997, *Religion in the Public Square: The Place of Religious Convictions in Political Debate*, Lanham, MD: Rowman & Littlefield.

Augustine, St. 1955, *Augustine: Confessions and Enchiridion* [397–401; 421–423] The Library of Christian Classics, vol. VII, trans. and ed. Albert C. Outler, Philadelphia: The Westminster Press.

1982, *The Literal Meaning of Genesis* [401–414], trans. J. H. Taylor, S. J., New York: Newman.

1984, *Concerning the City of God Against the Pagans* [413–427], trans. Henry Bettenson, intro. John O'Meara, London: Penguin Books.

Austin, Richard Cartwright 1987, *Baptized into Wildnerness: A Christian Perspective on John Muir*, Atlanta, GA: John Knox Press.

Ayala, Francisco J. 1985, "The Theory of Evolution," in McMullin (ed.), 59–90.

Baer, Richard 1971, "Ecology, Religion and the American Dream," *American Ecclesiastical Review* 165 (September): 46–47.

Baker, John Austin 1975, "Biblical Attitudes to Nature," in Montefiore (ed.), 87–109.

Barber, Benjamin R. 1984, *Strong Democracy*, Berkeley: University of California Press.

Barth, Karl 1958, *Church Dogmatics*, vol. III: *The Doctrine of Creation*, Pt. 1, trans. J. W. Edwards, J. Bussey, and Harold Knight, ed. G. W. Bromiley and T. F. Torrance, Edinburgh: T. & T. Clark.

1960, *Church Dogmatics*, vol. III: *The Doctrine of Creation*, Pt. 2, trans. Harold Knight, *et al.*, ed. G. W. Bromiley and T. F. Torrance, Edinburgh: T. & T. Clark.

1961a, *Church Dogmatics*, vol. III: *The Doctrine of Creation*, Pt. 3, trans. G. W. Bromiley, J. K. S. Reid, and R. H. Fuller, ed. G. W. Bromiley and T. F. Torrance, Edinburgh: T. & T. Clark.

1961b, *Church Dogmatics*, vol. III: *The Doctrine of Creation*, Pt. 4, trans. A. T. MacKay, *et al.*, ed. G. W. Bromiley and T. F. Torrance, Edinburgh: T. & T. Clark.

Basil, St. 1995, "Hexaemeron," in *Letters and Select Works*, trans. Blomfield Jackson, vol. VIII of *A Select Library of the Christian Church: Nicene and Post-Nicene Fathers*, ed. Philip Schaff and Henry Wace, Peabody, MA: Hendrickson. [330–379]

Beecher, Catherine E. and Stowe, Harriet Beecher 1869, *The American Woman's Home: or, Principles of Domestic Science being a Guide to the Formation and Maintenance of Economical, Beautiful and Christian Homes*, New York: J. B. Ford.

Beckley, Harlan and Swezey, Charles M. (eds.) 1988, *James M. Gustafson's Theocentric Ethics: Interpretations and Assessments*, Macon, GA: Mercer University Press.

Behe, Michael J. 1996, *Darwin's Black Box: The Biochemical Challenge to Evolution*, New York: The Free Press.

Belanger, Dian Olson 1988, *Managing American Wildlife: A History of the International Association of Fish and Wildlife Agencies*, Amherst: University of Massachusetts Press.

Bentham, Jeremy 1945, *Introduction to the Principles of Morals and Legislation* [1789], New York: Columbia University Press.

Berger, Peter L. 1969, *The Sacred Canopy: Elements of a Sociological Theory of Religion*, Garden City, NY: Anchor Books.

1970, *A Rumor of Angels: Modern Sociology and the Rediscovery of the Supernatural*, Garden City, NY: Anchor Books.

Berger, Peter L. and Luckmann, Thomas 1967, *The Social Construction of Reality: A Treatise in the Sociology of Knowledge*, Garden City, NY: Anchor Books.

Berman, Morris 1981, *The Reenchantment of the World*, Ithaca, NY: Cornell University Press.

Berry, Thomas 1990, *The Dream of the Earth*, San Francisco: Sierra Club Books.

Berry, Wendell 1977, *The Unsettling of America: Culture and Agriculture*, San Francisco: Sierra Club Books.

Blacker, Charles Paton 1952, *Eugenics: Galton and After*, Cambridge, MA: Harvard University Press.

Blackstone, William T. 1974a, "Ethics and Ecology," in Blackstone (ed.), 16–42.

Blackstone, William T. (ed.) 1974b, *Philosophy and Environmental Crisis*, Athens: University of Georgia Press.

Blake, William 1987, *The Essential Blake*, selected by Stanley Kunitz, New York: MJF Books. [1757–1827]

Bleich, J. David 1986, "Judaism and Animal Experimentation," in Regan (ed.), 61–114.

Blum, Lawrence A. 1980, *Friendship, Altruism and Morality*, London: Routledge & Kegan Paul.

1994, *Moral Perception and Particularity*, Cambridge: Cambridge University Press.

Bookchin, Murray 1991, *The Ecology of Freedom: The Emergence and Dissolution of Hierarchy*, rev. edn., New York: Black Rose Books.

Bostock, Stephen St. C. 1993, *Zoos and Animal Rights: The Ethics of Keeping Animals*, London: Routledge.

Bowden, Charles 1977, *Killing the Hidden Waters*, Austin: University of Texas Press.

Bowman, Leonard J. 1975, "The Cosmic Exemplarism of Bonaventura," *Journal of Religion* 55 (April): 181–198.

Bramwell, Anna 1989, *Ecology in the 20th Century: A History*, New Haven: Yale University Press.

Bratton, Susan Power 1986, "Christianity Ecotheology and the Old Testament," in Hargrove (ed.), 53–75.

1993, *Christianity, Wilderness and Wildlife: The Original Desert Solitaire*, Scranton, PA: University of Scranton Press.

Brennan, Andrew 1988, *Thinking about Nature: An Investigation of Nature, Value and Ecology*, Athens: University of Georgia Press.

Brooke, John Hedley 1991, *Science and Religion: Some Historical Perspectives*, Cambridge: Cambridge University Press.

Brown, Joseph Epes (ed.) 1971, *The Sacred Pipe: Black Elk's Account of the Seven Rites of the Oglala Sioux*, New York: Penguin.

Brown, Peter 1969, *Augustine of Hippo: A Biography*, Berkeley: University of California Press.

Bruggemann, Walter 1987, "Land, Fertility and Justice," in Evans and Cusack (eds.), 41–68.

Brumbaugh, Robert S. 1978, "Of Man, Animals and Morals," in Morris and Fox (eds.), 6–25.

Brunner, Emil 1946, "Nature and Grace," trans. Peter Fraenkel, with a reply by Karl Barth, in *Natural Theology*, London: The Centenary Press.

Bryan, Frank and McClaughry, John 1989, *The Vermont Papers: Recreating Democracy on a Human Scale*, Post Mills, VT: Chelsea Green.

Bultmann, Rudolf 1958, *Jesus Christ and Mythology*, New York: Scribner.

Burrell, David B. 1993, *Freedom and Creation in Three Traditions*, Notre Dame, IN: University of Notre Dame Press.

Butler, Joseph 1950, *Five Sermons Preached at the Rolls Chapel and A Dissertation Upon the Nature of Virtue* [1726; 1736], New York: Bobbs-Merrill.

Caldwell, Lynton Keith and Shrader-Frechette, Kristin 1993, *Policy for Land: Law and Ethics*, Lanham, MD: Rowman & Littlefield.

Callenbach, Ernest 1975, *Ecotopia: The Notebooks and Reports of William Weston*, New York: Bantam.

Callicott, J. Baird 1989, *In Defense of the Land Ethic: Essays in Environmental Philosophy*, Albany: State University of New York Press.

Callicott, J. Baird (ed.) 1987, *Companion to A Sand County Almanac: Interpretive and Critical Essays*, Madison: University of Wisconsin Press.

Calvin, John 1960, *Institutes of the Christian Religion* [1536–1559], Books I (ch. 1) to III (ch. 19), The Library of Christian Classics, vol. XX, ed. John T. McNeill, trans. and indexed Ford Lewis Battles, Philadelphia: The Westminster Press.

Cardenal, Ernesto 1974, *Love*, trans. Dinah Livingstone, preface by Thomas Merton, London: Search Press.

Carmody, John 1983, *Ecology and Religion: Toward a New Christian Theology of Nature*, New York: Paulist Press.

Carruthers, Peter 1992, *The Animals Issue: Moral Theory in Practice*, Cambridge: Cambridge University Press.

Catechism of the Catholic Church 1994, Washington, D. C.: United States Catholic Conference.

Chase, Alston 1987, *Playing God in Yellowstone: The Destruction of America's First National Park*, New York: Harcourt Brace Jovanovich.

Chase, Steve (ed.) 1991, *Defending the Earth: A Dialogue between Murray Bookchin and Dave Foreman*, Boston: South End Press.

Chertow, Marian R. and Esty, Daniel C. (eds.) 1997, *Thinking Ecologically: The New Generation of Environmental Policy*, New Haven: Yale University Press.

Child, Lydia Maria Francis 1972, *The American Frugal Housewife: Dedicated to Those Who are not Ashamed of Economy*, fascsimile of 20th edn. [1836], New York: Harper & Row.

Christian, William A., Sr. 1987, *Doctrines of Religious Communities: A Philosophical Study*, New Haven: Yale University Press.

Clark, Stephen R. L. 1982, *The Nature of the Beast: Are Animals Moral?*, Oxford: Oxford University Press.

  1984, *The Moral Status of Animals*, Oxford: Oxford University Press.

  1989, *Civil Peace and Sacred Order*, vol. I of *Limits and Renewal*, Oxford: Clarendon Press.

Cobb, John B., Jr. 1992, *Sustainability: Economics, Ecology and Justice*, Maryknoll, NY: Orbis.

Cohen, Michael P. 1984, *The Pathless Way: John Muir and American Wilderness*, Madison, WI: University of Wisconsin Press.

Collingwood, Robert George 1960, *The Idea of Nature*, Oxford: Oxford University Press.

Commoner, Barry 1971, *The Closing Circle: Nature, Man and Technology*, New York: Alfred A. Knopf.

Cragg, Kenneth 1975, *The House of Islam*, 2nd edn., Encino, CA: Dickenson Publishing Company.

Cupitt, Don 1975, "Some Evidence from Other Religions," in Montefiore (ed.), 159–168.

Curran, Charles E., and McCormick, Richard A., S. J. (eds.) 1991, *Natural Law and Theology*, Mahwah, NY: Paulist Press.

Dalton, Anne Marie 1999, *A Theology for the Earth: the Contributions of Thomas Berry and Bernard Lonergan*, Ottawa, Ont.: University of Ottawa Press.

Daly, Herman E. (ed.) 1980, *Economics, Ecology, Ethics: Essays Toward a Steady-State Economy*, New York: W. H. Freeman.

Darwin, Charles 1897, *The Descent of Man and Selection in Relation to Sex* [1871], New York: D. Appleton.

  1965, *The Expression of the Emotions in Man and Animals* [1872], Chicago: University of Chicago Press.

DeGrazia, David 1996, *Taking Animals Seriously: Mental Life and Moral Status*, Cambridge: Cambridge University Press.

Dembski, William A. 1998, *The Design Inference: Eliminating Chance Through Small Probabilities*, Cambridge: Cambridge University Press.

Dennett, Daniel C. 1978, *Brainstorms: Philosophical Essays on Mind and Psychology*, Montgomery, VT: Bradford Books.

Descola, Philippe and Palsson, Gisli (eds.) 1996, *Nature and Society: Anthropological Perspectives*, London: Routledge.

Devall, Bill and Sessions, George 1985, *Deep Ecology: Living as if Nature Mattered*, Salt Lake City: Peregrine Smith Books.

Dijksterhuis, E. J. 1961, *The Mechanization of the World Picture*, trans. C. Dikshoorn, London: Oxford University Press.

Dizard, Jan E. 1999, *Going Wild: Hunting, Animal Rights and the Contested Meaning of Nature*, rev. and expanded edn., Amherst: University of Massachusetts Press.

Dobbs, David, and Ober, Richard 1996, *The Northern Forest*, White River Junction, VT: Chelsea Green.

Dowey, Edward A., Jr. 1994, *The Knowledge of God in Calvin's Theology*, expanded edn., Grand Rapids, MI: Eerdmans.

Dupré, Louis 1993, *Passage to Modernity: An Essay in the Hermeneutics of Nature and Culture*, New Haven: Yale University Press.

Eckersley, Robyn 1992, *Environmentalism and Political Theory: Toward an Ecocentric Approach*, Albany: State University of New York Press.

Edwards, Jonathan 1989, "Concerning the End for Which God Created the World" [1765], *The Works of Jonathan Edwards*, vol. VIII: *Ethical Writings*, ed. Paul Ramsey, New Haven: Yale University Press.

Ehrenfeld, David 1978, *The Arrogance of Humanism*, Oxford: Oxford University Press.

1993, *Beginning Again: People and Nature in the New Millennium*, Oxford: Oxford University Press.

Eliade, Mircea 1977, *From Primitives to Zen: A Thematic Sourcebook of the History of Religions*, San Francisco: Harper & Row.

Eliot, T. S. 1935, *Murder in the Cathedral*, New York: Harcourt Brace Jovanovich.

1968, *Christianity and Culture: The Idea of a Christian Society and Notes Towards the Definition of Culture*, New York: Harcourt Brace.

Elliot, Robert 1986, "Faking Nature," in VanDeVeer and Pierce (eds.), 142–150; originally published in *Inquiry* 25.1 (1982): 81–93.

Erikson, Erik H. 1962, *Young Man Luther: A Study in Psychoanalysis and History*, New York: W. W. Norton.

1963, *Childhood and Society*, 2nd edn., New York: W.W. Norton.

Evans, Bernard F., and Cusak, Gregory D. (eds.) 1987, *Theology of the Land*, Collegeville, MN: The Liturgical Press.

Evans-Pritchard, E. E. 1965, *Theories of Primitive Religion*, Oxford: Clarendon Press.

Farley, Margaret 1986, *Personal Commitments: Making, Keeping, Breaking*, San Francisco: Harper & Row.

Feinberg, Joel 1970, "The Nature and Value of Rights," *The Journal of Value Inquiry* 4 (Winter): 243–257.

1974, "The Rights of Animals and Unborn Generations," in Blackstone (ed.), 43–68.

1978, "Human Duties and Animal Rights," in Morris and Fox (eds.), 45–69.

Fern, Richard 1982, "Hume's Critique of Miracles: An Irrelevant Triumph," *Religious Studies* 18 (September): 337–354.

1987, "Religious Belief in a Rawlsian Society," *Journal of Religious Ethics* 15 (Spring): 35–58.

1993, "The Internal Logic of Justice," *The Annual of the Society of Christian Ethics* (1993): 23–45.

Fiddes, Paul S. 1988, *The Creative Suffering of God*, Oxford: Clarendon Press.

Fischer, John Martin (ed.) 1989, *God, Foreknowledge and Freedom*, Stanford, CA: Stanford University Press.

Fleischacker, Samuel 1994, *The Ethics of Culture*, Ithaca, NY: Cornell University Press.

Fleming, John G. 1985, *An Introduction to the Law of Torts*, 2nd edn., Oxford: Clarendon Press.

Flew, Antony 1955, "Theology and Falsification," in Flew and MacIntyre (eds.): 96–99.

Flew, Antony, and MacIntyre, Alasdair (eds.) 1955, *New Essays in Philosophical Theology*, New York: Macmillan.

Forsyth, Neil 1987, *The Old Enemy: Satan and the Combat Myth*, Princeton: Princeton University Press.

Fowler, Robert Booth 1995, *The Greening of Protestant Thought*, Chapel Hill: University of North Carolina Press.

Fox, Michael Allen 1999, *Deep Vegetarianism*, Philadelphia: Temple University Press.

Fox, Michael W. 1986, *Agricide: The Hidden Crisis that Affects Us All*, New York: Schocken Books.

Fox, Stephen 1985, *The American Conservation Movement: John Muir and His Legacy*, Madison: University of Wisconsin Press.

Fox, Warwick 1990, *Toward a Transpersonal Ecology: Developing New Foundations for Environmentalism*, Boston: Shambhala.

Francione, Gary L. 1994, "Animals, Property and Legal Welfarism: 'Unnecessary' Suffering and the 'Humane' Treatment of Animals," *Rutgers Law Review* 46 (Winter): 721–770.

1995. *Animals, Property, and the Law*, Philadelphia: Temple University Press.

Frankena, William 1979, "Ethics and the Environment," in Goodpaster and Sayre (eds.), 3–20.

Franklin, Benjamin 2001, *The Autobiography of Benjamin Franklin and Selections from his Other Writings* [1789], intro. Stacy Schiff, New York: The Modern Library.

Frei, Hans W. 1974, *The Eclipse of Biblical Narrative: A Study in Eighteenth and Nineteenth Century Hermeneutics*, New Haven: Yale University Press.

Frey, R. 1980, *Interests and Rights: The Case Against Animals*, Oxford: Clarendon Press.

Frymer-Kensky, Tikva, Novak, David, Ochs, Peter, and Signer, Michael A. 2000, "Dabru Emet: A Jewish Statement on Christians and Christianity," *The New York Times* (September 10), Section A, 37.

Galston, William 1980, *Justice and the Human Good*, Chicago: University of Chicago Press.

Garner, Robert 1993, *Animals, Politics and Morality*, Manchester: Manchester University Press.

Geertz, Clifford 1973, *The Interpretation of Cultures*, New York: Basic Books.

Gendler, Everett 1993, "A Jewish Perspective on Creation," talk given at University of New Hampshire Conference: "God, the Environment and the Good" (November 12).

Gilbert, Margaret 1989, *On Social Facts*, Princeton: Princeton University Press.

1996, *Living Together: Rationality, Sociality, and Obligation*, Lanham, MD: Rowman & Littlefield.

Gilkey, Langdon 1993, *Nature, Reality and the Sacred: The Nexus of Science and Religion*, Minneapolis: Fortress Press.

Gilson, Etienne 1984, *From Aristotle to Darwin and Back Again: A Journey in Final Causality, Species, and Evolution*, trans. John Lyon, Notre Dame, IN: University of Notre Dame Press.

Glacken, Clarence J. 1967, *Traces on the Rhodian Shore: Nature and Culture in Western Thought from Ancient Times to the End of the Eighteenth Century*, Berkeley: University of California Press.

Goddard, Hugh 2000, *A History of Christian–Muslim Relations*, Chicago: New Amsterdam Books.

Goodpaster, Kenneth E. 1978, "On Being Morally Considerable," *Journal of Philosophy* 75 (June): 308–325.

1979, "From Egoism to Environmentalism," in Goodpaster and Sayre (eds.), 21–35.

Goodpaster, Kenneth E., and Sayre, Kenneth M. (eds.) 1979, *Ethics and Problems of the 21st Century*, Notre Dame, IN: University of Notre Dame Press.

Graham, Frank Jr. 1984, *The Adirondack Park: A Political History*, Syracuse, NY: Syracuse University Press.

Gray, Elizabeth Dodson 1981, *Green Paradise Lost*, Wellesley, MA: Roundtable Press.

Greene, John C. 1961, *Darwin and the Modern World View*, Baton Rouge: Louisiana State University Press.

1981, *Science, Ideology and World View: Essays in the History of Evolutionary Ideas*, Berkeley: University of California Press.

Gregory of Nyssa 1995, "On the Making of Man," in *Gregory of Nyssa: Dogmatic Treaties, Etc.*, trans. Henry Auston Wilson, vol. v in *A Select Library of the Christian Church: Nicene and Post-Nicene Fathers*, ed. Philip Schaff and Henry Wace, Peabody, MA: Hendrickson. [330–395]

Gregorios, Paulos 1978, *The Human Presence: An Orthodox View of Nature*, Geneva: World Council of Churches.

Griffin, Donald 1981, *The Question of Animal Awareness: Evolutionary Continuity of Mental Experience*, New York: Rockefeller University Press.

1984, *Animal Thinking*, Cambridge, MA: Harvard University Press.

1992, *Animal Minds*, Chicago: University of Chicago Press.

2001, *Animal Minds: Beyond Cognition to Consciousness*, Chicago: University of Chicago Press.

Guillaume, Alfred 1956, *Islam*, rev. edn., New York: Penguin Books.

Gunton, C. E. 1992, *Christ and Creation*, Grand Rapids, MI: Eerdmans.

Gustafson, James M. 1981, *Theology and Ethics*, vol. 1 of *Ethics from a Theocentric Perspective*, Chicago: University of Chicago Press.

1994, *A Sense of the Divine: The Natural Environment from a Theocentric Perspective*, Cleveland, OH: Pilgrim Press.

Gutmann, Amy (ed.) 1994, *Multiculturalism: Examining the Politics of Recognition*, Princeton: Princeton University Press.

Gutting, Gary 1999, *Pragmatic Liberalism and the Critique of Modernity*, Cambridge: Cambridge University Press.

Habermas, Jürgen 1994, "Struggle for Recognition in the Democratic Constitutional State," trans. Shierry Weber Nicholson, in Gutmann (ed.), 107–148.

Hall, Douglas John 1986, *Imaging God: Dominion as Stewardship*, Grand Rapids, MI: Eerdmans.

Hall, Kermit L. 1989, *The Magic Mirror: Law in American History*, Oxford: Oxford University Press.

Hargrove, Eugene 1989, *Foundations of Environmental Ethics*, Englewood Cliffs, NJ: Prentice Hall.

Hargrove, Eugene (ed.) 1986, *Religion and Environmental Crisis*, Athens: University of Georgia Press.

Hauerwas, Stanley, and Berkman, John 1993, "A Trinitarian Theology of the 'Chief End' of 'All Flesh'," in Pinches and McDaniel (eds.), 62–74.

Haught, John R. 1993, *The Promise of Nature: Ecology and Cosmic Purpose*, New York: Paulist Press.

Hauser, Mark D. 2000, *Animal Minds: What Animals Really Think*, New York: Henry Holt.

Hendry, George S. 1980, *Theology of Nature*, Philadelphia: Westminster Press.

Heschel, Abraham 1962, *The Prophets*, New York: Harper & Row.

Hesse, Mary 1975, "On the Alleged Incompatibility between Christianity and Science," in Montefiore (ed.), 121–131.

Hessel, Dieter T. 1992a, "Introduction: Eco-Justice Theology after Nature's Revolt," in Hessel (ed.), 1–18.

Hessel, Dieter T. (ed.) 1992b, *After Nature's Revolt: Eco-Justice and Theology*, Minneapolis: Fortress Press.

Hill, John Lawrence 1996, *The Case for Vegetarianism: Philosophy for a Small Planet*, Lanham, MD: Rowman & Littlefield.

Hooker, Brad, and Little, Margaret (eds.) 2000, *Moral Particularism*, Oxford: Clarendon Press.

Horwitz, Morton J. 1977, *The Transformation of American Law 1780–1860*, Cambridge, MA: Harvard University Press.

Hume, David 1948, *Hume's Dialogues Concerning Natural Religion* [1751–1776], ed. with an intro. by Norman Kemp Smith, 2nd edn., New York: Social Sciences Publishers.

Irenaeus of Lyons 1995, *Against Heresies*, in vol. 1 of *Ante-Nicene Fathers: The Apostolic Fathers, Justin Martyr, Irenaeus*, ed. Alexander Roberts and James Donaldson, rev. A. Cleveland Coxe, Peabody, MA: Hendrickson. [130–200]

Jackson, Wes 1996, *Becoming Native to this Place*, Washington, D. C.: Counterpoint.
Jaki, Stanley L. 1978, *The Road of Science and the Ways to God*, the Gifford Lectures 1974–6, Chicago: University of Chicago Press.
James, William 1961, *Varieties of Religious Experience: A Study in Human Nature* [1902], New York: Collier Books.
   1962, "The Will to Believe" [1898], in *Essays on Faith and Morals*, Cleveland, OH: Meridian Books.
Johnson, Edward 1984, "Treating the Dirt: Environmental Ethics and Moral Theory," in Regan (ed.), 336–365.
Johnson, Lawrence E. 1991, *A Morally Deep World*, Cambridge: Cambridge University Press.
Juliana of Norwich 1977, *Revelations of Divine Love*, trans. with an intro. M. L. del Mastro, Garden City, NY: Image Books. [1342–1413]
Kaminsky, Joel 1995a, *Corporate Responsibility in the Hebrew Bible*, Sheffield: Sheffield Academic Press.
   1995b, "Individual versus Communal Responsibility: Justice or Mercy," talk given at 1995 Annual Meeting of the Society of Biblical Literature.
Kant, Immanuel 1997, *Lectures on Ethics* (1780), ed. Peter Heath and J. B. Schneewind, trans. Peter Heath, Cambridge: Cambridge University Press.
Katz, Eric 1997, *Nature as Subject: Human Obligation and Natural Community*, Lanham, MD: Rowman & Littlefield.
Kaufman, Gordon 2000, "Re-Conceiving God and Humanity in Light of Today's Ecological Consciousness," *Cross Currents* (Spring/Summer): 103–111.
Kekes, John 1989, *Moral Tradition and Individuality*, Princeton: Princeton University Press.
   1993, *The Morality of Pluralism*, Princeton: Princeton University Press.
Kellert, Stephen R. 1996, *The Value of Life: Biological Diversity and Human Society*, Washington, D. C.: Island Press.
   1997, *Kinship to Mastery: Biophilia in Human Evolution and Development*, Washington, D. C.: Island Press.
Kelsey, David 1985, "The Doctrine of Creation from Nothing," in McMullin (ed.), 176–196.
Kepnes, Steven, Ochs, Peter, and Gibbs, Robert 1998, *Reasoning After Revelation: Dialogues in Postmodern Jewish Philosophy*, Boulder, CO: Westview Press.
Kierkegaard, Soren 1946, *Works of Love: Some Christian Reflections on the Form of Discourses* [1847], trans. David F. Swenson and Lillian Marvin Swenson, Princeton: Princeton University Press.
   1959, *Either/Or* [1843], 2 vols., trans. David F. Swenson and Lilliam Marvin Swenson (vol. i) and Walter Lowrie (vol. ii), with revisions and a foreward by Howard A. Johnson, Garden City, NY: Doubleday.
Kirkpatrick, Dow (ed.) 1971, *The Living God*, Nashville, TN: Abingdon Press.
Kohák, Erazim 1984, *The Embers and the Stars: A Philosophical Inquiry into the Moral Sense of Nature*, Chicago: University of Chicago Press.
   2000, *The Green Halo: A Bird's-Eye View of Ecological Ethics*, Chicago: Open Court.

Kowalski, Gary 1991, *The Souls of Animals*, Walpole, NH: Stillpoint Publishing.

Krieger, Martin 1973, "What's wrong with Plastic Trees?," *Science* 179 (February): 446–454.

Kupperman, Joel 1991, *Character*, Oxford: Oxford University Press.

Lao Tzu 1963, *Tao Te Ching*, trans. with an intro. by D. C. Lau, Baltimore, MD: Penguin Books. [6th century B. C. E.]

Larmore, Charles 1987, *Patterns of Moral Complexity*, Cambridge: Cambridge University Press.

1996, *The Morals of Modernity*, Cambridge: Cambridge University Press.

Leahy, Michael P. T. 1994, *Against Liberation: Putting Animals in Perspective*, London: Routledge.

Leiss, William 1974, *The Domination of Nature*, Boston: Beacon Press.

Leopold, Aldo 1970, *A Sand County Almanac with Essays on Conservation from Round River*, illus. by Charles W. Schwartz, New York: Ballantine Books.

Lewis, C. S. 1946, *The Great Divorce*, New York: Macmillan.

1947, *The Abolition of Man*, New York: Macmillan.

Lewis, Martin 1992, *Green Delusions: An Environmentalist Critique of Radical Environmentalism*, Durham, NC: Duke University Press.

Light, Andrew 1996, "Environmental Pragmatism as Philosophy or Metaphilosophy? On the Weston-Katz Debate," in Light and Katz (eds), 325–338.

Light, Andrew and Katz, Eric (eds.) 1996, *Environmental Pragmatism*, London: Routledge.

Lindbeck, George A. 1984, *The Nature of Doctrine: Religion and Theology in a Postliberal Age*, Philadelphia: The Westminister Press.

Linzey, Andrew 1987, *Christianity and the Rights of Animals*, New York: Crossword.

1995, *Animal Theology*, Urbana: University of Illinois Press.

Linzey, Andrew and Regan, Tom (eds.) 1988, *Animals and Christianity: A Book of Readings*, NY: Crossroad.

Lodrick, D. O. 1981, *Sacred Cows, Sacred Places*, Berkeley: University of Californian Press.

Lossky, Vladimir 1973, *The Mystical Theology of the Eastern Church*, trans. the Fellowship of St. Alban and St. Sergius, London: James Clarke.

Lovelock, James E. 1979, *Gaia: A New Look at Life on Earth*, Oxford: Oxford University Press.

Lynge, Finn 1992, *Arctic Wars, Animal Rights, Endangered Peoples*, trans. Marianne Stenbaek, Hanover, NH: University Press of New England.

McDaniel, Jay B. 1986, "Christianity and the Need for New Vision," in Hargrove (ed.), 188–212.

1989, *Of God and Pelicans: A Theology of Reverence for Life*, Louisville, KY: Westminster/John Knox Press.

McDonagh, Sean 1990, *The Greening of the Church*, Maryknoll, MD: Orbis Books.

McFague, Sallie 1993a, *The Body of God: An Ecological Theology*, Minneapolis: Fortress Press.

1993b, "An Earthly Theological Agenda," in Adams (ed.), 84–98.

McGrath, Alister E. 1994, *Christian Theology*, Oxford: Blackwell.

1998, *The Foundations of Dialogue in Science and Religions*, Oxford: Blackwell.

MacIntyre, Alasdair 1984, *After Virtue*, 2nd edn., Notre Dame, IN: University of Natre Dame Press.

McLean, George F. (ed.) 1978, *Man and Nature*, Calcutta: Oxford University Press.

McMullin, Ernan 1985a, "Introduction," in McMullin (ed.), 1–56.

McMullin, Ernan (ed.) 1985b, *Evolution and Creation*, Notre Dame, IN: University of Notre Dame Press.

Macquarrie, John 1974, "Creation and Environment," in Spring and Spring (eds.), 32–47.

Maimonides, Moses, 1963, *Guide of the Perplexed* [1190], intro. Shomo Pines, intro. essay Leo Strauss, Chicago: University of Chicago Press.

Mannison, D. S., McRobbie, M. A., and Routley, R. (eds.) 1980, *Environmental Philosophy*, Monograph Series 2, Philosophy Department, Australian National University.

Marcuse, Herbert 1964, *One-Dimensional Man: Studies in the Ideology of Advanced Industrial Society*, Boston: Beacon Press.

Marietta, Don E., Jr. 1994, *For People and the Planet: Holism and Humanism in Environmental Ethics*, Philadelphia: Temple University Press.

Maritain, Jacques 1966, *The Person and the Common Good*, trans. John J. Fitzgerald, Notre Dame, IN: University of Notre Dame Press.

Markus, R. A. 1954, "Pleroma and Fulfillment: The Significance of History in St. Irenaeus' Opposition to Gnosticism," *Vigiliae Christianae* 8 (no. 4): 193–244.

1970, *Saeculum: History and Society in the Theology of Augustine*, Cambridge: Cambridge University Press.

Mason, Jim, and Singer, Peter 1980, *Animal Factories*, New York: Crown.

Masri, Al-Hafiz B. A. 1986, "Animal Experimentation: The Muslim Viewpoint," in Regan (ed.), 171–197.

May, Larry 1987, *The Morality of Groups : Collective Responsibility, Group-Based Harm, and Corporate Rights*, Notre Dame, IN: University of Notre Dame Press.

May, Robert M. 1992, "The Modern Biologist's View," in Torrance (ed.), 167–182.

Merton, Thomas 1966, *Raids on the Unspeakable*, New York: New Directions.

Midgley, Mary 1978, *Beast and Man: The Roots of Human Nature*, Ithaca, NY: Cornell University Press.

1984, *Animals and Why They Matter*, Athens: University of Georgia Press.

1985, *Evolution as a Religion: Strange Hopes and Stranger Fears*, London: Methuen.

1986, "Persons and Non-Persons," in Singer (ed.), 52–62.

Mill, John Stuart 1969, "On Nature," *Three Essays on Religion* [1874], New York: Greenwood Press.

Miller, Richard W. 1987, *Fact and Method: Explanation, Confirmation and Reality in the Natural and the Social Sciences*, Princeton: Princeton University Press.

Milton, Kay 1996, *Environmentalism and Cultural Theory: Exploring the Role of Anthropology in Environmental Discourse*, London: Routledge.

Moltmann, Jürgen 1993, *God in Creation*, the Gifford Lectures 1984–1985, trans. Margaret Kohl, Minneapolis: Fortress Press.

Monod, Jacques 1971, *Chance and Necessity*, trans. Austryn Wainhouse, New York: Knopf.

Monsma, Stephen V. (ed.) 1986, *Responsible Technology. A Christian Perspective*, by the Fellows of the Calvin Center for Christian Scholarship, Calvin College, Grand Rapids, Michigan: Eerdmans.

Montefiore, Hugh (ed.) 1975, *Man and Nature*. London: Collins.

Moore, George Edward 1968, *Principia Ethica* [1903], Cambridge: Cambridge University Press.

Morehouse, Ward (ed.) 1989, *Building Sustainable Communities: Tools and Concepts for Self-Reliant Economic Change*, Turnbull, NY: The Bootstrap Press.

Morgan, Edmund 1966, *The Puritan Family: Religion and Domestic Relations in Seventeenth-Century New England*, 2nd edn., New York: Harper & Row.

Morris, Richard Knowles, and Fox, Michael W. (eds.) 1978, *On the Fifth Day: Animal Rights and Human Ethics*, Washington, D.C.: Acropolis Books.

Muir, John 1954, *The Wilderness World of John Muir*, ed. Edwin Way Teale, illus. Henry B. Kane, Boston: Houghton Mifflin. [1838–1914]

Murphy, Charles M. 1989, *At Home on Earth: Foundations for a Catholic Ethic of the Environment*, New York: Crossroad.

Nagel, Thomas 1979, *Mortal Questions*, Cambridge: Cambridge University Press.
   1980, "Ethics as an Automonous Theoretical Subject," in Stent (ed.), 198–205.
   1986, *The View from Nowhere*, Oxford: Oxford University Press.

Nash, James A. 1991, *Loving Nature: Ecological Integrity and Christian Responsibility*. Nashville, TN: Abingdon Press.

Nash, Roderick 1982, *Wilderness and the American Mind*, 3rd edn., New Haven: Yale University Press.

Nasr, Seyyed Hussein 1981, *Knowledge and the Sacred*, Albany: State University of New York Press.
   1996, *Religion and the Order of Nature*, Oxford: Oxford University Press.

Neihardt, John G. 1961, *Black Elk Speaks: Being the Life Story of a Holy Man of the Oglala Sioux*, Lincoln: University of Nebraska Press.

Niebuhr, H. Richard 1951, *Christ and Culture*, New York: Harper & Row.

Niesel, Wilhelm 1980, *The Theology of Calvin*, trans. Harold Knight, Grand Rapids, MI: Baker Book House.

Nilsson, Martin P. 1969, *Greek Piety*, trans. Herbert Jennings Rose, New York: W.W. Norton.

Noddings, Nel 1984, *Caring: A Feminine Approach to Ethics and Moral Education*, Berkeley: University of California Press.

Northcott, Michael S. 1996, *The Environmental and Christian Ethics*, Cambridge: Cambridge University Press.

Norton, Bryan G. 1991, *Toward Unity among Environmentalists*, Oxford: Oxford University Press.

1996, "The Constancy of Leopold's Land Ethic," in Light and Katz (eds.), 84–102.

Norton, Bryan G. (ed.) 1986, *The Preservation of Species: The Value of Biological Diversity*, Princeton: Princeton University Press.

Novak, David 2000, *Covenantal Rights: A Study in Jewish Political Theory*, Princeton: Princeton University Press.

Nozick, Robert 1974, *Anarchy, State and Utopia*, New York: Basic Books.

Nussbaum, Martha C. 1994, *The Therapy of Desire: Theory and Practice in Hellenistic Ethics*, Princeton: Princeton University Press.

O'Donovan, Oliver 1986, *Resurrection and Moral Order: An Outline for Evangelical Ethics*, Grand Rapids, MI: Eerdmans.

O'Neill, John 1993, *Ecology, Policy and Politics: Human Well-Being and the Natural World*, London: Routledge.

Ochs, Peter 1998, *Peirce, Pragmatism and the Logic of Scripture*, Cambridge: Cambridge University Press.

Oelschlaeger, Max 1994, *Caring for Creation: An Ecumenical Approach to the Environmental Crisis*, New Haven: Yale University Press.

Origen 1979, "Homily 27 on Numbers," *Origen*, trans. Rowan Greer, New York: Paulist Press. [185–254]

Orleans, F. Barbara, Beauchamp, Tom L., Dresser, Rebecca, Morton, David B., and Gluck, John P., 1998, *The Human Use of Animals: Case Studies in Ethical Choice*, Oxford: Oxford University Press.

Ortega y Gasset, José 1986, *Meditations on Hunting* [1942], New York: Macmillan.

Otto, Rudolf 1950, *The Idea of the Holy*, 2nd edn., trans. J.W. Harvey, Oxford: Oxford University Press.

Outka, Gene 1972, *Agape: An Ethical Analysis*, New Haven: Yale University Press.

1992, "Universal Love and Impartiality," in Santurri and Werpehowski (eds.), 1–103.

Page, George 1999, *Inside the Animal Mind*, New York: Doubleday.

Page, Ruth 1996, *God and the Web of Creation*, London: SCM Press.

Pannenberg, Wolfhart 1993, *Toward a Theology of Nature: Essays on Science and Faith*, ed. Ted Peters, Louisville, KY: Westminster/John Knox Press.

Partridge, Ernest (ed.) 1981, *Responsibilities to Future Generations*, Buffalo, NY: Prometheus Books.

Peacocke, Christopher 1979, *Creation and the World of Science*, the Bampton Lectures 1978, Oxford: Clarendon Press.

Penrose, Roger 1992, "The Modern Physicist's View of Nature," in Torrance (ed.), 117–166.

Pinches, Charles, and McDaniel, Jay B. (eds.) 1993, *Good News For Animals? Christian Approaches to Animal Well-Being*, Maryknoll, NY: Orbis Books.

Pluhar, Evelyn B. 1995, *Beyond Prejudice: The Moral Significance of Human and Nonhuman Animals*, Durham, NC: Duke University Press.

Polkinghorne, John 2000, *Faith, Science and Understanding*, New Haven, CT: Yale University Press.

Postman, Neil 1993, *Technopoly: The Surrender of Culture to Technology*, New York: Vintage Books.

Powell, T. G. E. 1958, *The Celts*, New York: Frederick A. Praeger.

Presbyterian Eco-Justice Task Force 1989, *Keeping and Healing the Creation*, Louisville, KY: Committee on Social Witness Policy Presbyterian Church (U.S.A.).

Rachels, James 1987, "Darwin, Species and Morality," *The Monist* 70 (January): 98–113.

1990, *Created from Animals: The Moral Implications of Darwinism*, Oxford: Oxford University Press.

Ramsey, Paul 1950, *Basic Christian Ethics*, Chicago: University of Chicago Press.

Rawls, John 1993, *Political Liberalism*, New York: Columbia University Press.

Regan, Donald 1986, "Duties of Preservation," in Norton (ed.), 195–220.

Regan, Tom 1982a, *All that Dwell Therein: Essay on Animal Rights and Environmental Ethics*, Berkeley: University of California Press.

1982b, "Environmental Ethics and the Ambiguity of the Native American's Relationship with Nature," in Regan 1982a, 206–239.

1982c, "On the Nature and Possibility of an Environmental Ethic," in Regan 1982a, 184–205; originally published in *Environmental Ethics* 3.1 (Spring 1981): 19–34.

1983, *The Case for Animal Rights*, Berkeley: University of California Press.

Regan, Tom (ed.) 1984, *Earthbound: New Introductory Essays in Environmental Ethics*, New York: Random House.

1986, *Animal Sacrifices: Religious Perspectives on the Use of Animals in Science*, Philadelphia: Temple University Press.

Regan, Tom, and Singer, Peter (eds.) 1976, *Animal Rights and Human Obligations*, Englewood Cliffs, NJ: Prentice Hall.

Reiger, John F. 1986, *American Sportsmen and the Origins of Conservation*, rev. edn., Norman: University of Oklahoma Press.

Rescher, Nicholas 1993, *Pluralism: Against the Demand for Consensus*, Oxford: Clarendon Press.

Richards, Robert J. 1992, *The Meaning of Evolution: The Morphological Construction and Ideological Reconstruction of Darwin's Theory*, Chicago: University of Chicago Press.

Richardson, W. Mark, and Wildman, Wesley J. (eds.) 1996, *Religion and Science: History, Method, Dialogue*, New York: Routledge.

Rifkin, Jeremy 1992, *Beyond Beef: The Rise and Fall of the Cattle Culture*, New York: Penguin Books.

Rodd, Rosemary 1990, *Biology, Ethics and Animals*, Oxford: Clarendon Press.

Rollin, Bernard E. 1992, *Animal Rights and Human Morality*, rev. edn., Buffalo, NY: Prometheus Books.

Rolston, Holmes 1981, "The River of Life: Past, Present, and Future," in Partridge (ed.), 123–132.

1986, *Philosophy Gone Wild: Essays in Environmental Ethics*, Buffalo, NY: Prometheus Books.

1988, *Environmental Ethics: Duties to and Values in the Natural World*, Philadelphia: Temple University Press.

Rorty, Richard 1989, *Contingency, Irony and Solidarity*, Cambridge: Cambridge University Press.

Rose, Herbert Jennings 1959, *Religion in Greece and Rome*, New York: Harper & Row.

Roszak, Theodore 1972, *Where the Wasteland Ends*, Garden City, NY: Doubleday.

Rouner, Leroy S. (ed.) 1984, *On Nature*, Notre Dame, IN: University of Notre Dame Press.

Rousseau, Jean Jacques 1993, "Preface to Discourse on the Origin of Inequality" [1754], in *The Social Contract and Discourses*, trans. and intro. E. D. H. Cole, New York: E.P. Dutton.

Routley, Richard and Routley, Val 1980, "Human Chauvinism and Environmental Ethics," in Mannison, *et al.* (eds).

Ruether, Rosemary Radford 1992, *Gaia and God: An Ecofeminist Theology of Earth-Healing*, San Francisco: Harper.

Runyon, T. 1971, "Conflicting Models for God," in Kirkpatrick (ed.).

Sagoff, Mark 1978, "On Restoring and Reproducing Art," *Journal of Philosophy* 75 (September): 453–470.

1988, *The Economy of the Earth: Philosophy, Law and the Environment*, Cambridge: Cambridge University Press.

Sale, Kirkpatrick 1991, *Dwellers in the Land: The Bioregional Vision*, Philadelphia: New Society Publishers.

Salt, Henry S. 1980, *Animals' Rights Considered in Relation to Social Progress* [1892], Clarks Summit, PA: Society for Animal Rights.

Santmire, H. Paul 1985, *The Travail of Nature: The Ambiguous Ecological Promise of Christian Theology*, Philadelphia: Fortress Press.

2000, *Nature Reborn: The Ecological and Cosmic Promise of Christian Theology*, Minneapolis: Fortress Press.

Santurri, Edmund N. and Werpehowski, William (eds.) 1992, *The Love Commandments: Essays in Christian Ethics and Moral Philosophy*, Washington, D.C.: Georgetown University Press.

Sapontzis, S. F. 1987, *Morals, Reason, and Animals*, Philadelphia: Temple University Press.

Schaff, Philip (ed.) 1996, *The Creeds of Christendom with a History and Critical Notes*, rev. David S. Schaff, vol. III: *The Evangelical Protestant Creeds*, Grand Rapids, MI: Baker Books.

Schrödinger, Erwin 1967, *What is Life? The Physical Aspect of the Living Cell and Mind and Matter*, Cambridge: Cambridge University Press.

Schumacher, E. F. 1973, *Small is Beautiful: Economics as if People Mattered*, New York: Harper & Row.

Schweitzer, Albert 1976, "The Ethic of Reverence for Life" [1923], in Regan and Singer (eds.), 133–138.

Searle, John R. 1994, *The Rediscovery of Mind*, Cambridge, MA: MIT Press.

Shapere, Dudley 1974, *Galileo: A Philosophical Study*, Chicago: University of Chicago Press.

Sher, George 1987, *Desert*, Princeton: Princeton University Press.

Shils, Edward 1981, *Tradition*, Chicago: University of Chicago Press.

1982, *The Constitution of Society*, Chicago: University of Chicago Press.

Simpson, George Gaylord 1967, *The Meaning of Evolution: A Study of the History of Life and its Significance for Man*, rev. edn., New Haven, CT: Yale University Press.

Singer, Irving 1984, *The Nature of Love*, vol I: *Plato to Luther*, 2nd edn., Chicago: University of Chicago Press.

Singer, Peter 1975, *Animal Liberation: A New Ethics for our Treatment of Animals*, New York: Avon Books.

1979, "Not for Humans Only: The Place of Nonhumans in Environmental Issues," in Goodpaster and Sayre (eds.), 191–206.

Singer, Peter (ed.) 1986, *In Defense of Animals*, New York: Harper & Row.

Sloan, Phillip R. 1985, "The Question of Natural Purpose," in McMullin (ed.), 121–150.

Smart, Ninian 1958, *Reasons and Faiths: An Investigation of Religious Discourse, Christian and Non-Christian*, London: Routledge & Kegan Paul.

Smith, John E. 1978, "Nature as Object and as Environment: The Pragmatic Outlook," in McLean (ed.), 50–57.

Smith, Mark J. 1998, *Ecologism: Towards Ecological Citizenship*, Buckingham: Open University Press.

Sober, Elliot 1984, *The Nature of Selection: Evolutionary Theory in Philosophical Focus*, Chicago: University of Chicago Press.

1986, "Philosophical Problems for Environmentalism," in Norton (ed.), 173–194.

Spring, David, and Spring, Eileen (eds.) 1974, *Ecology and Religion in History*, New York: Harper & Row.

Steck, Odil Hannes 1980, *World and Environment*, Nashville, TN: Abindon.

Stegner, Wallace 1987, "The Legacy of Aldo Leopold," in Callicott (ed.), 233–245.

1992, *Where the Bluebird Sings to the Lemonade Spring: Living and Writing in the West*, New York: Penguin Books.

Stent, Gunther (ed.) 1980, *Morality as a Biological Phenomenon*, rev. edn., Berkeley: University of California Press.

Stewart, Claude Y., Jr. 1983, *Nature in Grace: A Study in the Theology of Nature*, NABPR Dissertation Series, No. 3, Macon, GA: Mercer University Press.

Stoll, Mark 1997, *Protestantism, Capitalism, and Nature in America*, Albuquerque, NM: University of New Mexico Press.

Stone, Christopher D. 1987, *Earth and Other Ethics: The Case for Moral Pluralism*, New York: Harper & Row.

Strohmaier, David 2001, *The Seasons of Fire: Reflections on Fire in the West*, Reno, NV: University of Nevada Press.

Strong, Douglas H. 1988, *Dreamers and Defenders: American Conservationists*, Lincoln: University of Nebraska Press.

Swinburne, Richard 1970, *The Concept of Miracle*, London: Macmillan.

Tambiah, Stanley Jeyaraja 1990, *Magic, Science, Religion, and the Scope of Rationality*, Cambridge: Cambridge University Press.

Taylor, Charles 1989, *Sources of the Self: The Making of the Modern Identity*, Cambridge, MA: Harvard University Press.

1994, "The Politics of Recognition," in Gutmann (ed.), 25–73.

Taylor, Paul W. 1986, *Respect for Nature: A Theory of Environmental Ethics*, Princeton: Princeton University Press.

Teilhard de Chardin, Pierre 1965, *The Phenomenon of Man*, trans. Bernard Wall, New York: Harper & Row.

Telfer, Elizabeth 1996, *Food for Thought: Philosophy and Food*, London: Routledge.

Terrie, Philip G. 1993, *Wildlife and Wilderness: A History of the Adirondack Mammals*, Fleischmanns, NY: Purple Mountain Press.

1994, *Forever Wild: A Cultural History of Wilderness in the Adirondacks*, Syracuse, NY: Syracuse University Press.

Thomas, Keith 1983, *Man and the Natural World: Changing Attitudes in England 1500–1800*, London: Allen Lane.

Thompson, Paul B. 1995, *The Spirit of the Soil: Agriculture and Environmental Ethics*, London: Routledge.

Tillich, Paul 1952, *The Courage to Be*, New Haven, CT: Yale University Press.

Tolkien, J. R. R. 1965, *The Lord of the Rings*, Part I: *The Fellowship of the Ring*, New York: Ballantine.

Torrance, John (ed.) 1992, *The Concept of Nature*, Oxford: Clarendon Press.

Tribe, Laurence H. 1974, "Ways Not to Think about Plastic Trees: New Foundations for Environmental Law," *Yale Law Journal* 83 (June): 1315–1348.

Underhill, Ruth 1965, *Red Man's Religion*, Chicago: University of Chicago Press.

VanDeVeer, Donald 1986, "Interspecific Justice," in VanDeVeer and Pierce (eds.), 51–66; originally published in *Inquiry* 22 (Summer 1979): 55–70.

VanDeVeer, Donald, and Pierce, Christine (eds.) 1986, *People, Penguins and Plastic Trees: Basic Issues in Environmental Ethics*, Belmont, CA: Wadsworth Publishing Company.

Von Balthazar, Hans Urs 1988, *Dare We Hope "That All Men Be Saved?,"* with *A Short Discourse on Hell*, trans. David Kipp and Lothar Krauth, San Francisco: Ignatius Press.

1992, *The Theology of Karl Barth: Exposition and Interpretation*, trans. Edward T. Oakes, S. J., San Francisco: Ignatius Press.

Waldron, Jeremy (ed.) 1984, *Theories of Rights*, Oxford: Oxford University Press.

Wallace, James 1978, *Virtues and Vices*, Ithaca, NY: Cornell University Press.

Walzer, Michael 1983, *Spheres of Justice: A Defense of Pluralism and Equality*, New York: Basic Books.

1994, *Thick and Thin: Moral Arguments at Home and Abroad*, Notre Dame, IN: University of Notre Dame Press.

Ward, Keith 1982, *Rational Theology and the Creativity of God*, Oxford: Blackwell.

1996, *Religion and Creation*, Oxford: Clarendon Press.

Watt, W. Montgomery 1953, *The Faith and Practice of Al-Ghazālī*, London: George Allen and Unwin.

Wenz, Peter 1988, *Environmental Justice*, Albany: State University of New York Press.

1996, *Nature's Keeper*, Philadelphia: Temple University Press.

Westermann, Claus 1974, *Creation*, trans. John J. Scullion, S.J., Philadelphia: Fortress Press.

Westfall, Richard S. 1992, "The Scientific Revolution of the Seventeeth-Century: The Construction of a New World View," in Torrance (ed.), 63–93.

Weston, Anthony 1994, *Back to Earth: Tomorrow's Environmentalism*, Philadelphia: Temple University Press.

Westra, Laura 1994, *An Environmental Proposal for Ethics: The Principle of Integrity*, Lanham, MD: Rowman & Littlefeld.

Whitehead, Alfred North 1967, *Science and the Modern World* [1925], The Lowell Lecture 1925, New York: The Free Press.

Wilkinson, Loren (ed.) 1991, *Earthkeeping in the Nineties: Stewardship of Creation*, by the Fellows of the Calvin Center for Christian Scholarship, Calvin College: Peter DeVos, Calvin DeWitt, Eugen Dykema, Vernon Elders, and Loren Wilkinson, rev. edn., Grand Rapids, MI: Eerdmans.

Williams, Bernard 1985, *Ethics and the Limits of Philosophy*, Cambridge, MA: Harvard University Press.

Williams, Michael 1996, *Unnatural Doubts: Epistemological Realism and the Basis of Scepticism*, Princeton: Princeton University Press.

Williamson, Henry 1990, *Tarka the Otter* [1927], intro. by Robert Finch, illus. by C. F. Tunnicliffe, Boston: Beacon Press.

Wilson, Edward O. 1975, *Sociobiology: The New Synthesis*, Cambridge, MA: Harvard University Press.

1978, *On Human Nature*, Cambridge, MA: Harvard University Press.

1984, *Biophilia*, Cambridge, MA: Harvard University Press.

Wise, Steven M. 2000, *Rattling the Cage: Toward Legal Rights for Animals*, Cambridge, MA: Perseus Press.

Wittenberger, J. F. 1981, *Animal Social Behavior*, Boston: Duxbury Press.

Wittgenstein, Ludwig 1958, *Philosophical Investigations*, 2nd edn., trans. G. E. M. Anscombe, New York: Macmillan.

1972, *On Certainty*, trans. Denis Paul and G. E. M. Anscombe, ed. G. E. M. Anscombe and G. H. von Wright, New York: Harper & Row.

Wolterstorff, Nicholas 1995, *Divine Discourse: Philosophical Reflections on the Claim that God Speaks*, Cambridge: Cambridge University Press.

Worster, Donald 1985, *Nature's Economy: A History of Ecological Ideas*, Cambridge: Cambridge University Press.

1993, *The Wealth of Nature*, Oxford: Oxford University Press.

Wright, Larry 1976, *Teleological Explanation: an Etiological Analysis of Goals*, Berkeley: University of California Press.

Zizioulas, John D. 1993, *Being and Communion: Studies in Personhood and the Church*, with a foreward by John Meyendorff, Crestwood, NY: St. Vladimir's Seminary Press.

Index of names

Note: References to footnotes are not indicated where reference is made to the page. Bibliographical references are included only when the content is discussed or the author otherwise mentioned.

Index of subjects